To Herb Simon

In appreciation for
the years of advice
and inspiration.

John

CONSUMER BEHAVIOR: APPLICATION OF THEORY

McGRAW-HILL SERIES IN MARKETING

Consulting Editor
Charles Schewe
University of Massachusetts

Britt and Boyd: MARKETING MANAGEMENT
Buzzell, Nourse, Matthews, and Levitt: MARKETING: A Contemporary
    Analysis
DeLozier: THE MARKETING COMMUNICATIONS PROCESS
Howard: CONSUMER BEHAVIOR: Application of Theory
Lee and Dobler: PURCHASING AND MATERIALS MANAGEMENT:
    Text and Cases
Redinbaugh: RETAILING MANAGEMENT: A Planning Approach
Reynolds and Wells: CONSUMER BEHAVIOR
Russell, Beach, and Buskirk: TEXTBOOK OF SALESMANSHIP
Shapiro: SALES PROGRAM MANAGEMENT: Formulation and
    Implementation
Stanton: FUNDAMENTALS OF MARKETING
Star, Davis, Lovelock, and Shapiro: PROBLEMS IN MARKETING
Wright, Warner, Winter, and Zeigler: ADVERTISING

CONSUMER BEHAVIOR: APPLICATION OF THEORY

John A. Howard

George E. Warren Professor of Business
Graduate School of Business
Columbia University

McGRAW-HILL BOOK COMPANY

New York   St. Louis   San Francisco   Auckland   Bogotá   Düsseldorf
Johannesburg   London   Madrid   Mexico   Montreal   New Delhi
Panama   Paris   São Paulo   Singapore   Sydney   Tokyo   Toronto

To Lynn, Jeffrey, and Peter

*Without their support this
book could not have been written.*

658.834
H85n

CONSUMER BEHAVIOR: APPLICATION OF THEORY

1 2 3 4 5 6 7 8 9 0 KPKP 7 8 3 2 1 0 9 8 7

This book was set in Times Roman by University Graphics, Inc.
The editors were Rose Ciofalo and Susan Gamer; the cover was
designed by Joseph Gillians; the production supervisor was Milton
J. Heiberg. The drawings were done by Fine Line Illustrations, Inc.
Kingsport Press, Inc., was printer and binder.

Library of Congress Cataloging in Publication Data

Howard, John A
    Consumer behavior.

    (McGraw-Hill series in marketing)
    Bibliography: p.
    Includes index.
    1. Consumers. I. Title.
HF5415.3.H67   658.8'34   76-56122
ISBN 0-07-030520-X

Contents

v

Preface

The purpose of this book is to provide a systematic understanding of consumer behavior. Both the individual buyer and the organizational buyer will be considered.

To avoid a piecemeal approach, I have stressed a unified structure and the connections between certain carefully chosen and well-defined concepts. Each concept has been linked to the others so as to form a system; in this way, a comprehensive description of behavior is provided. Moreover, the number of concepts presented is adequate to deal with a wide range of consumer problems. Such problems are of three kinds: management (in both profit and nonprofit institutions), regulation, and actual purchasing. They exist within a wide range of social settings: preindustrial, industrial, and postindustrial. The concepts presented in this book can guide not only creative, practical problem solving but also productive basic research.

The book is designed to be versatile. I have recognized that great differences exist in students' backgrounds and have written this book for a wide range of students from undergraduate to graduate.

For students with little background in behavioral studies and little training in quantitative analysis, Chapters 1 to 11 (omitting Chapters 4 and 6) will provide a strong but not difficult course. These chapters include sections on application which will motivate students to use the principles.

For students with some background in behavioral studies, or a strong interest in this area, but with little or no interest in quantitative analysis, Chapters 1 to 11 will make a challenging course. These students will receive a strong foundation in modern information-processing theory.

For students with good training in quantitative work, Part One of the book offers a clear, theoretical structure, and Part Two will enable them to put it to use in building models for applied research.

Finally, for very advanced students, the book as a whole, with its combination of theory and method, can guide basic research. At present, there is an undue division between the extreme behaviorist who emphasizes the importance of hypotheses on theoretical grounds and the extreme quantitative researcher who emphasizes the sophistication of the quantitative tools used in testing the hypotheses. The behaviorist is often accused by the quantitative researcher of being careless in research; the quantitative researcher is accused by the behaviorist of testing hypotheses that don't matter. This book, which includes both theory and methodology, bridges the gap between these two points of view.

A number of special features have been included in this book to increase its usefulness for teaching. Each chapter contains several pages devoted entirely to application; each chapter is preceded by a table of contents that will improve comprehension and serve as a brief review after the chapter has been read; and each chapter concludes with a list of additional references which go more deeply into the topic or present an alternative point of view. Each chapter in Part One is followed by questions. Moreover, each concept is carefully defined, usually when it is first introduced; and these definitions are restated in a glossary at the end of the book.

Finally, it should be noted that four themes carry through the entire book. First (as has been mentioned), there are the three general problems of consumer behavior: management, regulation, and buying. Second (as has also been mentioned), these problems exist in each of three settings: preindustrial, industrial, and postindustrial. Third, there are three views of consumer behavior—economic, marketing, and psychological—which provide the foundation of the structure of consumer behavior. Fourth, there are three stages of development in the consumers' decision-making process: extensive problem solving, limited problem solving, and routinized response behavior. These three stages simplify and highlight the dynamics of consumers' behavior.

ACKNOWLEDGMENTS

I owe much to my colleagues and graduate students at Columbia University. In particular, my associates Professor John U. Farley and Professor Donald R. Lehmann were the finest of colleagues in our joint work in modeling consumer behavior, which has been a rewarding experience. Also, Professor Farley critically reviewed Chapter 13; and Professor Lehmann, Chapter 14. Professor Donald G. Morrison was most helpful with Chapter 12. In working with Professors Neil E. Beckwith and John U. Farley on a joint paper on public policy, I developed some of the ideas on which Chapter 11 is based. Chapter 6 was substantially improved with the help of Professor John O'Shaughnessy.

My joint work with Professor Morris B. Holbrook for the National Science Foundation project on a synthesis of consumer behavior research was indeed a stimulating experience. It influenced the work here, as the reader will readily perceive. Professor James Hulbert contributed to this book directly, but even more important was our joint work in the Federal Trade Commission project. Professor Kathryn B. Villani was a helpful colleague and, in her pragmatic way, has been an excellent source of ideas.

Many doctoral students have been generous with their time and ideas, especially A. S. Boote of Arthur D. Little, Inc., H. S. Jagpal of Rutgers University, and M. Laroche of Laval University.

Finally, I owe a fundamental intellectual debt of long standing to three people: William J. McGuire, Professor of Psychology, Yale University; the late Paul F. Lazarsfeld, Quetelet Professor Emeritus of Social Sciences, Columbia University; and Herbert A. Simon, Professor of Computer Science and Psychology, Carnegie-Mellon University. They have long been an inspiration, a source of helpful advice, and contributors of many ideas.

Bernice Schuddekopf has in numerous ways contributed to the book. Her remarkable typing skills were displayed in the repeated drafts of the manuscript. Equally important, however, she served as critic, grammarian, and chief administrative officer of the entire project. In the last role, she liberated me from endless hours of effort and detail.

I am grateful to two sources of financial support in doing the research that laid a foundation for this book. Their recognition of the need for development of theory is especially appreciated. First, General Foods Corporation, in 1966, financed the collection of the data that was the basis for much of the research in Chapters 13 and 14. In particular, I wish to thank James L. Beuide for having the imagination to perceive the potential of such data more than a decade ago. Also, I am indebted to the Food Center at Columbia University, which has been established by a seven-year General Foods grant made in honor of C. W. Cook and intended for research on the international food problem. Research on this topic has provided a stimulus and a setting for developing structure for the highly unstructured consumer decision process which appears to characterize much of the food problem.

Second, the Procter & Gamble Foundation has been generous in providing a series of grants which have been strategic to the development and completion of the book.

John A. Howard

Chapter 1

Introduction: The Nature of Consumer Behavior

CONTENTS

Stages of Consumer Behavior

Three Complementary Views of Consumer Behavior

Simplifying Assumptions

Application of Principles

Questions
Suggestions for Further Reading

In Adam Smith's vision of the good society, the consumer was given the central role in guiding economic activity. Although, in adapting Smith's ideas to a new land, Americans demoted the consumer from this eminent position, Adam Smith might still be pleased if he were to return today. Another Smith, Howard K., said on an ABC telecast:

> The evolution of real power in this country in this century has a certain symmetry to it.
> The first third of the century we were ruled by our politicians chosen by Business. . . . In the second third, Business had to accept . . . Organized Labor as a counterforce in power. . . .
> In the final third, now, it seems clear that 200 millions in between, the broad public, [are] moving in. . . . [There is a need for] every President and Governor to have a consumer advocate on his staff.[1]

Adam Smith would certainly like to see the consumer occupying a central role in the economy. However, he had supposed that it would be through the "unseen hand" of the market that the consumer would wield power—not through politics.

The increasing political power of the consumer is raising many problems for certain groups and for the society as a whole. Manufacturers and retailers are frustrated, for example. Managers see opportunities for bringing better products to consumers through improved technology (as with food) but are beset by demands that interfere. James L. Ferguson, Chairman, General Foods Corporation, said: "Efforts which could contribute to future human wealth and well-being—through better nutrition, less costly food, advances in controlling or preventing disease—could be frustrated by a regulatory system that was designed to protect them."[2]

Public policy makers are having to regulate something they understand poorly, and so they, too, are frustrated. They are also having to innovate; to enter entirely new areas of activity, as when they take action against the American Medical Association for prohibiting doctors from advertising. In such new areas, some of their actions are questionable, like the recommendation of the staff of the Federal Trade Commission that advertisers put on labels the extensive nutritional statement now required by the Food and Drug Administration.

[1] American Broadcasting Companies, Inc., 1975. Reprinted by permission.
[2] James L. Ferguson, in *Advertising Age,* December 22, 1975, p. 29.

Consumers are also frustrated. First, they are having difficulty in using their newfound political power to improve their lot through new political arrangements. Most consumer representatives want a department of consumer affairs, for example, somewhat analogous to the Department of Labor and the Department of Commerce. At the time of this writing, however, the President feels that the problem of consumer policy is so broad that the task is to make the entire bureaucracy more sensitive to consumers' needs. Second, buying has become more difficult because products are more complex: appliances are a good example. With a higher standard of living, consumers are facing a barrage of new products; and to buy these, consumers must first learn about them. Courses on how to buy are being offered in high schools; but even so, many consumers feel woefully inadequate.

Problems in these three areas—management, public policy, and buying—have a common base: a lack of understanding of consumer behavior. Of course, our understanding of human behavior in general is limited; but, beyond this, buying and consuming raise special issues. The purpose of this book is to provide better understanding of consumer behavior, by describing it and using the description to answer three kinds of questions:

1 How can a company selling a consumer product, or a nonprofit agency serving its clientele, better meet the objective of serving its consumers?

2 How can the government, in serving the consumer's interest, better regulate the seller?

3 How can consumers learn improved ways of buying to better serve their own needs?

The illustrative material presented will pertain mainly to the first question and will focus primarily on the private company; but the principles are equally applicable to any organization, including the arts, health care, and other nonprofit groups. Chapter 10 is specifically devoted to the second question. The third question is left largely implicit, ready to be developed; but knowing how consumers do buy is the foundation of recommending how they should buy.

For the purposes of application, bits and pieces of knowledge will be put into a systematic whole that can be more useful than the sum of its parts. The whole is put together from a single point of view, which gives it coherence and unity that will make it easier to understand and to apply to the three kinds of questions. In content, it is in a sense a further extension of my earlier views[3] but goes much beyond them, as will be seen in later chapters.

In this first chapter, a perspective is given for approaching the three types of problems. It has been partially provided by Daniel Bell's notion of three societies.[4] A number of additional ideas also contribute to it: product life cycle, the

---

[3]J. A. Howard, *Marketing Management,* Irwin, Homewood, Ill.; 1957; J. A. Howard, *Marketing: Executive and Buyer Behavior,* Columbia University Press, New York, 1963; J. A. Howard and J. N. Sheth, *The Theory of Buyer Behavior,* Wiley, New York, 1969.

[4]Daniel Bell, *The Coming of Post-Industrial Society,* Basic Books, New York, 1973.

marketer's stages of consumer buying, the psychologist's notion of concept learning, and the economist's notions of consumer demand. Finally, to give coherence and clarity to the presentation of complex ideas, I use the expository device of setting up a number of assumptions about the nature of the consumer and relinquishing them one by one so as to introduce the more complicated real world a piece at a time.

TYPES OF SOCIETIES

The concept of three types of societies—preindustrial, industrial, and postindustrial—facilitates the application of principles to different environments. By placing a consumer problem in its appropriate societal category, we gain understanding of consumers because we understand their environment and how it shapes their behavior.

Preindustrial

In a *preindustrial* society, agriculture (physical products) dominates, technological change is almost nonexistent, and communication among consumers is almost entirely confined to word of mouth with near neighbors. Consumers are oriented to the past and are guided in their buying decisions by common sense and expertise transmitted by the culture. They buy and consume almost exactly as their ancestors did 100 or even 1,000 years earlier. This type of society characterizes much of the developing world such as Asia, most of Africa, the Middle East, and South America.

Figure 1-1   Open market of a preindustrial society.

A characteristic of the preindustrial society is the open market seen in Figure 1-1. This illustration conveys much that is relevant for understanding consumers. Women, largely from homes without refrigerators, make their daily shopping trips to this market to meet their daily needs. They buy from the stalls products which are not standardized but which for the most part have been familiar for centuries; the culture has provided them with adequate knowledge of how to buy these products.

Industrial

In an *industrial* society, industrial production (physical products) dominates. Technological change—the foundation of new products—occurs but is guided by empiricism. Electronic communication is common, but it generally takes the form of undifferentiated mass communication. Consumers face a different environment from that of their parents. Radically new products do come into being and are increasingly apparent; but the markets for such products are still in their infancy. The consumer tends to be adaptive on an ad hoc basis. Industrial society characterizes Western Europe, the Soviet Union, Japan, Canada, Australia, New Zealand, and South Africa.

The mill towns of the industrial districts of Western Europe—Figure 1-2 shows an English mill town—represent modern industrial society. The consumers here are adapting in ad hoc fashion to changes in the products that confront them. Mass communication, indicated by the television aerials, introduces them to these changes; but the burden of introducing consumers to radically new products is not yet heavy.

Figure 1-2 Mass communication in an industrialized society.

Figure 1-3   Shopping at home in a postindustrial society of the 1980s.

Postindustrial

In a *postindustrial* society, services have begun to play a major role in production. Technological change and consequent new products, guided by theory, are a central phenomenon. This is a "communication society" with many forms of individualized communication. There is an orientation toward the future.

Sellers in a postindustrial society must find new ways of communicating to consumers a mass of information about radically new products. This is illustrated in Figure 1-3. Suppose that a man wants to buy a new lawn mower. He needs more information because there has been major change in the product since he last bought one. He telephones the Community Information Service. This service, transmitting by cable television, flashes on his screen the names of available lawn mowers and their characteristics, including their prices and where they are sold. This service is individualized: the consumer can get what he wants when he wants it, but he must pay for it. (Given the available information technology of the 1980s, the cost of this service is low.) Having evaluated each lawn mower against his needs, the consumer can simply telephone and have the one he wants delivered. Time and energy have been conserved.

Postindustrial society currently characterizes only the United States, where it grew out of World War II. The rapid rate of technological change causes products in a postindustrial socioeconomic structure to exhibit an accelerated life cycle. It is the concept of product life cycle which we examine next.

PRODUCT LIFE CYCLE

The concept of a product life cycle, which provides perspective on consumer behavior and is useful heuristically, can best be conveyed by means of a concrete example.

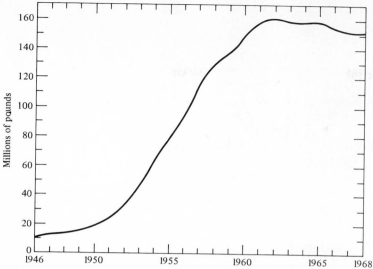

Figure 1-4   Portion of product life cycle for instant coffee.

In the late 1930s, Nestle Company introduced an instant coffee called Nescafe—a radically new product such as characterizes a postindustrial society. Previously, consumers had known only regular ground coffee. The new coffee was brewed at supernormal pressure and temperature and then sprayed into a column of hot air in a drying tower. When it fell to the bottom, it was a fine, soluble powder. As Figure 1-4 shows, Nescafe was somewhat slow in being adopted until about 1950, when it "took off." Rapid growth continued throughout the 1950s. By 1962, however, not only did the rate of growth decline, but the absolute level of consumption began to decline also.

By no means do all new products conform to this specific pattern of growth, but in general terms it is a useful description. Just as Nescafe did, most new products grow slowly at first, then rise rapidly, then level off, and finally begin to decline.

The last stage—inevitable decline—has come to be questioned, and the evidence for it is mixed.[5] Criticism of the concept of decline seems to arise largely because it is supposed that managers tend to assume a brand should be dropped once its sales have leveled off. Three comments are in order about the use of the concept in this book. First, it is used here in a particular way—not as a predictive concept, but as an explanatory concept. Second, we will be little concerned with the decline stage. Indeed, I could just as well use the term "product growth curve," except that it is less familiar. Third, I will use the term to describe the behavior of a product class, not an individual brand.

[5]M. L. Holbrook and J. A. Howard, "Consumer Research on Frequently Purchased Nondurable Goods and Services: A Review," Project on Synthesis of Knowledge of Consumer Behavior, RANN Program, National Science Foundation, April 1975 (original draft).

PRODUCT CLASS

The concept of a product class also is essential to understanding consumer behavior. Perhaps one reason why human beings are so remarkably effective is that they *group* something unknown with something known and then proceed to learn about the unknown by *distinguishing* it from known things within this limited set. Where a consumer product is concerned, they learn about it by placing it in a class and then distinguishing it from familiar brands in that class. Thus, "product class" is the group of brands that consumers view as close substitutes for each other. Economists have found the concept useful in defining a market, although they use the term "industry" instead, and traditionally they have not been concerned as much about brand comparisons as marketers are. Managers sometimes define an industry incorrectly because they do not know how consumers are grouping brands.

CONSUMERS OVER PRODUCT LIFE CYCLE

Having defined product life cycle and product class, let us proceed with instant coffee as an example of a product class over stages of the product life cycle. An important point here is that although Nescafe represented a radically new product, it was viewed as a type of coffee and thus was grouped with regular coffees. Its appearance in the market initiated a new class of brands, all called "instant coffee," which the consumer then had to distinguish from each other. These additional brands developed during the decade of rapid growth; their individual patterns of growth may have been quite different from that of the total product class shown in Figure 1-4.

It is this rise of a radically new product—the creation of a new product class—that characterizes a postindustrial society. In preindustrial societies, new products are almost nonexistent. In industrial societies, new products exist, but casual observation suggests that they are likely to fit into established classes; radically new products are not so frequent.

Consider the individual consumers who were buying instant coffee in the three decades from 1940 to 1970. In 1940, few had ever seen an instant coffee; to understand it so as to evaluate it in terms of their needs, they had to develop criteria by which to judge it. To do this required obtaining extensive information and taking substantial time to process it. Problems having to do with values confronted the consumer: was it good to want and buy such a convenient food, or would using instant coffee violate established values? This was a serious problem for the typical consumer, who was likely to be a homemaker proud of the ability to brew regular coffee. As was shown in a classic study by Mason Haire, a psychologist at M.I.T., almost half the homemakers surveyed felt that people would think them lazy and extravagant if they used instant coffee.[6] Today, such

---

[6]Mason Haire, "Projective Techniques in Marketing Research," *Journal of Marketing,* **14:**649–656, April 1950.

an attitude would be absurd; but then it was a very real problem for many consumers. An analogous problem is now being raised by fabricated foods.

Extensive Problem Solving (EPS)

There were two physically observable characteristics of consumers in this situation. First, they needed a great amount of information in order to decide whether to buy instant coffee. Second, they made up their minds slowly; that is, they exhibited a long decision time. This kind of behavior we call "extensive problem solving" (EPS). It occurs when consumers are confronted with a brand from a product class they have never before encountered. EPS is an important notion that will be used throughout the book.

Limited Problem Solving (LPS)

When another brand of instant coffee appeared on the market, as many did in the decade of the 1950s, the consumers' problem was much simpler. They had to decide how well the new brand measured up to their criteria for evaluating instant coffees, but they had these criteria readily available in mind. The criteria did not have to be learned, because they had already been learned for an earlier brand of instant coffee. Consequently, consumers needed less information than in EPS, and their decision time was faster. This kind of behavior we call "limited problem solving" (LPS). It occurs when the consumer encounters a new brand in a known product class.

Routinized Response Behavior (RRB)

By the 1960s, consumers had become familiar with most of the available brands of instant coffee. Brand concepts had been developed. Consumers had lost their reservations about convenience foods; in fact, convenience foods had become almost chic.[7] Purchase of a different brand from the one the consumer happened to be using at the moment was a simple task: the consumer mainly examined its price. He or she already knew its quality, having probably bought it before, and could compare its value in terms of price and quality with that of other brands. On this basis, a choice could be made. This kind of behavior is characterized by little need for information and by quick decisions. It is called "routinized response behavior" (RRB). If prices tend to be stable and suppliers consistently make products readily available in retail stores, consumers' behavior becomes habitual, automatic, unthinking. Each consumer simply buys the same brand as before. Consumers are "brand loyal."

In summary, our consumers passed through three stages of learning how to buy as they adapted the decision process to instant coffee, beginning with knowing nothing about instant coffee as a product class and probably ending as loyal buyers of particular brands of instant coffee. All consumer behavior can

---

[7]F. E. Webster, Jr., and F. von Pechman, "A Replication of the 'Shopping List' Study," *Journal of Marketing,* **34**:61–77, April 1970.

Table 1-1   Characteristics of Stages of Decision

Stage	Amount of information	Speed of decision
EPS	Large	Slow
LPS	Medium	Medium
RRB	Small	Fast

usefully be classified into one of the three stages, according to two observable characteristics: amount of information and speed of decision (Table 1-1).

Implications for Policy Makers

These stages are very useful for policy purposes because policy makers—private (company managers) or public (such as Federal Trade Commissioners)—are usually concerned with changing the consumer's behavior. To do this in a free society requires that the policy maker know how much information, and what kind of information, to provide to consumers, and how quickly consumers are likely to respond. For example, some consumers have become aware of the ill effects of too much sugar and so are looking for less heavily sweetened foods. Duffy-Mott Company produces a desirable unsweetened applesauce. Retailers stock it but do not sell it. Why? Few consumers are aware of its lack of sweetening. The company needs to advertise. Here is an example from the area of public policy: The Federal Trade Commission (FTC) is charged with protecting the consumer. One of its problems is to persuade consumers to make greater use of criteria having to do with nutrition—vitamins, proteins, etc. But who should be responsible for educating consumers? Commissioners must decide who should do this: the consumers themselves, private industry, some private third party like Consumers Union, or the government?

But using the stages of decision to describe types of consumer behavior does not go deep enough for some purposes, especially in a postindustrial society, where radically new products are common. It is adequate for the higher-level manager, but too superficial for the lower-level manager, who is closer to the market and more intimately involved with it and who plans market research. For a more fundamental understanding, we must turn to concept learning.

CONCEPT LEARNING

Psychologists have found that these three stages of consumer behavior characterize all human behavior. Concept learning includes three ideas that correspond to EPS, LPS, and RRB.[8] Furthermore, these ideas deal with *why*, in a very fundamental sense, behavior occurs.

[8]C. E. Osgood, "Psycholinguistics," in S. Koch (ed.), *Psychology: A Study of a Science,* vol. 6, McGraw-Hill, New York, 1963, pp. 244–316; P. C. Wason and P. N. Johnson-Laird, *Psychology of Reasoning,* Harvard University Press, Cambridge, Mass., 1972.

Concept Formation

The first idea, which corresponds to EPS, is called "concept formation." To buy a brand in an informed way, the consumer must have a concept of it. We can call this concept in the consumer's mind an "image." To learn to buy something which is entirely new, as instant coffee was in 1940, consumers must learn criteria by which to judge it. Humans learn by grouping and distinguishing, as was noted earlier. When consumers first encountered instant coffee, they grouped it with something it resembled. Since it was more like regular coffee than anything else, they grouped it with coffee. They then began to distinguish it from other things in that class; to do this, they used criteria—for example, convenience and taste. (It was more convenient but less tasty than regular coffee.) Such characteristics are *choice criteria*. In this way, consumers formed a concept of a product class called "instant coffee." This process of concept formation is the psychologists' counterpart of the policy makers' notion of EPS. As will be explained in later chapters, the psychologists' view of this process gives us a fuller understanding of the speed of decision and the information requirements.

Concept Attainment

When other new brands of instant coffee began to appear in the 1950s, consumers had to distinguish them from Nescafe, with which they were already familiar. Perhaps each brand was a little different, as in odor. Thus, to choose among brands, consumers had to add another choice criterion—smell—to the concept of the product class "instant coffee." Now, to judge a new brand, consumers only had to attain a *brand* image of it. Each consumer judged the new brand on each of the criteria and decided whether it was better than, the same as, or not as good as Nescafe. This the psychologist calls "concept attainment"; it is the counterpart of the managers' notion of LPS.

Concept Utilization

By the 1960s, consumers had an image of each of a number of brands of instant coffee, so that when a consumer considered another brand than the one he or she was buying at the moment, the decision was simple. All judgments about the quality of each brand had been made: the consumer had already formed a brand concept (brand image) of each brand. To decide, consumers merely considered the price and availability of the brand, which they had already learned to evaluate in forming the brand concept, and weighed these against their earlier judgment of quality. In other words, they used the brand concept that they had previously attained. They merely used an existing concept. This process is thus called "concept utilization." It is the counterpart of the managers' RRB.

STAGES OF CONSUMER BEHAVIOR

Figure 1-4 pictures the product life cycle of instant coffee as though one person went through each of the stages in the period between 1940 and 1970. This is, of course, a simplified, idealized version. One consumer does not require thirty years to pass through these stages, but only a matter of a few weeks or months, depending on how frequently he or she buys the product in question—which in turn depends on the amount consumed. What is true, however, is that in the 1940s most consumers were becoming familiar with this new product for the first time. They learned to generalize the notion of instant coffee to new brands and to discriminate between one brand and another. By the 1950s, most consumers knew about instant coffee and were simply evaluating new brands as they came along. By the 1960s, no new brands were appearing; most consumers had become familiar with a number of brands and were simply buying according to information on price and availability of the brand. Sheer availability of the brand—for example, how many jars of a brand were on the retailer's shelf— probably made a difference in whether a consumer bought one brand instead of another.

Yet even in the 1940s, there were probably some people who rather quickly came to like Nescafe, and thereafter for quite some time, perhaps the rest of their lives, bought Nescafe only, ignoring all new brands. Also, in the 1950s there were some people—in the more remote rural areas of the United States, for instance— who were first learning about this new product; there may even have been some in the 1960s. Consequently, by no means all the consumers had reached the same stage of learning at any point in time. Nevertheless, for a frequently purchased product there is a tendency for one of the three stages of decision to be typical at any time. As is shown in Figure 1-5, as regards instant coffee people in EPS were probably dominant in the 1940s, with some people in LPS and very few people in RRB.

In the middle 1950s, most buyers were in LPS; smaller numbers were in EPS and RRB, as is indicated in Figure 1-5. By the 1960s, most consumers were in RRB; new brands were not appearing and consumers had become familiar with all brands. When a choice was to be made, they already knew about quality, and the only information they needed was price and availability in local stores. This stage is also shown in Figure 1-5, with most consumers at the right side of the topmost graph (RRB), some at the middle (LPS), and almost none at the left side (EPS).

Important but infrequently purchased products—such as "consumer dura- bles" like refrigerators—probably do not conform to the straightforward picture of Figure 1-5. Choice criteria are probably forgotten in the interim between purchases. More important, technological change that occurs between purchases results in a new product design which often requires that new criteria be learned. Finally, the consumer's values may also change in the interim. All three of these effects tend to cause each purchase to be something of an EPS situation. Further, RRB seldom, if ever, exists for most consumers of infrequently purchased items.

In Chapters 2 to 5, we will examine each of these three stages of behavior as though they are quite discrete. In fact, they are not discrete. All three together make up a cycle which is a continuous learning process. To represent the three stages as forming a cycle, as in Figure 1-5, greatly facilitates our under- standing of the process as a whole. The continuity of the process will become

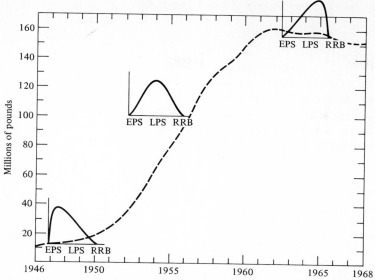

Figure 1-5 Product life cycle and stages of the decision process for instant coffee.

apparent in later chapters, where it will be shown that what appear to be three separate stages are really a complex stage (EPS) becoming simpler (LPS) and still simpler (RRB).

By integrating ideas of product life cycle, stages of decision, and concept learning, we pave the way for bringing together three historically disparate points of view: those of the manager, the psychologist, and the economist.

THREE COMPLEMENTARY VIEWS OF CONSUMER BEHAVIOR

Two different ways of looking at how the market changes over the product life cycle of a frequently purchased low-priced item have been presented: the manager's stages of decision by consumers, and the psychologist's concept learning. The economist offers a third view of the same thing, but uses still different terms. All three views are needed for the analysis of consumer behavior; they are summarized in Table 1-2.

Let us now examine the economist's view of a consumer buying a familiar brand (column 3 in Table 1-2). This is the consumer behavior you learned in your first course in economics; it is the counterpart of RRB.

It is characterized, first, by an unchanging utility function and, second, by unchanging consumer technology. To say that a consumer has a utility function is, roughly, to say that for any pair of brands presented, the consumer can tell which he or she prefers. The term "consumer technology" grows out of the desire of economists to draw an analogy between the consumer as an economic unit and the firm, which they view as characterized by "production technology."

Table 1-2 Three Views of the Stages of Consumers' Decision Processes

	1	2	3
Manager	EPS	LPS	RRB
Psychologist	Concept formation	Concept attainment	Concept utilization
Economist	Changing utility function	Constant utility function Changing consumer technology	Constant utility function Constant consumer technology

Consumer technology is the set of technical coefficients that relates a product to its want-satisfying characteristics.[9] In LPS, when the consumer prefers a new product, presumably this is because it is better than his or her regular product; that is, the technical coefficients have changed in a favorable way. The consumer's utility function, however, is unchanged. In EPS, the economist technically says that the utility function must be redefined so as to incorporate the radically new product, but "change in tastes" is the terminology more commonly used.

It is interesting to note in Table 1-2 that three differently oriented minds—the manager's, the psychologist's, and the economist's—have come to view the world in such a similar way and to provide such complementary views.

The economist's notion of a market is a remarkable mechanism for explaining how buyers and sellers adapt to change, as will be seen in the discussion of national consumer policy in Chapter 10. For dealing with changes in quantities of products, economists have splendid concepts. Prices of consumer goods and consumers' incomes are the chief variables. In preindustrial societies, these are probably the crucial variables. (The problem in such societies is keeping incomes high enough and food prices low enough to prevent mass starvation.) But it is only recently that significant developments have occurred in the concepts dealing with quality in this area.[10] Ideas have not been developed for dealing with changes in the consumer's response to the quality of products, particularly if this involves changes in utility, although Houthakker suggested changes in the direction of concept learning like those proposed here and in following chapters.[11]

The psychologist has developed a substantial amount of knowledge about response, although it tends to be in bits and pieces.

[9]Kelvin Lancaster, "Theories of Consumer Choice from Economics: A Critical Survey," Project on Synthesis of Knowledge of Consumer Behavior, RANN Program, National Science Foundation, 1975.

[10]Kelvin Lancaster, *Consumer Demand: A New Approach,* Columbia University Press, New York, 1971.

[11] H. S. Houthakker, "The Present State of Consumption Theory," *Econometrica,* **29**:704–740, 1961.

The manager's view (Table 1-1) may seem astoundingly simplistic, ambiguous, and (in the case of the terms "large" and "slow," for example) ill-defined. This can, however, be explained. "Manager," as used here, refers to a decision maker at the highest level, such as the chief executive officer of a corporation or the chairman of the Federal Trade Commission. Such people are dealing with problems pertaining to consumers at a level on which only such simplistic concepts can be handled. The reason for this is that the decision makers must bring together other, equally complicated, elements of a particular problem and combine them with their view of the consumer. Chief executive officers, for instance, must bring together cost, competition, and government policy with their understanding of the consumer. Once they learn their simplistic view, however, they can then associate with it as much detailed psychological or economic analysis as they find useful. People at lower levels of an organization, of course, need much more detailed concepts. Brand managers and market researchers, for example, can use the more detailed and operational view represented by concept learning to supplement the simplistic view of chief executive officers; they will also find the economists' vocabulary useful if they are concerned with public policy.

By integrating the stages of the consumer's decision process and concept learning with the notion of a product life cycle, I have brought together the manager's action-oriented view, the psychologist's information-oriented view, and the economist's welfare-oriented view. To use three different points of view separately is a burden on anyone attempting to apply the principles involved. For example, it was noted earlier that there are three kinds of consumer problems: those having to do with management, those having to do with public policy, and those having to do with how to buy. It was also noted that there are three kinds of consumer environments: preindustrial, industrial, and postindustrial. In each environment, all three kinds of problems exist. If we were to look at each of the three problems in each of the three environments from each of the three points of view the task would be complex indeed: since $3 \times 3 \times 3 = 27$, there would be twenty-seven possible situations. This complex picture is represented by the cube in Figure 1-6 (page 16).

If, however, we can bring the three points of view into a single, reasonably integrated set of concepts, the understanding of consumer behavior could be substantially simplified. The twenty-seven-cell cube would be reduced to a nine-cell plane. Making this integration is the task of the following chapters. Integration will be achieved not in a formal sense, but in the sense of a usable set of tools for dealing with each type of consumer environment.

SIMPLIFYING ASSUMPTIONS

Another way to gain perspective on the nature of consumer behavior and facilitate applying the principles is to assume away certain complications and thus present a simplified picture for analysis. Indeed, this is exactly what has

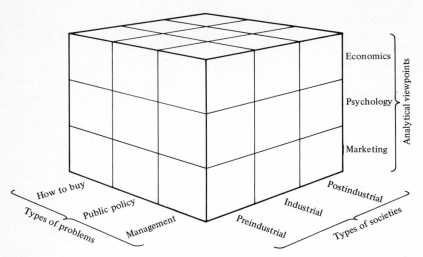

Figure 1-6 Permutations of problems, environments, and analytical perspectives.

been done—implicity—up to this point. For example, nothing has been said about the obvious fact that not all consumers are alike. Yet consumers do differ from each other, and this fact is important in two ways. First, companies selling to consumers try to *segment* the market. They try to put consumers into homogeneous groups and to provide a somewhat different marketing program for each group. Similarly, public policy makers segment the market: the Federal Trade Commission is particularly critical of the breakfast cereal companies because their advertising is directed at children, a special segment. Second, when research on consumers is being conducted, the differences among consumers may obscure very important general truths about their behavior. This is the problem of unexplained variance, or "noise," as it is often called.[12] It is often necessary to incorporate the differences explicitly into the analysis. If income is incorporated, for example, we may find that those who bought a certain product had high incomes and those who did not had low incomes; income would then explain buying.

It is common throughout the sciences to first assume away certain features of a phenomenon to obtain a simpler and clearer picture and then, later, to reintroduce these features as complications of the simple but clear picture. Simplifying by assuming away complications is, in fact, the essence of a model. I have made the following simplifying assumptions about consumer behavior in this chapter and later chapters; later, each of the corresponding complications will be introduced as necessary to give a complete picture.

---

[12]J. U. Farley and J. A. Howard (eds.), *Control of "Error" in Market Research Data,* Lexington Books, Lexington, Mass., 1975.

1 It is assumed that information received by consumers is very simple and precise; but in Chapters 3 and 4 it will be recognized that most messages to consumers are transmitted by human language, which is exceedingly complex.

2 Consumers are assumed to be passive receivers of information, responding only to that to which they are accidentally exposed. Chapter 7, however, will recognize the fact that consumers are very active receivers of information. Where an important product is concerned, they pay a great deal of attention and often search extensively. Also, two kinds of "nonrational" behavior that consumers sometimes exhibit—emotional and uninvolved behavior—will be included.

3 As was mentioned above, it has been assumed that all consumers are alike. In Chapter 8, the fact that consumers may differ substantially from each other will be incorporated.

4 It is assumed that other people are no more important than any other source of information available to consumers. In Chapter 9, it will be recognized that personal influence (that is, other people) is really a major source of information. This source will be introduced, and the more complicated real world of social structure will be dealt with. One social structure in which other people are the dominant influence is the formal organization; this structure will be used to introduce industrial buying and buying by other organizations, such as governments. (Actually, this book could just as well be called "Buyer Behavior," as will be seen in Chapter 9.)

5 It is assumed that our purpose in wanting to know about consumers is to serve the needs of the manager, private or public. If you are a member of the United Nations Food and Agricultural Organization, for instance, you might want to use the knowledge to persuade people in Africa to eat Incaparina, because various governments have decided that this is a good idea. If you are a brand manager for a company, you will want to use this knowledge to persuade consumers to buy your product. In Chapter 10, however, we will assume that our purpose is to use this knowledge to help consumers do whatever they believe is good for them. There we will assume that ours is a society where freedom of choice is an important value, and that the task of public policy is, at least in part, to help consumers exercise that freedom adequately.

APPLICATION OF PRINCIPLES

As you read this book and encounter increasing complication in each succeeding chapter, you may need some device to help you understand these complications quickly. Principles in any field of knowledge are usually much better understood when one can see how they are applied. This is certainly true of consumer behavior. At the end of each chapter, therefore, the relevance of the principles will be shown by applying at least some of them to particular problems.

The application is at the verbal level, and this is adequate for many, if not most, purposes. In this sense, Part One—Chapters 2 to 11—represents a self-contained presentation of the principles of consumer behavior. For some purposes, however, a more quantitative application is appropriate. Consequently, in Part Two—Chapters 12 through 15—the principles are applied quantitatively. (This application requires the reader to have had a course in statistics.)

QUESTIONS

1 What are the types of societies in terms of industrial development, and what is their significance for studying consumer behavior?
2 Why is it useful to think about stages in the learning process through which consumers pass as they learn to buy a radically new product?
3 Why do we need three different ways of describing the three stages through which consumers typically pass in learning to buy a radically new product?
4 What is the product life cycle, and how does it relate to the concept of product class?
5 Describe the two processes of grouping and distinguishing.

SUGGESTIONS FOR FURTHER READING

R. Ferber (ed.): *A Synthesis of Selected Aspects of Consumer Behavior,* U. S. Government Printing Office for National Science Foundation, Washington, D. C., in press.
G. Zaltman and B. Sternthal (eds.): *Broadening the Concept of Consumer Behavior,* Association for Consumer Research, 1975.

Part One

Theory and General Application

Routinized Response Behavior

CONTENTS

This chapter deals with RRB; Chapters 3 and 4 deal with LPS; and Chapters 5 and 6 deal with EPS. As we saw in Chapter 1, consumers learn these stages of buying behavior in the reverse order; however, it is easiest to begin our study with RRB, because this is the simplest stage. Once RRB is understood, the subtleties of the two earlier stages are more easily grasped, for the other two stages are mere extensions of RRB. Chapters 2 through 6 constitute the core of the principles of consumer behavior.

The observable characteristics of RRB—a limited search for information and a speedy decision (see Chapter 1)—are explained by the psychological process of concept utilization. Imagine someone reaching for a jar of coffee in the cupboard and finding it empty, or nearly so. Imagine someone walking back to the office after a mid-morning meeting and suddenly feeling hunger pangs. In both instances a need is being experienced. A "need" is defined as some event—internal or external to the consumer—that establishes motivation. It creates an insistent stimulus (arousal) that will continue until the demand is satisfied. In the examples just given, the demand will be satisfied by purchasing a jar of coffee or eating lunch.

Suppose further that the people we have used as examples have been buying the products in question—coffee and lunches—for some time. The chances are high that one will buy the same brand of coffee and the other will patronize the same restaurant as usual. This is because each has a clear brand concept—a distinct image—of each of the alternative brands. Thus, they know all about the various brands, and having found one brand satisfactory before, they will find buying it the easiest thing to do now.

The only differences which occur from choice to choice are minor changes in the consumer's environment, not in the brands but in the conditions of choice, such as in price of a brand or its availability. Thus, the consumer needs little information and can act quickly. Objects of choice for the consumer can be brands, stores, restaurants, and so on; but to simplify, we will assume that the object of choice is always a brand.

SYSTEM OF CONSUMER BEHAVIOR

This book is about principles of consumer behavior, and principles are applied theory. Theory is useful for solving practical problems even if we do not quantify it. It is often said, "There is nothing so practical as a good theory." A theory

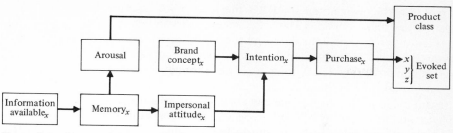

Figure 2-1   Consumer behavior model of RRB: utilization of brand concept.

helps us keep our thinking straight because it is merely a highly simplified picture of reality. A good theory includes only the most important elements of reality and ignores the others. In this way, it allows us to see a problem clearly.

Theory is also condensed knowledge. A theory is a synthesis of what is known, codified into a few simple statements. The synthesis is formulated as a set of constructs and the relations that connect them; Figure 2-1 is an example. A construct is a formally proposed concept with definition and limits. The boxes in Figure 2-1 represent constructs, and the arrows represent relations among the constructs. Figure 2-1 is the foundation upon which we will continue to build throughout this book.

A theory is useful because it can be laid upon a mass of seemingly unrelated facts, so that those facts become orderly and make sense to us in a way that they did not before. For our purposes, the facts are what a sample of consumers tell us about themselves; from these facts, we hope to find out why some bought a product and others did not. In this way, we may, for example, be able to change advertising so that those who did not buy will now buy. To get the correct facts, however, we must "operationalize" each construct: that is, develop a set of procedures by which the empirical counterpart of the construct can be measured. In Figure 2-1 for example "intention" (to buy) is a construct. To operationalize it, a question to ask the consumer is formulated: "How likely are you to buy brand x in the next month? Would you say you (1) definitely will, (2) probably will, (3) are not sure one way or the other, (4) probably will not, (5) definitely will not." Unless each construct has some such real-world counterpart, the theory— even though true—will not be very useful in guiding our thinking and quantification.

The relations among the constructs in Figure 2-1 are *causal:* it is assumed that a change in one of these constructs always causes one or more other constructs to change. The concept of causality is important because if you know the value of an antecedent or "causal" variable, you can predict the consequent or "caused" variable from it. If you know a consumer's intention to buy a brand, for instance, you can predict his or her purchase. These constructs put together into a total causal pattern make up a system—an interrelated set of parts—with an input and an output. Typically, information is the input and purchase the output. This system is the psychological process of concept utilization, which explains buying in RRB and which will become clearer as the chapter progresses.

As has already been noted, in RRB the search for information is short and decisions are made quickly. The total system is as shown in Figure 2-1.

Figure 2-1 can be considered as the counterpart of a consumer's central nervous system. To understand a person buying coffee, one can look at this diagram and envision what is going on in his or her head. It might be said that the system represented in the diagram is placed against the consumer's mind; thus, by reasoning from the system one can come to conclusions about the consumer's behavior and use these conclusions to decide what marketing policy will affect this behavior and in what way. We can do this because the relations between the constructs are invariant. For example, if the relation is positive, when one construct increases, the other always tends to increase, although the exact amount may vary from situation to situation. If it is negative, as one increases, the other always decreases. The relations making up a system are often called "mechanisms." Figure 2-1 shows several arrows which relate the constructs to each other—the mechanisms—and so show the paths of causation operating through the system.

Figure 2-1 also shows the construct "arousal," which, as is indicated by the arrow from it to "product class," supplies the push or motivation for the act of buying that product class. The subscript x indicates a particular brand, and "brand concept" is the degree of preference for brand x over competing brands. Just as arousal gives a push to behavior, preference gives it direction toward one brand instead of another. There are, in addition, some other constructs to complete the explanation of how the buyer uses a brand concept to buy. Let us take each of the constructs, define it, and explain how it fits into the system. At first, this system may seem very abstract—even devoid of meaning. But, as the boxes are described—the constructs are defined—it will come alive.

Information Available

Earlier, a person was described as finding the coffee jar empty. This discovery is new information. Before looking into the cupboard, this person did not know the jar was empty. The consumer is triggered to act because of having received some external information; and what further information is available will obviously make a great deal of difference in the consumer's behavior. "Information available" in Figure 2-1 is defined as some physical event in the consumers' environment to which they may be exposed, and to which they definitely could be exposed if they searched for information about the brand.

If we are to be effective in changing consumers' behavior, we must have a way of describing information that is available to the consumers. Otherwise, we will not know what information we are providing, and so cannot know whether it has the desired effect. The notion of "structure of information" is an objective, precise way to describe the information represented by the first box in Figure 2-1. As we examine the nature of the consumer's buying process, we will encounter the dimensions of this structure. These dimensions can be used to describe all types of information, including advertising.

Memory

The new bit of information has been lodged in the consumer's memory, as is shown by the arrow from "information available" to "memory," and has thus caused motives relevant to coffee to be stimulated, as is shown by the arrow from "memory" to "arousal." The subscript x in "memory" refers, of course, to brand x. In Chapter 4, the "memory" construct will be used extensively. For the present, we can say that this is long-term memory, the place where information is more or less permanently stored.

Arousal

Information stored in memory triggers the buyer's motives. Motives are fundamental and relatively permanent dispositions of the buyer to act, and they are manifested through arousal.

Buyers have physiological motives, such as sex and hunger; but they also have learned motives, such as achievement, affiliation, and power. For our purposes, the learned motives are more important. Some of these motives are served by purchasing some products, others by purchasing other products. People buy food because they are hungry; they buy an education because they have a strong motive for achievement. Whatever motive is applicable to a product is called a "relevant motive" when we are dealing with that product. What a motive is called is its "content"—for example, a hunger motive. At this point, we do not need to be more specific than this; but later the idea of content becomes essential.

More important here than the content of a motive is its intensity, whatever its content. How urgent is it for that relevant motive to be satisfied? The urgency of the motive is reflected in the consumer's level of arousal, which is defined as the readiness to respond and is physically measurable by various instruments. If the man has not eaten for several hours, the odor of food will trigger his hunger motive and arousal will increase; but if he has just finished eating, it will not. A brand that satisfies an intense motive we will call "important." Until Chapter 7, we will deal with the notion of importance only intuitively.

An increase in the intensity of a motive also causes consumers to pay attention to information about a product by interrupting what they have been doing. Before being interrupted, they would have ignored that information. This will be examined in Chapter 7. Here, the idea of motives and their manifestation in arousal is introduced only to explain that buying is energized; and that thinking about buying interrupts whatever other mental activity—and perhaps even physical activity—is going on. In one of our earlier examples a person was walking down the street to the office; but the trip to the office was interrupted by a heightened hunger motive, and instead, the person went into a restaurant.

The construct of arousal does not carry a subscript x, unlike the other boxes in Figure 2-1. Motive applies to all brands in a given product class rather than to a particular brand, since all brands in that class will satisfy that motive. Arousal determines *whether* the consumer will buy; brand concept influences *what* he or she buys—that is, which brand.

Brand Concept

As was noted in Chapter 1, human beings think by setting up categories into which they group similar things. When they encounter something, they identify it by placing (grouping) it in its appropriate category and then valuing (distinguishing) it in terms of the attributes which cause it to satisfy motives. All brands that are put into a single class—represented by "product class" in Figure 2-1—are identified and evaluated by the same criteria.

Definition   Let us now carefully examine "brand concept," because it is the most basic notion in this book. Brand concept can be defined as the subjective meaning of any homogeneous class of objects (physical products or services) of which consumers are aware. It is not directly perceived through one of the five senses, but rather is the result of manipulating sensory impressions. For example, one can directly perceive in Pringles potato chips certain properties such as color, taste, odor, texture, and sound, as one crunches them in the mouth. For Pringles to be a concept, however, one must also apprehend these properties as constituting part of the general notion of the characteristics of "potato chipness."

For a brand concept to develop in the consumer's mind, both abstraction and generalization are required. The consumer must *abstract* to isolate the properties that distinguish Pringles from all other potato chips. Then the consumer must be able to *generalize* these attributes to closely similar things so as to recognize that the concept can be ascribed to all other cans of Pringles, not just the particular can on the pantry shelf or in the retailer's display case. The manufacturer of Pringles helps, of course, by making every can just like every other can. A brand concept is, then, a category; but it is a subcategory of the category "product class." Finally, the discrete sensory data that make up a concept are linked by means of words and other symbols stored in memory. In this, we can see how central both language and memory are to a consumer's thinking about a brand; and it must be constantly remembered that most communication with the consumer is by means of human language.

In summary, a brand concept is more precisely defined as the subjective meaning of a brand that arises, not from sensory data about the brand per se, but from applying the processes of abstraction and generalization to the sensory data in such a way that the data are linked by words stored in memory.

Brand Concept in RRB   In RRB, the buyer has, from past experience, attained a concept of each of certain brands in a particular product class. He or she has a concept or image of brands x, y and z, as in Figure 2-1, but focuses only on x because it is preferred over y and z. Manufacturers strive very hard by means of quality control to ensure that each unit of a brand is just like all other units of that brand, so that customers will not confuse the preferred brand with other brands. This prevents the customer from putting the brand into some other category and so viewing it as a different brand. Thus, something which fits the class that is a subcategory of the product class is brand x. By merely categorizing it, the consumer knows from previous experience both what it is and how good it is for him.

Brand Concept and Brand Preference Brand concept contains an evaluative element. Consumers like a brand to a certain degree. They have a brand preference: they prefer brand *A* over brand *B,* perhaps because brand *A* tastes better. Preferences have to do with the characteristics of the brand—such as taste—that affect consumers personally. These make up the "liking" part of a brand concept.

Impersonal Attitude

Associated with a brand are conditions of purchase, such as its price and its availability. These, too, enter into consumers' liking of the brand. If the price is too high, they do not like it as well. Or if it is not readily available and they must shop around for it, their preference.will not be as high. In RRB, the consumers separate from their brand concept this liking toward these associated aspects of a brand, such as price.[1] Their feelings about these conditions of purchase are called "impersonal attitudes." Impersonal attitudes are defined as the consumers' degree of liking for the associated characteristics of a brand. Impersonal attitudes are formed—for example, consumers come to believe that a price is favorable—by means of information received from memory. This is shown in Figure 2-1 by the arrow from "memory" to "impersonal attitudes." The information involved here had earlier been received from "information available."

The distinction between brand concept and impersonal attitudes reveals the heart of RRB. We assume that a consumer in RRB has fully learned a concept of the brand and that it does not change. What may, and often do, change are impersonal attitudes, because the conditions of purchase are changing; price often changes, for example. Thus even in RRB the consumer must make some adjustments to the environment, but they are minor compared with adjusting the brand concept as is done in LPS.

Examples of impersonal attitudes are seen in Figure 2-2. It describes the RRB decision process of a woman living in New London, New Hampshire, who is buying gasoline. Bear in mind that she buys gasoline quite frequently, that she has been buying it for a long time, and that she therefore has a well-formed brand concept for each of a number of brands. Consequently, her decision in buying gasoline is so habitual that she is completely unaware of the nature of the process. Under close, extensive, and repeated interviewing, however, such a process can be elicited from her, as was done here. You should work through Figure 2-2 step by step to fully understand the meaning of the system of RRB.

The consumer's need for gasoline is indicated by box 1 in Figure 2-2. Getting into the automobile spurs her to look at her gasoline gage. If the tank is more

[1] H. S. Jagpal, "The Formulation and Empirical Testing of a Dynamic Consumer Decision Process Model: A Simultaneous Equations Econometric Model," unpublished doctoral dissertation, Columbia University, 1974, pp. 4–25.

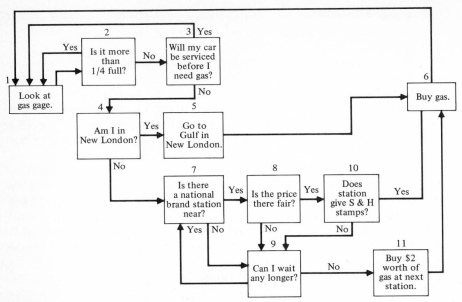

Figure 2-2   RRB stage of the decision process: motorist buying gasoline.

than a quarter full, she doesn't need gasoline (box 2). Even if it is less than a quarter full, if she is having her car serviced soon (box 3), she doesn't need gasoline, because she will have the tank filled when the car is serviced. Otherwise, she does need gasoline. Where she will buy it depends upon where she is. If she is in New London (box 4), she takes advantage of her favorable brand concept of Gulf—her high preference for it—and goes to the Gulf station (box 5).

If she is not in New London, she utilizes three impersonal attitudes. First, there is the availability of a standard (widely advertised) brand (box 7). Second, there is the question of price (box 8). Finally, there is the question of whether the station gives S & H trading stamps (box 10). She examines each of these boxes in sequence.

The construct "choice criteria" is useful here for explaining the process, but in order to simplify it is not included in Figure 2-1. Choice criteria are the mental counterparts of the attributes by which a consumer judges a brand. More specifically, they are a cognitive state of the buyer, which reflects those attributes of the brand that are salient in the buyer's evaluation of a brand and that are related to motives relevant for this product class, in the sense that brands in the product class have the potential for satisfying those motives. These are shown in Table 2-1 for the woman buying gasoline. It is essential to distinguish between the attributes per se and consumers' perceptions of these attributes, because consumers differ in their perceptions. It is the perception that effects behavior, not the attribute itself. "Attribute" is often used to mean choice criteria, but this leads to confusion. To use "attribute," when you mean not the attribute itself but the consumer's mental image of it, is to reify what is in the consumer's mind. That is analogous to thinking that people who are "thick-headed" have thicker heads than those who are not, or that "bluebloods" have no red corpuscles.

Where the consumer believes a brand is located on a choice criterion is called a "belief." Belief is defined as the cognitive state of the consumer, which reflects an evaluation of a brand in terms of a particular choice criterion.

Some key points of Figure 2-2 are summarized and highlighted in Table 2-1. This format will be useful later in comparing EPS, LPS, and RRB and in showing that all three are part of the consumer's continuous learning process. As the woman in our example works through her decision process and comes to box 7 in Figure 2-2, she finds that a Gulf station is not nearby, but that an Exxon and an Atlantic station are. She believes both to be "national" brands—that is, widely distributed and strongly advertised. She examines her brand concept of each brand and finds that she is more favorable toward Exxon than toward Atlantic, as shown in Table 2-1. Thus, one of her beliefs is that Exxon is good. Consequently, she takes it first through the remaining steps, and only if it fails at some step will she turn to consider Atlantic more fully.

She has implicitly applied the criterion of availability to Exxon when she found it nearby. Thus, "availability" is a criterion in Table 2-1, and her evalua-tion of this criterion is "yes." In box 8, she applies the criterion of price: Is it fair? Let us say that she finds it quite high and decides that it is too high. The evaluation of this criterion is "no"—that is her belief about the criterion "fair price." Exxon having failed this evaluation, she drops it from consideration and turns to consider Atlantic, to take it through the steps on the diagram. But if Exxon had been the only national-brand station in the area and it had failed the price criterion, she would check box 9 and then decide what to do next.

RRB, as shown in Figure 2-1, Figure 2-2, and Table 2-1, contains several important points. First, the consumer will examine various brands in order of preferences. Second, the choice criteria here are binary instead of multivalued; this is characteristic of an experienced decision process—the consumer has simplified the choice. Third, the criteria are applied in a definite order, presum-ably in order of decreasing importance. Fourth, a brand is dropped from further consideration if it fails one criterion. Finally, the complex process in Figure 2-2 has several boxes—it is factored into several parts, each quite simple—and this

Table 2-1 Routinized Response Behavior: Exxon versus Atlantic

Choice Criteria		Beliefs
Brand Concept		Exxon
Impersonal criteria		
Availability	(box 7)	Yes
Fair price	(box 8)	No
S & H Stamps	(box 10)	———

decision process, in spite of the simplicity of each step, ensures satisfactory results in choosing brands because of the large number of steps.

We will use the format of Table 2-1 to compare RRB with LPS and EPS, so that the nature of the learning process in each stage will be more apparent.

Some of the conditions of purchase, illustrated in Table 2-1, can change rapidly. In a period of inflation, prices go up from day to day. Thus consumers' beliefs about prices undergo change. In a period of shortages, a brand that was once readily available may suddenly be hard to find. Even in RRB—that is, even when one is buying a frequently purchased product—some conditions may have changed between purchases. Consequently, although a consumer prefers brand x and would buy it, he or she may find the price too high and so may turn to brand y instead. In RRB, changes in the values of impersonal attitudes—beliefs—are the only dynamic element in the system, but they can still necessitate substantial adjustment in the buyer's purchasing behavior from time to time.

Intention

If you ask a man whether he plans or intends to buy a brand, he can usually give you a fairly good answer. If he says he intends to buy it (his intention is high), the chances are good that he will. "Intention" is defined as a cognitive state that reflects the consumer's plan to buy some specified number of units of a particular brand in some specified time period.

This idea of intending to buy is useful in understanding consumers in a real market situation as contrasted with the laboratory. Consumers buy when they please, not to accommodate the researcher who tries to observe them. Without this measure of intention to buy, the observer must try to understand why consumers buy either by looking at their past history of purchases or by following them around and catching them at the moment of purchase. Neither approach is very satisfactory, for reasons which follow.

According to the system of RRB shown in Figure 2-1, brand concept and impersonal attitudes cause intention, and intention causes purchase. By obtaining a measure of brand concept and impersonal attitudes toward brand x, one should be able to predict whether, in fact, a consumer will buy x when he or she next experiences a need for the product class in which x falls. Past purchases cannot be used to verify the theory, because one would not have measures of brand concept and impersonal attitudes in the period preceding past purchases. If current purchases are to be used to verify the theory, one must follow the consumer around and observe the purchase; but then it is very difficult to get a measure of brand concept and impersonal attitudes just at the moment of purchase. A better procedure is to get three simultaneous measures: concept of x, impersonal attitude toward the external conditions, and intention to buy. One can then ask the consumer to record purchases that followed these measurements. This way is a much easier way to test the truth of the prediction that intention will cause a person to buy.

Intention to buy will not be a perfect predictor of future purchases, but it is always a usefully reliable predictor. As might be expected, the shorter the length of time between measurement of intention and subsequent purchase, the more reliable intention will be as a predictor. Also, intention can be used as a probability of purchase, which simplifies quantitative application.

Purchase

The act of purchasing—the arrow from "purchase" to x in Figure 2-1—requires definition. In fact, it is in most cases quite obvious, which is one reason why studying buying is such a fruitful way to study human behavior in general. Nevertheless, as we go along, certain situations will raise problems unless "purchase" is defined carefully. "Purchase," then, is the point at which a consumer has paid for a product or has made a financial commitment to buy some specified amount of it during some specified period. Consumers do not make such commitments until they are satisfied that the product is a good buy within their current framework of thinking. Thus, at this point a consumer will have gone completely through the decision process, even before taking physical possession of the product.

As can be seen in Figure 2-1, "purchase" is the end of the process. Thus, attitude, intention, and purchase form a means-end chain. A means-end chain is a series of links in which one end is the "ultimate" end and each succeeding link toward the other end is a means to the preceding link. Purchase is the means by which the consumer satisfies a motive (an end). In Figure 2-1, brand concept and impersonal attitudes reflect motives and so are the "end end" of the means-end chain. Specifically, in this case, attitude-intention-purchase is the complete means-end chain. As we move on to LPS and EPS, we will find that the means-end chain both widens and lengthens. By examining the means-end chain, you can better understand what is happening in the consumers' buying process as they move from EPS to LPS and from LPS to RRB.

Product Class

Another construct in Figure 2-1 is "product class," which was introduced in Chapter 1 and referred to earlier in this chapter. Product class is one order higher than brand concept. This definition will be adequate until Chapter 5, where product class will be more fully defined.

A product class contains a given brand and all similar brands—that is, all those brands that the buyer will readily substitute for each other. The term "generic" is sometimes used in this context. Competition, an important idea in marketing and public policy, is defined in terms of product class. Marketers strive to make their brands more attractive to customers than competitors' brands. Indeed, this is how the fruits of technological progress are passed on to the consumer. The concept is essential to economists studying competition, but they put another label on it, using "industry" to describe what we mean by product class. In practice, industries are sometimes misdefined: for example, a company thought it was selling soup, only to find that consumers were putting condiments in it and calling it a cocktail spread. For some purposes, such as forecasting, we are often interested only in whether consumers buy a product class, not in whether they buy a brand. This will be dealt with in Chapter 5.

We can now relate product class to motives. Brands that serve the same motive (or set of motives) for a consumer are, by definition, those brands that make up his or her product class. Specifically, motives connect to choice criteria, as will be developed at length in Chapter 5, and a product class is a group of brands all judged by the same choice criteria and with the same weight given to each criterion. When information about a need—an empty coffee jar, for example—triggers a particular motive or motives which underlie arousal, it is these brands that are evoked in the consumer's mind. Thus, a product class exists because it serves a set of motives.

Evoked Set

When a consumer in RRB needs to buy, say, gasoline, not all brands that he or she is aware of come to mind, or, as we say, are evoked. Instead, the consumer selects out those two, three, or four brands which best meet the need: only these will be evoked. These constitute the "evoked set." Therefore, evoked set is defined as the subset of brands that a consumer would consider buying out of the set of brands in the product class of which he or she is aware.

In this way, when a need stimulates a buying process in RRB, the consumer does not have to get information on every brand in the product class, as might be suggested by the arrow in Figure 2-1 from "memory" to "impersonal attitudes." The consumer must get information only about price and availability, for example, on two brands—x and y. In this way, the choice process is substantially simplified.

Table 2-2 gives an example of the number of brands in a consumer's evoked set. As you can see, it varies much across product classes. One of the reasons for this could be that some product classes are more important than others (the consumer is more involved in them); and the more important a class, the larger

Table 2-2   Mean Number of Known Brands and Average Evoked Set Size for Six Product Classes

Product class	Mean brands known	Mean evoked set	N	Mean evoked set/ mean brands known
Coffee	10.2 (1.3)*	4.2 (2.2)	102	.41
Dishwashing liquid	15.2 (3.2)	5.6 (3.6)	102	.37
Table napkins	7.3 (1.6)	5.0 (1.9)	102	.64
Toothpaste‡	10.4 (2.2)	3.1 (2.1)	186	.30
Laundry detergent‡	19.3 (3.0)	5.0 (2.9)	187	.26
Cakemix¶	7.8 (N/A)	3.2 (N/A)	202	.41

*( ) = Standard deviation.
‡Reported by Campbell.
¶Reported by Jacoby and Olson.
    Source: L. P. Jarvis and J. B. Wilcox, "Evoked Set Size—Some Theoretical Foundations and Empirical Evidence," mimeographed, 1974.

the evoked set. Jarvis and Wilcox's study supports this conclusion.[2] Consumers can differ from each other in the size of the evoked set. This is sometimes called a difference in "cognitive style." (It is also supported by Jarvis and Wilcox's study.)

Again, we see illustrated here a basic principle of all human behavior. Wherever conditions will permit, human beings will simplify a situation and make life easier for themselves—just as was noted earlier in the case of binary choice criteria and breaking decisions into several subprocesses.

APPLICATION OF PRINCIPLES

The principles discussed here can be applied to a number of managerial decisions: informing the consumer, allocating funds to inform the consumer, setting prices, and designing marketing channels.

Informing the Consumer

Let us assume for now that the system shown in Figure 2-1 is a reasonably good description of how the buyer thinks, so that we can apply it and thereby improve our decisions as managers. Remember that our purpose here is to apply the principles to our thinking about a practical problem.

We study consumer behavior so that we can better inform the buyer about external conditions. What information do we need to supply consumers who are in RRB? Price and availability have been suggested, for example. These are the consumers' choice criteria, and information about them will enable consumers to form beliefs which constitute impersonal attitudes. Information about availability, however, can also jog a consumer's memory—act as a reminder that the brand may be needed—and in this way both motivate and guide the consumer. But when a consumer is in RRB, the contribution of information to motivation is less significant; hearing the name of the product class probably suffices to motivate the consumer.

When we speak of "better informing" consumers, we mean giving them the information they need in a more economical manner and in a form that can be easily and quickly understood. It may be an advertisement on radio or television, a personal letter, or a call by a salesperson. Let us first examine the informational aspects, because unless consumers know the price of a brand and whether it is available, they are unlikely to buy it. Also, we want to develop the notion of structure of information in the simplified case of RRB, where this important idea can be more easily understood.

How information is symbolized makes a difference in how easily and quickly the buyer will understand it. Information can be transmitted by words, pictures, or music—that is, by linguistic, pictorial, or musical symbols. Words are, of course, the most common form. Pictures, although they can stimulate a buyer's sense of needing something (for this purpose, "one picture is worth more than

---

[2]L. P. Jarvis and J. B. Wilcox, "Evoked Set Size—Some Theoretical Foundations and Empirical Evidence," mimeographed, 1974.

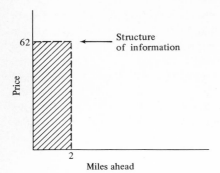

Figure 2-3   Structure of information.

ten thousand words"), are limited. Imagine trying to tell a buyer the price of gasoline and where the filling station is located by pictures alone.

A great amount of effort goes into selecting messages. To talk about messages, we need certain concepts and words to label them. For example, "structure of information" is a description of a message in quantitative terms. In our example of the woman buying gasoline, the theory suggests a simple information structure as regards content, particularly if we assume away the step involving S & H stamps. The theory specifies only the price of gasoline and location of the filling station. If the message is on a highway billboard, it could read something like this: "Sinclair gas, 2 miles ahead, 61¢." Here, the structure of information in terms of content would be a point in a two-dimensional space, indicated in Figure 2-3.

The concept of structure of information should help us analyze and evaluate an advertisement, a salesman's message to a client, or any other information intended for the consumer. People who have taken an M.B.A. are criticized by many employers for their unfamiliarity with advertising and their inability to feel some confidence in evaluating it; this concept can help. In LPS, the content of the structure of information is more complicated than Figure 2-3, however, and in EPS it is more complicated still. The form of the structure of information will be dealt with in Chapter 4.

Allocating Funds for Informing Consumers

An important question for the manager is whether giving customers the content of a message is worth the advertising cost. Will it make that much difference in their behavior? To answer this question according to our principles of consumer behavior, we would ask ourselves whether the product matters to the consumer. Suppose, for example, that you are at a supermarket checkout counter. You notice chewing gum on display and suddenly have a yen for it. If you noticed that the price seemed comparatively high, would you consider stopping at a number of stores on the way home? Probably not. You would either take the gum at the supermarket's price or forget it. It isn't important enough for you to go to much trouble. Importance of the product class is a concept developed in Chapter 7.

Another factor to be considered is how well the consumer is able to distinguish among brands. The better consumers can distinguish, the more worthwhile it will be to advertise. In a stable, mature industry, the product is often almost a commodity; all suppliers' offerings are identical. When this is so— and consumers know it is so—informing consumers about differences in price will pay off. If consumers are not sure whether or not brands are alike, giving credible information that your brand is better will pay off; but this implies changing consumers' concept of your brand and thus moving from RRB into LPS. LPS is covered in Chapter 3.

Setting Prices

How consumers respond to changes in price is obviously important to company policy. But price changes come in various forms. A price, for instance, can be "59¢"—a simple, absolute figure—or it can be the somewhat more complicated "10¢ reduction" (from 69¢). It can be still more complicated: a coupon can be issued, which, with a box top, will give the consumer a 25¢ reduction off the listed price. Furthermore, a price change can apply to the retailer or to the consumer. Such pricing approaches can be expanded into an almost infinite variety. Taken together, they make up what is called "promotional pricing." Let us first examine simple pricing in RRB.

Simple Pricing   When consumers are not well informed about the quality of a product, its price can affect their belief about it, but this would be LPS. The most dramatic example occurs when a major change in price causes consumers to view a product as being in a different product class from the one in which they originally perceived it.[3] In RRB, however, the consumer is fully informed about the quality of the brand, as is assumed in classical economic theory, and price is viewed only as a sacrifice: what is paid for this product is not available for buying something else.

How quickly do consumers respond to direct price changes? Examining gasoline, Claycamp concluded that for each percentage point of differential between a station and its competitors, a station lost 0.743 percent of its normal daily revenue on the first day.[4] By the second day and for subsequent days, this rose to 2.72 percent per day. Thus, after the first day that a price differential was created, consumers shifted their purchase by almost three times as much as the differential. The response was quick and large.

How well informed are consumers about prices? The proportion of consumers who do not know the exact prices of items is often surprising. Goldman points out, however, that studies in which this phenomenon have appeared have examined inexpensive, branded grocery products such as coffee, margarine,

[3]Carolyn Sherif, "Social Categorization as a Function of Latitude of Acceptance and Series Range," *Journal of Abnormal and Social Psychology,* **67**:148–156, 1963.
[4]H. F. Claycamp, "Dynamic Effects of Short Duration Price Differentials on Retail Gasoline Sales," *Journal of Marketing Research,* **3**:176–178, May 1966.

rice, flour, and toothpaste.[5] It has been found that consumers of lower socio-economic status are often less well informed than consumers of higher status. In a study of knowledge of meat prices in Jerusalem, however, it was clear that lower-status consumers were better informed than higher-status consumers. For many people, meat is an important food representing a significant proportion of the food budget. Also, it is a highly repetitive purchase, so that consumers come to learn much about its quality. Finally, the product is not subject to much change. These three conditions favor the development of an RRB stage of buying.

Promotional Pricing Price-related devices form a large part of the market-ing activity for relatively inexpensive, widely distributed, frequently purchased products, where consumers are in RRB. Such devices can be an important marketing tool, particularly when a product class reaches maturity in the product life cycle. As much money may be spent on promotion as on advertising.

For example, a common practice, especially in the package goods industry where products are sold through grocery stores, is the use of coupons, called "deals." A coupon is often inserted in the product package or sent through the mail to the consumer. The consumer uses it to purchase, or at least partially purchase, an item. It is, in effect, a price cut, but it has two advantages over a simple price cut. First, consumers probably do not respond, on the average, as sharply as they would to the same reduction in the form of a direct price cut. Everyone is inclined to take advantage of a direct price cut, but not everyone will redeem a coupon. Furthermore, a small proportion of consumers account for a large proportion of the deals,[6] so that the effect is not so general as that of a direct price cut. In one study, people who took advantage of deals tended to be young, better-educated families with above-average incomes.[7] Also, because consumers do not respond as quickly, competitors are less likely to respond. Second, the coupon is informative. When a coupon is mailed, a piece of advertising literature accompanies it. In summary, promotional pricing produces milder competitive effects and provides consumers with additional information.

Designing Marketing Channels

Marketing channels are designed to make a brand as available to the consumer as possible within cost constraints. How available a brand is to a consumer has two major aspects.

First, is it available in stores in which the consumer regularly shops? This is particularly important for grocery items. For example, there is evidence that 25 percent of homemakers shop in no more than two stores; only 10 percent shop in seven or more stores.[8] People living in urban areas tend to shop in a greater number of stores. For frequently purchased, unimportant products and when

[5]Arieh Goldman, "Do Lower-Income Consumers Have a More Restricted Shopping Scope?" *Journal of Marketing,* **40**:46–54, 1976.
[6]F. E. May, "Buying Behavior: Some Research Findings," *Journal of Business,* **38**:379–395, 1965.
[7]Ibid.
[8]R. S. Tate, "The Supermarket Battle for Store Loyalty," *Journal of Marketing,* **25**:8–13, 1961.

consumers are mostly in RRB, marketing channels that expose a product to a large number of people, perform only this service, and do it cheaply are the most desirable from management's point of view.

Second, within the store, where is the brand located? Location can make a difference in consumers' response. The amount of shelf space devoted to a brand can affect sales, as with Coffeemate, an impulse item widely accepted by consumers. For staple items like salt, however, this is probably not the case.[9] A manufacturer can usually get ("rent") more space in the retail store by a "trade deal," such as giving a free case of the product to the retailer who buys ten cases of it. Also, putting items in gondolas (large, barrel-like containers) at various central locations in the store tends to increase sales.[10]

CONCLUSIONS

RRB is a complex choice process; but because it is made up of a number of simple individual steps, it appears simple. It shows how human beings are able to function effectively, making complex decisions with a minimum of conscious effort, as long as their environment is not changing too rapidly, by making use of habit and routine.

RRB is typical where frequently purchased, relatively unimportant products—such as package goods sold in grocery stores—are concerned. It is probably seldom found where appliances are concerned, because these are usually important and infrequently purchased, and in the time between purchases consumers can forget.

In terms of the types of societies discussed in Chapter 1, RRB probably characterizes almost all markets in preindustrial societies such as are typical in the less developed countries that make up most of the world. Technological change is lacking, so that the same products exist year after year. The only changes are those affecting impersonal attitudes, such as price and availability. Also, choices are few because income is generally low. Changes in income obviously can make profound differences, but these are outside the system of Figure 2-1. Differences in income among consumers will be treated in Chapter 8.

We can see how profoundly the marketing problem differs in the less developed countries and in a postindustrial society like the United States. In a preindustrial society, behavior tends to be habitual; products are not as standardized, and the alternatives are not nearly as great, as in more developed societies. More important, the marketing problem is to make the price low enough that people can afford the product and to make the product available (to provide channels of distribution). Information such as advertising and indirect pricing such as promotion are irrelevant. The most important factors in whether consumers buy are prices and income. Given the prices, do they have the necessary income?

[9]Keith Cox, "The Effect of Shelf Space upon Sales of Branded Products," *Journal of Marketing Research,* 7:55–58, 1970; R. E. Frank and W. F. Massy, "Shelf Position and Space Effects on Sales," *Journal of Marketing Research,* 7:59–66, 1970.
[10]F. E. May, op. cit.

In this situation, therefore, the economists' tools for dealing with prices and income are the most relevant. Readers familiar with economic theory will recognize in RRB the situation implied in classical demand theory, described in Chapter 1 as the case of unchanging utility function, constant consumer technology, and identical brands. In economics, however, the emphasis is on the act of choice; here, it is on the process of choice. In this simple choice situation, we can see why economists are content to focus their attention on price and income and assume away other, complicating features of consumer behavior. For more complex situations, such as LPS and particularly EPS, this may be a serious oversimplification, as we will see later. Further, economic theorists are usually much more concerned with choices among product classes than with brand choice, which will be discussed in Chapter 5. (Industrial-organization economists, who concern themselves with antitrust issues, do think in terms of brand choice, however.)

A theory of a particular type of buying behavior—RRB—has now been delineated. It provides principles to act upon. The theory in its verbal form can be useful in explaining behavior and providing terminology with which to discuss it. Whenever we are concerned with setting policy, the ability to discuss the behavior affected by the policy is most useful. When one lacks a theory, one is forced to concoct one in order to talk about the problem; this is what we call an "ad hoc" or "intuitive" theory. The difficulty with such a theory is that its assumptions are not obvious and, because it is never fully articulated, it is never laid open to inspection and thus cannot benefit from criticism.

Much, if not most, of marketing is concerned with providing information. In order to describe such information, the practical concept of structure of information has been developed.

QUESTIONS

1   A number of constructs make up the system of consumer behavior shown in Figure 2-1. What do we mean by a "construct," and what purpose does it serve?
2   One of the most essential constructs is the brand concept. Describe it.
3   Another central construct in the system is attitude. What is meant by "impersonal attitudes," and why are they important in understanding RRB?
4   What is the means-end chain in Figure 2-1, and how does it relate to the other two stages of the consumer decision process, LPS and EPS?

SUGGESTIONS FOR FURTHER READING

J. R. Bettman: "Information Processing Model of Consumer Behavior," *Journal of Marketing Research,* **7:**370–376, August 1970.

G. H. Haines, Jr.: "Process Models of Consumer Decision Making," in G. D. Hughes and M. L. Ray (eds.), *Buyer/Consumer Information Processing,* University of North Carolina Press, Chapel Hill, N.C., 1974, pp. 15–23.

Chapter 3

Limited Problem Solving: Brand Concept and Associated Constructs

CONTENTS

Pricing
   Association of price and quality
   Range of prices
   Pricing new products

Conclusions

Questions
Suggestions for Further Reading

Limited problem solving (LPS) is the second stage of learning to buy a brand. A buyer is confronted with a new brand in a product class with which he or she is already familiar, and must attain a concept or image of this new brand. Thus, attaining a concept is the psychological process that underlies the observable characteristics of LPS: a considerable search for information, most of which is presented in human language, and a substantial length of time for decision making. LPS is merely an extension of RRB; but, as will be made clear in this chapter and in Chapters 4, 5, and 6, the amount of information processing required is much greater than with RRB and much less than with EPS. Because of the greater role of information in LPS, we must become more realistic and drop the assumption, made in Chapter 1, that the information received by consumers is simple and precise.

Information processing is often discussed at two different levels, and both are essential for understanding consumers' behavior. Information processing is one way to describe in sociopsychological terms how communication operates to change attitudes.[1] Information processing is identified with the concept of a flow-chart used in Chapter 2, which has information as its input and change in buying behavior as its output. The sociopsychological approach is particularly useful because it is highly operational in the field and is excellent for dealing with information content, as in designing a message like advertising copy. It is sometimes held that this approach is limited by omitting motivation, but the approach does not necessarily omit motivation, as will be seen in Chapter 7, Attention and Search.

A deeper view of information processing which emphasizes human beings' limited capacity to receive information involves memory, especially short-term memory (STM). STM is the key to much of limitations on the human ability to process information and to think. Consequently, if we are concerned with how well consumers can handle certain kinds of information—and we often are— STM becomes an essential construct, and this deeper view becomes necessary. For example, as was shown in Chapter 1, consumers in a postindustrial society will probably do much of their buying by requesting that certain information be shown on their television screens. When we consider what kind of information will be most effective and how long must it be left on the screen, questions about

---

[1]W. J. McGuire, "The Guiding Theories behind Attitude Change," in C. W. King and D. J. Tigert (eds.), *Attitude Research Reaches New Heights,* American Marketing Association, New York, 1971, pp. 26–48.

the human ability to process information are raised. Another instance of this problem is unit pricing. This was strongly urged in Congress as a means of helping the consumer; but it has not been very effective, as several studies have shown. Is this because the information is not displayed so as to facilitate the consumer's comprehension? Understanding the deeper level of processing by considering STM is especially useful in designing the *form* of a message, as opposed to the content.

Both views of information processing—sociopsychological and STM—are highly useful, and the two do not overlap much; therefore, it would seem sensible to merge them. The sociopsychological view will be covered in this chapter; the limitations of human beings as information processors will be covered in Chapter 4. Merging the two views will substantially improve our ability to deal with the whole chain of information processing.

The need to deal with the entire chain of information processing has been pointed out by the social psychologist W. J. McGuire. Writing about one link in the chain, McGuire said: "One of the scandals of social psychology . . . is the low correlation between attitudes and action."[2] McGuire believes that we must not confine our attention to the simplistic relationship between attitude and behavior: ". . . The communicators should develop persuasive material that maximizes the likelihood of evoking each of the steps in information processing from exposure, reception, comprehension, etc., down to the ultimate step in action."[3] If consumers are to buy a brand, they must understand it. To understand it, they must (1) have received its meaning and (2) have made a judgment about whether it serves their needs better than alternative brands. Let us now examine the concept of "meaning."

MEANING OF A BRAND

The total meaning of a brand is called its "semantic structure." It can be represented by a tree. To illustrate, we will examine a consumer product (freeze-dried coffee) and an industrial product (self-drilling screws). For a consumer, the "meaning" of Maxim coffee looks like Figure 3-1. There are, say, four kinds of breakfast beverages, one of which is coffee; there are three kinds of coffee, and for each kind there are a number of brands.

For an industrial buyer, the semantic structure of "brand *C*" self-drilling screws might look like Figure 3-2. Self-drilling screws perform two operations: drilling the hole and tapping the thread. Self-tapping screws merely tap the thread in a hole bored by some other means. Regular screws neither drill the hole nor tap the thread. For each type of screw, there are a number of brands.

These hypothetical examples will help us to define the semantic structure of a brand. A brand concept implies a semantic structure; but typically we think of a brand concept in a more limited way, as involving only the relationship between

---

[2]W. J. McGuire, "Psychological Factors Influencing Consumer Choice," Project on Synthesis of Knowledge of Consumer Behavior, RANN Program, National Science Foundation, April 1973, p. 76.

[3]McGuire, "Psychological Factors," p. 79.

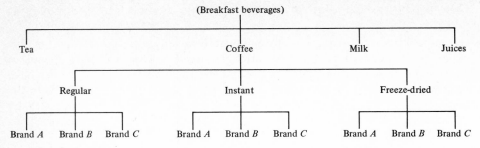

Figure 3-1 Hypothetical semantic structure of a consumer product: Maxim coffee.

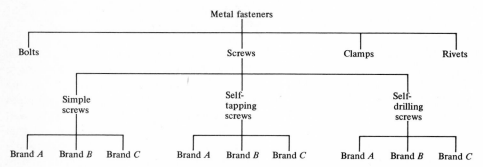

Figure 3-2 Hypothetical semantic structure of an industrial product: brand *C* self-drilling screws.

the brand—the physical object—and the consumer. A brand concept is not itself sensory data; rather, it is the result of sensory data to which thinking has been applied generally—a system which is the product of past responses to characteristic stimuli. It is made up of words and other symbols that link discrete experiences, as we saw in Chapter 2. Further—and here we move to semantic structures—the meaning of a brand does not stand alone. As our hypothetical examples have shown, it is related to several other class concepts. The semantic structure, then, is the relation between the structure of each of these related concepts and the structure of the brand concept. Taken together, these various structures constitute the semantic structure of a brand and the particular meaning that it holds for the buyer. Thus, a semantic structure brings together a wider range of objects, words, and meanings than does brand concept alone.

ANALYSIS OF SEMANTIC STRUCTURE: A WORD-ASSOCIATION STUDY

A real example of semantic structure will give us a much fuller understanding of what we mean by phrases like "giving information to the consumer" and "communicating with the consumer."

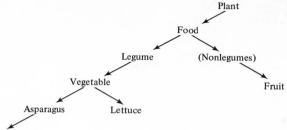

Figure 3-3 Hierarchy of nominal words elicited by "asparagus." The brand name "Del Monte" was not actually elicited in the study cited in the text; it has been added here to indicate the relationship between product class and brand concept.

The meaning of a brand can be elicited from a consumer who already has attained the brand concept. Free association is one way to do this. To illustrate, we will take the product class "asparagus." A study of word association was made with fifty Johns Hopkins students.[4] They were given the stimulus noun "asparagus," for example, and asked what words came to mind. The following words were elicited:

caesar	fruit	plant
can	green	shute
echh	hate	stringy
esophagus	legume	thin
food	lettuce	vegetable

These words can be sorted into four meaningful groups: (1) nominal words of the same type, (2) nominal words of a different type, (3) attributive words, (4) other words. Let us examine these groups in turn.

1 Nominal (naming) words of the same type: "food," "vegetable," "fruit," "lettuce," "legume," "plant." These nouns can be intuitively arranged in a hierarchy or tree (Figure 3-3).

Suppose that we are shown a piece of asparagus and asked what it is. Presumably, we could answer by giving any of the words in the list above. But in fact what word is given depends upon where in the superordinate-subordinate tree "asparagus" is being considered (conceptualized). That is, the term chosen will depend on the level at which the concept is to be categorized. For our purposes, the term chosen will also depend on function.[5] Someone shopping for dinner will probably categorize asparagus as a "vegetable," not a "legume," because it serves the function of being eaten. A farmer, however, concerned with

---

[4]James Deese, *The Structure of Associations in Language and Thought,* Johns Hopkins Press, Baltimore, Md., 1965, pp. 145ff.

[5]Roger Brown, *Social Psychology,* Free Press, New York, 1965, p. 319.

the fertility of the soil, might (mistakenly) call it a "legume." At this level, asparagus will be categorized with things (other products) that serve the same function, such as beans, peas, and spinach.

If one were thinking of the next lower level of the tree, one would be dealing with brands of canned asparagus. Thus, the level where asparagus is categorized is the functional or nonlinguistic equivalent of the brand. In marketing terminology, we say "in the same product class or competitive in the choice." By giving something a name, we match linguistic and nonlinguistic cues;[6] we match the meaning of words with the meaning of a thing.

What name—what symbol—we attach to a category in the first place is arbitrary. To learn the meaning of a thing, we may at first need the support of nonlinguistic experiences (like petting a cat and learning that it is a small furry animal that purrs), including experiences having to do with function (such as having a cat that serves the role of a household pet). But once learned, a name can be combined with the systematic properties of linguistic phonology; this lightens the burden that memory must bear, as we will see in Chapter 4, and also reduces the need for perceptual vigilance (for paying attention), as will be seen in Chapter 7.[7]

How objects are grouped and, consequently, labeled varies among cultures, because different cultures naturally have different needs. Languages reflect these different needs, particularly as regards degrees of discrimination. For example, seven colors are named in English, four in Shona (Rhodesia), and two in Bassa (Liberia).[8] Speakers of Bassa distinguish only the colors on the blue-green end of the color spectrum and the colors on the red-orange end. Thus, for them everything is either one color or the other. Similarly, English has only one word for rice; Hanunoo (Phillipines) has ninety-two words for rice. This indicates that the world of rice is vastly more complex for a speaker of Hanunoo than for a speaker of English. Grouping of the objects also indicates the importance of objects: the more important, the more careful the discrimination and the larger the number of groups. Rice is the dominant food for speakers of Hanunoo.

Economists and marketers are very much interested in substitution because of its implications for competition among companies—not only among brands but at higher levels in the semantic structure as well. For instance, how readily will the buyer substitute various vegetables for each other at various prices? How will the consumer choose between spending and saving? It is becoming more and more important to educate consumers to make product substitutions as the world's food supply becomes less and less adequate and new types of food must be found and accepted. Soybeans can be substituted for meat; they are equally nutritious and much cheaper, but not as tasty. Substitution in the semantic structure at the level of product class and higher is dealt with in Chapter 5.

[6]Ibid.
[7]Brown, op. cit., p. 321.
[8]Brown, op. cit., pp. 315–317.

2   Nominal words of a different type: "esophagus," "can," "shute," and "caesar." These words are related to "asparagus" and represent the physical or conceptual environment in which asparagus tends to be used. Perhaps "caesar" was given because the subject thought of asparagus as part of Caesar salad. Shute may have referred to "shoot," a stem with its leaves. Nominal words tend to be elicited in a word-association test instead of descriptive or attributive words. However, descriptive relationships do underlie the choice of these words.[9] For example, if we ask people to give the adjectives they associate with both asparagus and its associated nouns, we find that asparagus shares certain attributive words—"green," "sweet," etc.—with these associated nouns. Thus, they share meaning.

3   Attributive words: "green," "stringy," "thin." Attributive words both identify and evaluate a brand. These words and the attributes they describe are therefore crucially important for our purposes. We saw in Chapter 2, when brand concept was defined, that attributive ideas are formed by abstraction and generalization. For the buyer it is these attributes that directly give additional meaning to a product. By far most of the attributive words are adjectives, and most appear to be evaluative. Evaluative adjectives combined with adverbs (e.g., "very sweet") provide a quantitative description of *how* the consumer likes the brand. They represent the central construct of attitude toward a brand, which—as we saw in Chapter 2—is one of the elements of the brand concept.

4   Other words: "echh," "hate." These happen to be evaluative (they express dislike) but in general terms: that is, they do not name specific attributes.

We can now see why attaining a brand concept is such a powerful way for the buyer to receive information, make sense of it, and act upon it. As soon as a piece of asparagus is labeled "asparagus," it is placed in that category in our minds where all asparagus goes—and we immediately know immensely more about it than we did before we categorized it. The mere act of categorization adds tremendously to our knowledge. The situation is very different when one must *learn* each of the many relations exemplified in the word-association study before coming to the meaning of any new brand of asparagus. This occurs when a person has never seen or heard of asparagus; it is dealt with in Chapter 5, Extensive Problem Solving.

In LPS—by definition—the consumers already have the surrounding structure in mind. They know what asparagus is: they have acquired its meaning. What they do not know are the attributes of the new brand of canned asparagus that will fit into this category or class of things; they have not yet learned the *concept* of this new brand.

In summary, the word-association study shows how much meaning is in fact

<hr>

[9]Deese, op. cit., p. 150.

associated with the simple notion "asparagus." First, there are hierarchical relationships. Second, there are functional relationships. Third, there are associational relationships: that is, relationships having to do with perceived attributes of an object. These three kinds of relationships make up the fundamental process by which people use words in thinking.

Although the word-association study involved a group of people, we have drawn from it conclusions about the individual. A report by Fillenbaum and Rapoport suggests that although each individual's semantic structure is not as extensive as that of the group, this approach is nevertheless valid.[10] Finally, it must be pointed out that free word association is a rough but context-free method of identifying the meaning of a concept,[11] and that there are alternative methods. One alternative, multidimensional scaling, has come to be familiar in market research.[12]

ELEMENTS OF BRAND CONCEPT

In Chapter 2 brand concept was described in general terms; it will now be discussed more specifically. When we say that consumers do not have a brand concept, what exactly do we mean? What are they lacking? What must they acquire in order to have a brand concept? Let us return to asparagus: what information must be transmitted if our consumer is to acquire a concept of the new brand? To answer this question in terms of factors that we can do something about, such as advertising, we must take a closer look at the idea of a brand concept.

A brand concept is made up three parts: ability to identify a brand, liking of the brand, and the strength of the concept. These are called brand identification,[13] attitude, and confidence, respectively. (See Figure 3-4.) Our discussion of these elements begins with brand identification, instead of the familiar attitude construct, because brand identification is an essential foundation of attitude and because discussing it helps clarify the nature and source of the attitude construct.

Brand Identification

Brand identification is a denotative or referential description of a brand: we refer to it by means of referential attributive words. It is defined as a cognitive state of the consumer that reflects the extent to which he or she has sufficient knowledge to exhibit well-defined criteria for identifying—not evaluating—a particular brand. It is a specific image in the mind. As has already been implied, when we want to know what something is—including a new brand—we must first deter-

[10]S. Fillenbaum and A. Rapoport, *Structures in the Subjective Lexicon,* Academic Press, New York, 1971.

[11]James Deese, *Psycholinguistics,* Allyn and Bacon, Boston, 1976, pp. 110–112.

[12]P. E. Green, Y. Wind, and A. K. Jain, "Analyzing Free-Response Data in Marketing Research, " *Journal of Marketing Research,* **10**:45–52, February 1973.

[13]This construct was labeled "brand comprehension" in earlier work, including J. A. Howard and J. N. Sheth, *The Theory of Buyer Behavior,* Wiley, New York, 1969.

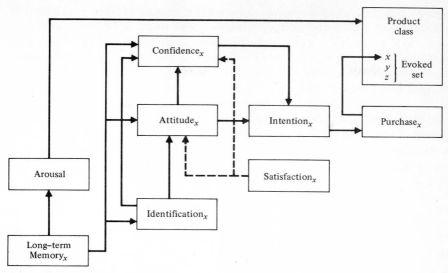

Figure 3-4   Partial model of LPS.

mine its identifying characteristics. For automobiles, these may include the wheelbase, width, height, and shape. For instant breakfast food, the identification would be "a powder that is put in milk, comes in several flavors, and is drunk, not eaten with a spoon." These attributes typically seem to have nothing to do with what the buyer likes about a product. They are merely ways of making an identification which must precede any decision about whether or not the product is liked. How do you know whether you like something until you are sure what it is? The need to know "what it is" becomes especially important when one wants to discuss the product.

For purposes of identification, marketers almost always use a brand name, such as Del Monte. They may go beyond the name and attach a picture—a trademark. René Lacoste, for example, places a crocodile on his tennis shirts. Brand identification is formed by information from long-term memory, as is shown in Figure 3-4.

One way of obtaining a precise understanding of brand identification is to consider a standard experiment used to study concept attainment.[14] The correct concept the experimenter wishes the subject to identify could be, for example, "two green squares with two borders," but the subject does not know this. The subject is presented verbally with possible combinations of four attributes, each having three values: *shape* (square, triangle, circle), *color* (green, red, black), *number* of figures (one, two, three), and *number of borders* (one, two, or three). Thus, there are eighty-one possible concepts ($3^4 = 81$). At each presentation— e.g., "one green circle with one border"—the experimenter tells the subject

[14]P. C. Wason and P. N. Johnson-Laird, *Psychology of Reasoning,* Harvard University Press, Cambridge, Mass., 1972, pp. 202–203.

"positive" (an instance of the correct concept) or "negative" (not an instance of the correct concept), depending upon whether one or more of the four attributes is correct. "One green circle with one border" would be called "positive" because "green" is correct (the other three dimensions are negative). The test proceeds with additional combinations of attributes labeled "positive" or "negative" until the subject has completely identified the correct concept.

This experiment is analogous to actual identification of a brand. For example, six attributes—"a small, two-door, hatchback coupe, getting 25 to 29 miles per gallon of gas, with horsepower of 80 to 99 and four cylinders"—was used by consumers to identify a certain car in 1970. A car is a complex, important item and therefore likely to require more identifying dimensions than many other products.

Such laboratory studies have produced several findings which bear on the problem of informing the buyer:

1 Attaining a concept becomes more difficult as the number of relevant attributes increases, the number of values of attributes increases, and the salience of the attributes decreases.

2 Attaining a concept becomes more difficult as the information load (number of attributes × values of attributes) increases and as more information is expressed in negative, rather than positive terms.

3 There are various strategies for handling the information load, some more successful than others in the long run.

These points summarize what was known in 1964,[15] and little research of this type has been done since. The experiments have placed on a much firmer foundation the idea of a brand identification as a part of the consumer's information-processing mechanisms. They also support the notion of three stages in the decision process—EPS, LPS, RRB—as will be seen later.

It seems likely that an attitude construct should also be considered part of the consumer's information-processing mechanisms; if so, it would be intimately related to brand identification. Unfortunately, research into concept formation and research into attitudes have—with minor exceptions[16]—remained separate. The attributive words used in studies of concept attainment are descriptive, whereas those used in attitude studies are evaluative. Yet, both are part of the concept that consumers acquire in order to identify brands, evaluate them, and act on their knowledge. Attitude dimensions are more abstract, but this probably does make them more difficult to learn.[17]

Before examining the attitude element of a brand concept, we will find it helpful to look at the total system we are assembling, construct by construct. Figure 3-4 shows all the mechanisms that are required in concept attainment (LPS), supplementing those shown when we discussed RRB: brand identifica-

[15]J. B. Carroll, "Words, Meanings and Concepts," in J. A. Emig, J. T. Fleming, and H. M. Popp (eds.), *Language and Learning,* Harcourt Brace and World, New York, 1966, pp. 86–87.
[16]R. J. Rhine, "A Concept-Formation Approach to Attitude Acquisition," *Psychological Review,* **65**:362–370, 1958.
[17]Wason and Johnson-Laird, op. cit.

tion, attitude, confidence, satisfaction, short-term memory, and long-term memory. Short-term and long-term memory are particularly important in communicating with the consumer. The dotted lines represent feedbacks in the system: if consumers buy and like a product, their satisfaction will increase their liking and confidence, and they will be more likely to buy it again.

Attitude

Attitude is shown in Figure 3-4 as building partly from long-term memory and causing intention to buy. It is defined as a cognitive state of the consumer which on a number of dimensions reflects the extent to which that consumer prefers, in terms of individual motives, each brand he or she is familiar with. It develops from evaluative, attributive words such as those cited in the example of asparagus. An attitude implies an expectation of satisfaction.

Attitude contains both personal and impersonal elements. The personal element is an evaluative, cognitive state of the consumer that has to do with the intrinsic qualities of the brand per se; this is contrasted with the impersonal elements which, as was noted in Chapter 2, have to do with external conditions associated with the brand. In LPS we expect the two elements to merge, instead of affecting intention quite separately as in RRB.

This view of attitude is a unidimensional or multidimensional notion which has an evaluative nature: "liking or disliking." The notion of a unidimensional attitude results when attributes of a brand are considered all together; the notion of a multidimensional attitude results when such attributes are considered separately. The unidimensional notion is convenient and simple; but the multidimensional notion is more useful, because when we like a brand, it is for particular reasons having to do with its particular attributes, and the multidimensional notion takes the mental counterparts of these attributes into account. These mental counterparts, as was seen in Chapters 1 and 2, we refer to as "choice criteria." The concept of choice criteria provides a much deeper understanding of consumer behavior, as economists are beginning to recognize.[18] The multiattribute model is the common way of describing this more complex view.

Multiattribute Model   A consumer evaluates a brand by a number of choice criteria—typically, three or four. He or she has a belief about where the brand is located on each criterion. Table 3-1 shows the elements of attitude in tabular form. The attitude is formed by beliefs about each of the choice criteria (column 1): personal and impersonal attributes. Column 2—salience—indicates the importance of each criterion to the consumer. The more important criteria have a greater influence upon behavior than the less important ones. Column 3—belief—represents the consumer's perception of facts about a product. If we want to determine consequences of behavior, we must weight each belief by the salience of the criterion. In this way column 4—contribution to attitude—is derived. The various elements contributing to behavior can be summed to yield a single estimate

---

[18]Kelvin Lancaster, *Consumer Demand: A New Approach*, Columbia University Press, New York, 1971.

Table 3-1   Evaluation of a Brand

Choice Criteria (1)	Salience (2)	Beliefs (3)	Contribution (4)
Personal criteria			
Mileage			
Ease of start			
Pickup			
Cleans engine			
Impersonal criteria			
Price			
Availability			
S & H stamps offered			
Attitude =			

called "attitude." Consumers are likely to buy the brand for which their attitude is most favorable.

Figure 2-2 (page 28) showed an actual example of impersonal beliefs toward gasoline, given in terms of the three criteria at the bottom of column 1 in Table 3-1. The four personal criteria are shown at the top of column 1. (In defending itself in 1973 against a charge by the Federal Trade Commission of untruthful advertising, the Sun Oil Company held that these four criteria were in fact used by many people to determine the "quality" of gasoline.) To simplify matters, let us assume that personal and impersonal beliefs do not operate independently of each other in affecting intention. Thus, there is one "attitude" box in Figure 3-4 and one "attitude" in Table 3-1.

The relationships indicated in Table 3-1 can also be shown in the format of the consumer behavior model which we began developing in Chapter 2. This is done in Figure 3-5 (for the sake of simplicity, the impersonal beliefs have been omitted). For each of the four criteria shown, information from long-term memory causes a belief to form.

The description given here of the multiattribute approach has been somewhat simplified. This approach is currently an active area of research, and questions are in the process of being answered. Researchers are trying to determine, for example, how many criteria are used, whether or not the criteria are independent of each other, how the consumer integrates information about them to form an attitude, and how salience affects this process.

Content of Choice Criteria   The source of choice criteria is discussed in Chapter 5; their actual content is a matter of some debate, and we will deal with content here. Lancaster, who has pioneered the use of choice criteria in economics but labeled them "characteristics," views choice criteria as the mental counterpart of "objective" characteristics of a brand.[19] He has in mind criteria

[19]Ibid. He also assumes that the consumer is perfectly informed.

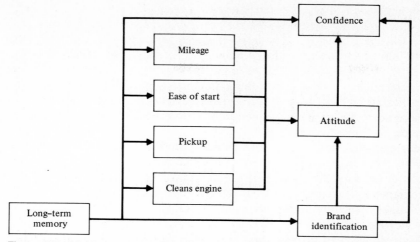

Figure 3-5 Multiattribute version of LPS in terms of the consumer behavior model.

that can be measured in conventional units such as distance, weight, and volume in inches, ounces, and pints. Economists who take this so-called objective view are probably motivated by at least two considerations.

First, they have found it useful to conceptualize the world as being made up of firms and households and to see the household as the counterpart of the firm. They therefore think in terms of "consumer technology"—which, like production technology, they take as a given. Consumer technology is defined as the ratio between a product and its capacity to satisfy a want. A change in technology is said to occur when the consumer views a brand as having a different want-satisfying capacity from what it had before the change. Traditional economists have been unconcerned with changes in consumers' preferences. Rather, they have taken given preferences as a starting point and examined how consumers would respond to changes in price and income. Recently, however, they have begun to deal with advertising, which can change preferences; and Lancaster predicts that economists will be more and more concerned with changes in preference.

The second consideration has to do with the sophisticated statistical techniques of econometrics, which are less effective with ordinal data than with interval or ratio data. With ordinal data one can say only that something is greater or smaller than another thing on some dimension such as size. The economist thinks of psychological data—e.g., "I like *A* very much"—as necessarily ordinal in nature.

Psychologists, on the other hand, consider the formation of preferences— that is, the attainment of concepts—as a central problem. They tend to be highly operational in their thinking and are experienced in attempting to get operational measures of subjective feelings, such as liking. Also, because they are finding that human language is a precise instrument for conveying meaning, they favor measures which may not appear on the surface to be equal-interval but which in fact can be treated as such.[20] Equal-interval scales tell us that if a woman rates brand A "4" on a like-dislike scale and brand B "2," she likes A twice as much as she likes B. Whether the content of choice criteria really is equal-interval is yet to be determined. I believe that the economist is more correct as regards brand identification, which probably does have objective content, and the psychologist is more correct as regards evaluation or attitude, which probably is more often in terms of subjective content.

Besides personal and impersonal choice criteria, there is a third type: interpersonal. Consumers often act partly for social reasons—to be better liked, for instance, or to be more respected by others. As will be discussed in Chapter 5 and later chapters, each person has a self-concept which is primarily, if not entirely, a concept relating himself or herself to others. We all receive satisfaction from viewing ourselves favorably in relation to other people, particularly people whom we like and respect—that is, people with whom we *identify*.

The purchase and consumption of certain brands can affect our self-concept. A recent advertisement for the Cadillac illustrates this idea: owning a Cadillac is "a good way to show the world the kind of person you are." The brand, or the purchase situation, in this case has attributes which supposedly contribute to one's self-concept. Consumers' mental counterparts of these socially originated attributes are among their choice criteria.

Interpersonal beliefs are like personal beliefs in that they probably change infrequently (impersonal beliefs change more frequently); but they are different in that interpersonal beliefs have to do with either the quality of the brand or the external conditions of purchase and consumption. These social effects on buying will be more fully developed in Chapter 9.

Choice Criteria and Language   The choice criteria can be related to language. As was noted earlier in this chapter, attributive relations are adjectival. Adjectives are powerful words. Many of them have opposites, e.g., "bad-good," "black-white," "dark-light," "hard-soft." Out of 278 commonly used adjectives, Deese found thirty-nine pairs of opposites.[21] Such opposites are used when we form concepts. Adverbs are used to intensify or enumerate. "Very sweet," for example, is more intense than "somewhat sweet." The role of adverbs appears to be multiplicative instead of additive.[22] Thus, adverbs increase the precision with which adjectives can be used in conceptualizing a brand— in building a brand image. The association of a noun with its modifying adjectives and adverbs in the mind of the buyer constitutes a brand concept. The criteria in Figure 3-5 are in fact evaluative adjectives. Thus, we can begin to see how

[20]C. E. Osgood, "Psycholinguistics," in S. Koch (ed.), *Psychology: A Study of A Science,* McGraw-Hill, New York, 1963, p. 271.

[21]Deese, *The Structure of Associations in Language and Thought,* p. 124.

[22]N. Cliff, "Adverbs as Multipliers," *Psychological Review,* **66**:27–44, 1959.

the meaning or semantic structure of the brand provides a vocabulary that can accurately describe the brand to someone who is unfamiliar with it.

Attitude and Brand Identification   Attitude is formed from two sources. First, as is shown in Figure 3-4 by the arrow from "long-term memory" to "attitude," it is formed from information either previously stored or recently received. Second, the evaluative—attitudinal—level of cognition is more abstract than the brand-identification level; but this abstract level must rest upon—be formed from—the level of concrete identification. "The more abstract process must originate with a concrete process and cannot exist without it."[23] Brand identification, then, is the foundation upon which attitude is built, as was suggested by the arrow leading from "identification" to "attitude" in Figure 3-4. This may seem to go without saying: obviously, consumers must identify the brand toward which they have an attitude; attitude is meaningless except in terms of an object. But unfortunately, much attitude research has probably been weakened because the attitude object was not well specified and the consumers were left unsure about the thing toward which they were being asked to express an attitude.

Figure 3-6 (page 54) shows how information (F) and brand identification (B) interact in shaping attitude (A). It can be seen that if $B = 0$ or 1, F has no effect on A; but as B increases, F has a greater and greater effect. B has both a direct effect (as is suggested by the increase in A with increasing B) and an interactive effect with information (as is indicated by the increasing slope with higher values of B). These data are consistent with the hypothesis that identification must precede attitude. The correlational study from which the data were taken is discussed at greater length in Chapter 14.

Brands without Differences in Quality   In the discussion of the multiattribute model, it has been assumed that differences, real or imagined, exist among the brands from which the consumer is choosing. Yet most of us can think of brands between which there probably are no relevant differences, as the consumer knows. Differences among brands probably tend to diminish, for example, as a product reaches the maturity stage of its life cycle. The situation becomes more and more like that assumed in classical demand theory: brands are all alike. Cases involving infringement of copyright provide instance after instance where every attempt has been made to make one brand like another. Advertising in such areas is often substantial. How can this advertising be explained if, as we have implied, the purpose of advertising is to tell consumers about differences among brands?

There is a growing body of evidence that mere exposure to neutral information about an object will improve a person's attitude toward it. Figure 3-7 (page 55) shows the results of a field experiment in which five Turkish words were randomly

[23]D. O. Hebb, personal communication, April 25, 1975.

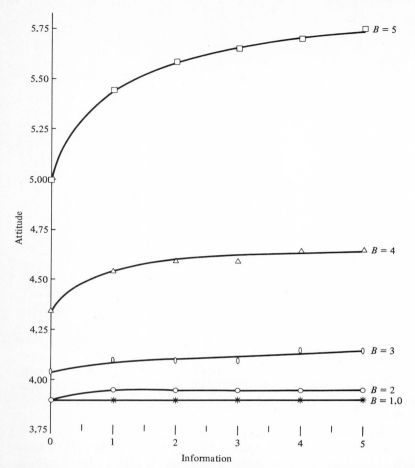

Figure 3-6 Interaction between identification and information affecting attitude. (*M. Laroche and J. A. Howard, "Nonlinear Relations in a Complex Model of Buyer Behavior," Graduate School of Business, Columbia University, mimeographed, 1975.)*

assigned to appear 1, 2, 5, 10, and 25 times within a twenty-five-day period in two university newspapers. "Single words were printed in unadorned column-inch boxes. On some days, only one word was printed; on other days, two or three words appeared. At no time were there more than three words shown on a given day. During the exposure period, there was no editorial mention of the stimuli, and readers' queries were met with the reply that the purchaser of the displays wished anonymity."[24] Within three days after the series of Turkish words had appeared, 206 attitude questionnaires at one university and 74 at the other were distributed and collected in undergraduate classes. In addition, 1,000 names were

[24]R. B. Zajonc and D. W. Rajecki, "Exposure and Affect: A Field Experiment," *Psychonomic Science,* **17:**216–217, 1969.

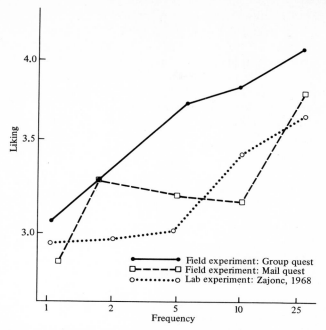

Figure 3-7 Effects of repeated exposure on liking. (*R. B. Zajonc and D. W. Rajecki, "Exposure and Affect: A Field Experiment,"* Psychonomic Science, **17:216, 1969.**)

chosen from the student directories of the two schools, and each of these students was mailed an attitude questionnaire.

The log-frequency monotonic relation is comparable to the results shown from the laboratory experiment, as seen in Figure 3-7, and also to a number of other laboratory experiments by Zajonc and his colleagues at the University of Michigan in a research program (extending over a decade) on the effect of frequency of exposure on attitude. These monotonic results were achieved when a "good-bad" response scale was used. One can hypothesize that this is the reason for the relation between attitude and exposure to a neutral stimulus suggested in Figure 3-4 by the arrow from "brand identification" to "attitude." It is one reason why advertising is used even when there are no differences between brands.

When other scales were used, such as "interesting-boring," that contained a component reflecting the subject's curiosity instead of an evaluative judgment, an inverted-U relation was found (this topic is taken up in Chapter 7, which deals with attention).

Confidence

The third element of consumers' concept or image of a brand is their confidence in their ability to judge its quality. This is defined as the degree of certainty that a consumer subjectively experiences with respect to satisfaction *expected* from a brand. This capacity has nothing to do with whether, in fact, the buyer concludes that the brand is good or bad; it is merely the capacity to judge. Confidence is the strength of this capacity. If two people hold equal beliefs about the quality of a brand, the one with higher confidence in that judgment is more likely to buy it.[25] This is not always so, but it usually is; the reason for this will be shown in Chapter 7.

Confidence arises from information stored in long-term memory and causes intention, as is seen in Figure 3-4. This information answers three types of questions. First, how distinctive is the brand being considered? Is it unique, or is it similar to competing brands? Second, how consistent over time is the evidence that has been received? Third, how widespread are the beliefs about it? What is the consensus?

First, let us examine the distinctiveness of a brand. There is a commonsense idea that the greater the difference between two objects, the greater a person's confidence in judging them. Unfortunately, evidence on consumers is limited, but this idea has been documented experimentally in the laboratory.[26] Statistically naive subjects were required to estimate which of two decks of cards had, on the average, the larger numbers on their faces. As the difference in the means of the numbers on the two decks became greater, the subjects' confidence in judging them increased. It is also well known that decision time is inversely related to the magnitude of differences between stimuli.[27] The relationship between distinctiveness and confidence is implied by the positive relation between attitude and confidence indicated by the arrow in Figure 3-4. As attitude intensifies, the distinctiveness of the brand from the consumer's point of view increases. Similarly, as identification increases, the distinctiveness of the brand increases; this is implied by the arrow from "identification" to "confidence" in Figure 3-4. Confidence will be increased by information only if identification has been developed. In other words, confidence—like attitude—rests upon identification. This is supported by the data in Figure 3-8: with low identification, information has little or no effect on confidence; but at high levels of identification, information has a strong effect on confidence.

Second, let us consider the consistency of evidence over time. The more consistent the information, the greater its effect on confidence. Again, we must go to the laboratory for support. In Irwin, Smith, and Mayfield's experiment, as the variance of the decks of cards increased, the subjects' confidence decreased. In less technical terms, when the numbers varied more from card to card, the subjects were less sure that their guess about the average of all the cards was correct.

Third, let us consider consensus. Many experiments have shown that consensus creates a basis for confidence in one's judgment. Support from others tends to increase our adherence to our opinions; disagreement with others tends to reduce certainty and to increase the likelihood of change.

[25]G. S. Day, *Buyer Attitudes and Brand Choice Behavior,* Free Press, New York, 1970.
[26]F. W. Irwin, W. A. S. Smith, and J. F. Mayfield, "Tests of Two Theories of Decision in an 'Expanded Judgement' Situation," *Journal of Experimental Psychology,* **51**:263–268, 1956.
[27]F. W. Irwin and W. A. S. Smith, "Further Tests of Theories of Decision in an 'Expanded Judgement' Situation," *Journal of Experimental Psychology,* **52**:345–348, 1956.

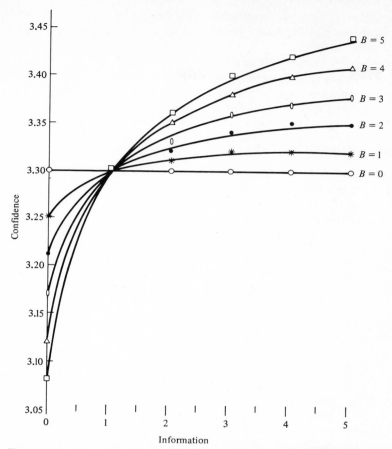

Figure 3-8 Interaction between brand identification and information affecting confidence. *(M. Laroche and J. A. Howard, "Nonlinear Relations in a Complex Model of Buyer Behavior," Graduate School of Business, Columbia University, mimeographed, 1975.)*

SATISFACTION

One vital type of information we have neglected to this point is that derived from experience. Satisfaction is defined as the consumer's mental state of being adequately or inadequately rewarded for the sacrifice he or she has undergone. The degree of adequacy results from comparing actual past experience with the reward that was expected from the brand in terms of its potential to satisfy motives served by its product class. We all believe, and it is true, that the *satisfaction* we get from buying and using a brand influences our liking for it, and therefore whether we will buy it again. For this reason, sastisfaction is incorporated into Figure 3-4 and an arrow connects "purchase" to "satisfaction."

We see here a "feedback" phenomenon. What happens today to one of the constructs will later in time have an effect upon a construct that is positioned earlier in the system. In this way, a loop is formed. Specifically, satisfaction from the brand today affects attitude and confidence favorably tomorrow, as is shown in Figure 3-4, and this in turn increases the probability of purchase the day after tomorrow.

It has been noted that attitude is an expectancy, an anticipation of satisfaction. What happens when this expectancy is disappointed? The answer to this question has to do with a consumer's level of aspiration, a topic that will be discussed in Chapter 7 as a determinant of attention and search.

APPLICATION OF PRINCIPLES OF LPS

A theory is not useful unless it can be applied. Application of a body of principles, however, does not come easily at first. In the following pages, examples will be given of how the principles can be applied. The applications will necessarily be incomplete, because the purpose here is to introduce the task, not to carry out full analyses. Also, the applications will be verbal, not quantitative, since quantitative application is reserved for Part Two of this book.

The areas of application to be discussed are as follows:

1 Product space
2 Product design
3 Package design
4 Message design
5 Pricing

Product Space

The idea of a product space is one way of sharpening and applying the concepts of LPS discussed in this chapter. First, each brand has an evaluative meaning. A consumer evaluates it by means of the choice criteria—the qualities on which it tends to differ from competing brands. These qualities are expressed by some of the attributive words (adjectives) of brand meaning, and they can be used as dimensions in Euclidean space.

Second, competition is usually important in a market. Your brand and the competing brands implied by the term "competition" can be arranged in a product space as in Figure 3-9. Assume that you, as a manager for Ford, are marketing the Pinto. The competing brands are, of course, other subcompacts. Let us simplify matters and assume that you find consumers evaluating a subcompact on only two dimensions: gasoline consumption and riding comfort. (In actuality, of course, for such an expensive and socially significant item, we would expect more than two dimensions to be used.) Pinto, Toyota, and Vega, let us suppose, occupy the positions shown in Figure 3-9. Assume that the positions are based on average figures taken from a sample of 200 people of an age and income group likely to buy a subcompact.

What we see is that Pinto is viewed as being more like Vega than it is like Toyota. This tells you that you are competing more with Vega than with Toyota. More specifically, it tells you that, if you wish to be more effective in the market,

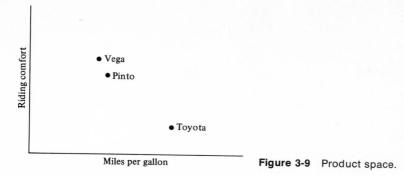

Figure 3-9   Product space.

you should consider redesigning your car to make it more comfortable riding; or, if the consumers' judgment is incorrect, to advertise that it rides easily.

The purpose of a product space is to indicate where a given brand stands in relation to competitors, and why the brand is located there, in terms of factors the manager can do something about—such as changing the brand or changing information about the brand. This information is, of course, the foundation for *positioning* a brand. "Positioning" and "repositioning" are two of the most important terms in the vocabulary of marketing managers. In their efforts to attain a better market share and meet other goals, such as profit, they are continually considering how a major brand can be repositioned. They may not necessarily think in the terms of Figure 3-9, but doing so would help them articulate the problem and clarify their thinking.

Figure 3-9 ignores differences among individual consumers in how the subcompacts are viewed. In Chapter 8 these individual differences are included in the idea of a market space so that market segments can be incorporated into the positioning decision.

Product Design

Analyzing a brand in terms of product space often suggests that the brand should be redesigned. Since redesigning can be a costly and time-consuming operation, it is important to understand how this decision is made. By definition, when consumers are involved in LPS, their choice criteria are fixed; it is therefore in terms of these criteria that we must design a product if we are to expect consumers to want it. For example, consider instant breakfast food. If consumers like the product class for reasons having to do with taste and nutrition, then we must design a product which is tasty and nutritious.

The problem is more complicated, however, Since the consumers have already formed the concept of a product class, they know about other brands in this class. Thus, our brand must be not only tasty and nutritious, but also tastier and more nutritious—or else cheaper—than these other brands. Otherwise, why should consumers buy it? Knowing where we are weak and where we are strong in comparison with competitors is an essential preliminary to redesigning the product.

An even more fundamental problem than redesign is building new products that will be accepted by the consumer. The failure rate is typically very high; for example, it was found to be 60 percent, even after test marketing, in a study by Booz, Allen, and Hamilton of fifty companies in 1964. The *test market* is an important concept: a potential new product is introduced into some medium-size city by being placed in retail stores and given the usual advertising. This is a realistic but expensive test of acceptance by consumers. The *concept test* is a faster, cheaper, but less accurate measure, which is often used before a test market will be considered: the product is described to consumers, who are perhaps shown drawings of it and are sometimes even given a package of the product itself and are then asked their evaluations of it.

Package Design

Human beings conceptualize more easily at the concrete level than at the abstract level, as was noted earlier. As a result, the physical characteristics of a product can facilitate or hinder the development of a brand concept. A distinctive package can help the consumer form an image of the physical brand upon which to build an attitude. If the package is too distinctive, however, the brand may not be viewed as belonging in the particular product class: it would fall outside the acceptable range.[28] The consumers would not look on it as meeting the needs satisfied by brands in this class. To accommodate it in their thinking, they would have to form a new product class (this is the topic of Chapter 5).

Message Design

In this chapter we have suggested the information that a message should contain if it is to transmit meaning to consumers that will allow them to form a brand concept. It must give identifying elements and belief elements (positions on choice criteria) and present this information in a consistent manner, indicating to what extent relevant beliefs are shared by the consumers' peers, thus strengthening their confidence. This gives us a great deal of guidance for designing the content of messages in any form: advertising, labels on packaging, or what the salesman tells the customer. (It does not, however, tell us the form in which the message should appear. This is the major purpose of Chapters 4 and 6.)

It is necessary to deal here with the situation where there are no differences in quality among the brands confronting the consumer. This situation is represented in Figure 3-4 by the arrow from "brand identification" to "attitude." It was noted earlier that advertising may be justified even when there are no evaluative differences among brands because consumers form a favorable attitude toward a stimulus merely from frequency of exposure. But there are probably very real limits to the amount of contribution that advertising, or any medium of communication, can make. When no evaluative information is being fed in to allow consumers to perceive one brand as distinctive, the brand image is likely to be weak.

---

[28]C. W. Sherif, "Social Categorization as a Function of Latitude of Acceptance and Series Range," *Journal of Abnormal and Social Psychology,* **67**:148–156, 1963.

Pricing

In discussing the consumer's response to price in RRB, we concluded that price seems to be an important influence and that there seems to be no reason to expect great complexity here. To consumers involved in LPS, however, the effects of price may become much more complex. This is shown especially in three ways: the association of price and quality, the notion of a range of prices, and the pricing of new products.

Association of Price and Quality   It is widely believed that a high price will cause the consumer to think that the quality of a brand is higher. In the economics books this is usually called the "price-quality association." Whether this association exists depends to a great extent upon how well-informed consumers are about the brand. If the only thing they know about the brand is price, they do decide that the quality is better when the price is higher.[29] As their information about the brand increases, they seem to be less inclined to associate price with quality. On this point, however, the conclusion is less firm, in spite of a great amount of research.

Range of Prices   The range of prices is another dimension by which the consumer conceptualizes all brands in a product class. The two extremes of the range represent anchor points. If the price set for a brand is outside this range, the consumer will not perceive the brand as belonging in the product class and so may not accept it as meeting the needs satisfied by that class.

Pricing New Products   An important question is whether a company should introduce a new product with a "skimming" price or a "penetration" price. A skimming price is a high price which skims off those willing to pay it. A penetration price is one that is low enough to attract many customers and so penetrates the market. If a penetration price is set, the company may find later that it wants to raise the price. A field study involving mouthwash, toothpaste, aluminum foil, light bulbs, and cookies has provided good evidence that it is unwise to raise a price once the product is introduced.[30] When confronted with a price increase, consumers tended to conclude that it was unwarranted and switched to other brands. Those confronted with a higher initial price bought and continued to buy the brand.

CONCLUSIONS

In Chapter 1, we introduced two basic cognitive operations: grouping and distinguishing. Now that we have discussed each of the elements of the brand concept—brand identification, attitude, and confidence—it is clear that

---

[29]D. M. Gardner, "The Role of Price in Consumer Choice," Project on Synthesis of Knowledge of Consumer Behavior, RANN Program, National Science Foundation, April 1975.

[30]A. N. Doob, J. M. Carlsmith, J. C. Freedman, T. K. Landauer, and S. Tom, Jr., "Effect of Initial Selling Price on Subsequent Sales," *Journal of Personality and Social Psychology*, **9**:3–8, 1969.

distinguishing a brand is substantially more complex than might have been thought from Chapter 1. Nevertheless, the basic ideas of grouping and distinguishing still describe the process. The consumer distinguishes at two different levels—identification and evaluation (attitude)—and on several dimensions at each level. When we know the content of a brand concept, we can specify what information consumers must have in order to attain the brand concept. It is such information that enables consumers to build each of the three elements, to acquire the meaning of a brand, to form the brand into a semantic structure. We have seen how the brand concept relates to the model of consumer behavior in Figure 3-4.

In LPS the means-end chain described in Chapter 2 is broadened. As originally presented, it included brand concept and impersonal beliefs. Here it is broadened by the introduction of choice criteria underlying the general notion of attitude. In later chapters, the means-end chain will be lengthened.

To provide perspective, three types of societies were described in Chapter 1: preindustrial, industrial, and postindustrial. The notion of product change is largely irrelevant in a preindustrial society. In an industrial society, the role of the consumer's income in shaping a buying decision should be considered. Changing income over the business cycle is particularly significant for the acceptance of new products. There is some evidence that a decline in income will substantially reduce a consumer's interest in new products. Presumably, so-called "discretionary income" declines much more than total income; this leaves the consumer with less freedom to buy additional products. Buying in postindustrial society will be dealt with in Chapter 5, Extensive Problem Solving.

So far, we have examined why consumers buy only at one level of explanation: that they buy because they have received information which caused them to form a favorable concept of a brand, which in turn supports the purchase of that brand. This process of buying, however, can be examined at a more basic level that will reveal more of the nature of the information that should be made available to consumers if we are to influence their buying behavior. This more fundamental level—which has to do with deeper information processing—will be dealt with in Chapter 4, where some of the form elements of the message are described.

QUESTIONS

1 In most design of marketing strategies and plans, a central issue is the meaning of the brand to the buyer. But we seldom ask ourselves what we mean by the "meaning of a brand." How would you describe it?

2 Describe the three elements of a brand concept and how they relate to each other.

3 The notion of information structure is used several times in this chapter and elsewhere. How is it related to the brand concept?

4 The design of marketing strategies and plans might, in large measure, be called the art of using human language. How do choice criteria as a part of the brand concept relate to human language?

5 What kind of information is likely to affect the consumer's confidence in judging the quality of a brand?

SUGGESTIONS FOR FURTHER READING

A. B. Ryans: "Estimating Consumer Preferences for a New Durable Brand in Established Product Class," *Journal of Marketing Research,* **11**:434–443, November 1975.

W. L. Wilkie and E. A. Pessemier: "Issues in Marketing's Use of Multi-Attribute Attitude Models," *Journal of Marketing Research,* **10**:428–441, November 1973.

Limited Problem Solving: Deeper Information Processing

CONTENTS

Summary

Questions
Suggestions for Further Reading

Having examined the elements of a brand concept and the words associated with it, let us now examine the more fundamental information processing that gives rise to the concept. In particular, we will deal with the *form* of the structure of information, since its content was discussed in Chapter 3. More specifically, we will examine in depth the nature of some of the barriers to communicating to the consumer. Naturally, consumers differ substantially in their capacity to process information; but this is dealt with in Chapter 8, where individual differences are taken up.

Language, memory, and inference are the foundation of deeper information processing. Let us illustrate how these three overlapping processes interrelate with each other and guide us in designing the form of information.

In the late 1960s, many consumer advocates believed that unit pricing would simplify the consumer's task in buying and that therefore it should be required by law. The principle of unit pricing is simple. Each price is stated not only in absolute terms, as is conventional, but also in terms of some unit of weight or volume of the product. Its effect is to standardize price in terms of package size. In some states, unit pricing was made mandatory; in others, retail stores often use it voluntarily as a service to consumers. A number of studies have indicated, however, that unit pricing has been relatively ineffective.[1] Only about one-third of the total population used it. When it is examined in light of the limits of consumers' information-processing capacity, its ineffectiveness is not surprising.

The unit price of a brand is usually given on a tag located where the brand is shelved. To compare prices, the consumer, while standing at the display, must first take each unit price into short-term memory (STM) and then hold each price there until all the prices to be compared are accumulated. Holding these prices in STM requires effort, as we will see later. Alternatively, the consumer can transfer the prices to long-term memory (LTM); but this too takes effort and time, as will also be discussed later. Furthermore, the consumer can hold a maximum of only about five prices in STM. Thus it is difficult to hold the information necessary for making an inference about which brand is cheapest. The limits of the consumer's information-processing capacity are being exceeded; or, at least, the consumer is feeling "cognitive strain." "Cognitive strain" is a term coined by Bruner, Goodnow, and Austin to refer to the sense of effort required to process information.[2]

---

[1] J. M. Carman, "A Summary of Empirical Research on Unit Pricing in Supermarkets," *Journal of Retailing,* **48**:63–71, Winter 1972–1973; and R. C. Stokes, *Unit Pricing Differential Brand Density and Consumer Deception,* Consumer Research Institute, Washington, D.C., June 1973.

[2] H. A. Simon, *The Sciences of the Artificial,* M.I.T. Press, Cambridge, Mass., 1969, p. 34n.

Now the *content* and *form* of information can be contrasted. Here, the content is the unit price, since we assume that price is a choice criterion, a position on which represents an element of attitude. The form is the way in which the information is presented. In this case, the form is a series of bits of information, each located some 2 or 3 feet from the next, which must be accumulated by the consumer in an excessive amount under pressure of time, and in a situation where the consumer is ill-equipped to process information with ease.

In discussing unit pricing, we are dealing only with numerical symbols, which are precise in meaning: 8 is always less than 9 but more than 7. Most information, however, is received by means of linguistic symbols, whose meaning is much less precise and which put a greater cognitive strain upon the consumer: for example, one brand is "very sweet," another "somewhat sweet," and a third "exceedingly sweet." Drawing an inference as to which brand is sweetest makes substantially more demands on STM than numerical symbols do. Also, the linguistic information that the consumer typically receives is probably much more ambiguous than the example given here. Nevertheless, the example of unit pricing can give us an intuitive understanding of the interrelations between language, memory, and inference, and the meaning of the *form* of structure of information. Language, memory, and inference will be discussed in detail, and, in the process, the characteristics of the consumer's information processing that should influence the form of the message will be identified.

TRANSMISSION OF BRAND MEANING BY LANGUAGE

Linguistic transmission is emphasized for a number of reasons. First, it helps us understand how the form of a message—grammar, for example—influences its effectiveness in communicating meaning. Second, language makes heavy demands on short-term memory, a fact we must recognize in order to discuss how quickly information can be processed. Third, because language makes demands on STM, the nature of language influences our capacity to make inferences and so form a brand concept. Fourth, language affects the nature of attention and search, as will be shown in Chapter 7. Fifth, the background given in this chapter lets us take advantage of the research in psycholinguistics that is applicable to consumers' behavior. Unfortunately, we use language so constantly, so habitually, and so mechanically that we seldom stop to consider the task it is accomplishing for us.

Advertising is one of a number of media used to transmit the meaning of a brand to a consumer. What is meant by "transmitting meaning"? As was discussed in Chapter 3, the meaning of a brand—the brand concept—is retained in the consumer's memory and can be represented as a tree. This was illustrated briefly with Maxim coffee and self-drilling screws, and in detail with asparagus. The question now is, "How do we transmit that meaning to a person who, say, knows about subcompact cars but not about a particular brand called 'Subaru'?" How essential is language in communicating the meaning of a Subaru?

Figure 4-1 An ambiguous sentence can be clarified by a picture.

In communucation, linguistic cues represented by words are often supplemented by pictorial symbols. Pictures can draw attention, add detail, and avoid ambiguity. Here is an example of how an ambiguous sentence can be clarified by a picture:

I saw the man on the hill with the telescope.

The question is, "Does the man or the speaker have the telescope, or is it just lying on the hill?" Figure 4-1 immediately clarifies the ambiguity: the speaker has the telescope. Musical symbols, too, can supplement linguistic cues. Music obtains greater attention for a message because hearing it satisfies certain motives irrelevant to buying. Also, it makes the message easier to remember because it provides an external structure. How many times have you noticed that hearing a musical passage reminds you of a set of words, e.g., "See the U.S.A. in a Chevrolet"?

The discussion here, however, will be confined to linguistic cues because language is by all odds the most important way to communicate a brand concept. The linguistic transmission of meaning described in general terms is accomplished by means of phonetic, grammatical, and semantic structures.

Phonetic Structure

The phonetic structure is the meaningless, *physical* sounds of the language. These are called "phonemes." Phonetic structure may be illustrated by the following sounds:

> th e man likes a blu car

These symbols are the vowels and consonants of a particular language and carry no meaning whatsoever. Linguists are concerned with a vast phonological literature,[3] but only a small portion of it is relevant for our purposes.

Grammatical Structure

The grammatical system links sound and meaning. That is, it moves us from sound—the acoustical level—to meaning. This is obviously an important step. The grammatical system is, in turn, made up of morphology and syntax. Morphology consists of rules for building words; syntax consists of rules for building sentences.

Morphology At the morphological level, meaningless phonemes are grouped into morphemes—the minimum forms of meaning. For example:

> the man like/-s a blue car

Morphemes are essentially sounds that constitute words, such as "the" and "man." We will focus not on morphology but on syntax, because in the English language most rules operate at the syntactical rather than the morphological level.

Syntax There are two types of syntactical rules: sequencing and hierarchical.

Sequencing rules. These rules have to do with the order of words in a sentence. For example, in French the noun usually precedes the modifying adjective: *la maison blanche* ("the white house"). A language in which this rule obtains is more easily understood because the noun is heard first and the modifying adjective second, so that the hearer has a "conceptual peg" upon which to hang a complex series of attributive words— as the rest of the sentence is heard.

Hierarchical rules. These are one of the fascinating features of human language. Consider the following sentence, constructed from a flow of phonemes: "The Vega goes very fast." How does a hearer—for our purposes, a consumer—process this flow of words in order to distill meaning from the sentence and form a brand concept of Vega? The ability to process words separates human beings from animals. It has long been considered mysterious; but our understanding of it is now beginning to grow, as linguists and psychologists share their knowledge in the field of psycholinguistics.

[3]Roger Brown, *Social Psychology,* Free Press, New York, 1965.

Do we receive and analyze sentences from left to right, as we seem to read them? For a number of reasons we do not. The best way to describe how we analyze sentences as we receive them is to say that we use "structural grammar"—that is, hierarchical rules. The notion of structural grammar was developed by Chomsky[4] and has profoundly influenced the way we think about language. In structural grammar, an entire sentence is manipulated as a unit by the hearer, who operates (transforms the sentence) from the "top down," so to speak, as it is received.

We can use a simple structural grammar to illustrate the process used to analyze a sentence and so extract its meaning.[5] This simple grammar is made up of six rules. Let us apply it to the sentence "The Vega goes very fast," a sentence which is intended to communicate with consumers.

Rule 1 is: "Break the sentence into a noun phrase and a verb phrase."

$$S = NP + \quad VP$$
$$\text{The Vega} \quad \text{goes very fast}$$

Note that the sentence includes a choice criterion, which is represented by an adjective—"fast"—and further specified by an adverb—"very"—which gives the Vega a specific position on that criterion.

Rule 2 is: "Break the noun phrase into the article and the noun."

$$NP = \text{article} + \text{noun}$$
$$\text{The} \quad \text{Vega}$$

Rule 3 is: "Perform an operation on the verb phrase similar to that performed on the noun phrase."

$$VP = \text{verb} + \text{noun phrase}$$
$$\text{goes} \quad \text{very fast}$$

Rule 4 is: "Set out the verb."

goes

Rule 5 is: "Set out the nouns."

Vega

Rule 6 is: "Apply the articles (more generally, the determiners)."

the   very

---

[4] N. Chomsky, *Syntactic Structures,* Mouton Press, The Hague, 1957; and *Aspects of the Theory of Syntax,* M.I.T. Press, Cambridge, Mass., 1965.
[5] J. Deese, *Psycholinguistics,* Allyn and Bacon, Boston, 1970, pp. 18–21.

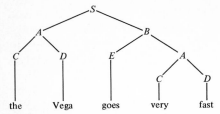

Figure 4-2   Tree diagram of simple structural grammar.

It is helpful to show the same process in the form of a tree, as is done in Figure 4-2.

That people do in fact process language in some such way as this is shown by the existence of "phrase markers." Each node, or switching point, in the tree is a phrase marker. You will recall that rule 1 broke the sentence into a noun phrase and verb phrase. Thus, in a simple, active, positive, declarative sentence, the hearer perceives a gap—a break—at the phrase marker between the two phrases. If subjects in an experiment listen to a sentence and simultaneously hear clicks occurring at random in the sentence, they will perceive these clicks as occurring, roughly, at the sentence breaks (the phrase markers) instead of where they actually occur.[6] In fact, as you may have observed, a speaker who pauses in the middle of a phrase, instead of between phrases (at the natural break), will be heard by other people as pausing at the break, not in the middle of the phrase. The ability of a receiver to structure an irregular flow of sounds by means of markers tremendously improves verbal communication.

"The Vega goes very fast" is a "kernel sentence," that is, a simple, active, affirmative, declarative sentence. Such a sentence can be contrasted with its opposite, a complex, passive, negative, interrogative sentence. The function of structural grammar is to convert the incoming flow of language to kernel sentences, because kernel sentences are the form in which meaning is stored in long-term memory (LTM).

Another important notion of structural grammar is that every sentence has a "surface" structure and a "deep" structure. The surface structure is the physical form of the sentence, the form in which it is received by eye or ear. The deep structure is the form of the sentence which conveys the meaning. It consists of the kernel sentences, derived from the surface structure. Surface structure is linguistic reality, and deep structure is meaning or psychological reality. As Greene puts it, "The kernel sentence has psychological reality."[7] It is the form by which meaning is conveyed and to which the surface structure of a sentence must be converted if it is to convey meaning.

According to the theory of structural grammar, the conversion from surface

[6]Deese, op. cit., p. 37.
[7]J. Greene, *Psycholinguistics,* Penguin Books, Baltimore, Md., 1972, p. 136.

structure to deep structure is achieved by the strictly linguistic rules illustrated above. For example, suppose that the incoming flow (surface structure) is a complex, passive, negative, interrogative version of the sentence given above as an example. It might then read:

Is it that the car which does not go slow is a Vega?

If this were to be converted to "The Vega goes very fast," it might be supposed that the amount of time required to process the information would be in direct proportion to the number of transformations required to make the conversion to the kernel sentence. But the situation is not that simple. It is true, in fact, only where a negative is concerned. It does not hold true for the complex, the passive, or the interrogative: elements of meaning can enter in and modify the strictly linguistic predictions about processing time for these three characteristics. We now believe that there is some similar process operating to perform this conversion, but it is not solely linguistic; it includes psychological elements.

Semantic Structure

Now, how does the semantic, or meaning, structure of language take over from the grammatical structure to enable a consumer to form brand identification, attitude, and confidence as the designer of the message intended? Currently, we do not know; but this is a field of very active research. Newell and Simon view their theory of problem solving as a theory of the nature of deep structure; but their work, though highly interesting, does not include learning of a concept, which is our concern in LPS and EPS.[8]

Whatever process occurs when we come to understand a sentence, it is essential to capturing the meaning of the brand concept. There are several ways to characterize this process of coming to the meaning of a sentence or segment of a sentence. One might say, for instance, that it is the assignment of information to semantic categories, such as were represented by Figure 3-3 for the example of asparagus: categories in the semantic structure which, in terms of words, is the meaning of a brand. Understanding a sentence, then, means assigning its subject to one of the categories in that structure. Then, consumers would use facts about the subject to form brand identification (B^1), attitude (A) and confidence (C) and so come to distinguish it from other objects in the same category.

Unfortunately, with the current state of knowledge, we cannot predict in advance how a given person will conceptualize a specific brand in a specific situation: that is, in which category in the semantic structure the brand will be placed. For this reason, much of our specific information about a person's brand meaning must be derived empirically, from people who have already developed

[8]A. Newell and H. A. Simon, *Human Problem Solving,* Prentice-Hall, Englewood Cliffs, N.J., 1972, p. 38.

that meaning from their own experience of conceptualizing the brand. It is for this reason that the elicitation of meaning was emphasized at the beginning of Chapter 3. Again, the familiar processes of grouping and distinguishing are useful. When grouping brands, consumers think in terms of similarities: they group a brand with other brands that have similar attributes (are in the same product class). Much work has been done on multidimensional scaling, using data having to do with similarities. When asked to distinguish a brand, however, consumers do not reveal the importance of attributes. Rather, they think of the brand as being classified in some common way. Classification is in terms of superiority or subordinacy: consumers think of a product as being in some category, higher or lower, in the relevant semantic structure, as we saw with the example of asparagus.

Conclusions about Language

We have seen that a message made up of a particular kind of symbols—human language—can carry meaning, and that linguistic factors (e.g., affirmatives as opposed to negatives) can affect the transmission of meaning. Nothing has been said about how individuals differ in their ability to handle language; but these differences are great, and this fact should influence the analysis of consumers' behavior, as will be seen in Chapter 8.[9]

The processing of language is done mainly by short-term memory. Thus, our next step is to examine how memory facilitates the flow of meaning into information storage, from which referential (identification) and evaluative (attitudinal) inferences about a brand can be made. Finally, to complete the chain of information processing that leads to identification, attitude, and confidence—and so underlies buying behavior—we will deal with these same processes as a problem of inference. This will also provide a better understanding of the psychological processes that make up the linguist's notion of deep structure.

TRANSMISSION OF BRAND MEANING BY MEMORY

Obviously, memory is required to a great extent in processing language to extract the meaning of a sentence. For a number of reasons, memory requirements impose severe limitations upon the buyer's ability to process the flow of information when it is received in the form of language. Hence, memory must be considered if we are to understand how a buyer receives information to shape a brand concept and a concept of a product class. Knowing the nature of this process can help us design messages that are more likely to "get through" and to be retained in the buyer's memory.

In addition to allowing the manipulation of words and sentences so that meaning can be extracted, memory serves another very important function: it is a selector. Consumers are confronted with far more information than they can

---

[9]L. R. Gleitman and H. Gleitman, *Phrase and Paraphrase,* Norton, New York, 1970, pp. 137–141.

possibly use. Even when a consumer lacks certain *kinds* of information to form a brand concept, overall there is continually far more information than he or she can handle. This flow must be reduced to a manageable amount; the consumer must carefully select out of the total flow what will best serve his or her motives. Three memories largely accomplish the two difficult functions of selecting input and extracting meaning from it: sensory memory (SM), short-term memory (STM), and long-term memory (LTM).

Sensory Memory

Sensory memory (SM) automatically receives all information that the senses come into contact with. If you walk into a room, your sensory memory takes in everything received by your eyes. Material is held there, however, only for a few milliseconds; unless it is transferred into short-term memory by that time—which most of it is not—it is lost. The material is stored as a representation of the physical message itself—as the sounds or phonetics of a verbal statement, for example—not as a meaningful unit. SM plays an important, automatic role as an encoder, but it is not so influential as the other two memories. Indeed, we will disregard it in order to focus upon short-term and long-term memory, which have more immediate relevance for the transmission of meaning.

Short-Term Memory

Figure 4-3 shows how short-term memory (STM) can be visualized in relation to other elements of the process by which consumers receive meaning. STM receives information from the environment ("information available") to which the buyer is exposed by the senses and processes it for transmission to permanent memory (LTM). STM is defined as a working memory, receiving information from sensory memory and transmitting it to long-term memory. Controls within STM monitor these processes.

Information is stored in STM in meaningful units, and in STM the surface

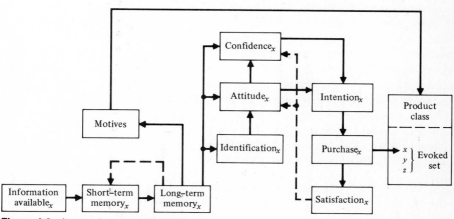

Figure 4-3 Incomplete model of LPS.

structure of sentences is converted to deep structure. Material is stored in STM for no more than eighteen seconds, unless one consciously tries to retain it by rehearsing it.

Here is an example of the rehearsal of content in STM. Suppose that you are telephoning a person whom you never expect to call again. You look up the number in the directory, and upon finding it you proceed to say it to yourself (you rehearse it) as you dial. Once someone answers at the other end, you forget all about the number. A few hours later, you cannot recall it. You never expected to use it again and so did not bother to store it, but you did rehearse it so that it would be available the one time you did need it. The phenomenon of rehearsal is essential to STM.

You will recall the "top down" analysis of our simple structural grammar by which meaning is derived. The demands that this processing places on STM are obvious. For example, rule 1 breaks the sentence into a noun phrase and a verb phrase; and rule 2 breaks the noun phrase into the article and noun. Clearly, the verb phrase must be held in memory storage while rule 2 is being applied. Our example is an exceedingly simple structural grammar, however; we did not deal with the more complex processes of converting normal conversation into meaning.

Imagine the storage required for processing the complex, passive, negative, and interrogative sentences that characterize much normal writing and conversation. The evidence is clear that constituent structure affects the way a sentence is memorized. This is seen in transformation studies, which indicate that the greater the number of "phrase markers" in a sentence, the more difficult the sentence is to remember.[10] For example, contrast two sentences: "The boy hit the ball," and "The ball hasn't been hit by the boy." The second is harder to remember because it has two additional markers: a negative and a passive.[11] Further evidence is provided by the fact that the ability to describe a color is related to the ability to remember it.[12] Finally, consider sentences in which clauses are complexly embedded. For example, "The Vega, which has yellow that is bright upholstered seats, goes very fast." This double self-imbedded sentence will cause many listeners to stumble.

The consumer must receive the flow of information at a given pace—as it emanates from television, for example. If the sentence is coming too fast, it becomes unintelligible; the human information-processing capacity is too slow to keep up with it. On the other hand, if it is received at too slow a rate, the constituent grammatical groupings fall apart; this also makes it unintelligible— one hears a meaningless string of sounds (not even words, much less sentences), as can be seen when the speed of a record player slows down.

It must also be noted that the consumer processes information in series, not in parallel.[13] To process one piece of information—e.g., to receive a new piece of

[10]G. A. Miller and D. McNeill, "Psycholinguistics," in G. Lindzey and E. Aronson (eds.), *The Handbook of Social Psychology,* vol. 3, Addison-Wesley, Reading, Mass., 1969, pp. 704–709.
[11]Miller and McNeill, op. cit., p. 706.
[12]Miller and McNeill, op. cit., pp. 736–741.
[13]Newell and Simon, op. cit., p. 796.

information—one must interrupt one's current processing. This does not, however, seem to preclude the reception in parallel of information about different attributes of the same brand.[14]

Can we say anything further about the constraints on STM than that information is stored in STM for no more than eighteen seconds? We can. First, the capacity of STM is between five and seven chunks of information. A "chunk" is a standard measure, but the "size" of a chunk can vary. A single letter can be a chunk. On the other hand, several words, if grouped in a meaningful pattern, can also be a chunk. "Q," "U," and "V" are each a chunk, but "C-A-T" is a single chunk. A phrase is also a chunk. A chunk is defined as "the quantity that short-term memory will hold five of."[15] Its psychological reality has been well established. Second, about five to ten seconds are required to fix a chunk in LTM after it leaves STM.

Although meaningfulness is the most important characteristic of content, affecting the ease of transfer to LTM, it is not the only characteristic. Other nonlinguistic factors are familiarity and similarity.[16] If the content is familiar, it is more likely to be transferred and stored. If elements of the stimulus are similar to what was previously retained, it is also more likely to be stored. These effects occur because there is a feedback from LTM to STM, as shown in Figure 4-3. Information can be meaningful only in terms of being related to meanings previously stored in LTM. Similarly, information is familiar only in terms of its relation to items previously stored in LTM and similar only in terms of previously received information. Thus, there is constant feedback from LTM to STM as a stream of information is received by STM from sensory memory. This feedback strongly influences the nature of STM processing and whether the incoming stream is transferred into LTM for permanent storage.

Long-Term Memory

Long-term memory is defined as existing where an event recalled from the past has been absent from consciousness and belongs to the psychological past. It is full of gaps and distortions. Retention is more or less permanent.

The organization of material is really the key to long-term memory (LTM). In general, I will give here only the principles of human learning of which we are at least intuitively aware from our own experiences, such as studying for important examinations. Learning is a matter of chunking and categorizing information.[17] The following principles obtain:

1 *Small basic units:* The material must be divisible into self-contained sections with no more than four or five items (chunks) in a section.

2 *Internal organization of the material:* Within the message itself, all the parts (chunks) should fit together in a logical, self-ordering structure. Meaningfulness is the most common ordering relationship.

[14]D. Kahneman, *Attention and Effort,* Prentice-Hall, Englewood Cliffs, N. J., 1973, p. 110.
[15]H. A. Simon, "How Big Is a Chunk?" *Science,* **183**:482–488, 1974.
[16]Simon, *The Sciences of the Artificial,* p. 38.
[17]D. E. Norman, *Memory and Attention,* Wiley, New York, 1969, p. 122.

3 *External organization of the material:* Some relationship should exist between the material to be learned and material which has already been learned, so that one fits neatly with the other.

The common factor operating in external organization, of course, is simply meaningfulness. An advertisement says, "Vega gives good gas mileage," and you are likely to remember it because you already know about Vega. Vega is a part of a semantic structure in your mind. Mnemonic devices are also examples of external organization. For instance, if you want to remember ten things—and especially if you want to retain their particular order in LTM—you might try the following device. First memorize these rhymes:

One is a bun	Six are sticks
Two is a shoe	Seven is heaven
Three is a tree	Eight is a gate
Four is a door	Nine is a line
Five is a hive	Ten is a hen

These ten short lines are easily memorized and, once memorized, can be used indefinitely thereafter. Second, associate each of your ten things with the noun in one of the sentences, allowing about five seconds for each association. Now, what was number seven on your list? You will have no trouble remembering it.

Information is almost never stored in LTM in exactly the same form as the original message. It is far more likely to be a paraphrase, in kernel sentences; in the process of admitting information, consumers transform it into their own words in as simple a form as possible. By paraphrasing it, they understand its meaning, and meaningfulness—as was already noted—greatly facilitates storage.

Another characteristic of a message which influences whether it will be transferred to LTM is its relevance. In discussing attention in Chapter 7, we will deal with this at length. Here it is necessary to say only that "relevance" refers to the degree to which information relates to a concept the buyer values highly. Specifically, it is information that will serve a buyer's motives in making a choice. Thus, putting a name on a brand that serves such motives lightens the burden on memory, because information associated with that name will then be more easily processed.

Model of LTM   An important characteristic of LTM is the ease with which information can be retrieved from it. Retrieval is, of course, implied in the feedback from LTM to STM shown in Figure 4-3, where in order for the information to feed back it must first be retrieved from LTM. Retrieval will also be implied in discussing inference: how a consumer infers a brand concept from facts retrieved from LTM combined with new facts just received.

The notion of retrieval, although not explicitly mentioned, was dealt with at length at the beginning of Chapter 3, in the discussion of a consumer's semantic structure. When subjects were asked what words they associated with "aspara-

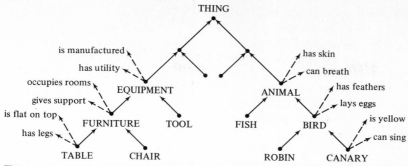

Figure 4-4   Model of LTM. (*D. E. Meyer and R. S. Schvaneveldt, "Meaning, Memory Structure and Mental Processes,"* Science, **192**:29, 1976.)

gus," for example, they retrieved the associations from LTM. Earlier, we were concerned only with the content of retrieval. But the *speed* of retrieval can also be used as a measure of recall. Specifically, it can be used to map where consumers locate information in LTM; and location will influence how easily a particular piece of information can be retrieved.[18]

Figure 4-4 is a view of semantic structure in terms of memory rather than meaning. (The example of asparagus in Figure 3-3 was given in terms of meaning.) As with semantic structure, Figure 4-4 is made up of categories of objects in a hierarchy from the general to the specific. It exhibits four kinds of relations: subset, superset, overlap, and disjoint. In the experiment from which this diagram was drawn up, subjects were given sentences like "Some birds are animals." In this sentence, the subject ("birds") is a *subset* of a higher category ("animals"). If the sentence was "Some animals are birds," the first category would be a *superset* of the second. If the sentence was "Some birds are female," the relation between the first category and the second would be *overlap,* because both animals and birds can be female. Finally, if the sentence was "Some birds are tools," the relation would be *disjoint,* because one category ("birds") bears no relation to the other ("tools").

The subjects, when presented with each of the sentences, were to respond "true" or "false." By recording the response time, the experimenters obtained estimates of retrieval time. Their conclusion was that the *nearer* categories are in meaning, the *shorter* the response time is. Specifically, subset relations were closest in meaning, and response time was shortest for these. Superset relations were second closest; overlap relations were third closest; disjoint relations were least close. Response times varied inversely with closeness of the relationship. Thus, support was given to the idea that memory is arranged hierarchically by categories. People cannot recall instantaneously; instead, they take time to sift their memories for stored information, and the time taken varies inversely with proximity of meaning of the word being recalled to the stimulus.

[18]D. E. Meyer and R. W. Schvaneveldt, "Meaning, Memory Structure and Mental Processes," *Science,* **192**:27–33, 1976.

An interesting point was noted, however. When universal affirmative sentences—e.g., "All birds are animals"—instead of existential affirmative sentences—e.g., "Some birds are animals"—were used, the results were somewhat different. We cannot go into the evidence here; but the conclusion was that universal affirmative sentences require extra mental processing. One reason for this is that in addition to the initial identification of category names, there is a subsequent check for links that connect the location of each category to a collection of basic defining attributes, shown as dotted lines in Figure 4-4, which must all be possessed by members of the category. We are already familiar with the notion of defining (identifying) attributes; see Chapter 3, page 46. In the case of universal affirmative sentences, these defining attributes are probably necessary to help verify whether the first category mentioned is a subset of the second category. In Figure 4-4, for example, canaries are yellow and can sing, while birds have feathers and lay eggs. It appears that a close relation between categories—e.g., "canaries" and "birds" instead of "canaries" and "animals"—actually slows down the process of retrieval. The similarity of categories necessitates the defining attributes; they are needed to determine whether the first category mentioned in a universal affirmative is a subset of the second category. "All birds are canaries" would elicit the response "false"; presumably this requires finding a defining attribute of the first category that is generally not an attribute of the second category, e.g., having many colors. Birds are of many colors, but canaries are not.

This model of LTM allows us to relate semantic structure (with its characteristic hierarchical form), concept attainment, and inference to memory. Next, we will deal with inference in greater detail. In Chapter 5, we will find that values (motives) share this hierarchical form with semantic structure and memory; these constitute the foundation of complex choice found in EPS.

Conclusions: Interaction of Language and Memory in Processing Information and Transmitting Brand Concept

As we have seen, language, memory, and their interactions are crucial in the processing of information. If we as private or public policy makers are to design messages, work with media, and decide the amount of resources to be used in disseminating information, we must understand concept, language, and memory—and especially their interaction. Concept is related to language by virtue of its meaning, contained in its identifying and evaluative attributes, which are adjectives. For the consumer to attain that meaning, language is first received in the form of sound—phonetic structure. Grammatical structure converts meaningless sounds into meaningful units of sound, which are words and sentences. The process of receiving meaningless sounds and converting them to meaning is carried out in the three memories: sensory, short-term, and long-term. In each of these, there are factors that can hinder the flow from meaningless sound to meaning stored in LTM. From LTM and currently received information, meaning is derived by inference, as is suggested by the model of memory given on pages 76 and 77.

TRANSMISSION OF BRAND MEANING BY INFERENCE

Inference, language, and memory make up the chain of information processing that underlies buying behavior. Inference is the process by which buyers convert information received from words and sentences and stored in LTM into a judgment of what a brand is (brand identification) and whether or not it is good for them (attitude), to a point where they are reasonably certain of their judgments about it (confidence).Inference was described loosely earlier in this chapter in order to convey some idea of its nature. Now, we will be more precise.

Inference is the process of coming to a conclusion about the referential and evaluative nature of a brand by drawing upon one or more other judgments. It takes place in short-term memory. In terms of logic, LPS (concept attainment) requires relational inference because the consumer has only to conclude that a new brand is rated "more" or "less" on certain identifying criteria and evaluated as "better" or "worse." A relational inference is a particular type of syllogism, a linear syllogism in which the conclusion depends upon the relations *within* the facts presented and *between* the sentences presented. An example is the three-term series problem,[19] two of which are given below. These examples could just as well be stated in terms of information a consumer has received about the positions of three brands—A, B, and C—on identifying criteria (brand identification) and on evaluative criteria (attitudes).

> A is larger than B.
> B is larger than C.
> A is larger than C.

> A is better than B.
> B is better than C.
> A is better than C.

In this form, the problem of inferring to attain a brand concept looks very simple. But the problems in the real world are often more complex in at least three major ways. First, the consumer may not have the facts stored in memory in their natural order, as shown above. Instead, the facts might be stored as follows:

> B is better than C.
> A is better than B.

If so, the facts must be reordered before the inference can be made:

> A is better than B.
> B is better than C.
> A is better than C.

---

[19]P. C. Wason and P. N. Johnson-Laird, *Psychology of Reasoning,* Harvard University Press, Cambridge, Mass., 1972, chap. 9.

Second, it may be necessary to compare more than three brands, and the number makes a difference. The greater the number of brands compared, the more difficult the inference. As we saw in Chapter 2, the evoked set can simplify this problem.

Third, the facts may be obscured in sentences—a possibility familiar to all of us who may have struggled with the ambiguities of human language. Here is a simple case:

A is larger than B.
C is smaller than B.

The second premise must be *converted* into:

B is larger than C.

Obviously, the difficulty is increased with complex sentences.

Experience with a specific problem also makes a difference and is a strong explanatory factor. When consumers first experience a problem, they seem to try to build a mental representation of the problem as it actually is and to handle all aspects of it more or less simultaneously. With further experience, however, they begin to elaborate the problem in ways appropriate to its particular constraints and its natural sequence and to develop a more mechanized approach.[20] Slovic and Lichtenstein suggest that a single criterion may first be used, with other criteria being adapted to it (something like the halo effect), but with experience other beliefs come to be more accurately inferred.[21] This suggests that the halo effect studied by Beckwith and Lehmann could be much greater early in LPS than later.[22]

Research on relational inference gives some evidence that referential and evaluative judgments are formed by processes which are not really dissimilar.[23] There is little evidence on whether identifying judgments are more easily formed than evaluative judgments; but some evidence is given in Chapter 6 from which it is concluded that identification is easier because it is less abstract.

Conclusions on Inference

Logical inference tells us how, working from information in long-term memory, the consumer decides where a brand is located on identifying and evaluative criteria. This is merely a beginning, but it gives us some additional hints (as we saw above) about how the form of a message, as contrasted with its content, can facilitate or hinder the process. Ease of retrieval is another factor, as indicated in the model of LTM; but it is omitted here in order to simplify.

[20]Wason and Johnson-Laird, op. cit., pp. 126–127.

[21]P. Slovic and S. Lichtenstein, "Comparison of Bayesian and Regression Approaches to the Study of Information Processing in Judgment," *Organizational Behavior and Human Performance,* **6**:712–713, 1971.

[22]N. E. Beckwith and D. R. Lehmann, "The Importance of Halo Effects in Multi-Attribute Attitude Models," *Journal of Marketing Research,* **12**:265–275, August 1975.

[23]Wason and Johnson-Laird, op. cit.

APPLICATION

In contemplating message design it is well to bear in mind the role of managers. Managers are not supposed to be able to create messages; this task is left to "creative people." The manager is, however, expected to formulate strategies and marketing plans, and these can be meaningful only insofar as their implicit assumptions about what can be created are valid. Equally important, managers are expected to be competent in evaluating advertising and other types of information transmitted to consumers. Consequently, message design is a central problem.

Unit pricing illustrates how useful the understanding of information processing can be in designing a message. As was noted earlier in this chapter, unit prices are usually stated on a tag located near the brand. The results of this method have not been what consumer advocates had hoped. Only a small proportion of consumers, mainly those in the upper income brackets, have changed their behavior as a result of unit pricing. Russo et al., in an experiment in a chain of supermarkets, compared the method of displaying unit prices shown in Table 4-1 with the usual tag method.[24] As Table 4-1 shows, the raw price was given in the middle column of the display and the unit price in the right column. The stores in the experiment had been using separated shelf tags for some time; for the experiment, records were maintained on brand sales with the tag method for three weeks, and then the new method was applied for two weeks. The two methods were compared on a weekly basis. When the new method was used, consumers showed a significantly greater tendency to shift to cheaper brands. Presumably, they shifted because the data for comparing brands were close together, permitting them to bypass LTM. That is, consumers did not have to store the data in LTM to make comparisons. Furthermore, to the extent that comparisons were made among homogeneous brands in a product class, the effect of unit pricing was greater. Most categories of brands contained a relatively homogeneous group and a less homogeneous group; for example, dog food was made up of dry foods and moist (canned) foods. It seems fairly obvious that grouping by homogeneous brands further decreases the burden on STM—that is, the cognitive strain of transmitting information to LTM.

This example illustrates a change in the form of a message. The content of the message—the price—remained the same. In the discussion of language, memory, and inference, a number of characteristics of form were identified. Following are some of them.

Whether or not the elements of the content are in their natural order makes a difference to the consumer's ability to infer accurately. This is seen in the following two examples:

$A > B$ $C < B$
$B > C$ $A > B$
(Therefore $A > C$)   (Therefore $A > C$)

[24]J. E. Russo, G. Krieser, and S. Miyashita, "An Effective Display of Unit Price Information," *Journal of Marketing*, **39**:11–19, April 1975.

Table 4-1 Experimental Display of Unit Prices

List of unit prices (listed in order of increasing price per quart)		
Par 48 oz.	54¢	36.0¢ per quart
Par 32 oz.	38¢	38.0¢ per quart
Sweetheart 32 oz.	55¢	55.0¢ per quart
Brocade 48 oz.	85¢	56.7¢ per quart
Sweetheart 22 oz.	39¢	56.7¢ per quart
Supurb 32 oz.	59¢	59.0¢ per quart
White Magic 32 oz.	59¢	59.0¢ per quart
Brocade 32 oz.	63¢	63.0¢ per quart
Brocade 22 oz.	45¢	65.5¢ per quart
Supurb 22 oz.	45¢	65.5¢ per quart
White Magic 32 oz.	45¢	65.5¢ per quart
Brocade 12 oz.	27¢	72.0¢ per quart
Supurb 12 oz.	29¢	77.3¢ per quart
Ivory 32 oz.	80¢	80.0¢ per quart
Dove 22 oz.	56¢	81.5¢ per quart
Ivory 22 oz.	56¢	81.5¢ per quart
Lux 22 oz.	56¢	81.5¢ per quart
Palmolive 32 oz.	85¢	85.0¢ per quart
Ivory 12 oz.	32¢	85.3¢ per quart
Palmolive 22 oz.	60¢	87.3¢ per quart
Palmolive 12 oz.	34¢	90.7¢ per quart

Source: J. E. Russo et al., "An Effective Display of Unit Price Information," *Journal of Marketing,* **39**:14, April 1975.

The "kernel sentence" is another characteristic of form. This receives much attention in English composition courses. Brand meaning encapsulated in a kernel sentence—a simple, affirmative, active, declarative sentence—can most easily reach LTM. If the sentence contains a negative, it becomes more difficult. Complexity, passivity, and interrogation also make sentences more difficult. Logically, it would appear to follow that if you are forced to use a negative, then a polar adjective should be used, because the opposite of the negated adjective should come to mind readily.

There are severe limits to how meaning can be received in memory. For the acceptance of every chunk of information into LTM, five to ten seconds are required; this holds even when other conditions are favorable and the material is well organized. Mnemonic devices such as rhymes and music can help by imposing external structure; we constantly see examples of such devices in advertising.

Another characteristic of form is the uncertainty of the message; this will be discussed in Chapter 7.

Finally, there is the general symbolic vehicle—pictoral, musical, or linguistic—that is used.

These dimensions of form—supplemented, of course, by content, as specified in Chapter 3—can guide us in the design of messages. Thus, a piece of advertising copy for a brand should contain information pertinent to the dimensions of personal and impersonal criteria, brand identification, and confidence. This would be presented in accordance with the form of the structure of information. Finally, considerations having to do with competition, which we have recognized only implicitly, must be kept in mind: where are we weak and where are we strong? The notion of competition becomes explicit when we recognize that the brand concept determines what other brands our brand will be grouped with. It will be grouped with things that are functionally equivalent; that is, it will be grouped with the competitors' brands. The concept of product space is helpful here.

It is on these principles that we can begin to develop an analytical basis for evaluating advertising copy. Incapacity to judge advertising has been the greatest criticism of the modern M.B.A. by practitioners. Those who hold the M.B.A. are highly regarded for quantitative skills but are found wanting as far as this more creative role is concerned.[25]

SUMMARY

The notion of brand meaning brings together three seemingly unrelated ideas—brand concept, language, and competition. Through the nature of information structure, brand meaning provides a basis for making decisions in many areas of marketing. First, that portion of the meaning that must be received by a consumer in LPS in order to attain a brand concept of it has to do with the three

---

[25]V. P. Buell, *Practices in Advertising Decision-Making and Control,* Association of National Advertisers, Inc., New York, 1973, pp. 91–92.

elements of the concept: brand identification, attitude, and confidence. Second, this meaning can best be transmitted by the words that consumers use to conceptualize the brand. We cannot predict what these words will be, but we can obtain them from a sample of people who have attained the concept, and then use the words to inform others about the brand.

Brand meaning is transmitted by information processing. Here the overlapping processes of language, memory, and inference change the elements of the consumer's concept of the brand. In information processing, a number of factors affect cognitive strain. As regards language, these factors are the characteristics of the sentence: simple or complex, active or passive, positive or negative, declarative or interrogative. As regards short-term memory, they are the maximum time of storage in STM, the maximum amount of storage, and the time required for transfer to LTM. In long-term memory, they are the necessity for sentences to be in kernel form and for the material to be meaningful, familiar, and similar to previously acquired material. As regards inference, they are the requirement that material be in its natural order, the number of brands involved, whether or not facts are obscured in sentences, and ease of retrieval.

Language is surprisingly precise, but accuracy in communication depends upon how many associations people have in common. Thus, it should not be surprising to find substantial "noise" in a quantitative analysis. Customers' experiences differ, for example, and hence the meanings they associate with a brand probably differ. This leads to differences among consumers in their behavior. Probably more important are the differences among consumers in their capacity to process language and to make the inferences that lead to a brand concept. (This happens because information processing involves cognitive strain, and people differ in the capacity to deal with it.) By using these individual differences it is possible to operationalize STM as a part of the consumer behavior system, as will be shown in Chapter 8.

Understanding the communication process is important in an industrial society where new products are common and mass communication is readily available. It is less essential in preindustrial countries; but where such societies are striving to industrialize, changes will come that will make this analysis appropriate.

QUESTIONS

1 What do we mean by the "form" of structure of information, and what is its significance?
2 What is meant by "structural grammar"?
3 What is a "kernel sentence," and what is its significance in understanding how the meaning of a brand concept is transmitted?
4 Short-term memory is often viewed as a bottleneck in transmitting the meaning of a brand concept. Why should this be so?
5 How would you design a message to facilitate the drawing of inferences about the brand concept from meaning stored in LTM?

SUGGESTIONS FOR FURTHER READING

S. Banks and E. W. Hart: "Factors Influencing Consumer Choice: Promotional Methods," in R. Ferber (ed.), *A Synthesis of Selected Aspects of Consumer Behavior,* U.S. Government Printing Office for National Science Foundation, Washington, D.C., in press.

R. W. Chestnut and J. Jacoby: "Consumer Information Processing: Emerging Theories and Findings," Purdue Papers in Consumer Psychology, No. 158, 1976.

Extensive Problem Solving: Concept Formation

CONTENTS

Identification

Evaluation

Two Levels of Choice

An Example of Concept Formation

Information Processing: Generating Alternatives

Application of EPS Analysis

In extensive problem solving (EPS), the third stage of learning to buy, the consumer is confronting a radically new thing. Consequently, the consumer requires much information and comes to a decision slowly. Never having seen a brand that is closely similar, the consumer must form a new product class— that is, must form the product space described in Chapter 4. In common parlance, the consumer must perform the task of identifying the problem. In order to evaluate alternative solutions to the problem in terms of motives, one must form criteria by which to identify and judge all things in the class as they are encountered.

The product-class concept is the next higher-level analogue of the brand concept and is defined analogously. It is the subjective meaning of a class of similar brands. This meaning arises not from sensory data as such, but from application of the processes of abstraction and generalization to the sensory data so as to link them by means of words stored in memory.

Economists do not help us in dealing with this higher level of choice, even though they have probably devoted more research to it than to choice at the brand level. The economists sometimes call EPS "change in consumers' tastes," or, more technically, "redefinition of the utility function," but they have no analysis to offer. The psychologists offer a little more. The psychological process that underlies EPS has to do with the formation of the criteria I have mentioned; it is called "concept formation." It explains the observable characteristics of EPS: an extensive search for information and a long decision time. Concept formation is defined as the process of developing the criteria for identifying and evaluating a radically new brand, a brand from an unfamiliar product class. In principle, concept formation occurs when a consumer has not formed criteria; concept attainment occurs when the consumer has formed criteria. In the real world, however, the two processes are not entirely separate; rather, there is a continuum of learning in which concept formation evolves into concept attainment.

Because EPS requires a great deal of information, it causes cognitive strain in information processing. As was noted in Chapter 3, information processing can go on at two levels: attitude formation and deeper processing. In designing the content of messages, it is appropriate to examine the level of attitude formation. In designing the form of a message, it is appropriate to consider the deeper level, where human limitations are recognized. This chapter takes up attitude formation; Chapter 6 deals with deeper processing.

IDENTIFICATION

It is probable that product-class concepts are seldom formed *in vacuo,* but rather arise through a process of choice among existing product classes that the buyer encounters. This comes about as follows: when consumers observe a new thing and try to identify and evaluate it, they first group it with things that it is like; having found the proper group, they proceed to distinguish it from other brands in that group (we saw this in discussing semantic structure in Chapter 3). To the extent that the consumer has a well-defined meaning or semantic structure for that group already in memory (from previous experience), the process of identification and evaluation will proceed smoothly. For example, if the new thing were a baboon, and one's meaning structure could be represented by a well-developed "tree" of living things, like Figure 5-1, one's task would not be difficult. One would locate the appropriate branch in the tree and follow it down to the appropriate level of living thing and on to the node which the new thing was most like. Thus, EPS is more concerned with grouping than LPS, and less concerned with distinguishing. But having grouped the baboon, one would probably find

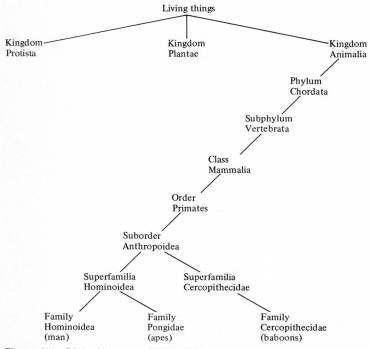

Figure 5-1　Biologist's tree of living things.

that baboons are not all alike and would proceed to distinguish the given type of baboon from other types of baboons.

The biologist's "tree" of living things in Figure 5-1 represents a referential or identifying structure, not an evaluative structure. That consumers do identify according to a referential structure is shown in Stefflre's work.[1] He found that when consumers are asked to group according to judgments about similarity, there is substantial agreement among consumers. When they are asked to group according to judgments about preference, however, there is much less agreement. Referential criteria are necessary for communication; therefore, they would be expected to have more common meanings than preferences.

Figure 5-1, of course, is an exaggeration if it is taken as showing how well equipped consumers typically are to deal with new product classes. Human beings probably never have such a systematically worked-out meaning structure. To the extent that they are not experienced in areas related to a new thing, they develop a local structure by processing information and then proceed to group and distinguish.

Up to this point we have been speaking of grouping and distinguishing in rather loose terms. We learned from Chapters 2 and 3, however, that the processes are complicated by at least two factors. First, grouping is in terms of specific criteria. Second, these criteria are of two kinds, referential and evaluative, and both sets of criteria must be formed. For our purpose here, we will deal mainly with evaluative criteria, which will be called "choice criteria."

EVALUATION

Source of Choice Criteria

A buyer who prefers one brand over another must believe that in some way the first brand serves his or her motives better; but the connection between motivation and choice is complex. It is a means-end chain, with motives as the "end" and purchase as the "means" or, as it is sometimes called, the "instrumental end." In such a chain each link is a means to satisfying the preceding end, as will be seen later. The means-end chain is longer in EPS than in LPS.

Consumer's Self-Concept Motives are the energizing or "dynamizing" aspect of behavior. In Chapter 3 it was noted that they are manifested in physical tension, called "arousal." We can think of them as being represented in the consumer's self-concept. Your self-concept is how you view and think about yourself. Just as you have a concept of a brand, you have a concept of yourself. To the extent that you are what you believe you ought to be, you are a satisfied, happy person. I suspect that there is not usually a great difference between what you are and what you think you ought to be. When you are not successful at the things you think you should do in order to become what you want to be, you are

---

[1]Volney Stefflre, "Market Structure Studies: New Products for Old Markets and New Markets (Foreign) for Old Products," in F. M. Bass, C. W. King, and E. A. Pessemier (eds.), *Applications of the Sciences in Marketing Management,* Wiley, New York, 1968.

dissatisfied and will search for different ways to behave—if you are mentally healthy. (This kind of searching will be discussed in Chapter 7.) This explanation of behavior is a modified version of the "consistency theory" of motivation: inconsistency between self-cognitions having to do with morality and competence produces tension, and tension creates motivation.

There is a connection between self-concept and buying behavior—indeed, between self-concept and all behavior. This is supported by research.[2] Dolich's work will serve as an example. Subjects were presented with a number of pairs of adjectives used to describe four product classes: beer, cigarettes, bar soap, and toothpaste. Then, the subjects were asked to use the same pairs of adjectives to rate themselves. For each subject, the two sets of ratings were compared to see if subjects rated the products in the same way they rated themselves. This comparison is crucial to the self-concept theory: the theory that a consumer buys brands which are similar to his or her self-perception.

The adjectives were taken from magazine advertisements and television commercials for the products. They were converted into adjectival pairs as follows:

Evaluation: good-bad, safe-dangerous, superior-inferior, clean-dirty, tasty-distasteful
Potency: hard-soft, robust-fragile, strong-weak, brave-cowardly, masculine-feminine
Activity: active-passive, lively-calm, exciting-dull, impulsive-deliberate, complex-simple
Stability: stable-changeable
Novelty: modern–old-fashioned
Receptivity: colorful-drab
Miscellaneous: sophisticated-unsophisticated, expensive-inexpensive, reliable-unreliable, conforming-unconforming.

The meaning of each concept for an individual subject is defined operationally as the set of scores for the scales made from adjectival pairs representing that concept. The operational concepts are two brands for each of four products and two self-images, real and ideal. The "ideal" self-concept is what the subject would like to be; the "real" self concept is what he or she is. The subjects were 200 students, each of whom used all four products. They were free to select the most preferred and least preferred brands within each product class.

The degree of congruence between a self-image and a brand image was estimated by computing the absolute arithmetic difference, scale by scale,

[2]A. E. Birdwell, "Automobiles and Self-Image: A Reply," *Journal of Business,* **41**:486–487, October 1968; I. J. Dolich, "Congruence Relationships Between Self-Images and Product Brands," *Journal of Marketing Research,* **6**:80–84, February 1969; E. L. Grubb and H. L. Grathwohl, "Consumer Self-Concept, Symbolism and Market Behavior: A Theoretical Approach," *Journal of Marketing,* **31**:22–27, October 1967; I. Ross, "Self-Concept and Brand Preference," *Journal of Business,* **44**:38–50, 1971; P. C. Vitz and D. Johnston, "Masculinity of Smokers and the Masculinity of Cigarette Images," *Journal of Applied Psychology,* **49**:155–159, 1965.

Table 5-1

The person I am*										
Scale		(1)	(2)	(3)	(4)	(5)	(6)	(7)		Code
1	impulsive	__	__	X	__	__	__	__	deliberate	3
2	simple	__	__	__	__	X	__	__	complex	5
(to scale 22)										

The brand of beer I most prefer is										
1	impulsive	X	__	__	__	__	__	__	deliberate	1
2	simple	__	__	__	__	X	__	__	complex	5
(to scale 22)										

Calculation of congruence scores			
Scale	Real self-image	Brand most preferred	Difference
1	3	1	2
2	5	5	0
Total			2

*The ideal self-image was measured similarly, under the concept title "The person I would like to be."

between two sets of scales. For example, a subject's ratings of real self-image and the brand of beer most preferred would be as shown in Table 5-1.

The absolute differences between the ratings shown in Table 5-1 were 2 for scale 1 and 0 for scale 2. Summing these differences gives a value, 2, that represents the congruence of the real-self image and the brand of beer most preferred by the respondent. A low score indicates a greater congruence than a high score.

The congruence scores for one respondent are shown in Table 5-2. Such scores were the basic data used in variance analysis to detect differences in congruence.

Table 5-2   Congruence Scores for Self-Image and Product Brands for One Subject*

Product	Real self-image		Ideal self-image		Total
	Brand most preferred	Brand least preferred	Brand most preferred	Brand least preferred	
Beer	22	55	23	56	156
Cigarettes	24	68	21	75	188
Bar soap	23	51	26	70	180
Toothpaste	22	42	23	45	132
Total	91	226	93	246	656

*A low score indicates greater congruence (similarity) than a high score.
Source: I. J. Dolich, "Congruence Relationships between Self-Images and Product Brands," *Journal of Marketing Research,* **6**:80–84, February 1969.

This study shows clearly that there is congruence between a subject's preferences for brands and his or her self-concept. Whether it is likely to be greater for the real self-concept than for the ideal self-concept is not yet clear, however, although there is some evidence that the real self-concept will produce greater congruence. Thus there is a relation between a consumer's self-concept and his or her preferences. The link between self-concept and preferences is values.

Consumer's Values   That values are the source of choice criteria has been held for some time,[3] but the idea has been systematically developed only recently.

A consumer's self-concept is served by his or her values. A value is defined as an enduring belief that a specific mode of conduct or state of existence is personally and socially preferable to the opposite mode of conduct or state of existence. Values guide behavior in a direction (toward purchasing a brand) which will keep the elements of the self-concept (self-cognitions) consistent with one another. Values can be separated into terminal values ("being") and instrumental values ("doing").[4] In terms of the means-end chain, terminal values are closer to the ultimate end, which is self-concept, and are more abstract than instrumental values. Instrumental values are closer to the "means," which is purchase, and less abstract than terminal values.

For a fuller understanding of values, let us examine Table 5-3, which lists eighteen terminal and eighteen instrumental values that have been systematically developed.[5] They were obtained, in part, by asking people to rank values according to their importance; it was felt that eighteen was the greatest number a person could meaningfully rank. Whether they are as generally applicable as Rokeach believes remains to be seen: for example, the value structure should be verified if the group in question is from outside the United States, or even if it is American but has been little studied.[6] For most purposes, however, this list is probably adequate.

In the means-end chain, values are served by choice criteria, with which we are already familiar. Furthermore, values determine the salience of a choice criterion. To the extent that some aspect of a consumer's self-concept is not being served—i.e., when two self-cognitions are inconsistent (when what one is differs from what one ought to be)—values will become more intense and the corresponding choice criteria will become more salient.

As we know, an attitude toward a brand is positions on choice criteria, and attitudes lead to intention to buy and purchase. Thus, we have now completed our description of the means-end chain that begins with the purchase and ends with motives (self-concept).

[3]M. J. Rosenberg, "Cognitive Structure and Attitudinal Effect," *Journal of Abnormal and Social Psychology,* **53**:367–372, 1956.

[4]R. P. Barthol and R. G. Bridge, "The ECHO Multi-Response Method for Surveying Value and Influence Patterns in Groups," *Psychological Reports,* **22**:1345–1354, 1968.

[5]M. Rokeach, *The Nature of Human Values,* Free Press, New York, 1973.

[6]Barthol and Bridge, op. cit.

Table 5-3 Terminal and Instrumental Values

Terminal value	r*	Instrumental value	r
A comfortable life (a prosperous life)	.70	Ambitious (hard-working, aspiring)	.70
An exciting life (a stimulating, active life)	.73	Broadminded (open-minded)	.57
A sense of accomplishment (lasting contribution)	.51	Capable (competent, effective)	.51
A world at peace (free of war and conflict)	.67	Cheerful (lighthearted, joyful)	.65
A world of beauty (beauty of nature and the arts)	.66	Clean (neat, tidy)	.66
Equality (brotherhood, equal opportunity for all)	.71	Courageous (standing up for your beliefs)	.52
Family security (taking care of loved ones)	.64	Forgiving (willing to pardon others)	.62
Freedom (independence, free choice)	.61	Helpful (working for the welfare of others)	.66
Happiness (contentedness)	.62	Honest (sincere, truthful)	.62
Inner harmony (freedom from inner conflict)	.65	Imaginative (daring, creative)	.69
Mature love (sexual and spiritual intimacy)	.68	Independent (self-reliant, self-sufficient)	.60
National security (protection from attack)	.67	Intellectual (intelligent, reflective)	.67
Pleasure (an enjoyable, leisurely life)	.57	Logical (consistent, rational)	.57
Salvation (saved, eternal life)	.88	Loving (affectionate, tender)	.65
Self-respect (self-esteem)	.58	Obedient (dutiful, respectful)	.53
Social recognition (respect, admiration)	.65	Polite (courteous, well-mannered)	.53
True friendship (close companionship)	.59	Responsible (dependable, reliable)	.45
Wisdom (a mature understanding of life)	.60	Self-controlled (restrained, self-disciplined)	.52

*Numbers are test-retest correlation coefficients.
Source: M. Rokeach, The Nature of Human Values, The Free Press, New York, 1973, p. 28.

Values and Attitudes Using Table 5-4, which is an extended, complete version of Table 3-1, let us illustrate the role of values in the choice process. The table shows choice operating at two levels: product class and brand.

The first four criteria of Table 3-1 had to do with choosing among brands of gasoline in terms of personal criteria or requirements. The last three dealt with more situational conditions, conditions external to the brand (impersonal choice criteria), having to do with particular gasoline stations, each of which stocks a particular brand. To simplify, let us consider only one of the first four criteria.

Table 5-4   Extensive Problem Solving Elaborated

	(1) Instrumental values	(2) Choice criteria	(3) Salience	(4) Beliefs	(5) Contributions to attitude
Elements of the means-end chain	Logical	Mileage			
			Attitude		

A buyer's relevant motive may be achievement, to use David McClelland's terminology,[7] and in order to achieve the terminal values of a comfortable life and family security one tries to serve the instrumental value of being logical and thus doing those things—buying those brands—that are as logical as possible. To be logical is to be consistent and rational (Table 5-3). One could interpret this as being economical; then one would distinguish sharply among gasolines, for example, according to miles per gallon obtained. The fuller version of Table 3-1 shown in Table 5-4 is designed to incorporate more complete motivational elements. To simplify, these were only implied in Chapter 3, and the choice criteria which reflect such elements were assumed to be already established.

In extensive problem solving, however, the table is empty except for instrumental values. The consumer has not yet developed any choice criteria. We will assume that the consumer's values, both terminal and instrumental, are fixed or given during the period of our analysis. Later, in Chapter 9, we will deal with changing values. Forming a concept is the process of providing content for the blanks in column 2. Imagine a man who has never even thought about buying gasoline before. He has driven a car, however, and knows what the car does in terms of satisfying his values. Faced with the problem of buying gasoline, he reasons that mileage per gallon of gasoline is an important consideration because gasoline is costly and he is frugal. In column 1 of Table 5-4, doing logical things—in this case, being economical—is an instrumental value, and in this case it is served by good gasoline mileage. Thus, the relevant choice criterion in column 2 is mileage per gallon.

Column 3, "Salience," as we know from Chapter 3, refers to the importance or weighting of one criterion as compared with other criteria used in making a choice. It comes from the importance of the instrumental values served by the criterion of good gasoline mileage.

Column 4 is the buyer's belief about where a radically new brand lies on a given criterion—in this case, mileage. Thus, to obtain an attitude measure operationally, we multiply salience by belief. This gives the contribution of the criterion "mileage" to an overall measure of attitude toward a brand of gasoline,

---

[7]D. C. McClelland, *The Achieving Society,* Free Press, New York, 1961.

which is the content of column 5. As in Chapter 3, the contributions of all criteria are summed to obtain a measure of attitude toward a brand. As consumers learn more about the relationship between a particular value and a particular choice criterion, their certainty that the relationship exists increases and their confidence also increases. Also, as the learning process proceeds, it can change the salience of a choice criterion, as well as the position of a brand on a choice criterion.

Nature of Choice Criteria

So far, we have neglected one important aspect of the choice criteria that make up a product space. Are the criteria discrete or continuous? If they are discrete, of how many units is each made up? This is to ask, "How 'long' is a choice criterion?"

A choice criterion is a consumer's reference scale, "which he uses in sizing up particular stimuli, placing each in one of several categories."[8] Thus, it is considered discrete. A key question, then, is, "How many categories make up each criterion?" Linguistically, as we learned from Chapter 3, this is asking how many adverbs must be used to describe the criterion.

The number of categories making up a criterion depends upon, among other things, the importance of the object being evaluated. The greater its importance, the greater the number of categories. Cultural factors are also influential. You will recall from Chapter 3 that different languages have different numbers of words for describing objects; for example, one Philippine tribe has ninety-two names for rice whereas English speakers have only one. Cultural differences like this would be expected to cause differences in the number of categories.

Another aspect of choice criteria was suggested in Chapter 3. In the discussion of pricing, it was noted that the end points of a criterion are called "anchor points." Objects that fall outside the anchor points are seen as dissimilar to those that fall inside and tend to be less preferred.[9] To put it another way, the object falling outside is not seen as being in the same product class.

Conclusions on Choice Criteria

Choice criteria are so important because they are central to a product-class concept. They are established by concept formation. The basic idea of concept formation is that the choice criteria required to evaluate a radically new brand are formed because they relate it to the values its purchase will serve.

Values are the specific source of choice criteria and so represent links in the consumer's means-end chain. Concept formation is defined to include not only the formation of the original choice criteria, but also the reweighting—the change in salience—of choice criteria which sometimes takes place in choosing a

[8]M. Sherif and C. W. Sherif, *Social Psychology,* Harper & Row, New York, 1969, p. 323.

[9]C. Sherif, "Social Categorization as a Function of Latitude of Acceptance and Series Range," *Journal of Abnormal and Social Psychology,* **67**:148–156, 1963.

familiar brand in a known product class; this change in weighting can come about because of a change in the buyer's values or environment.

TWO LEVELS OF CHOICE

In concept formation, choice occurs at two levels. Therefore, we can perhaps best represent concept formation as developing two product spaces, one at each of two levels of choice.

The first level of choice is a higher-level product space; typically, it exists in the consumer's semantic space at the level at which the product is first grouped—as "a coffee" or "a bacon," for example. The space here consists of a class of product classes. The consumer distinguishes and chooses from among product classes: an instant coffee versus a regular coffee, or a regular bacon versus a vegetable bacon.

The second level of choice is the familiar product space discussed in Chapter 3. It consists of a product class. In EPS, the consumer does not have to distinguish among brands, because there is only one brand in the class at the time. Consequently, the spatial dimensions at this second level are probably not as extensive as they will become later, when other brands appear. Nevertheless, they must have some content, because the consumer must decide whether the brand is worth buying at all. (The class could be better than other product classes but still not be worth the cost and effort necessary to buy it.) The concept of information structure was used in earlier chapters as a guide to designing messages; it specifies the information a consumer must acquire to form this space. Here, however, the information requirements are broadened to include information about relevant choice criteria. By means of the information structure, we bring together the concept formation and information requirements.

An example of concept formation is presented next. It is followed by a description of the information processing that is required for concept formation to take place. Finally, various applications of the principles will be shown.

AN EXAMPLE OF CONCEPT FORMATION

In Chapter 3, a consumer's semantic structure—a bundle of related concepts in which a brand concept is nested—was illustrated with asparagus. A hierarchy of superior-subordinate relations is central to semantic structure. It was noted in Chapter 3 that a consumer groups a new brand at the appropriate level—the product class—and then proceeds to distinguish it from competing brands at the next lower level—the level of brand choice. This same hierarchical structure of categories was seen in the model of memory in Chapter 4. Hierarchy has been emphasized by Simon as a common way of handling very complex relations.[10]

If consumers place products in classes in a hierarchical fashion and if they choose from among classes, as I have been suggesting, then there must be a

[10]H. A. Simon, *The Sciences of the Artificial,* M.I.T. Press, Cambridge, Mass., 1969, chap. 4.

hierarchical evaluative structure corresponding to the hierarchical identifying or semantic structure. This leads me to hypothesize that the consumer has an evaluative structure corresponding to his or her semantic structure and memory structure. At each level in the evaluative structure there are values which generate choice criteria for the corresponding level of his or her semantic structure. For example, the lowest level in the evaluative structure (instrumental values) generates choice criteria for choosing among brands and the next higher level (terminal values) generates choice criteria for choosing among product classes, one of which contains the brand being considered. In this, I go beyond Rokeach, who deliberately leaves the nature of the relationship between instrumental and terminal values unspecified.[11]

This important hypothesis will shape our thinking throughout much of the rest of the book, especially in discussing market segmentation. Is there independent evidence for it? Such evidence is provided by a study of consumers buying a number of household appliances. For several reasons, I believe that this example represents concept formation, even though the product classes were not new to the consumers. Household appliances are bought infrequently; refrigerators, for instance, may be bought only once in eight to ten years. In the interim between purchases, consumers forget their experiences and must therefore rebuild the product-class concept. Also, consumers' values may change, so that new criteria, or at least differently weighted criteria, are needed. Finally, appliances change fairly rapidly, so that consumers are often faced with a product quite different from the last one purchased and therefore requiring different choice criteria.

Before the study is discussed, the model used to guide the study—development of questionnaire, analysis, and interpretation of results—will be presented. This will provide an overview of the application of the principles of EPS. After the details of the study are given, the conclusions will be stated.

Model for the Study: Product-Class and Brand Choice

If two levels of choice—brand choice and product-class choice—occur in EPS, as Figure 5-2 and the hypothesis of an evaluative hierarchy suggest, then instrumental values must be instrumental to the attainment of terminal values. This requirement is met if the terminal values (such as a comfortable life and family security) serve as the source of criteria for product-class choice (like the choice of small or large automobiles) and the instrumental values (such as being logical) serve as the source of criteria for brand choice (like the choice of a brand of small cars). Terminal values are used to select among product classes, and the chosen class provides the criteria for choosing among the brands. Thus a brand chosen according to these criteria will, indirectly, best serve the terminal values. In this way, instrumental values serve terminal values. The idea of levels of choice was implied in the discussion of semantic structure, with its hierarchy of superior and subordinate relations, and in the model of memory.

[11]Rokeach, op. cit., p. 12.

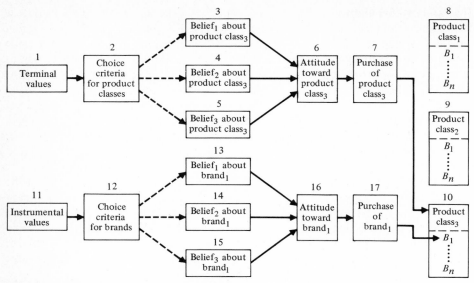

Figure 5-2 Specifications of structure of EPS.

The model of two levels of choice will be described by reference to Figure 5-2. Whenever a construct of the model is mentioned, it will be followed by a number in parentheses which refers to the appropriate box in Figure 5-2. As Figure 5-2 shows, terminal values (1) are the source of choice criteria for product classes (2), and instrumental values (11) are the source of choice criteria for brands (12). Broken lines connect choice criteria for product classes (2) with beliefs (3, 4, 5) about where a product class is located on a choice criterion, because these are obviously not the usual causal relations implied in a flowchart. Instead, beliefs about a product class imply positions on choice criteria which the consumer uses in evaluating that product class. Similarly, at the level of brand choice, choice criteria for brands (12) are connected to beliefs about brands (13, 14, 15) by broken lines. In order to simplify, salience of choice criteria has been omitted from Figure 5-2.

That individual beliefs cause attitude is the basic assumption of all multiple-attribute models, as was discussed in Chapter 3. In Figure 5-2 this principle is applied both to attitude toward product class (6) and to attitude toward brand (16).

That attitude causes purchase is the usual assumption of attitude theory. When this principle is applied at each level, we obtain the decision to purchase product class 3 (7) and brand 1 (17) within that class.

Finally, I hypothesize that the two-level choice structure is quite general and can be moved up and down to apply at any two adjacent levels in the consumer's conceptual hierarchy shown in Figure 3-3. This hypothesis implies that there can be more than two levels of values, however—a point that will be developed later, especially in Chapter 8.

Description of the Study

The study described here was designed to test the truth of this two-level conceptualization.[12] The sample consisted of 124 women homemakers in Norwalk, Connecticut. Each subject affirmed that either she or her husband was considering the purchase of one or more of the following household appliances within the next three months:

> Color television set
> Black-and-white television set
> Sewing machine
> Clothes washer
> Clothes dryer
> Dishwasher
> Vacuum cleaner
> Food freezer
> Refrigerator

The sample was relatively homogeneous in terms of age, income, and ethnic background.

Operational definitions were developed for terminal values, instrumental values, choice criteria, beliefs, attitude, and purchase. The terminal values were derived from a number of sources and operationalized as follows:

> To have household possessions which are different from those of other people I know.
> To make or do things which express my distinctive personality or talents.
> To have something to do to entertain myself when I have leisure time at home.
> To enjoy a high level of physical comfort at home.
> To have a feeling of accomplishment with everything I do.
> To have plenty of food on hand at all times to meet my kind of requirements.
> To have a beautiful home.

These are values of "being"—for example, "being the kind of person who has household possessions which are different from those of other people I know." Measurements taken were the importance ratings or salience of these values.

The following operational instrumental values were derived from reducing a list of thirty-eight original values by factor analysis:

> Rationality
> Appearance
> Independence
> Novelty
> Traditionality
> Social consciousness

[12]A. S. Boote, "An Exploratory Investigation of the Roles of Needs and Personal Values in the Theory of Buyer Behavior," unpublished doctoral dissertation, Columbia University, 1975.

These are values of "doing"—for example, "doing those things which are rational." Again, the measurements were importance ratings. These two lists of values are similar, though not identical, to Rokeach's standard lists. They are not as clearly distinguished according to "being" and "doing" as Rokeach's lists.

The two levels of choice were models of appliances, designated "product class," and brands. In clothes washers, for example, there were four models with brands of each:

Full-size automatic, 1 or 2 cycles
Full-size automatic, 3 or more cycles
"Mini" automatic, 1 to 3 cycles (small enough to store in closet)
Compact (portable, on casters); semiautomatic spinner is usually in a separate compartment

The choice criteria at both levels were derived by asking each subject to rank each characteristic in terms of its importance to her at that level of choice. The choice criteria for product class were:

Reputation for dependability
Good style and appearance
Good value for the money

At the level of brand choice a fourth criterion was added:

Reputation for modern, up-to-date features

At both levels of choice, the measurements were importance ratings.

Beliefs were measured as a consumer's belief about the extent to which the product and brand possessed the quality specified in a choice criterion.

Attitude measures in both cases were unidimensional like-dislike ratings of each product class or brand.

Purchase was defined as buying a particular product class and brand four to six months after the initial interview, in which the other variables in the system shown in Figure 5-2 had been measured.

Conclusions of the Study

As is predicted by Figure 5-2, terminal values are related much more strongly than instrumental values to the product-class level of choice. Furthermore, terminal values are not related at all to the level of brand choice; instrumental values are related to brand choice. The most important results of the study are consistent with Figure 5-2, which describes two levels of choice, with terminal values guiding choice among product classes and instrumental values guiding choice among brands.

You will recall from the earlier discussion that only three choice criteria

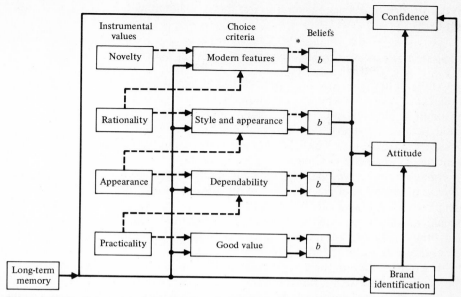

Figure 5-3   Partial model of EPS. Broken lines indicate a relation which is not causal.

operate at the more abstract level; four operate at the more concrete level. This is consistent with the accepted notion that concrete ideas are characterized by more detail than abstract ideas.[13] Other sources lead me to believe that the two levels of choice operate differently, as will be seen in Chapter 8.

EPS can now be shown as part of the model of consumer behavior introduced in Chapter 2. This is done in Figure 5-3, which, for simplicity, is confined to the level of brand choice. Concept formation requires adding two more sets of mechanisms. First, information from LTM brings relevant instrumental values and criteria together for brand choice. This is the inference problem, which will be discussed in Chapter 6. Second, information from LTM also creates a belief (*b*) on each choice criterion. Again, broken lines indicate relations which are not causal relations in the usual sense.

We have seen an example of how a brand is grouped and distinguished. By grouping a brand in a class of product classes, the consumer immediately endows the brand with a great amount of meaning. But must this grouping and distinguishing be confined to two levels of choice? The notion of semantic structure would imply no such limitation. In fact, it suggests that several levels of choice can exist. Thus, the data supporting Figure 5-2 can be considered as confirming the hypothesis of semantic structure and so suggesting that multilevel choices exist. In our primitive state of thinking, it is convenient to discuss terminal and instrumental values as though only two levels of choice can be dealt with within

[13]D. O. Hebb, "Concerning Imagery," *Psychological Review*, **75**:466–477, 1968.

the framework of a value structure. But this is a simplification; values, too, are multilevel.

INFORMATION PROCESSING: GENERATING ALTERNATIVES

Up to now, it has been assumed that being confronted with a radically new brand is an event that initiates the consumer's effort to form a concept. But the consumer could, instead, search for an alternative. If so, the initiating event would be the discovery that existing choices are inadequate in terms of the consumer's aspirations. Thus, level of aspiration can be considered the initiating event, as will be seen in Chapter 7.

Imagine that a woman who uses an automobile is confronted with a large increase in the price of gasoline. From observing automobiles and assessing her own personal and family requirements, this woman could decide that she wanted a small, sturdily constructed station wagon which used considerably less gasoline than other available cars. She would thus have hypotheses about relations between choice criteria and terminal values.

It would seem that the task of concept formation is much easier for a person who is confronted with a radically new alternative than for a person who must formulate choice criteria and then search for a means to satisfy them. When confronted with a new brand, a person has the physical object to "work from." The discussion in Chapter 6 of the difficulties of dealing with abstractions suggests that it is substantially easier to work backward in the means-end chain, from physical object to choice criteria and their underlying values, than to work forward from values to the choice criteria.

As was mentioned at the beginning of this chapter, the formation of product space is usually called "identifying alternatives" or "formulating alternatives." This is an extremely important process, especially in postindustrial society, with its high rate of technological change and frequent new products. Guilford has referred to the process as "divergent thinking";[14] Berlyne describes its overt manifestations as "diversive exploratory behavior."[15] Wickelgren has proposed seven search strategies.[16] McGuire believes that before search strategies can be understood, the organization of memory must be determined; once the organization of memory is better understood, our understanding of search strategies will fall into place.[17]

When we think of EPS as concerned with generating alternatives, we seem to be getting close to what is meant by "identifying the problem." This process was long recognized as central in studying such practical problems as designing market research studies, but no conceptualization as sharp as the one given here had been obtained.

[14]J. P. Guilford, *The Nature of Human Intelligence*, McGraw-Hill, New York, 1967.

[15]D. E. Berlyne, "Curiosity and Exploration," *Science,* **153**(3731):25–33.

[16]W. Wickelgren, *How to Solve Problems: Elements of a Theory of Problems and Problem Solving,* Freeman, San Francisco, 1974.

[17]W. J. McGuire, *Psychological Factors Influencing Consumer Choice,* Project on Synthesis of Knowledge of Consumer Behavior, RANN Program, National Science Foundation, April 1975.

APPLICATION OF EPS ANALYSIS

What do the principles of information processing and behavior in EPS tell us about practical problems? These principles have two types of implications. First, they complete the system of consumer behavior that was introduced verbally in Chapter 1 and thereafter elaborated upon by means of flowcharts. The fact that this is a total system is important for setting corporate strategy, as we will see. Second, knowing about EPS itself enables us to deal with types of marketing decisions that cannot be dealt with otherwise, because EPS involves two levels of choice (product class and brand) rather than just a single level (brand). These two types of implications will be distinguished from each other throughout the discussion of application.

Marketing Concept

The "marketing concept" evolved in the 1950s, as managements paid increasing attention to the marketing operations of their companies. "Marketing concept" was a label for the idea that a company should strive to meet consumers' needs. The concept received a great deal of discussion in academic and trade publications. The modern generation, of course, probably accepts the concept without even thinking about it. Its evolution, however, was a part of a general development of marketing, which included such ideas as market research, emphasis on new products, organization in terms of brand managers, and more carefully coordinated marketing activities.

For our purposes here, the important point is that the articulated concept of EPS is a further manifestation of the marketing concept. EPS is the extreme case of serving the consumer's values and reflects the rapid technological change that characterizes postindustrial society.

One obvious implication of this is a greater emphasis upon marketing planning and a longer planning horizon. In turn, this leads to emphasis on strategy and on the relationship between marketing strategy and corporate strategy, to which we turn next.

Design of Corporate Strategy and Long-Term Planning

One of the most important top-level decisions in a company is setting a master strategy, more often called a "corporate strategy." Such a strategy guides all aspects of the company; thus, marketing strategy and plans flow out of it.

Since corporate strategy guides the long-term future development of a company, we should ask, "How is it determined?" The nature of an appropriate corporate strategy may depend more strongly on anticipated markets than on anything else. In speculating about anticipated markets, it would be useless to consider consumers' current brand concepts. Most brand concepts change too rapidly in a postindustrial society to provide any sort of base from which to speculate.

Alternatives for corporate strategy can be viewed as in Table 5-5. Underly-

Table 5-5   Alternatives for Corporate Strategy

Markets	Products	
	Existing	New
Existing	Penetration	Expansion by product development
New	Expansion by market development	Diversification

ing the selection of a corporate strategy are corporate objectives, which can be thought of as growth with adequate profit. To simplify, let us assume either a single-product company or the average product-development stage in a multi-product company.

If the product is in the stage of maturity, penetration—seeking to obtain a larger share of the established market—is hardly a feasible corporate strategy. Competitive response will usually drive prices down and costs up. The advantages are slight, and there is only a short time left for payoff on investment. The probable alternatives are product development or market development, unless the company has a management team made up heavily of innovators or entrepreneurs—in that case, diversification is an alternative. The nearer the product is to the stage of initiation, the more practical is the strategy of penetration.

The choice between product or market development depends upon how far along the product class is in the stage of growth. The further along it is, the more product development should be planned. This will provide a replacement when the current product reaches the stage of inadequate profit and drop. When a product is at an early stage of growth, the company can pick up growth with less risk by exploiting new markets than by exploiting new products, for two reasons. First, new markets probably pose fewer unfamiliarities than new products. Second, by carrying out market development, the company is provided with more time for the product development that must ultimately come.

Marketing Decisions

We have examined the nature of EPS and its relevance for corporate strategy, both in the sense of how consumers behave in EPS and how behavior changes over the whole learning process, of which EPS is only the initiating stage. Now let us discuss both aspects of EPS for each of the areas of marketing decisions: design of distribution channel, product design, and pricing. Design of communication will be discussed in Chapter 6.

Channel Design   Knowing the distribution channels to be used can give guidance in designing a product, because the constraints imposed upon the product by the channel can be incorporated.

We saw in Chapter 1 that consumers' information requirements change over the product life cycle. This suggests that marketing channels should be changed in response to changes in how the consumer buys. When buyers are in EPS, the manufacturer would want heavy promotion from his retailers, not only telling consumers that this radically new thing is available, but going into great detail about how it looks (brand identification) and how it will benefit them (attitude). Price, although relevant, is much less important than it will be later. Specialty stores provide this kind of service, particularly through cooperative advertising arrangements (by which the manufacturer pays a part of the cost); supermarkets do not.

As the manufacturer's product moves toward LPS, promotion becomes less important, and coverage—that is, exposure—becomes more important. Price is slightly more important.

When the buyers are in RRB, coverage is very important and price still more so. Mass distribution may be essential.

How to secure these changes in channels raises many problems of relations with retailers, wholesalers, brokers, etc. To mention one: If retailers work with you to get a new product accepted, they will be unhappy if it is taken away from them later on to be handled by retailers who better meet your needs when consumers are in LPS and RRB.

Product Design   In LPS, in designing a product we can be guided by the "holes" in the consumers' product space. In EPS, consumers have yet to form a product space, and it is necessary to go behind the choice criteria and explore their source, which is values. Instrumental values should give the most specific guidance; but terminal values should not be ignored, because they determine the criteria which make up the class of product classes.

The concept test of ideas for new products, which is done most systematically with conjoint measurement techniques, may not be very useful, because consumers have not yet learned to think about the new brand. You will recall that thinking about a new brand is complicated because the basic comparison is probably at the level of choice among product classes.

Consider bacon, for example. A bacon made of cereal is possible; it would cost one-half to one-third of regular bacon, and its nutritional values would presumably be just as good. The potential consumer of such a product in any analysis would not compare it with, say, Armour bacon but rather with a general class—"regular bacon" or "Canadian bacon." In this way, the consumer would begin to form choice criteria.

The concept of values is probably most relevant for product design. By observing trends in changes in values, it should be possible to extrapolate those trends as a foundation upon which to build new products. That this is possible is suggested by the fact that Daniel Yankelovich, Inc., along with other firms, has for a number of years provided a syndicated service which makes available periodic surveys of American values on a wide range of topics. To make such data useful to a product designer undoubtedly requires detailed knowledge of a particular market. A product group director of a large company that subscribes to such a service says:

In fact, the only people who use this information are the brand management groups and upper marketing management. . . . In general, however, I would have to say that the middle management marketing people use this information only slightly and then not nearly to its potential for existing brands. In regards to upper management's use of the materials, I see absolutely no evidence of its application beyond the Marketing Director level.[18]

Pricing   As was mentioned earlier, EPS has two kinds of implications: first, it is a part of the general learning process; second, it labels a certain kind of behavior.

For pricing, the first kind of implication is that as a product matures, price becomes an increasingly sensitive and important element in the marketing mix. Consequently, a pricing strategy should be developed which recognizes these changes and encourages a consistent pattern of price change.

The second kind of implication is that the price range becomes one way for the consumer to identify the product. If price is changed, the new price may fall outside that range and cause the brand to be viewed as belonging in a different product class. Also, if consumers' information is limited, they may associate price with quality: the higher the price, the better the product. This is more likely in LPS, however, where consumers are choosing among brands.

Expanding and Forecasting Industry Demand

In the preceding chapters, we were directly concerned only with choices among brands. For two purposes, however, it is important to know the nature of choices among product classes, and here the EPS model is essential. One of these purposes is to expand a total industry, or, as we would say, a product class. The second purpose is to forecast this demand.

Expansion   Companies working through an industry association sometimes want to expand generic or industry demand. Citrus growers, wool producers, and milk producers, for example, often have extensive advertising campaigns for the product class as such, unrelated to any particular brand. Strawberry producers in California recently began to advertise and are apparently finding advertising profitable:

California Strawberry Advisory Board, delighted with its first strong ad effort last year when it spent $95,000 in 18 markets, has decided to jump into 44 markets with $250,000 in 1975.[19]

What are the implications of EPS principles for expanding industry demand? An effect on terminal values will have a greater payoff than an affect on instrumental values, since terminal values are more strongly related to choice

---

[18]Personal communication.
[19]*Advertising Age,* March 10, 1975, p. 51.

criteria for product classes than they are to choice criteria for brands. Thus, a given change in terminal values will have a greater effect upon purchases of the product class than will the same change in instrumental values. Marketing, however, has a less active role, since company managers are less likely to be able to change terminal values than to change instrumental values. (Terminal values, being more abstract, are harder to change.) Also, consumers' skepticism about the motives of advertisers probably adds to the difficulty.

Forecasting Thus far, we have not been concerned about the timing of choices. Yet a buyer's intention (plan) to purchase a product class can be useful for forecasting purposes if it has some degree of reliability. It can be a lead-lag indicator: a change in intention today indicates a change in purchases tomorrow. Managers find such forecasts useful for intermediate and short-term planning because they can make an assumption about their market share and thus arrive at a prediction of sales for some future period. In many instances, the market share does not change significantly. If it does, managers may be much better able to predict their share than to predict total industry sales, even when they are well-informed.

Makers of economic policy, charged with the responsibility for maintaining some national level of employment, are interested in forecasts of a particular class of products—consumer durables. These products represent heavy expenditures and are a volatile element of the economy because they are purchased infrequently and their purchase can usually be delayed if funds are short. If these expenditures are expected to be large, governmental efforts to help the economy can be decreased.

Unfortunately, attempts to use consumers' intentions to predict the purchase of product classes (e.g., automobiles) have not been successful. Intentions have not been a sufficiently good predictor of future purchase of a product class. The United States Bureau of the Census has been collecting such data for several years but has recently decided, in the face of budget cuts, to discontinue the service. Some nongovernmental institutions are continuing to collect these data, however. The decision of the Census Bureau has occasioned a careful review of the history and performance of data on intentions.[20] More than a decade ago, Cohen and Modigliani wrote:

> Actually the problem of how anticipations (intentions) are formed and revised falls on the borderline of traditional economics, and it may well be that advances in this area will require closer cooperation between economists, psychologists, and other social scientists.[21]

[20]J. McNeil, "Federal Programs to Measure Consumer Purchase Expectations, 1946–1973: A Post-Mortem," *Journal of Consumer Research*, 1:1–15, December 1974.

[21]F. Modigliani and K. J. Cohen, *The Role of Anticipations and Plans in Economic Behavior and Their Use in Economic Analysis and Forecasting,* University of Illinois Bulletin 58, January 1961, p. 152.

What evidence is there on the relation between intentions and purchase of a product class? The Census Bureau's quarterly *Survey of Consumer Buying Expectations* (CBE), begun in July 1966, was an intentions measure stated probablistically on a ten-point scale. In late 1969, CBE failed to reflect the decline in sales of new cars, let alone to predict it. In an earlier period, 1959–1961, the simple intentions survey had correlated well with actual purchases. But this was a period of strong upward movement in most economic data. These results could be interpreted as indicating that when contradictory cues begin to appear, buyers become more sensitive to the environment and let internal structure (intentions) play a smaller role relative to environmental cues.

At the product-class level, identification and confidence should develop and exert their influence much as their counterparts do at the brand level. In this discussion, however, they have been omitted for the sake of simplicity.

CONCLUSIONS

EPS represents a new area of study of the decision process and behavior. We have begun here to clarify important concepts which have been used ambiguously—for example, values, definition of the problem, and change in consumers' tastes.

The notions of semantic structure (from Chapter 3) and memory structure (from Chapter 4) raise the possibility that there are several levels of values, one for each level of generality of the product hierarchy presented in Chapter 3, rather than simply terminal and instrumental values. More will be said about this in Chapter 8.

The means-end chain is substantially lengthened in EPS. Here, values were introduced as a part of that chain.

The stage of economic development of a society would appear to be relevant to where EPS would be expected. EPS would be expected far more frequently in postindustrial society than elsewhere.

The reader must note that important areas have been assumed away. As a consumer creates a product space, he or she probably begins searching for other alternatives; for this, see Chapter 7. Also, the discussion here has been limited to that portion of EPS where change occurs in choice criteria but where the consumer's values are unchanging. It may also be possible to secure change in choice criteria by changing values; this is dealt with in Chapter 9. Finally, nothing has been said about the role of family budget, a role which is emphasized by economists as constraining the acceptance of products in EPS that are not a substitute (replacement) for currently used products. Changes in family income over the business cycle can be an important influence on whether a radically new product is accepted.

One final point should be made about postindustrial society. Earlier, social philosophers considered the "good society" to be one without scarcity: physical products would exist in such abundance that no one would be needy. This might imply that consumers' efforts in choosing would be greatly reduced, since they would not have to economize, to choose among competing alternatives. In fact, though, this has not happened. There are three areas where effort is forced upon the consumer by scarcity even in the affluent postindustrial society. First, services are scarce. The consumer durables that we buy—television sets, houses, automobiles, boats, etc.—require maintenance. The consumer needs more income to buy these maintenance services. Second, consumption takes time: it takes time to read a book, play tennis, talk to a friend on the telephone, drink a cup of coffee, travel abroad, go to a concert, etc. Thus, consumers must allocate scarce time. Third, time saving becomes a more and more important criterion for choice. Consumers may do their own maintenance to save money, or they may want to spend money to save time. They must calculate: "Man, in his leisure time, has become homo economicus."[22]

Finally, the discussion of EPS is significant for methodology because it bounds the field of consumer behavior. We are now better equipped to answer the question, "What is consumer behavior?"

QUESTIONS

1 What is meant by "self-concept"? Is there evidence for its validity?
2 Choice criteria were emphasized in Chapters 2 and 3. What is the source of choice criteria? Explain.
3 What are the content dimensions of information required in EPS?
4 Describe how each of the stages of choice by consumers—EPS, LPS, and RRB—relates to the marketing concept.
5 Practitioners often criticize market research courses because not enough attention is given to the important task of "identifying the problem." What does identification of the problem involve?

SUGGESTIONS FOR FURTHER READING

N. T. Feather: *Values in Education and Society,* Free Press, New York, 1975.
M. Rokeach, *The Nature of Human Values,* Free Press, New York, 1973.

[22]D. Bell, *The Coming of Post-Industrial Society,* Basic Books, New York, 1973, p. 474.

Extensive Problem Solving: Deeper Information Processing

CONTENTS

The model of EPS in Figure 5-2 gives us a background for discussing the information-processing requirements of the concept-formation process implied in Table 5-4 and Figures 5-2 and 5-3. In designing the form of a message, we must consider human limitations in processing information. Unfortunately, however, our basic knowledge is itself limited. Almost all research on concept learning has dealt with concept utilization or concept attainment.[1] But although there has been substantial related research on cognition, thinking, concept identification, problem solving, etc., the recent research that bears directly on concept formation has dealt with the learning of attributes and rules, specifically where "a concept is defined in terms of certain stimulus attributes and of a rule connecting or integrating these attributes."[2] Not only has research been confined to concept utilization or concept attainment; it has dealt almost exclusively with concepts at the level of identification, not evaluation. Research on buying in LPS, such as was illustrated in Table 3-1 and Figure 3-5, however, gives us reason to believe that these two levels develop similarly.

PRODUCT LIFE CYCLE AND CHANGING INFORMATION REQUIREMENTS

To bring the information requirements of EPS into focus, let us first briefly review the stages of the decision process and the information requirements for LPS and RRB. The product life cycle introduced in Chapter 1 gives us a realistic context for thinking about how information requirements change. The life cycle for instant coffee, which you will recall from Chapter 1, is shown in Figure 6-1. The proportion of consumers in each stage changes drastically over the cycle. At the maturity stage, most consumers would be in RRB, as is indicated by the topmost graph in Figure 6-1. In the growth stage, most are in LPS (the middle graph); and at the introduction stage, most are in EPS (the bottom graph).

The information requirements for RRB, discussed in Chapter 2, are shown in the bottom half of Figure 6-1 at the right. They are few: just enough information to let the consumer infer the magnitude of changing impersonal beliefs about price and availability. Brand concept is firm.

The requirements for LPS (at the middle of the lower half of Figure 6-1) involve forming evaluative beliefs about a new brand and summing the beliefs (weighted by salience); this sum is attitude toward the brand. Also, consumers must have information in order to form brand identification and confidence.

In EPS, information requirements (at the lower left of Figure 6-1) are substantial. The consumers must have information in order to group a brand in the correct class of product classes and then to distinguish it from among the other classes. Bear in mind that it is assumed throughout this chapter that consumers' instrumental values are given; changing values will be discussed in

[1]J. P. van de Geer and J. F. W. Jaspars, "Cognitive Functions," *Annual Review of Psychology,* **17**:149–150, 1966.

[2]L. E. Bourne and R. L. Dominowski, "Thinking," *Annual Review of Psychology,* **23**:117, 1972.

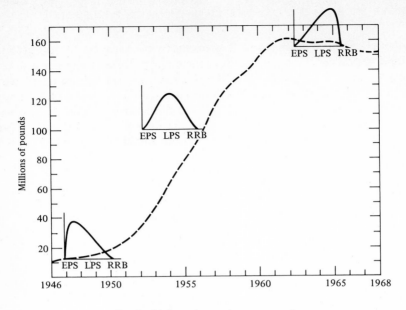

Details of information requirements at each stage

Product class choice

	Terminal values	Choice criteria for product class	Salience of criteria	Beliefs about product class	Contribu- tion
EPS	▬▬ ▬▬ ▬▬	▬▬ ▬▬ ▬▬	▬▬ ▬▬		
	Attitude toward product class				

Brand choice

	Instru- mental values	Choice criteria for brand	Salience of criteria	Beliefs about brand	Contribu- tion
	▬▬ ▬▬				
	Attitude toward brand				

LPS

Choice criteria for brand	Salience of choice criteria	Beliefs about brand	Contribu- tion
▬▬ ▬▬	▬▬ ▬▬		
Attitude toward brand			

RRB

Choice criteria	
Brand concept	Nescafe
Impersonal criteria Availability Price	 Yes No
Attitude toward brand	

Figure 6-1 How consumers' information requirements change over the product life cycle.

Table 6-1   Consumers' Feelings toward Nescafe

Ascribed characteristics	Purchaser of Nescafe	Purchaser of Maxwell House
Lazy	48%	4%
Poor planner	48%	12%
Thrifty	4%	16%
Spendthrift	12%	0%
Bad wife	16%	0%
Good wife	4%	16%

Source: F. E. Webster and F. von Pechman, "A Replication of the Shopping List' Study," *Journal of Marketing*, April 1970, pp. 61–77.

Chapter 9. Consumers must also have information in order to relate their instrumental values to the appropriate criteria for brand choice, to determine the salience of each criterion, and to locate a new brand on the various choice criteria. In EPS not only the content but also the form of information is important; consumers should receive the information with ease. These points will be developed further as we go along.

Finally, consumers in EPS not only do not know about a new thing, but are often opposed to it when they learn about it because it requires new behavior patterns which may violate their values. That this was the case with instant coffee in the late 1940s has been documented by Mason Haire.[3] Haire's study was referred to earlier; it will now be described in detail because it is the earliest study to document these contrary values in EPS. Haire presented fifty subjects (women homemakers) with a typical shopping list, one item of which was Nescafe (instant coffee). He presented another fifty with a list that was identical except that it substituted Maxwell House coffee (drip grind) for Nescafe. He asked each subject to describe the kind of homemaker—in terms of personality and character—who would buy the list. The replies, shown in Table 6-1, clearly indicate the subjects' feelings. Such feelings must be laid to rest before wide acceptance can be expected, but advertising may be ineffective in changing the values that give rise to them.

With the information requirements in mind, let us deal with language, memory, and inference in turn.

LANGUAGE IN EPS

As in LPS, language carries the burden of communication to the consumer in EPS. Pictures can support but not supplant it. Sound waves must be transmuted into meaningless sounds (phonemes) and then into meaningful words and sen-

---

[3]M. Haire, "Projective Techniques in Marketing Research," *Journal of Marketing*, **14**:649–656, April 1950.

tences. The same "top-down" analysis of sentences occurs. The details of information processing described in Chapter 4 need not be repeated here; we need only note that in EPS there is considerably more information to be transmitted. Also, sentences that can easily be transformed into kernel sentences—simple, active, affirmative, and declarative sentences—are probably even more important in EPS than in LPS. This is true because the information in EPS is likely to be less meaningful, less familiar, and less similar to known information than in LPS, as will be emphasized in Chapter 7. Polar adjectives will probably be substantially more effective than nonpolar or independent adjectives because polar adjectives probably convey information more precisely. Also, the choice of adjectives makes a difference; for example, "better" and "taller" convey relative positions, whereas according to psychologists "worse" and "shorter" convey, in addition, something about absolute positions.[4]

MEMORY IN EPS

When we turn to memory, however, we encounter additional complexities arising from both the quantity and the quality of information. Presumably, sensory memory operates similarly in EPS and LPS. In short-term memory, however, the differences between EPS and LPS probably become apparent, because in EPS the consumer lacks the structure of even a product-class concept. In long-term memory, the lack of a product-class structure probably is a major influence on the speed and ease with which information can be processed. In EPS there is no feedback of words stored in long-term memory (since there is no existing product-class structure); hence there are no readily available labels for choice criteria, and this makes it difficult for short-term memory to select the most relevant parts of the flow of incoming information. This will be discussed in Chapter 7. Also, the incoming flow will not be nearly as meaningful, familiar, or similar as in LPS.

The incoming words and sentences will have to be associated by inference, not by concrete choice criteria as in LPS but rather by personal values (which are more abstract). This means that the same physical volume of input will probably become many more chunks of information in EPS than in LPS, because without feedback from long-term memory each word is less meaningful. (A chunk, as was noted in Chapter 4, can be a letter, a word, or a group of words, as long as it is a meaningful pattern.) Processing time and effort will go up correspondingly. Whether the exact words that are finally stored are contained in the message— whether one finds the particular words appropriate to one's own way of thinking or must paraphrase them to feel comfortable—will probably matter considerably more in EPS than in LPS.

Information processing will be more difficult still if there is no appropriate semantic structure into which a consumer can categorize (group) a new thing—

---

[4]P. C. Wason and P. N. Johnson-Laird, *Psychology of Reasoning,* Harvard University Press, Cambridge, Mass., 1972, pp. 108 and 126.

that is, if the consumer must build a new local structure. This is implicit in the model of memory discussed in Chapter 4. The retrieval time—the time spent in searching for the appropriate category in LTM—would be much longer, because the new thing and the retrieved thing would at first be unrelated (the relation would be disjoint).

INFERENCE IN EPS: INFERRING CHOICE CRITERIA

Is inferential information processing substantially different in EPS and LPS? Is it different when consumers are forming a product space (EPS) and when they are identifying a brand's position in that product space (LPS)? In general, when we ask such questions we are asking about the process by which a consumer decides that certain choice criteria cause satisfaction—that is, satisfy instrumental values. This phrasing brings us back to the question dealt with in Chapter 3, of how confidence forms. Here we are concerned with confidence in judgment at the level of choice among product classes; but distinctiveness, consistency, and consensus should still be relevant. To simplify, let us omit confidence from this discussion, as we omitted brand identification from the study of appliances (pages 97 to 102).

To develop a connection between evaluative criteria (means) and instrumental values (end), buyers group a new thing with related product classes and use currently received information and storage in LTM to represent in their minds an image of the new alternative. First, they compare the new brand with their image of each of the existing product classes and infer whether the new brand will better serve their choice criteria for these product classes. Second, if they find that the new brand is better, they must then decide whether it is worth the cost and trouble of purchasing it. To do this, however, they must have at least loosely formulated some criteria for brand choice; that is, they must have some hypotheses about what are acceptable brand criteria. We will examine two possibilities: first, what happens when the buyer has hypotheses about the relevance of particular criteria to instrumental values; second, what happens when the buyer has no such hypotheses.

Inference with Hypotheses about Criteria

In most instances we would expect normal, adult buyers to have some ideas, however vague, about whether the perceived attributes of a brand matter for their instrumental values. They would probably generalize from buying similar product classes; for example, someone who has never bought a subcompact car has probably at least bought a regular car. In such a situation consumers will call upon information stored in LTM: their experiences have left traces in their memory which they can call upon. These traces will also facilitate getting consumers' attention—that is, getting them to take in information about a new product. (This will be discussed in Chapter 7.) Whether a consumer has a hypothesis would seem to depend upon how much of a relevant semantic structure he or she already has.

Practically, the consumer is often faced with choosing between two kinds of evaluative criteria: those with high predictive value and those with high confidence value.[5] An illustration will help clarify this distinction. Technical information about the electronic parts would be predictive of the performance of a hi-fi set; but the consumer, not being an engineer, may not have confidence in his or her ability to use such a criterion and may therefore prefer to use the salesperson's statement, which is at least understandable. Cox concludes, "Predictive value seems to be the basic force determining information value and hence cue (criterion) utilization. . . . But confidence value . . . acts as a qualifying variable and carries a strong veto."[6]

By what process does a consumer take information about these cues from LTM and infer from it whether particular brand attributes conform to certain choice criteria and serve particular instrumental values? Here we must move from the relational inference (linear syllogism) of LPS that was implied in the model of memory (Chapter 4) to the more complex, quantified inference of the regular syllogism. We do this by inserting degree, amount, and quantity.

For example, consider this question: "Will high-protein food make me more effective?" Let us assume that "being effective" would serve two instrumental values: ambition and capability (see Table 5-3). The question can, of course, be viewed as a hypothesis ("high-protein food will make me more effective") which the consumer tests by retrieving information in LTM or obtaining new information. To answer this question in determining choice criteria for vegetable bacon, one could reason in the following way:

1 Meat foods contain high proportions of protein.
2 Protein will give me energy.
∴ Meat foods provide me with high energy.

This method of reasoning is a syllogism. Its conclusion rests on hypotheses 1 and 2. Further information is required if one is to be confident of the conclusion and willing to act on it in accordance with the following inference:

1 I want to have more energy, to work harder and be more effective.
2 Protein will give me energy, and meat contains high protein.
∴ I will eat meat.

Information is needed to give assurance that if one chooses food based on "proteinness," one will be able to work harder; and that this will in turn contribute to the instrumental goals of being ambitious and capable. In studying a complex problem such as this, where so little that goes on is observable, the

[5]D. F. Cox, "The Measurement of Information Value: A Study in Consumer Decision-Making," in W. S. Decker (ed.), "Emerging Concepts in Marketing," *Proceedings of the Winter Conference of the American Marketing Association,* 1962, pp. 413–421.
[6]Ibid., p. 419.

buyer's behavior is often compared with a model. The model used here is the syllogism given above.[7]

The following sections will, first, illustrate the syllogistic model by means of a real-world problem, the appliance study discussed earlier; second, illustrate the model in a laboratory context; third, examine what this type of research reveals about the nature of the inference process in order to bring the available evidence to bear on problems of consumers' behavior; fourth, discuss the significance of the findings in terms of information to meet consumers' needs.

A Real-World Example of the Syllogistic Model   Let us use here the appliance study presented earlier. Assume that a buyer has gone through the following syllogistic reasoning process:

1 Appliances with modern features usually are novel.
2 We find novel things satisfying.
   ∴ Appliances with modern features will be satisfying.

The buyer now has a hunch, a hypothesis, that modern features in, say, a television set will serve the instrumental need for novelty quite well. To make sure, however, the buyer needs more information—friends and shopping, for example. Such information will confirm or disconfirm the hypothesis, so that the buyer can accept or reject the connection between modern features and novelty with enough confidence to act on the conclusion. The question, then, is: What information will confirm the hypothesis and what will disconfirm it? The answer to this question should tell us something about the information he thinks he needs, which is the information he will search for.

A Laboratory Example of the Syllogistic Model   A laboratory experiment can provide an analogue to the real-world example and thus give us firmer evidence on whether a syllogism really does describe what goes in in a buyer's mind when he or she tries to match choice criteria and instrumental values in order to form a product-class concept. We will discuss a laboratory-type experiment in terms of the conditions of the appliance study.[8] Then, we can move directly to actual laboratory experiments to determine what evidence they provide on the nature of the consumer's reasoning process.

If one has a hypothesis about something, a piece of evidence can either confirm it, disconfirm it, or contribute nothing to determining its truth. Now, imagine that in a laboratory, a subject is presented with four cards, each with a letter on one side and a number on the other. When placed on a table in front of the subject, the cards read as follows:

E   K   4   7

---

[7]Wason and Johnson-Laird, op. cit., chap. 11.
[8]Wason and Johnson-Laird, chap. 13.

A hypothesis is now put to the subject: "Cards with a vowel on the visible side have an even number on the other side." The subject is asked which cards he or she should pick up to confirm or reject this hypothesis.

Now let us describe our problem of matching instrumental values and choice criteria in terms of this abstract model; in this way, we will see the relevance of the model to consumers' problems. Our real-world problem is to determine the truth of this hypothesis: "If the appliance has modern features, it serves my novelty value." (The conditional "if" may sound strange, but it is implicit in all statements of relation.) Our problem, then, corresponds to the laboratory model in the following way:

E = "appliance has modern features"
K = "appliance does not have modern features"
4 = "it serves the value of novelty"
7 = "it does not serve the value of novelty"

The significance of each of the four conditions can be amplified as follows:

Condition E: We look at an appliance and find that it does have modern features. We can look at it (search by looking at the other side of the card) to see if it really does serve our needs. When we do, we can find either that it does (even) or that it does not (odd). If it does, we have confirmed the hypothesis only for this particular brand of appliance, however. It tells us nothing about other brands. This is verification.

Conditions K and 4: Neither card K nor card 4 tells us anything about the truth of the hypothesis implied in our problem, as we will see below.

Condition 7: Checking a brand which does not serve the value of novelty, such as is indicated by 7, would let us know if there is ever an instance where such a brand does have modern features. If in this one case, where the value of novelty is not served, the appliance does have modern features, we have disproved the hypothesis (we have falsified it). Thus, the important conclusion is that we should logically be searching for disconfirming—falsifying—evidence instead of confirming evidence.

Now, having seen the relevance of the model to our problem, let us examine it more carefully to see what light it throws on the consumer's capacity to make valid inferences about the relationship between choice criteria and values.

If the subject picks up card E and finds an even number on the other side, the hypothesis will be *confirmed.* But to be absolutely sure the hypothesis is *true,* all possible cards with vowels must be checked to ensure that there is no exception. The purpose in picking up card E was to determine whether there was an even number on the other side. A more efficient purpose for picking up E might have been to *falsify* the hypothesis. If the subject finds an odd number on the other side of E, the hypothesis will have been falsified with a single card. This is a much more efficient rule of search.

In terms of action, both purposes—confirmation and falsification—yield the same result, namely, picking up *E*.

When we turn to the other cards, however, the objective of falsification would cause the subject to pick up 7, not *K* or 4. If a vowel is found on the other side of 7, the hypothesis is known to be untrue. Again, falsifying is the efficient rule of search. If 7 has a vowel on the other side, then by a single card—with just one piece of information—the hypothesis is falsified and can be rejected. This reduces the effort required for search and the information requirements. Falsification is thus the most efficient way to determine whether a hypothesis is true.

In this situation, to be sure that the hypothesis is correct, the subject should pick up both *E* and 7. A subject who picks up only *E* will miss an opportunity to falsify. But the subject should not pick up 7 only, because *E* does contribute some information: It tells whether this particular instance is true. Having this information is better than having no information.

Evidence from Applying the Syllogistic Model   Can we expect buyers to use logical inference to determine whether there is a relation between choice criteria and instrumental values? That is, will consumers attempt to falsify hypotheses? What is the empirical evidence? To answer this, we can see what people do when confronted with the cards. Does their behavior conform to the method that we are using as a model? It does not. When the card experiment was actually done, only a few subjects used the method of the model. The results of the experiment are shown in Table 6-2; note that fifty-nine subjects made the mistake of picking up cards *E* and 4. Only five subjects out of 128 applied both confirmation and falsification and so used logical inference properly.

Why do we find this discrepancy between behavior and logic, these departures from good logic? Why do so many subjects pick *E* and 4, the wrong cards? Card 4 contributes no evidence whatsoever, because the hypothesis does not say that even-numbered cards have a vowel on the other side. Subjects who pick

Table 6-2   Results of Card Experiment

Cards	Number of subjects choosing cards	Results
E and 4	59	Illicit conversion of the original premise
E	42	Confirmation
E, 4, and 7	9	Excess information resulting from illicit conversion of premise
E and 7	5	Falsification
Others	13	
Total sample	128	

Source: P. C. Wason and P. N. Johnson-Laird, *Psychology of Reasoning,* Harvard University Press, Cambridge, Mass., 1972, p. 182.

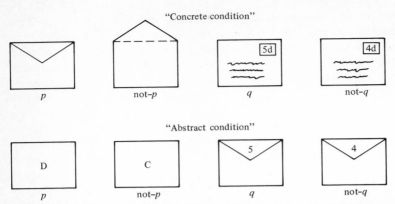

Figure 6-2   Concrete versus abstract conditions of choice. (*P. C. Wason and P. N. Johnson-Laird,* Psychology of Reasoning, *Harvard University Press, Cambridge, Mass., 1972, p. 192.*)

card 4 have "illicitly converted the premise" (the hypothesis). Similarly, *K* tells nothing about the truth of the hypothesis, because the hypothesis says nothing about consonants.

Why do people err? In large part, abstractness of the material is the reason: it creates cognitive strain. This explanation is supported when the same type of problem is given with envelopes—four "concrete" envelopes and then four "abstract" envelopes.[9] This form of the experiment is shown in Figure 6-2 (top). In the concrete condition, the subjects were instructed to assume that they were doing the practical job of sorting letters in a British post office. The hypothesis was, "If a letter is sealed, it has a 5d stamp on it." To add to the realism of the task, envelopes were used instead of cards. In standard logic, the notation *p* means "true" and *q* means "false." In Figure 6-2 (top) the back of a sealed envelope is *p;* the back of an unsealed envelope is not-*p;* the front of an envelope with an address and a 5d stamp is *q;* the front of an envelope with an address and a 4d stamp is not-*q*. As in the card study, the subjects were asked to choose those envelopes which would tell them the truth of the hypothesis. In this "practical" situation, twenty-one of twenty-four subjects used correct logical inference by selecting both and only *p* and not-*q*. These results are markedly different from those of the card study, in which only five out of 128 subjects reasoned correctly.

The results of this experiment can be contrasted with those of a very similar experiment which incorporates abstract conditions. The abstract conditions are shown in Figure 6-2 (bottom). Here subjects are given the following hypothesis: "If a letter has a *D* on one side, then it has a 5 on the other side." The material used was more abstract: the front of an envelope with a *D* on it was marked *p;* the front of an envelope with a *C* on it was marked not-*p;* the back of an envelope with a 5 on it was marked *q;* the back of an envelope with a 4 on it was marked not-*q*. In this more abstract situation, only two of the twenty-four subjects reasoned correctly. The difference in the results of these two very similar studies

[9]Wason and Johnson-Laird, chap. 14.

is remarkable, and it is abstractness that has clearly made the difference. The results are even more impressive when we learn that the subjects had been exposed to the concrete experiment before the abstract one. They learned nothing from the concrete experiment that helped them; there was no transfer of learning.

Another reason why people do not use logical inference is the belief in causality. In much of life, when things occur together it is because one causes the other. The assumption of causality is one of the reasons why the subjects in these experiments went astray and did not falsify. If the subjects assume causality between p and q, then 1 and 4 amount to the same thing. The symbol p would always be followed by q and never by not-q or not-p. More important, p and q would be the correct choices because picking q under conditions of causality would be a means of falsifying the rule. In the appliance study, a consumer who found a q card without a p on the other side would be falsifying the hypothesis that the choice criterion "modern features" is associated with the "novelty" value.

Following is a summary of the logical errors found in the studies of inference:

1 Illicit conversion of premises. We observed this above when the hypothesis was mistakenly interpreted as saying that even-numbered cards had a vowel on the other side.

2 Bias toward verification. This is encouraged by the abstractness of a situation. It can also result from assuming causality—for example, assuming that "modern features" caused "novelty"—which of course is to assume away the problem.

Two other logical errors, blocking on negatives in the premises and ignoring implied content of the premises, have also been observed.

Significance of Evidence from the Syllogistic Model   What can we conclude about how we ought to prepare messages if we want to help the consumer in EPS make correct inferences? Also, what rules of search might we advise consumers to use?

Avoiding abstract statements and stating information in concrete terms will clearly aid inference. By presenting consumers with concrete material, we encourage them to falsify instead of confirm. This not only simplifies their task but prevents them from illicitly converting premises. A description of possible levels of abstraction will help clarify this important dimension. Following are four levels:

1 Concepts so abstract that it is almost impossible to give an intuitive representation, much less a visual representation. E.g., certain mathematical problems in n-dimensional space can be manifested only in a symbolic way. Imagine that you could not use the concept of product space in two- or three-dimensional terms but only in *n*-dimensional terms. The concept would be far less useful to you.

2　Arbitrary geometrical configurations, like the four cards of the experiment or the "abstract" envelopes in Figure 6-2, that do not represent anything concrete.

3　Familiar, everyday causal relationships. E.g., "If heat is applied to water, the water becomes warmer." Giving consumers favorable information about a brand will cause their attitude toward it to improve.

4　Actual objects in a familiar setting. E.g., the "concrete" envelopes of Figure 6-2.[10]

In addition to providing concrete instead of abstract material, we can delete negatives from the message. We can also be explicit rather than implicit. Implicit statements encourage a person to ignore essential elements of the information.

We have seen that inference can be much more difficult in EPS than in LPS or RRB. Not only is the consumer confronted with much information, but the actual process of inference is also more difficult. In EPS, inferences are made about which choice criteria serve which instrumental values. In LPS, the task is much simpler: "Is X more than or less than Y on a choice criterion?" In RRB, the task is analogous to LPS, except that the choice criteria are fewer and are probably substantially more concrete than those in LPS. In summary, the inferential aspects of the linguist's "deep structure" are much more complex in EPS, as was indicated at the bottom of Figure 6-1 where the information requirements of EPS were compared with those of LPS and RRB.

Historically, philosophers taught that inference was a matter of logic; only the *structural characteristics* of a problem mattered. In layman's language, only logic matters. That is:

1　Major premise
2　Minor premise
　　∴ Conclusion

Specifically, once a problem is properly set up in terms of logic, the conclusion must be correct. This implies that what is fed into this logic machine does not matter. But what is fed in is the facts of a situation and the form in which they are presented; and we have seen that information does make a great difference in how accurate a consumer's inference is. Indeed, the nature of the facts being fed in make all the difference in the world. Thus, if we want consumers to infer correctly, we feed them a particular type of material—e.g., concrete, not abstract. This situation opens up a great opportunity for us as consumer experts to learn how to help people make good choices by providing them with information that is better both in content and in form; here, however, we have dealt only with form.

[10]Wason and Johnson-Laird, pp. 342–343.

Inference without Hypotheses about Criteria

We now examine the situation where the buyer has no hypothesis about what evaluative criteria for a new brand should be. In this case, the buyer must search for and retrieve from memory—that is, from new information and past experience —hunches about what may be relevant to forming a hypothesis. An experienced buyer would be expected to develop some hunches from stored experience. An inexperienced buyer will probably have to search extensively for the input needed.

A market researcher's experience illustrates generating a hypothesis. Alfred Politz, working as a marketing consultant for an automobile company, found that people valued acceleration in a car. He wondered how they had developed this criterion, because he thought that acceleration was difficult to identify. The question, then, was: "How did they know that a particular car had acceleration?"

Politz remembered that only when he was in a jet airplane had he felt a sense of acceleration—never in a car. If this was also true of other people, then automobile drivers must be using some surrogate or substitute measure. What could such a surrogate conceivably be? Politz hypothesized that it was the tension on the accelerator spring. In other words, he hypothesized that automobile buyers went through the following syllogism:

1   Some cars exhibit high acceleration.
2   These cars usually have soft accelerator springs.
    ∴ Cars with soft accelerator springs exhibit high acceleration.

To check the truth of this, he conducted a survey. Respondents were asked whether they thought their automobiles had high acceleration and whether the accelerator spring was soft or stiff. Politz found that, on the average, those people who felt their automobiles had high acceleration also thought that the accelerator spring was soft. He concluded that having a soft accelerator spring gave people the impression of high acceleration. This was the essential cue; it also illustrated a high confidence but a low predictive value.

Conclusions on Inference in EPS

Some of the consumer's difficulties with logical inference have been shown. A primary reason for these difficulties is the abstractness of the information. We know that both choice criteria and, particularly, values are abstract entities; thus it is not surprising that they often raise serious difficulties for consumers who are attempting to form a product space. We would also predict that consumers experience much greater ease in forming identifying criteria than evaluative criteria. The formation of product-class and brand concepts would seem to be more difficult for a service than for a physical product, because a service is less concrete. The concreteness-abstractness dimension is related to a number of cognitive characteristics on which people differ but which were not discussed here: category width, leveling, assimilation and contrast, cognitive simplicity, and open- and closed-mindedness (dogmatism).[11]

This discussion has ignored the role of different sources of information, which receives so much attention in studies of diffusion. Specifically, other people are a very important source of information for consumers. In EPS, we would expect social influence to be by far the dominant source.

Our discussion has implicitly assumed that new choice criteria are being formed. There is also the possibility of change in existing choice criteria—that is, change in weightings. We would, of course, expect this to be much easier than the forming of new criteria. The discussion has also implied that it is easier to change attitudes (beliefs) than to change choice criteria. But the evidence for this is limited, although Lutz found that attitude appeared easier to change.[12]

APPLICATION

The practical implications of the consumer's limited capacity for processing information are not well understood. A good example, unit pricing, was given in Chapter 4. The improved method of stating unit prices should be much more relevant for EPS.

Because our knowledge is incomplete, we cannot easily separate effects of the content of information from the effects of the form. The two probably interact anyway. Consequently, no attempt will be made here to distinguish them sharply. In Figure 6-1, the product life cycle was used to illustrate how information requirements change. Let us develop this topic further now.

Product Life Cycle and Stages of the Decision Process

By using the total system for describing the consumer and placing the three stages of the decision process—EPS, LPS, and RRB—in the perspective of the product life cycle (as in Figure 6-1), we can better understand both the stages of decision and the product life cycle (PLC). The PLC of instant coffee was introduced in Chapter 1 to illustrate the three stages of decision—EPS, LPS, and RRB—for a frequently purchased, rather unimportant product. Now that we have discussed each of these three stages, they can be related to each other to explain the continuous learning process that a consumer undergoes.

Figure 6-1, by highlighting the changing information requirements as the PLC advances, shows that the consumer has been the missing link in understanding the PLC. This explains why, for example, Cox found that in 70 percent of forty-five drug items, "promotional effort . . . rises to a peak in the Growth stage and declines to a moderate level . . . in the Maturity stage";[13] and Buzzell found

[11]R. B. Zajonc, "Cognitive Theories in Social Psychology," in G. Lindzey and E. Aronson (eds.), *Handbook of Social Psychology,* vol. 1, Addison-Wesley, Reading, Mass., 1968, pp. 333–335.

[12]R. J. Lutz, "Changing Brand Attitudes Through Modification of Cognitive Structure," *Journal of Consumer Research,* 1:49–59, March 1975.

[13]W. E. Cox, Jr., "Product Life Cycles as Marketing Models," *Journal of Business,* **40**:380, October 1967.

Table 6-3 Optimal Advertising over Product Life Cycle

Year	Sales*	Actual advertising	Optimal advertising
1886	68,697	$ 68,961	$372,949
1887	79,834	74,238	405,719
1888	76,070	66,546	495,226
1889	94,059	110,466	495,005
1890	108,888	174,149	497,386
1891	127,247	147,191	483,184
1892	134,588	117,631	460,972
1893	133,530	187,857	426,517
1894	137,349	176,923	392,601
1895	133,635	190,522	342,208
1896	144,012	223,740	306,146
1897	145,512	230,195	268,843
1898	147,391	224,916	224,841
1899	156,878	251,284	192,546
1900	168,097	210,084	163,536
1901	174,158	237,689	134,049
1902	189,424	334,808	112,789
1903	207,419	227,382	92,139
1904	215,824	273,403	74,639
1905	231,275	327,615	60,064
1906	230,123	325,131	47,169
1907	206,890	323,383	37,999
1908	195,003	292,426	30,370
1909	182,109	266,015	23,274
1910	167,868	255,834	17,533
1911	165,779	252,014	12,695
1912	147,078	248,129	8,704
1913	140,568	263,097	5,862
1914	119,968	140,221	3,073
1915	111,958	67,984	1,790

*Sales are in units of one-half gross.
Source: L. J. Parsons, "The Product Life Cycle and Time-Varying Elasticities," *Journal of Marketing Research,* **12**:477 and 479, November 1975.

evidence of falling advertisement-to-sales ratios and declining prices over the cycle of grocery products.[14] Parsons reanalyzed the actual data for sales and advertising for Sapolio; see Table 6-3.[15] The level of advertising indicated by the estimated advertising elasticity of sales that varied over time can be contrasted with the actual level of advertising. There are remarkable discrepancies between "actual advertising" and "optimal advertising"; and these are consis-

[14]R. D. Buzzell, "Competitive Behavior and Product Life Cycles," in J. S. Wright and J. L. Goldstucker (eds.), *Proceedings of American Marketing Association,* 1966, pp. 46–88.
[15]L. J. Parsons, "The Product Life Cycle and Time-Varying Elasticities," *Journal of Marketing Research,* **12**:476–480, November 1975.

tent with the theory that heavy brand advertising should occur early in the product life cycle and decline over its life, or at least until repositioning is attempted. The reader should be aware that the method gives some downward bias to advertising at the end of the period but does not apply to most of the period. The nature of the consumer's information requirements could at least partially explain these changing marketing plans.

It is important to note that in this situation, not only should the marketing *plan* for a brand change from year to year over the PLC, but the marketing manager should also change the brand *strategy* periodically—e.g., moving the brand to a more favorable position in product space by redesigning the product, changing information about the brand, or both. The possibility of repositioning a brand to salvage it was suggested by research on 754 drug products by Cox.[16] He found less support than other researchers for the concept of PLC; for example, six different forms of equations were needed to fit the life cycles of 258 successful products. In fact, the fourth-degree (oscillating) form best represented at least 39.1 percent of these products. This suggests that additional marketing effort can often revive a product which has entered the decline stage. An example of the repositioning of an old product is Bon Ami, a glass cleaner which has been repositioned to a number of new uses. Another outstanding example is Seven-Up. This slow-growth, special-occasion drink was repositioned beginning in 1968 to a general soft drink; it now ranks third in the soft-drink industry, with large increases in sales and profits.

Ultimately, the typical corporate objective of growth with adequate profit may make it necessary to drop a brand. Ideally, the brand can be replaced and the excess personnel can be absorbed by a well-timed introduction of a new product. The need to change strategy is especially great because the market structure is probably changing at the same time that the demand structure—the stage of decision process—is changing.

For example, in the late 1930s the Nestle Company was a monopolist. Being a monopolist means being able to ignore competitors. This leaves managers free to concentrate their attention on consumers, a possibility which immensely simplifies market planning. But by the early 1950s, the market was probably "monopolistically competitive." Numerous new companies entered the industry, usually making an improvement upon the original product. Differences among brands continued to exist; later, however, mergers began to produce a state of differentiated oligopoly. Finally, by 1965, the differences among brands had begun to diminish as technology became standardized; consequently, the instant coffee market probably approached a pure oligopoly. Competitive response became sharp.

This analysis probably applies to frequently purchased, unimportant products which fill the shelves of groceries and drugstores. When we turn to consumer durables, however—especially heavy durables such as automobiles—the analysis is probably less valid. RRB is probably seldom attained; EPS is more

---

[16]M. B. Holbrook and J. A. Howard, "Consumer Research on Frequently Purchased Nondurable Goods and Services: A Review," Project on Synthesis of Knowledge of Consumer Behavior, RANN Program, National Science Foundation, April 1975, p. 69.

common, because these products are purchased infrequently, consumers forget, and values change. Nevertheless, consumers of durables do pass through similar stages of learning, and the concept of PLC is useful for thinking about their changing information requirements.

Design of Messages

EPS has the two kinds of implications for designing information messages: change and current content and form.

As regards change, a message strategy must be developed which will guide changes and help consumers by giving them a consistent picture. Consistency of information is an essential element of confidence, as you will recall from Chapter 3.

As regards content, what does the discussion of EPS processes tell us about how to design it so that it will be more effective in serving the process of concept formation? First, the concept of the structure of information required by the process implies that we should transmit to the consumer the information content specified in the EPS process shown at the bottom of Figure 6-1. Second, we can now compare the three stages in terms of structure of information. This will allow us to sharpen the distinction between information at different stages. In Chapter 2, structure of information was defined as a point in n-dimensional space but was discussed in terms of the typical two-dimensional space. There, information was so simple that it did not significantly involve form. In LPS, additions were made to content dimensions—namely, the content of brand identification, attitude, and confidence. At this point dimensions of form were introduced, such as negatives and the natural order of elements. EPS has carried us substantially further in developing a complex information structure. Two additional content dimensions—the connections between choice criteria and terminal values—were introduced. Let us now examine the dimensions of form in EPS.

Language per se raises few new problems at this stage. Memory, however, does raise important new problems. First, less of the information the consumer receives is likely to be relevant, because in EPS motivation is not precisely defined. Motivationally relevant information has to do with the relation between instrumental values and choice criteria rather than with positions on choice criteria. Second, the information is likely to be less meaningful, in the sense that consumers have less information in their memory about a new thing to associate with the new information. Third, the new information is less familiar. Fourth, the new information will probably be less similar to existing information than it is in LPS. All four of these conditions would imply that the message should carry greater redundancy and should be received more slowly, because a greater number of chunks of information are to be processed. Both greater redundancy and reduced speed of presentation can be reflected in the form of the message.

The process of inference in EPS creates additional complications. First, the abstractness of the message impedes inference. We must recognize that the very nature of the task is more abstract: values are more abstract than choice criteria. Abstractness leads to the illicit conversion of premises and a bias toward verification. Usually, the design of a message can either exaggerate or alleviate this limitation. Use of kernel sentences may help, for example. Second, to the extent that premises are implicit instead of explicit, inferences may suffer. The message can make premises more explicit. Third, because of the difficulty of handling the information, consumers may tend to avoid it. Therefore, problems of attention and search are substantially greater in EPS than in LPS or RRB. But the stronger the buyer's hypothesis about a relation between a possible choice criterion and a value, the less these complications apply. (Issues of attention are dealt with in Chapter 7.)

CONCLUSIONS

Information processing differs substantially in EPS and LPS. For one thing, the linguist's "deep structure" can be immensely more complicated in EPS. Most of the differences, however, appear to lie in short-term and long-term memory and, especially, in inference, rather than in language. Some of the characteristics of information that should shape the form of a message were identified. The effect of abstractness is the most striking. Belief in causality was probably another factor. Although this chapter has focused upon the consumer's limitations as an information processor, using the concept of the product life cycle, it has also brought together the form and content of the information structure. (Content had been specified in Chapter 5.)

   Finally, according to the theory of consumer behavior, the effects of language and inference are captured in short-term memory instead of being shown as separate variables in the system. This simplification is essential to maintaining a mentally manageable theory. Short-term memory can be operationalized directly in the laboratory. Under field conditions, however, which characterize most applications, it can be indirectly operationalized if it is treated as a difference among individual consumers. This will be seen in Chapter 8.

QUESTIONS

1   Why should both marketing strategy and marketing plans for a brand change over the life of a product class?
2   Explain at some length why short-term memory (STM) should be so much more heavily burdened in EPS than in LPS.
3   Illustrate how you might write a message telling a consumer about a brand in such way that the concreteness of the message will help the consumer make correct inferences from it.
4   Does the syllogism capture enough of the important features of buying in EPS to justify using the conclusions from its application to guide the development of marketing strategy and plans?

SUGGESTIONS FOR FURTHER READING

D. A. Norman: *Memory and Attention: An Introduction to Human Information Processing,* Wiley, New York, 1969.
M. I. Posner, *Cognition: An Introduction,* Scott, Foresman, Glenview, Ill., 1973.

Attention and Search

CONTENTS

The Interrupt System

Exceptions to Normal Attention and Search
    Low Involvement
        Learning without involvement
        Cognitive response to information
    Excessive Arousal

Attention, Search, and the Stages of the Decision Process

Application
    Interpretation of Data
    Product Design
    Design of Messages
    Design of Media
    Design of Channels

Conclusion

Questions
Suggestions for Further Reading

So far, it has been assumed that consumers take in all information to which they are exposed, but the significance of this assumption was not obvious. If consumers simply passively accepted all information that they accidentally encountered, they would, for example, probably die of starvation because they would be unable to carry out the act of purchasing food. They would be lost in information. The assumption, then, must be abandoned.

First, consumers are, and must be, very selective as regards the information they take in, because they are confronted with massive amounts of information, most of it irrelevant. Suppose that to pass each course, you tried to memorize (put into long-term memory) the entire textbook. This would be virtually impossible. Instead, you are highly selective in the information that you retain. You probably never memorize even a single sentence, much less the whole text; you retain in long-term memory only relevant, paraphrased sentences—the meaning of the text content put into your own words.

Second, consumers must be highly adaptive to changing information needs and changes in the environment. At one moment a consumer is buying chewing gum; at the next, buying an automobile. The difference in information requirements is almost astronomical. Also, the environment is continually changing with respect to the information that it provides. Often, almost no effort is required to process the information; this is especially true of advertising. The sentences are largely kernel sentences, whose meaning is easily captured and which allow the irrelevant to be distinguished quickly from the relevant. On the other hand, in some situations—like buying an automobile—new vocabulary is usually encountered and much information comes from normal conversation, where, for example, complicated sentences (like the double self-embedded sentence of a clause within a clause cited in Chapter 4) are frequent. In a situation like this, substantial effort is required to process information. Going to the library to read *Consumer Reports* requires still more effort. Consumers must continually adapt to this changing environment.

Without the characteristics of selectivity and adaptability of effort, the consumer would be handicapped indeed. Thus, to be realistic, we must drop the assumption made in Chapter 1 that the consumer is a passive information-processing machine of unlimited capacity.

Consumers get information from their surroundings—their environment—and this environment is very complex. In fact, it is probably the complexity of the environment, rather than the complexity of the buyer, that makes understanding consumers' behavior so difficult:

> A man, viewed as a behaving system, is quite simple. The apparent complexity of his behavior over time is largely a reflection of the complexity of the environment in which he finds himself.[1]

Consider the enormous number of sources of information that a consumer could use for almost any product in the technologically advanced culture of postindustrial society. For example, suppose you are buying a television set. You can discuss it with friends. You can read the newspaper advertisements. You can shop at many stores. You can watch television. You can read *Consumer Reports*. You can read some of the family magazines and newspapers which run articles on various products, especially when there are significant product changes.

Because of the complexity of the environment, what buyers pay attention to in the environment and where they search in that environment make a great difference to their purchasing behavior. This fact has at least two implications.

First, we must attempt to understand the processes of attention and search. The remarkable capacity of human beings for selective attention and search is especially pertinent to understanding the effects of mass media, which offer a wide scope for this selectivity to operate. The viewer of television has enormous freedom to "tune out," which we all do; but it is important to know just what we tune out and why. Selectivity explains, for instance, the surprising conclusion (see Chapter 3) that a consumer's confidence and intention usually increase together; we would expect that a consumer could become equally confident in disliking a brand, so that confidence and intention could move in opposite directions.

Second, because of the environmental differences among consumers, we should not be surprised at the great amount of variability—"noise"—that we encounter when we analyze data about them. Consumers have had quite different experiences. Their individual differences will be discussed in Chapter 8.

---

[1]H. A. Simon, *The Sciences of the Artificial*, M.I.T. Press, Cambridge, Mass., 1969, p. 52.

MEANING OF ATTENTION AND SEARCH

To understand what is meant by attention and search, let us look at their physical manifestations. We have already seen simple examples of attention and search in the laboratory experiments on inference discussed in Chapter 6: the subject, in making inferences, chose a card or envelope that would tell whether a hypothesis was valid: that is, the subject paid attention to and searched for specific relevant information.

Definition

"Attention" is defined as the active selection of, and emphasis on, a particular component of a complex experience, and the narrowing of the range of objects to which the consumer is responding. In general, when consumers are "paying attention," their sensitivity to one sense modality—e.g., the auditory—is heightened, and their sensitivity to the other modalities decreases. In addition, memory is facilitated when one pays attention.

"Search" is defined as movement of the body, including the head, to obtain information. Body movement incorporates a great variety of activities: talking, shopping, reading advertisements, reading news reports, reading *Consumer Reports,* etc. In these ways, the consumer changes the informational environment.

Information Available

The consumers' environment is the source of information to which they might be exposed. It is indicated by the construct "information available" (about brand y) introduced in Chapter 2 and shown in Figure 7-1, which shows mechanisms that operate in paying attention to and searching in the environment. It is these sources to which consumers *could* be exposed if they searched enough. Search exposes consumers to new information, giving us the construct "information exposed" (relevant to brand y), which is also shown in Figure 7-1. Information exposed is defined as those stimuli with which the consumer's sense organs have come into contact. The stimuli are typically symbols that represent the brand. They may be linguistic (spoken words), orthographic (printed words) or pictorial (pictures or cartoons); they may also be the physical brand itself. An important question is: To what informational environment did search expose the consumer?

Sources of information can be classified as *interpersonal* (excluding salespersons), *commercial* (including salespersons, advertising, etc.), and *neutral* (that is, neutral with respect to values). Television, radio, magazines, newspapers, billboards, salespersons, and advertising brochures are commercial sources. Friends, people at work, servicemen, and relatives are interpersonal sources. *Consumer Reports* is a neutral source. People appear to respond quite differently to these three sources. The data in Table 7-1 give some idea of this difference. To determine the nature of sources used in buying automobiles, the following question was asked of a sample of consumers: "How willing are you to

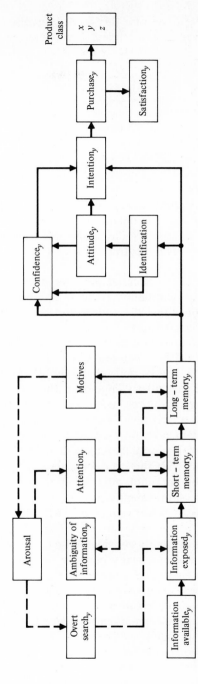

Figure 7-1 Consumer behavior model: some attention and search mechanisms.

Table 7-1   Sources of Information for Buying Automobiles
(Percentages Indicate the Proportion of the Sample That Rated
Each Source as More than 50 on a Scale of 0 to 100.)

1 Television: 25%	7 Automobile salespersons and dealers: 20%
2 Radio: 12%	8 Friends: 64%
3 Magazines: 25%	9 People at work: 58%
4 Newspapers: 30%	10 Gasoline station attendants: 43%
5 Billboards: 20%	11 Garage mechanics
6 Advertising brochures: 22%	12 Relatives: 62%
	13 *Consumer Reports:* 78%

be guided by each of the following sources of information about cars?'' It would appear from these results that the interpersonal sources—friends, people at work, and relatives—shown in the column on the right are more effective than the commercial sources (television, radio, magazines, billboards, brochures, and salespersons and dealers). The neutral source, *Consumer Reports,* is most effective, however.

This difference between commercial and interpersonal sources probably has to do. with their credibility. Credibility is made up of two elements: trust and competence. Does the buyer feel the source can be trusted? Does the source have integrity? Is the source competent to provide the information it is offering to the buyer? This entails competence in telling buyers which choice criteria are appropriate to their values (EPS), where a brand is located on their identifying criteria and choice criteria (LPS), and where the brand can be found (RRB). Trust and competence are particularly important where interpersonal sources are concerned. Friends are useful sources because they are trustworthy (if they were not, they would not be your friends). Sometimes they are competent. Equally important, and more fundamental, they are very likely to have the same values that you have. If so, you can simply take over their choice criteria, especially if they have had experience with the product class and you have not. Finally, friends are convenient: you are much more likely to see them than anyone else. To summarize: friends can conveniently provide trustworthy and perhaps even competent information about belief ratings in RRB and LPS and about choice criteria in EPS cases.

Consumer Reports is evidently considered both trustworthy and competent. Presumably it is viewed as trustworthy because the buyer is paying for it and assumes that it exists to serve the consumer. It is most probably viewed as competent because it does some testing of the products that it rates. There remains the question of whether *Consumer Reports* is using criteria that are adequate to the buyer's requirements; for example, how neighbors value a brand—information not included in *Consumer Reports*—can be a perfectly legitimate criterion for a consumer who wants to get along socially.

This discussion has omitted shopping, which is often an important source of information. Considerable research has been done, but it is difficult to make generalizations.[2] One sensible conclusion is that people who are satisfied with their last purchase of a brand are less inclined than others to shop around. The larger the number of sequential purchases, the less shopping is done; this is probably related to satisfaction.

The most extensive shopping is done for consumer durables—radios, televisions, washing machine, automobiles, etc. But the great differences among shoppers are striking. For example, in one study 39 percent of television buyers and 22 percent of furniture buyers visited only one store; but 44 percent of the television buyers and 22 percent of the furniture buyers visited three or more stores.[3]

Consumers of "soft" goods, especially clothing, also shop extensively; for example, in one study 25 percent of the subjects shopped in seven or more stores for eight clothing and household items which were listed.[4]

Buyers of food do not tend to shop quite as much. In one study, 54 percent of the subjects shopped in a single store, 37 percent visited two or more stores, and 9 percent shopped around with little consistency.[5] Of working women, 71 percent shopped once a week; of nonworking women, 43 percent shopped once a week.

One serious social question is whether the poor and disadvantaged shop as carefully for basic foods as the richer and more advantaged. Granbois has reviewed the research on this issue, and one can conclude from his review that there is considerable truth in the belief that the poor do not shop as carefully as others do. The problem is complex, however; for example, significant differences exist among the disadvantaged minority groups.

In-home shopping, such as telephone ordering, mail ordering, and purchasing from door-to-door salespeople, is common, but it varies much from product to product.[6]

Studies of shopping, it should be noted, probably understate the actual amount of shopping, especially for infrequently purchased items, because the data are collected by means of recall, and our memories are fallible.

CAUSE OF ATTENTION AND SEARCH: AROUSAL

What are the mechanisms that give rise to attention and search? Like all behavior, attention and search are motivated. Motivation is varied, of course.

[2]Donald Granbois, "Consumer Shopping Behavior and Preferences," Project on Synthesis of Knowledge of Consumer Behavior, RANN Program, National Science Foundation, April 1975.

[3]B. Le Grand and J. G. Udell, "Consumer Behavior in the Market Place," *Journal of Retailing,* **40**:32–40, 47–48, Fall 1964.

[4]S. U. Rich, "Shopping Behavior of Department Store Customers," Division of Research, Graduate School of Business, Harvard University, Boston, Mass., 1963, p. 98.

[5]Bryan Thompson, "An Analysis of Supermarket Shopping Habits in Worcester, Massachusetts," *Journal of Retailing,* **43**:17–29, Fall 1967, p. 18.

[6]Granbois, op. cit., p. 35.

Indeed, it must be if the consumer is to adapt to a complex environment with varied sources of information. This is particularly true in postindustrial society, where change (such as change in the price and availability of new products) is frequent and much information is available if the consumer wants to take advantage of it. (Nevertheless, information is usually not in the exact form needed, nor does it appear at the best time. Rather, it often appears in the form of casual conversation with a friend, has all the inadequacies of conversational speech, and is not available when the consumer is actually buying.) The pyschological motives must also be diverse, for much the same reasons.

One way to develop both diversity of attention and search and diversity of is sources is to begin with the physiological condition of arousal. Arousal, defined as the degree of tension in the body, gives rise to attention and search. An overview of the mechanisms by which this is accomplished is given in Figure 7-1, but many details are omitted (these are added in Figure 7-2). Near the left of Figure 7-1 is a box labeled "arousal." "Arousal" feeds into "attention," which positively affects the two memories. Also, "arousal" causes "search," which, in turn, changes the informational environment to which the consumer is exposed ("information exposed"). "Information exposed" is defined as objects and symbols for objects with which the consumer's sense organs have come into contact. This environment is only a portion of the total environment to which the consumer could be exposed in searching ("information available"). "Information available" was defined earlier in this chapter.

Arousal is a general effect, specific not to any particular brand but only to a product class. Hence, unlike the other constructs, it does not carry the subscript y, which refers to a particular brand. It energizes or provides push to attention and search. Direction—specific focus—of attention and search is given by the same kind of learned preferences for some information over others that give direction to choice among brands. Further selectivity is provided by the feedback from LTM to STM, as described in Chapter 4. The consumer pays attention to and searches for that which is relevant, and LTM tells STM what is relevant. Thus, consumers have two problems: (1) to exert enough effort in attention and search to handle the information that they are exposed to, and to expose themselves to additional information; (2) to allocate their efforts in such a way that attention and search will be selective enough to obtain information about a particular brand. The amount of effort is a function of the amount of arousal (up to a point), and the amount of arousal is a function of the demands of the tasks one is confronted with. Excessive arousal, however, can inhibit the effort to pay attention and to search, as it can any form of behavior.

The demands of the task of exerting effort will change from minute to minute. Much of the information input makes little demand; but suddenly one may encounter, for example, some long, awkward sentences in conversation, which increase the cognitive strain on STM (whose capacity is measured by chunks, as was noted in Chapter 4). Arousal increases because the burden on short-term memory has increased (as a result of the additional chunks). I emphasize the linguistic factor as a burden on STM because the linguistic content of a message is more important than graphics (form) in getting attention.[7] When the limited capacity of short-term memory is exceeded, cognitive strain results and arousal increases.

Given this theoretical background, let us examine the causes of arousal—the demands of the task of obtaining adequate information. Next, we will develop the process of the allocation of attention and search, and then turn to the consequences of arousal.

Causes of Arousal

We have discussed how buyers pay attention and search when they need information, and how increasing arousal causes these behaviors. Now let us ask more specifically: What causes arousal? Another way to put this is: How is the need for information reflected in psychological mechanisms? Since arousal is not specific to a particular need, we must also ask: What are the mechanisms for allocating attention and search? This question, however, will be dealt with after we have discussed the causes of arousal.

Four mechanisms are the source of arousal: intensity of relevant motives, ambiguity of the information, confidence in judging the quality of a brand, and level of aspiration. Let us now explore the nature of each of these mechanisms.

Intensity of Relevant Motives   Motives served by a product class are a dominant source of arousal; this relationship is shown by the feedback from "motives" to "arousal" in Figure 7-2, which presents a more complete picture than Figure 7-1. These motives specify what information is relevant. Relevant information is that information which pertains to how a particular set of motives can be satisfied.

Feedback has already been mentioned several times. Because it is such an essential part of the way consumers unconsciously regulate their information input, let us examine this subtle idea more carefully. In Figure 7-2, LTM is the source of change in motives (values); the increased intensity of the motives stimulates arousal; and, finally, arousal causes the consumer to pay attention, which affects what is held in short-term memory. Thus, the system feeds back upon itself; there is movement from a later part of the system to an earlier part. This is a "feedback loop." Other feedback loops are also operating, but for the moment it will suffice to describe just one. The important point is that information going from LTM to motives ends up, via the loop, changing how LTM will respond to future information. To put it technically, the state of the system has changed.

Motives consist of the innate motives of hunger and sex and the learned motives of fear and other cognitively based goals of values. Fear has substantial potential for motivating consumers, but its effects can also be inhibiting.[8] It is

<hr>

[7] J. B. Haskins, "Predicting Interest in Messages," *Journal of Advertising Research,* **15**:31–35, October 1975.

[8] M. L. Ray and W. L. Wilkie, "Fear: The Potential of an Appeal Neglected by Marketing," *Journal of Marketing,* **34**:54–62, January 1970; B. Sternthal and C. S. Craig, "Fear Appeals: Revisited and Revised," *Journal of Consumer Research,* **1**:22–34, December 1974.

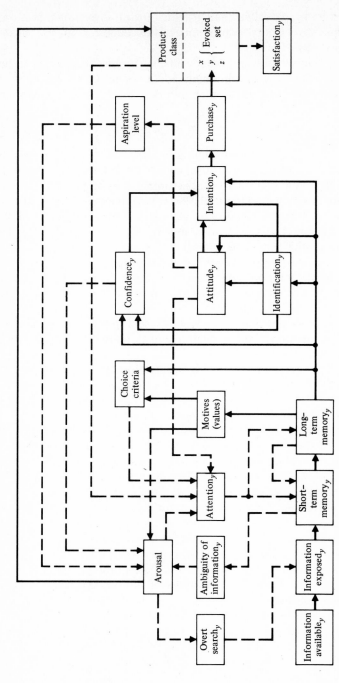

Figure 7-2 Consumer behavior model with additional search and attention mechanisms. (Satisfaction feedbacks have been omitted.)

easier to think in terms of values (see Figure 4-3 and Table 5-4) as motivators. In fact, I treat learned (cognitively based) motives and values as synonymous.

Values are related to beliefs about product classes and brands, as was shown in Figure 5-2; this relationship involves choice criteria. We assume that conflict or inconsistency among important beliefs will cause arousal; this is especially true of inconsistency of beliefs about self, called "self-cognitions." Inconsistency in beliefs about one's competence and morality are the strongest motivators of all.[9] Inconsistency among the intrumental values of competence and morality that support these particular beliefs also leads to arousal. For example, conflict between the instrumental values of behaving imaginatively (competence) and behaving logically (competence) and conflict between acting politely (morality) and offering intellectual criticism (competence) both lead to arousal. Thus, we are using a strongly modified version of the "cognitive consistency" theories which have until recently been the dominant models for changes in attitudes. This modified version is suggested because most people do not place a high value on inconsistency as such. Rokeach, analyzing values, writes, "The average adolescent and adult American care little indeed about being logical, and college students care only a little bit more about it."[10]

An important point about the learned or cognitively based (learned) goals represented by values, which distinguishes them from the innate goals (such as hunger and sex), is that they are not satiable. Also, they are not periodic. They do vary in importance, as was shown in Chapter 5, and they are subject to slow change.

Learned goals thus contrast sharply with the innate motives and with fear, which are subject to momentary changes in intensity. For instance, hunger can come on suddenly, as when one sees an advertisement for food just before dinnertime. Most psychologists have dealt with rapidly changing intensities and conceptualized motive intensity by means of an "equilibrium" model.[11] Imagine, for example, a man who at the outset is in equilibrium with regard to hunger. When he is confronted with visual and olfactory cues that he has come to associate with food, however, a disequilibrium is created. Hunger stimulates tension and the potential for action (arousal) within his body. Equilibrium will return when hunger is satisfied or is replaced by a more compelling set of motives.

Variations in arousal that underlie attention and search, expecially attention, can be still more momentary. For example, suppose that a consumer is confronted with two pieces of information, one relevant and one irrelevant to his or her motives. The first will cause an increase in arousal, and the consumer will focus attention on it until it is processed into LTM or discarded.

In summary, innate motives and needs for attention and search operate within the motivational framework of a fairly stable value structure that guides

[9]M. Rokeach, *The Nature of Human Values,* Free Press, New York, 1973, p. 225.
[10]Rokeach, op. cit., p. 78.
[11]C. N. Cofer and M. H. Appley, *Motivation,* Wiley, New York, 1964, pp. 810–813.

attention and search. For example, a buyer who is, at the moment, hungry will focus attention on food—not on just anything having nutritional value, however, but only on those sources of food that are consistent with his or her values. Snake meat has nutritional value, but not many Americans will pay attention to this food.

Ambiguity of Information   The ambiguity of a stimulus is another informational feedback effect on arousal (see Figure 7-2) and guides attention and search. Ambiguity of information is defined as a lack of clarity in a stimulus in communicating the content dimensions of that stimulus. Ambiguity can occur in a number of ways: the message can be physically unclear; its meaning can be unclear; or it can be novel and unexpected. Any of these three—lack of clarity, novelty, and unexpectedness—can give an impetus to arousal. The reason for this is that the buyer needs additional information to clarify the message, and attention is increased to accommodate this need. In a laboratory study of buying a new car, Holbrook found that uncertainty of the message did enhance attention to and perception of the product.[12]

Novelty of a stimulus is similar to ambiguity and is treated like ambiguity in Figure 7-2. Substantial research indicates that the human being is attracted by the novel event, the unfamiliar event.[13] Some psychologists would prefer to call this a motive. Whatever one calls it, the important point is that it causes arousal to increase. The novelty of a new brand, then, has the advantage of stimulating attention. As we saw in Chapter 3 in discussing the case of identical brands, the relation between exposure and attitude is positive when a "good-bad" measure is used, but an inverted U when other scales, such as "interesting," are used.

Confidence   A buyer's confidence is low when the meaning of a brand concept is unclear as regards its capacity to meet his or her needs. Low confidence gives rise to arousal, as is shown by the feedback from "confidence" to "arousal" in Figure 7-2.[14] The three sources of conceptual clarity were discussed in Chapter 3: distinctiveness of a brand, consistency of the evidence, and consensus on the facts. This can also be expressed in terms of the function of information (rather than the nature of the message): the consumer needs additional information to clarify criteria for judgment (EPS), to decide where on given criteria a brand is placed (LPS), or to judge a brand on a particular subset of criteria (RRB).

Empirical evidence for the relationship between confidence and search has been gathered under field conditions, and search was measured in terms of word of mouth (WOM). But the relation tended to be positive, not negative as

[12]M. B. Holbrook and J. A. Howard, "Consumer Research on Frequently Purchased Non-Durable Goods and Services: A Review," Project on Synthesis of Knowledge of Consumer Behavior, RANN Program, National Science Foundation, April 1975, p. 96.

[13]D. E. Berlyne, "Motivational Problems Raised by Exploratory and Epistomic Behavior," in S. Koch (ed.), *Psychology: The Study of a Science,* vol. 5, McGraw-Hill, New York, 1963, pp. 284–364.

[14]Berlyne, op. cit.; J. T. Lanzetta, "Uncertainty As a Motivating Variable," mimeographed, Conference on Experimental Social Psychology, Vienna, Austria, 1967.

implied here.[15] In this uncontrolled field study, though, search was probably motivated not only by the need for information but also by the need for social interaction, and the two were not separated. The results obtained by Coleman et al. are more consistent with our hypothesis.[16] These researchers found that total WOM (not the WOM for each individual) decreased as confidence increased. Bennett and Mandell found that for automobiles, the larger the number of previous purchases of the brand that was ultimately purchased and the larger the number of sequential purchases of the brand, the less search took place.[17]

Level of Aspiration   The need for information also arises when some of the brands which consumers want to consider (those in the evoked set) do not meet their standard of what is acceptable. To replace the inadequate brands, consumers must search for additional brands. How do buyers decide when a brand or set of brands is good enough to be considered at all? They must have some sense of what is "good enough" in order to decide when to stop searching for better brands in a product class. (This problem was mentioned in Chapter 4.) The notion of an "ideal point" in a consumer's ideal brand, derived in multidimensional scaling, is perhaps related to this issue, but the relationship has never been developed.

The key element in this attention-and-search decision is the construct "level of aspiration," which is defined as the standard of adequacy. For each of their choice criteria, consumers have a standard of adequacy. When all known brands are below that level, a consumer is stimulated to pay attention and search. The causal relations are shown in Figure 7-2 by the arrow from "attitude" to "aspiration level" and from "aspiration level" to "arousal."

Aspiration level is apparently reflected in one's satisfaction in using a brand, as described in Chapter 3, or in one's attitude (which is an expectation of how well one would be satisfied by a brand, as is discussed in Chapter 3), or in both. Some evidence cited in Chapter 14 suggests that the relation between purchase and satisfaction is concave upward. This can be interpreted as evidence that level of aspiration is reflected in satisfaction. On the other hand, some evidence cited by Sethna suggests that level of aspiration is reflected in attitude.[18] He found that discrepancies between belief on a choice criterion and the salience of that choice criterion showed a strong negative relation to attitude defined unidimensionally. The effects of aspiration level upon satisfaction and attitude are perhaps both operative, and they have not been distinguished.

[15]S. I. Lampert, "Word-of-Mouth Activity During the Introduction of a New Food Product," unpublished doctoral dissertation, Columbia University, 1969.

[16]J. Coleman, E. Katz, and H. Menzel, "Social Processes in Physicians' Adoption of a New Drug," *Journal of Chronic Diseases,* **9**:1–19, January 1959.

[17]P. D. Bennett and R. M. Mandell, "Pre-purchase Information Seeking Behavior of New Car Purchasers—The Learning Hypothesis," *Journal of Marketing Research,* **6**:430–433, November 1969.

[18]B. N. Sethna, "A Control System Approach to Consumer Behavior," unpublished doctoral dissertation, Columbia University, 1976.

Conclusions about Causes of Arousal   Motive intensity is triggered by brand meaning represented in product class, attitude, and specific choice criteria. Intensity of motives, along with ambiguity and novelty of information, confidence in ability to judge the quality of a brand, and aspiration level, leads to arousal. These are the sources of selective regulation of information. They enable the consumer to adapt with remarkable effectiveness to the dynamic environment of postindustrial society.

It is often useful to group these sources of arousal into the more functional categories of arousal-evoking situations: relevance, conflict, and novelty.[19] Motive intensity is related to relevance; ambiguity of a stimulus, confidence, and level of aspiration are related to conflict. Finally, of course, novelty of a stimulus is related to novelty.

We see here an explanation of the apparent paradox stated in Chapter 3: that confidence and intention are related only positively. This is contrary to the commonsense notion that a consumer could be just as confident in disliking a brand as in liking it, so that confidence and intention could be negatively correlated. The explanation is that information about a disliked brand is irrelevant, because the disliked brand is not in the evoked set. Consequently, the consumer is more inclined to take in information only about a liked brand, and this information will on balance add to intention.

Allocation of Attention and Search

Arousal is taken as a measure of the need for attention and search, and we just discussed the sources of arousal. Because arousal is nonspecific to a brand, we must now discuss how it is allocated to information about a particular brand. Increasing arousal (1) narrows attention to a more restricted range of cues, (2) increases the flexibility of attention to roam within that restricted range of cues, (3) leads to greater difficulty in making fine discriminations, and (4) causes shifts in strategy—for example, from accuracy to speed.[19] Thus, arousal allocates attention by narrowing the range of cues attended to and improving scanning within that range. Beyond a certain point, however, increasing arousal can inhibit performance by causing less fine discrimination and shifting attention strategy, as to speed.

Product-Class Concept   The need to form a product-class concept is reflected in confidence, which is negatively related to arousal as shown in Figure 7-2. The concept forms from information received as a result of the importance of this product class, reflected in the intensity of motivation. In the process of formation, structure is created in long-term memory (LTM). This additional structure will be reflected in the feedbacks from LTM to short-term memory (STM), and information related to the product-class concept will be highly likely

---

[19]R. Lynn, *Attention, Arousal and the Orientation Reaction,* Pergamon Press, New York, 1966, p. 12.

to get through to LTM and be stored there. Selectivity occurs in this way: attention is *allocated* to information that is relevant to the particular product class.

Attitude   As with the product-class structure, when an attitude forms, additional structure is created in LTM. This structure serves to further direct or allocate information within the product-class structure to information about a particular brand, as is implied by the arrow from "attitude" to "attention" in Figure 7-2.

Choice Criteria   Obviously, the product-class concept is a bundle of choice criteria. Attention is allocated to particular choice criteria within that bundle much as with attitude and product class, as is shown in Figure 7-2 by the arrow from "choice criteria" to "attention." It would also seem that the more salient criteria would, when information concerning the attribute is attended to, increase arousal by increasing the intensity of motives. This is consistent with Holbrook's finding (mentioned earlier) that more attention is given to information about a salient attribute of a brand than to less salient attributes. We are dealing here, however, with a complex set of relations.

Consequences of Arousal

The general consequences of arousal are, of course, attention and search. Earlier in the chapter we noted the physical manifestations of attention and search. Now we must examine some more fundamental aspects of attention and search in the complex system for receiving and acting upon information shown in Figure 7-2.

Arousal and Attention   Arousal has been much studied,[20] but we are here extending it to the new area of consumer behavior in a natural or field setting. Arousal has three effects. First, it increases the consumer's sensitivity to information. The pupils of the eyes dilate; there are photochemical changes in the retina; the threshold for intensity of light is decreased; the auditory threshold is lowered on the order of 4 to 10 decibels. Second, it not only encourages the receipt of relevant information but actually inhibits the effect of irrelevant information, blocking or reducing it at a very peripheral level, specifically in those nerves that are farthest from the brain and spinal cord. Third, general muscle tone increases, so that the person is prepared for sudden actions.

Arousal and Search   The easiest way to search is to plumb LTM instead of using up time and energy in a physical, overt search. Retrieval from memory is obviously an important source of information for the highly experienced consumer. To understand how past information is brought to bear on a current decision, it is necessary to know how that past information was stored. The

[20]D. Kahneman, *Attention and Effort,* Prentice-Hall, Englewood Cliffs, N.J., 1973, pp. 37–42.

nature of the storage and retrieval processes was developed in the model of memory and related ideas in Chapter 4.

In an actual, overt search, an experienced consumer obviously makes use of much learned behavior. Some of this behavior was described earlier in the chapter (e.g., word of mouth and shopping). Search is postulated to be a function of the consumer's perceived risk; Granbois concludes that this is a plausible hypothesis after carefully reviewing the various theories of search.[21] Perceived risk is the product of the importance of the product class (intensity of motives served) and the consumer's subjective uncertainty about what the brand is expected to contribute to his or her satisfaction, which is the inverse of confidence. Thus, the consumer's perceived risk is implied in Figure 7-2 by the combination of the value construct which connects with "arousal" and the feedback from "confidence" to "arousal."

Arousal and Purchase   In Figure 2-1, brand purchase was shown as being affected by motives manifested in arousal. It was noted that motives give a push to that behavior. Now we can be more specific. In Chapter 5, we saw that inconsistency in self-cognitions, especially those having to do with competence and morality, determines the timing and intensity of the act of purchasing. Values give direction to behavior by focusing attention on more valued brands and more valued attributes of each brand. Values operate by means of the importance of choice criteria, presumably at both levels of choice in EPS.

Conclusions on the Consequences of Arousal   Arousal strongly influences the consumer's input of information. It not only stimulates attention on information related to a brand but also inhibits information encountered but deemed irrelevant. For the experienced consumer, search of long-term memory is an important source of information. Arousal underlies overt search, just as it underlies all behavior, but much remains to be discovered about the nature of the complex processes of attention and search.

THE INTERRUPT SYSTEM

Often, a consumer must get information by a certain time in order to act by a given deadline; this gives rise to time pressure. In computer terminology, this is a "real-time" demand. If the need for information is to be met in real time, there must be an interrupt system of some kind, especially for the insatiable needs represented by values. Such an interrupt system is reflected in "motives" in Figure 7-2. It has two requirements:

1   A certain amount of processing must go on continuously in order for the buyer to *notice* (to pay attention) when conditions have changed so much that ongoing RRB programs must be interrupted. Consider the example of the woman

---

[21]Granbois, op. cit., pp. 4–9.

buying gasoline in Chapter 2. She may be thinking about buying a house, for example; but when she gets into her car, this program must be interrupted in order to check the gasoline.

    2   The interrupt system must be able to set aside the ongoing decision process so that the new decision process can be put into action. The process set aside is stored and may be abandoned permanently or resumed once the more urgent process is completed.[22]

The notion of interruption of an ongoing stream of behavior is further developed by Birch et al.[23]

EXCEPTIONS TO NORMAL ATTENTION AND SEARCH

A large proportion of buying behavior is uneventful and unemotional. The consumer switches from buying task to buying task with ease and displays in each situation one of the information-processing approaches described in the preceding chapters: RRB, LPS, or EPS. But there are two exceptions, two situations where this highly rational information processing may not occur. One occurs when the involvement of the consumer—the intensity of motives—is too low to support this type of rational information-processing behavior. The second occurs when the involvement—the tension—is too high to permit normal information processing. Let us examine each exception in turn.

Low Involvement

Some products do not involve us enough to justify thought and consideration in buying. These have come to be called "impulse products" and are defined as products which the consumer does not plan to buy. Low involvement has implications not only for immediate buying but also for learning.

    Learning without Involvement   Learning a concept does not always require arousal.[24] "Learning without involvement" seems to contradict what we have been discussing; but as we examine attention more carefully, it will become consistent. When people are subjected to information while the intensity of their motives is low, there is evidence that they learn information irrelevant to the motives.[25] Thus, when our attention is low, we do not "tune out" effectively. When an advertisement interrupts a television program, the people whose involvement in the program is low do not have their ongoing pattern of thought interrupted but merely take in the advertising as a part of the entertainment. They are vulnerable, but probably mainly to information that identifies rather than evaluates the brand.

    [22]H. A. Simon, "Motivational and Emotional Controls of Cognition," *Psychological Review,* **74**:29–39, 1967.
    [23]D. Birch, J. W. Atkinson, and K. Bongort, "Cognitive Control of Action," in B. Weiner (ed.), *Cognitive Views of Human Motivation,* Academic Press, New York, 1974, pp. 71–84.
    [24]Kahneman, op. cit., pp. 9–12.
    [25]Simon, "Motivational and Emotional Controls of Cognition," p. 38.

Krugman accepted this idea of uninvolved learners and stated specifically that such consumers would learn factual information, but that attitude would be learned only after they had bought a brand.[26] This distinction between the two levels of learning—brand identification and attitude—can be developed further by viewing it as a difference in the consumer's cognitive response to incoming information.

Cognitive Response to Information   The mechanisms that regulate the consumer's input of information relating to attention and search have been outlined. In these mechanisms, we see the very active role of the consumer in selecting and shaping the nature of the information input. This active role is so strong that it is useful to think of the person as cognitively responding to the information.

In LPS, for example, incoming information, regulated by attention and search, causes changes in the consumer's concept of a brand. Specifically, it causes changes in identification and evaluation of the brand. It is useful, then, to have measures of the effect of the information. *Identifying response* and *evaluative response* can be used for this purpose.

The distinction between active and passive roles is important because substantial research indicates that a consumer can recall a message without its having an effect on attitude. Is there always a relation between the content of the message that a buyer remembers and a change in the buyer's attitude? Doubting that this relationship exists may seem contrary to common sense; but in fact there is good evidence that there is often no such relation.[27]

What is the role of memory in this process in which the content of a message is not related to attitude development? Clearly, the information is learned— stored in LTM—even though it has no effect on attitude; this is indicated by the fact that people can recall it accurately. Does attention explain why there may be no relation between information and attitude? That is, could it be that more attention is required to learn abstract evaluative information than concrete identifying information? Greenwald believes that the intensity of cognitive response is an essential factor.[28]

There is some evidence that a consumer's identifying response is positively related to recall of the message and that an evaluative response is positively related to the thinking that took place when the message was received. From this, we can hypothesize that since evaluative effects are more abstract than identifying effects, greater responding occurs only when a brand is involving enough to get attention. One might say that to the extent that a message evokes from LTM the evaluative adjectives appropriate to a product class (choice criteria), the response is strong enough to create an attitude toward the brand.

[26]H. E. Krugman, "The Impact of Television Advertising: Learning without Involvement," *Public Opinion Quarterly,* **29**:349–356, Fall 1965.
[27]A. G. Greenwald, "Cognitive Learning, Cognitive Response to Persuasion and Attitude Change," in A. G. Greenwald, T. C. Brook, and T. M. Ostrom (eds.), *Psychological Foundations of Attitudes,* Academic Press, New York, 1968, p. 150.
[28]Greenwald, op. cit., p. 150.

Excessive Arousal

The second exception to normal information processing occurs when arousal is too high to permit it. According to our earlier analysis, this would occur when a brand involves very important motives, when a consumer has not yet begun to learn the brand concept (when confidence is low, such as in EPS), and when information is unclear (the stimulus is ambiguous). The desire to process information would be high, but the task would be difficult, causing severe cognitive strain. We saw in Chapter 6 that an abstract message can distort good judgment considerably. In fact, one might wonder how much of what is labeled "pathological reasoning" may simply be a matter of perfectly normal people responding to extreme cases of cognitive strain.[29] Studies of cognitive dissonance and perceived risk are relevant here.

When arousal is excessive, emotion and its manifestation in tension seem to occur. Here is an example. A woman, who happened to be a very careful buyer, was shopping for wall-to-wall carpeting. After spending about four days collecting information on the various materials available, the types of weaves, their durability, the quality of service offered by each dealer, and the range of prices, she suddenly stopped in frustration and refused to think about the matter or discuss it. Her state of tension was clearly observable. A month later, she returned to the task of buying and made her choice. Let us see how we can incorporate this sort of situation into the system given in Figure 7-2—an information-processing system that, so far, seems to be singularly devoid of emotion. Emotion is related to the interrupt system.

Three kinds of real-time needs are served by the interrupt system:

1 Needs arising from unexpected environmental events; e.g., "loud" stimuli
2 Physiological needs; e.g., hunger
3 Cognitive associations—loud stimuli evoked not by sensory events but by associations in memory; e.g., arousal of anxiety

Sudden intense stimuli have these effects:

1 They supplant present goals—choice criteria—with new goals in RRB and LPS, and with instrumental values in EPS.
2 They have large effects on the autonomic nervous system; e.g., on heartbeat.
3 Consumers report emotions; e.g., tension (arousal).

Emotion is thus associated with the interruption of behavior. Usually, emotion is adaptive: a person learns to handle it by developing a program (an RRB decision process) for it. But when the emotion-producing stimuli are persistent as well as intense, they become disruptive and result in nonadaptive behavior. The woman buying carpeting knew herself well and so had the good

---

[29]P. C. Wason and P. N. Johnson-Laird, *Psychology of Reasoning,* Harvard University Press, Cambridge, Mass., 1972, chap. 18.

sense to delay. But what if the circumstances had not permitted a delay? No purchase, or a poor decision, would probably have been the consequence. Predictions about cognitive dissonance, which received much attention in marketing studies in the 1960s, could be relevant here.[30]

If consumers behave adaptively, short-term changes in the intensity of arousal cause them to focus upon particular information, information about a product class, a brand, and even particular attributes of a brand, as we have seen. Increased arousal causes, not random search, but directed search. By focusing upon relevant information—information about evoked brands in the product class in RRB and LPS—the buyer becomes highly selective in attention and search.

ATTENTION, SEARCH, AND THE STAGES OF THE DECISION PROCESS

Thus far, in order to simplify, there has been no systematic discussion of the important distinction between RRB, LPS, and EPS. Most of our discussion has applied implicitly to LPS, as is indicated by the references to the role of feedback from attitude, confidence, and product class. These would not exist in EPS because neither brand concepts, choice criteria, nor product-class concepts exist in the consumer's mind.

This implies that in EPS, attention and search activities would be much less sharply focused. They would be guided by feedback from motive intensity to arousal, but they would lack the specific direction of feedback from stored meaning in LTM to STM—product class, brand evaluation (attitude), and choice criteria—to make the information relevant. Whether a choice criterion relates closely or not at all to a set of values is probably often uncertain, and what information is relevant in clarifying the relationship is correspondingly unclear. The discussion of inference in EPS (in Chapter 6) indicates some of the reasons for this lack of clarity. In summary, LPS has much greater automatic selectivity than EPS but within a much narrower range of attention and search. And, of course, RRB exhibits the greatest selectivity of all.

Thus, when consumers are in EPS, it is difficult to get their attention so that they can learn that a product (and information about it) is relevant to their values. It will help if they have a related, well-developed semantic structure. The example of asparagus in Chapter 3 will illustrate this. To the extent that consumers have a well-developed semantic structure for "vegetables," they will find it much easier to construct a structure for a radically new brand of vegetable of which they have never heard before. In our terminology, they will have something with which to group the new thing. Without this opportunity to group it, they would have to complete a new local structure independent of any surrounding structure. This process of grouping and distinguishing a brand, even when some semantic structure exists, is probably complicated by the fact that con-

[30]J. W. Brehm and A. R. Cohen, *Explorations in Cognitive Dissonance*, Wiley, New York, 1962, pp. 302–309.

sumers use one set of criteria to identify it and another set to evaluate it, as was noted in Chapter 3. It would seem possible for the new thing to be inconsistent with consumers' previous experience as regards the identifying criteria associated with evaluative criteria for a particular product class.

APPLICATION

The consumers' environment, especially in a postindustrial society, is complex, and whether they obtain information from it makes a substantial difference in their behavior. Marketers can also make a difference, by the extent to which they make a product easily available and tell consumers about it. We have seen that consumers have a remarkable capacity to regulate input—that is, to filter out and select. Here, too, marketers can make a difference in the way they design a product, a message, a media pattern for disseminating the message, and a channel for distributing the product.

Interpretation of Data

The importance of the feedbacks that we have been discussing can be seen in a recent market research study. A well-known company used coupons as a device in a test market. To measure the effects of the coupons, each respondent in a survey of the test market was asked whether he or she had received a coupon. In fact, almost everyone in the test area had received a coupon. But the following results were obtained from questioning people:

Of those who did not try the product, 10 percent recalled receiving the coupon.
Of those who tried the product but were not repeat purchasers, 45 percent recalled the coupon.
Of repeat purchasers, 55 percent recalled the coupon.

We can assume that those who did not try the product were not interested in it and so ignored the coupon. Self-report was an undependable measure.

Product Design

Having seen some of the problems of getting attention implied by the psychological mechanisms underlying attention and search, we know that we must, in every way possible, design a product so as to facilitate the process. The high rate of failure among new products (60 percent, even after passing a test-market criterion) suggests the magnitude of the problem. Unfortunately, we do not know whether failure differs empirically in LPS and EPS, because these distinctions have been made only intuitively. One fair guess is that the rate of failure is much higher for a product in EPS.

The design of a product often is, and always should be, related to the intended positioning. In EPS, it is especially important that careful attention be given to positioning. Communication to consumers is so difficult that positioning a radically new brand near a product class which consumers already know can enormously facilitate communicating the new product class and brand concept. If consumers perceive the product as being like something they already know, our task is far easier.

Design of Messages

We have learned that three conditions of a message—conflict, novelty, and relevance—influence the amount of arousal the consumer shows. Arousal determines the amount of attention consumers pay to whatever they are exposed to; it also determines what they expose themselves to through search.

The most obvious criterion for the content of a message is relevance. Does the message tell the consumer that the product will meet an urgent set of choice criteria in the case of RRB and LPS, or that it will satisfy values in EPS?

Conflict is a less obvious criterion. If consumers receive information that is contrary to—conflicts with—existing information, arousal results. An example is ambiguity of a stimulus; Holbrook found that attention and perception are increased by the uncertainty of the message.[31]

The least obvious criterion is novelty. The unexpected, the unusual, creates arousal. Copywriters obviously believe this, as is indicated by the sometimes bizarre devices they use to get attention.

Design of Media

To the extent that consumers are exposed to information in the normal course of their activities and so do not have to search for it, the probability is higher that they will take it in. Thus, the task of media design is to select the combination of media which will best expose a selected audience in terms of reach and frequency measures.

Consumers must, however, also perceive this information as relevant, conflicting, or novel, or else they may tune it out—unless they are completely relaxed and have nothing else to do but attend to it. Not only should the medium be relevant; it should also be credible, viewed as both trustworthy and competent. Design can sometimes influence these characteristics.

Design of Channels

Channels are intimately connected with the consumers' attention and search efforts because channels strongly influence the amount of search necessary and also the amount of information available in the market. Some types of retail stores provide the service of disseminating information; others do not.

The study of marketing has a long history of trying to classify products so as to obtain a rationale for distributing them—that is, for deciding what channels to use. Economists have traditionally explained the number of retail stores in terms of distance traveled and the production function, and have predicted a uniform distribution of stores.[32] If travel time and search are incorporated, however,

---

[31]Holbrook and Howard, op. cit.

[32]P. Nelson, "Information and Consumer Behavior," *Journal of Political Economy,* **78**:311–329, 1970.

Table 7-2   A Classification of Goods Based on Consumer and Product Characteristics

	High clarity
	High specific self-
	  confidence
	Mental effort during
	  shopping (brand
	  comparisons)
		Low clarity
		Low specific self-
		  confidence
		Mental effort before
		  shopping (information
		  seeking)

Low magnitude Low ego involvement Low physical shopping effort	Convenience goods	Preference goods
High magnitude High ego involvement High physical shopping effort	Shopping goods	Specialty goods

Source: M. B. Holbrook and J. A. Howard, "Consumer Research on Frequently Purchased Non-Durable Goods and Services: A Review," Project on Synthesis of Knowledge of Consumer Behavior, RANN Program, National Science Foundation, April 1975, p. 121.

clustering of stores results. Consequently, the criteria traditionally used by marketers in classifying products were (1) the effort the consumer devoted to traveling to the place of purchase and (2) the effort the consumer devoted to comparison shopping. These criteria omitted a dimension that has become increasingly important: preshopping effort, that is, efforts such as paying attention to advertising and collecting information. Brand insistence or brand preference can arise from preshopping efforts.

As the principles of attention and search imply, consumers search to relieve uncertainty. This can be clearly conceptualized in terms of perceived risk, which has two elements: the importance of the product (motive intensity or involvement) and confidence in judging the brand.[33] Lack of confidence is caused by lack of clear characteristics distinguishing a brand from competing brands; this in turn arises because a brand lacks distinctiveness, or because information or consensus is lacking.

Combining these consumer characteristics (ego involvement and confidence) with product characteristics (magnitude of purchase and clarity of characteristics) and consumers' responses (shopping and mental effort) gives us Table 7-2.[34]

Table 7-2 shows the relation between product classification and marketing strategy, which is derived by adding consumer characteristics to the more traditional view. The upper row implies intensive distribution: put the product in as many outlets as possible (in grocery stores, for example). The lower row

[33]R. A. Bauer, "Consumer Behavior as Risk Taking," in D. F. Cox (ed.), *Risk Taking and Information Handling in Consumer Behavior,* Graduate School of Business Administration, Harvard University, 1967, pp. 23–33.

[34]Holbrook and Howard, op. cit., pp. 112–122.

implies selective distribution: put the product in a limited number of stores selected according to some set of criteria, including their tendency to disseminate information. The left column implies limited dissemination of information (advertising); the right column implies extensive dissemination of information. This classification gives us a more complete description of channel alternatives than the traditional view does. For a product that is easily understood and not very important, the cell at the upper left would be appropriate; this is exemplified by the supermarket. If the product is easily understood but important, the cell at the lower left is appropriate; the product should be placed in a retail store characterized by extensive comparison shopping and limited distribution, such as a furniture store. If the product requires much mental effort but is not very important, the cell at the upper right is appropriate; and the product should be placed in a store that advertises heavily but represents wide distribution, such as a department store. Finally, if the product is difficult to understand and is important, the cell at the lower right is appropriate; and the product should be placed in a specialty shop, such as an appliance store.

CONCLUSION

The incorporation of attention and search activities into the analysis of information processing requires the addition of other dimensions of form to the structure of information. Novelty (ambiguity of a stimulus) and conflict (confidence), for example, should be added. Notice that these particular dimensions have to do with motivation rather than with cognition, language, memory, or inference (these other dimensions are discussed in Chapters 4 and 6). Also, the importance of the dimensions of content is emphasized as providing relevant information, which in RRB and LPS will get attention for a product.

Arousal is the central construct in a number of mechanisms, largely having to do with feedback, which regulate the flow of information and give the consumer a remarkable ability to adapt to the dynamic environment of postindustrial society.

Attention and search differ substantially in EPS, LPS, and RRB. This fact is obviously relevant in our own postindustrial society, but it is also helpful in thinking about other societies. It suggests that in industrial societies, even for new products, the problem of obtaining information is not great, because for most of new products consumers are in LPS. In preindustrial societies, where consumers are typically in RRB, information in the market is also no great problem, although standardization of products often brings efficiency, partly because it simplifies choice for consumers by requiring them to have less information. However, if one attempts to change the information in such situations, the problems raised are probably great, far greater even than in EPS. The reasons for this will be dealt with in Chapter 9.

In Chapter 1, it was noted that one goal of this book is to merge the marketing, economic, and psychological views of the consumer. The inadequacy of the economic theory of demand for the kinds of problems discussed in this chapter is obvious. The theory was designed, however, for dealing only with income and changes in price; thus it is appropriate only for RRB, although Lancaster has begun to introduce into economics the LPS notion of choice criteria, as was discussed in Chapter 3.

QUESTIONS

1 Why should you, as a student of consumer behavior, be concerned about the extent to which the consumer pays attention to and searches for information?

2 It was asserted in this chapter that a consumer's state of arousal is a central explanatory construct in how the consumer pays attention and searches. Develop this notion of the role of arousal.

3 What is meant by a "cognitive response," and what is its significance for explaining whether a consumer will buy a brand?

4 Earlier in this book, the emphasis was upon how consumers behave in a more or less rational manner by processing information. Yet, one often hears comments about the "irrational consumer." Is there such a thing as an irrational consumer? If so, under what conditions might such a consumer be found?

5 Is there a connection between the form of a message and whether the consumer pays attention to that message? If so, explain.

SUGGESTIONS FOR FURTHER READING

D. Granbois: "Consumer Shopping Behavior and Preferences," in R. Ferber (ed.), *A Synthesis of Selected Aspects of Consumer Behavior,* U.S. Government Printing Office for the National Science Foundation, in press.

D. Kahneman, *Attention and Effort,* Prentice-Hall, Englewood Cliffs, N.J., 1973.

Individual Differences

CONTENTS

The notion of the product life cycle (PLC) was introduced in Chapter 1 and then used in Chapter 7 to describe in some detail how consumers' information requirements change over its course. This description brought us closer to reality, as portrayed in the economists' idea of a market with many consumers. Our earlier, simplistic view was of a single consumer in contact with a number of sellers of closely substitutable products. But once we are dealing with a number of consumers, the differences among them become relevant. We must therefore drop the assumption that consumers are homogeneous and begin to deal with the important fact of differences among consumers. Until recently, research on consumers has been predominantly devoted to this subject.

Different consumers are exposed to different environments and (as was noted in Chapter 4) have different values. In turn, these differences lead to differences in the way consumers respond to marketing inputs. If this is to be understood, consumers' environments and values must be integrated into the concept of market space in terms of what consumers like and how they perceive brands. Market space is the basis for applying the notion of differing responses. First, however, the nature and significance of the differences will be elaborated.

SIGNIFICANCE OF INDIVIDUAL DIFFERENCES

The reader may wonder why there has been so much research on individual differences when it would seem that in order to develop a theory the more fruitful approach would be to try to find similarities—common patterns—in buying behavior. In fact, it was the practical need for at least an ad hoc theory, an explanation of particular events observed, that stimulated much of the research. Managers hoped to find in these differences clues about causality, although they seldom if ever articulated the problem in just this way. Like all policy makers, public and private, they wanted to know that if they did something in the market—changed advertising, for example—consumers would respond in certain ways.

The same sort of search for causality—for a theory—is now being followed in research on cancer. This is not a pleasant example, but it illustrates dramatically that attention to individual differences is basic to our thinking. It has been found that in one region of the People's Republic of China, cancer of the esophagus is so prevalent that it is the chief cause of death from all sources. This finding has led to a very detailed and costly study of this region in the hope of isolating the cause.[1] In the process, the characteristics of this region will be compared with those of regions where cancer is low. The aim is to formulate hypotheses about the causes of cancer. The medical scientists will formulate an ad hoc theory by finding people who differ on one characteristic—the predominance of a particular form of cancer—and then examine their other characteristics. These other characteristics will be used to explain why the differences in the first characteristic occurs.

There is a second reason for the emphasis on individual differences: the desire to segment markets—that is, to place consumers in more homogeneous groups. The purpose of segmenting a market is to enable the manager to adapt the marketing effort to each particular group. Better still, a manager may find in these categories a particular segment that his or her company could serve better than the competitors, and thus be protected from competition. In fact, there is a body of economic theory, developed in connection with price discrimination, that gives unambiguous rules for doing just this.

The concept of segmenting is useful not only to marketing management but to almost any policy maker, public or private. It is probably one of the most important contributions that the field of marketing has made to the general "sciences of the artificial," as Simon calls the theory of design that should underlie the activities of any professional school.[2] A professional school is basically concerned with how something *should* be done—how a medical operation should be carried out, how a legal case should be developed, etc.—not with how it actually *is* done.

If research into segmenting of markets was motivated by the need for a theory, how does segmentation relate to the model of consumer behavior which is developed throughout this book? To answer this, a distinction between endogenous and exogenous variables must be introduced. With one exception, all the variables (boxes) in the system have been endogenous; that is, all changes in them are explained from within the system. Changes in one variable are caused by changes in some other variable within the system. Attitude is changed by changes in brand identification and information, as is shown in Figure 8-1. The one exception is information. It can be an exogenous variable; it comes from the outside and is not explained from within the system. What is exogenous to a system, however, depends upon the way the system is specified. Thus before Chapter 7 no distinction was made between information available and information exposed. Information available is exogenous. But through search the con-

[1]*Washington Post,* June 18, 1975, p. A-2.
[2]H. A. Simon, *The Sciences of the Artificial,* M.I.T. Press, Cambridge, Mass., 1969.

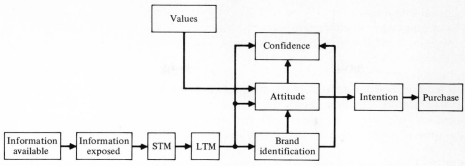

Figure 8-1 Incomplete consumer behavior model: individual differences.

sumer actively regulates information exposed (as was seen in Chapter 7); when this fact is incorporated in the model, information exposed is endogenous.

The concept of exogenous variables allows us to tie in individual differences and thus convert the consumer behavior model, which we have been treating as a model of the individual, into a model of a large number of consumers. For example, we would expect consumers with different values to have different choice criteria, which would, in turn, lead to different attitudes. We would therefore insert in Figure 8-1 an exogenous variable called "values," and it would affect attitude.

This brings us to a third reason for the interest in individual differences among consumers: to reduce the unexplained variance in the analysis of data about consumers.[3] If we were to estimate quantitatively how much a given increase in information would change attitude in a sample of consumers, we would find substantial error in the estimate. A major cause of this unexplained variance—or "noise," as it is often called—is probably that different consumers have different values. Inserting the exogenous variable "values," to explain some of this variance in attitude, reduces the noise. That is, it allows us to explain more of consumers' behavior than we could otherwise.

There is, finally, a fourth reason for wanting to know about individual differences. If you are constructing multiple-equation models of consumer behavior, as will be done in Part Two, individual differences are needed to identify the system. This identification has to do with the requirement that a simultaneous system must have as many equations as it has unknowns.

CLASSIFICATION OF INDIVIDUAL DIFFERENCES

Having examined the significance of individual differences, let us now try to classify them.

[3]J. U. Farley and J. A. Howard (eds.), *Control of "Error" in Market Research Data,* Lexington Books, Lexington, Mass., 1975.

External Influences

The discussions of information processing, attention, search, etc., have contained the implicit belief that the consumers' environment makes a substantial difference in the nature of their behavior. Since we are attempting to classify influences upon consumers' behavior, environmental influence is one important set; let us define it as including all influences external to a buyer during the period of observation. The condition "during the period of observation" is necessary because if we choose a large enough period, some influences that are external at one time may become internal at another.

Internal Influences

The other general influences operating on the buyer are internal. These can be subdivided into two classes. First, there are influences that change during the period of concern—attitude, for example. The theory set forth in this book has been designed to capture these, and they are treated as endogenous in the figures in Chapters 2 to 7. But the fact that they are treated there as endogenous does not mean that they must always be endogenous. When we apply the theory to a specific problem, we may find it convenient to express the system in a simpler form by omitting some of the less critical constructs.

Second, there are internal influences that do not change during the period of concern. These are our major interest in this chapter. They may often cause a consumer to respond to information differently from other consumers. By using these influences to classify consumers into groups which are alike in their responses, we may be able to devise an appropriate information program for each group. This is, you will recall, what is meant by market segmentation.

Let us now investigate the two major types of differences among consumers that give rise to differences in purchasing behavior: environment and values. A third difference—the capacity to process information—will be examined more briefly.

ENVIRONMENTAL FACTORS

In Chapter 7, where attention and search were discussed, the complexity of the consumer's environment was emphasized. Environmental differences have come to be called "situational" differences. Traditionally, researchers have not focused on the environment in explaining consumers' behavior—unlike economists, who focus entirely on the environment (on changes in prices and income, for example). The researchers' approach can be understood if we consider the tendency of actors in a situation to explain their own behavior in terms of situational requirements but to explain other people's behavior in terms of personal dispositions. Researchers are observers, not actors. Their approach probably differs from that of actors because of differences in the information available and the salience of the information. Actors in a situation ordinarily have more information about their own behavior in similar and related circumstances than observers would have. Actors know what the distinctive properties of a situation are, and information about these is highly salient to them. Observers, on the other hand, lack situational information; they are more informed about persons than about the situation. As a consequence, they emphasize the uniqueness of a person's behavior and attribute it to something inside the consumer, not to the consumer's environment.

"The consumer's environment," however, is a vague term. Just what is meant by it? As regards information, Chapter 7 showed how broadly environment must be defined. This is indicated by the construct "information available" in Figure 8-1. Information structure, with its content and form, is a way to specify the construct. The content elements are those having to do with the formation, attainment, and utilization of a brand concept; they are specified by certain constructs in the system of consumer behavior, such as identification, attitude, and confidence. Mass media obviously make up a part of that information. Social structure, "word of mouth," is perhaps an even more significant part of the consumers' information (it is developed in Chapter 9), and it too is incorporated in "information available." In addition to information, there is the "market," which includes the product and competing products or close substitutes. (In LPS it is competing brands; in EPS it is competing product classes.) Both quality and conditions of purchase of these competing products should be included as a part of the environment.

It is easy to illustrate environmental or situational conditions, but not easy to define them. There is a growing awareness of the importance of external conditions in shaping behavior, and considerable debate about how best to define the consumers' environment.[4] The need for a general definition is now recognized.

VALUES

Internal Factors Related to Values

A variety of internal factors have been used to describe and explain differences among consumers. A few years ago research on internal factors dominated the field of consumer behavior. Such factors have usually been called "personal factors"; they are sometimes distinguished according to whether they are stable and general across consumers or situational (situation-specific). They include demographic and socioeconomic variables and variables having to do with personality and life-style.

Although the conclusions are somewhat controversial, in many cases these variables were not related at all to product usage.[5] In other studies, the relationship clearly existed. A number of reasons may explain this discrepancy. For example, almost all the studies dealt with frequently purchased nondurables.

---

[4]For example: R. W. Belk, "Situational Variables and Consumer Behavior," *Journal of Consumer Research*, R. G. Barker and A. W. Wicker, "Commentories on Belk, Situational Variables," *Journal of Consumer Research*, 2:57–168, December 1975.

[5]M. B. Holbrook and J. A. Howard, "Consumer Research on Frequently Purchased Nondurables and Services: A Review," Project on Synthesis of Knowledge of Consumer Behavior, RANN Program, National Science Foundation, April 1975.

As regards these, the consumer is probably well informed (from previous experience), and the product is not very important. Durables appear to be more affected by personality and socioeconomic variables, but even here the evidence is far from conclusive. (There are some methodological issues which are beyond the scope of this discussion.)

Can the numerous stable internal differences be simplified and dealt with more coherently by subsuming them under "values," as introduced in Chapter 5? The theory has been developed that consumers go through stages of decision—EPS, LPS, and RRB—and that the buyer's means-end chain is a central element in this process. How can we relate the idea of stable, internal individual differences to this basic theory? Rokeach states, "Differences between cultures, social classes, occupations, religious or political orientations are all translatable into questions concerning differences in underlying values and value systems."[6] Can the longer-term internal differences in buying be related to values? Rokeach clearly thinks so. With this possibility in mind, let us examine personal factors and their relation to values.

Personality Traits   Extensive research in psychology and considerable research in consumer behavior has been given to personality traits. A trait is "any enduring or persisting character or characteristic of a person by means of which he can be distinguished from [other persons]. . . . Personality trait attempts to distinguish a special class of traits, though unfortunately it is usually not clear just which traits are to be so named."[7]

Personality traits, considered as a cluster making up an individual personality, can be reformulated as a system of values. A man identified as an introvert on an extraversion-introversion scale, for example, might identify himself in terms of his own values as a person who cares more for wisdom and a life of the intellect than for friendship, prestige, and being cheerful.

Psychological research on personality traits has not been particularly fruitful. When the available studies were carefully reviewed by Peterson, only two traits appeared consistently: neuroticism (perceived adjustment) and extraversion-introversion. As Peterson puts it:

> Available evidence now suggests that the most dependable dimensions drawn from conventional factor analysis of ratings and questionnaires are simple, familiar dimensions of broad semantic scope (cited above). It also appears that most of the initially obscure, apparently more precise, more narrowly defined factors many investigators have claimed to reveal are either trivial, artifactual, capricious, or all three.[8]

Life-Style   If we use the concept of social structure given in Chapter 9, we can consider life-style a subculture. What used to be called "social class" is now

---

[6]M. Rokeach, *The Nature of Human Values,* Free Press, New York, 1973, p. 26.

[7]H. B. English and A. C. English. *Psychological and Psychoanalytical Terms,* McKay, New York, 1958, p. 560.

[8]D. R. Peterson, "Scope and Generality of Verbally Defined Personality Factors," *Psychological Review,* 72:48–59, 1965.

often called "life-style," largely because the term "social class" implies a sharper structure than actually can be found. Roger Brown states, "A style of life is manifest in occupations, possessions, recreation, manner and the like." After reviewing research on social class, he concludes: "The style of life of a family unit in this country depends chiefly on the occupation of the father. There seems to be nothing in the prestige ratings given occupations to suggest a class structure and there seem to be no discontinuities in style of life that are great enough to suggest such a structure."[9] Myers and Guttman however, concluded that life-style and social class give somewhat different results empirically.[10]

Research on life-style must be distinguished from psychographics, which has received much attention, especially from practitioners. Psychographic studies focus on more abstract, theoretical personality traits; life-style studies focus more on specific activities, interests, attitudes, and values, which are held to be more directly tied to consumer behavior.[11] The consumer's activities, interests, and opinions are often abbreviated AIO.

Life-style can be related to the consumer's system of values. In one study, "hippies" and "nonhippies," as they were called in the 1960s, were contrasted in terms of their values.[12] For example, on the average, hippies rated the terminal value of "a world of beauty" eighth and nonhippies rated it sixteenth. The instrumental value of being "responsible" was rated twelfth by hippies and second by nonhippies. A more complete picture of the two groups is as follows:

Hippies	**Nonhippies**
Terminal values:	*Terminal values:*
Exciting world	Comfortable life
World at peace	Sense of accomplishment
World of beauty	Family security
Equality	National security
Pleasure	Salvation
	Self-respect
Instrumental values:	Social recognition
Broadminded	*Instrumental values:*
Cheerful	
Forgiving	Ambitious
Imaginative	Obedient
Independent	Polite
Loving	Responsible
	Self-controlled

[9]R. Brown, *Social Psychology,* Free Press, New York, 1965, p. 133.

[10]J. H. Myers and J. Gutman, "Life Style: The Essence of Social Class," in W. D. Wells (ed.), *Life Style and Psychographics,* American Marketing Association, Chicago, Ill., 1974, pp. 243–253.

[11]W. D. Wells, "Life Style and Psychographics: Definitions, Uses, and Problems," in W. D. Wells (ed.), *Life Style and Psychographics,* American Marketing Association, Chicago, Ill., 1974, p. 320.

[12]Rokeach, op. cit., pp. 140–142.

Table 8-1   Values and Religion

	Rank		
Value	Catholics	Protestants	Jews
Imagination	12	9.8	8
Independence	5.4	4.8	2.9
Intellectuality	9.8	8.1	6.5
Obedience	10.4	14.6	16.5
Politeness	10.5	11.9	14.3
Self-control	10.9	11.3	13.3

Source: Gary Bridge, Julie Blackman, and Martin Lopez Morillas, "How Parents Choose Schools in Multiple Option Systems," American Education and Research Association, April 1976.

Socioeconomic Characteristics   Socioeconomic factors include such demographic characteristics as education and income. There are some value differences in both education[13] and income,[14] so that these too can be at least partially translated into values. Whether they can be fully translated is a question yet to be answered.

Economists emphasize the value of time and postulate that higher-income people have a stronger motivation to save time.

Religion   Religious differences can be translated, at least in part, into value differences. This was indicated by a study of parents in the Mamaroneck, New York, school system. These parents were asked to rank Rokeach's eighteen instrumental values according to their importance. The responses were then sorted according to the subjects' religion. Table 8-1 shows the results; the higher the rank (i.e., the lower the number), the more important the value. There is a striking consistency for each of the six values: Catholics are at one extreme, Jews are at the other, and Protestants are in the middle.

Translating Internal Factors into Values

Insofar as these internal characteristics can be translated into values, a very complex area can perhaps be simplified and made more orderly.

For example, if the purpose of an analysis requires a stable independent variable, as in segmentation, the independent variable should be selected from the more abstract part of the means-end chain. Specifically, it is not useful to classify consumers according to their beliefs about a brand, because tomorrow those beliefs may be different. It is true that attitudes have sometimes been used in segmentation studies, on the theory that any consumer moving into a given level of attitude will behave in a specified way. But when the concern is with choice of a product class, as opposed to choice of a brand, it is more appropriate to work with abstract values. This was suggested by the notion of semantic struc-

[13]Rokeach, op. cit., pp. 64–65.
[14]Rokeach, op. cit., pp. 60–61.

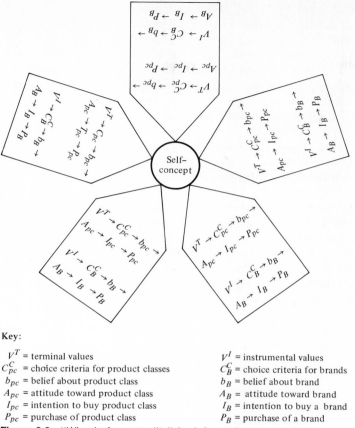

Key:

V^T = terminal values V^I = instrumental values
C^C_{pc} = choice criteria for product classes C^C_B = choice criteria for brands
b_{pc} = belief about product class b_B = belief about brand
A_{pc} = attitude toward product class A_B = attitude toward brand
I_{pc} = intention to buy product class I_B = intention to buy a brand
P_{pc} = purchase of product class P_B = purchase of a brand

Figure 8-2 "Wheel of personality" for information processing.

ture (Chapter 3) and the empirical analysis of values at two levels of choice (Chapter 5).

To the extent that personal characteristics can be fully integrated into a system of values, grouping consumers by values will amount to grouping them by the salience of choice criteria. That large differences exist in choice criteria is shown by Slovic and Lichtenstein in a review of how people weight criteria.[15] Thus, we should be able to determine individual values, group consumers by these values, and so simultaneously be grouping them by choice criteria and basic behavioral tendencies.

At each level of choice for each homogenous group, there will be a means-end chain providing for choice. This is shown in Figure 8-2, which incorporates the same ideas as Figure 5-2. Let us assume that consumers are in LPS. The

[15]P. Slovic and S. Lichtenstein, "Comparison of Bayesian and Regression Approaches to the Study of Information Processing in Judgment," *Organizational Behavior and Human Performance*, **6:**712–713, 1971.

blades of the "wheel of personality" for information processing radiate out from the consumer's self-concept. The outer end of each blade represents the semantic structure for a brand choice within a particular product class. The attributive words—the adjectives—of the semantic structure provide its identifying and evaluative elements. That is, the means-end chain for *brand* choice is outermost on the blade. The blade is made up of successive levels, each level constituting a means-end chain. Each level becomes more abstract, more and more terminal, as it approaches the hub of self-concept. These different levels of means-end chains taken together constitute the semantic structure for a given product class. Thus, "personality," as far as choice is concerned, refers to the description of a particular configuration of semantic structure, the structure that is relevant for that choice. For each product class that the consumer considers buying, there is a blade in the wheel.

If a consumer has a relatively full meaning structure, this suggests that he or she conceptualizes and makes explicit choices at the more abstract levels of that structure. Accordingly, the consumer's value structure would have to be "longer" than a simple structure of terminal and instrumental values, in order to serve these abstract levels of choice.

Obviously, the "wheel of personality" differs from person to person. If A is familiar with a wider range of products than B, A's "wheel" will have more blades. Also, the length of a blade depends on how important a product is to a consumer—the more the product involves a consumer, the longer the blade. Thus the wheel for any one person is certain to have blades of varying lengths.

Values and Arousal

So far, we have been concerned with the content of the values. Another dimension of values is their salience, intensity, or importance. In Chapter 7, the degree of involvement was discussed as the total intensity of all relevant values for a particular product class.

People differ on the intensity of their values, and the intensity of motives is an important source of arousal, as was seen in Chapter 7. Therefore, it should be possible to use differences in the intensity of values to operationalize arousal partially and indirectly.

Implications of Values

The importance of values in individual differences has implications for the segmenting of markets. To simplify our discussion, let us refer to lower-level (more concrete) values as connected with or "hooking into" higher-level (more abstract) values. As was shown in Chapter 5, this hierarchical relationship is actually much more complex. In fact, the higher-level values limit the number of choices at the next lower level; that is, higher-level values serve as selectors from among product classes, and lower-level values serve as selectors from among brands within the selected subset. This complexity should be borne in mind in the following discussion. In practice, a great variety of psychographic and other

variables are used for segmenting stable consumers in LPS into more homogeneous groups.[16] Theoretically, these more concrete characteristics of consumers
are hooked to their values, so that consumers are in fact being classified by their
values. Thus, using psychographics may be a sensible expedient, but only so long
as consumers are in LPS and, by definition, have the product space firmly fixed
in their minds.

The following list is an illustration of AIO values developed for food items:

A well-balanced meal for the family is important to me.
I look for good buys when I shop.
I try to wash dishes right after a meal.
I am in a big hurry in the morning.

However, segmenting by choice criteria would seem to yield even better results
than using such AIO values. AIO values are probably used more often for
creating an ad hoc theory than for segmenting. I would argue that it is better to be
explicit in theorizing—but this is not typically the case when ad hoc theories are
created. The purpose for ad hoc theories is to provide a basis for changing
behavior, as in providing copy points for advertising. Thus one is concerned with
identifying words, the brands for which those words are labels, and the way
people identify and value those brands. This brings us back to the example of
asparagus to illustrate semantic structure as the source of meaning and of words
that are labels for brands and related brands, and to the process of attaining a
brand concept and its mechanisms for identification and evaluation. In fact, AIO
values are probably an intuitive way of measuring semantic structure.

When we turn to EPS, however, it is inexpedient to use AIO, for four
reasons. First, the consumer does not yet have a product space in mind. To
purchase and consume a new brand representing a new product class may
require a class of new behaviors. This is illustrated by Haire's study of instant
coffee, discussed in Chapter 5.[17] Women homemakers who bought Nescafe in
the late 1940s were considered by almost half of Haire's sample to be lazy and
poor planners; about one-seventh of the sample thought of them as spendthrifts
and bad wives. Such concrete characteristics as are represented in psychographics would probably not be associated with these behaviors. Hence, classifying
consumers by means of them would lead to erroneous conclusions.

Second, when consumers are in LPS the only course of action available to
the decision maker is segmentation. For consumers in EPS, however, the
decision maker also has the alternative of communicating to consumers which
choice criteria will best serve their values. Consequently, the decision maker

---

[16]W. D. Wells, "Psychographics: A Critical Review," *Journal of Marketing Research,* **12:**
196–213, May 1975; F. Hansen, "Psychological Theories of Consumer Choice," Project on Synthesis
of Knowledge of Consumer Behavior, RANN Program, National Science Foundation, April 1975.

[17]M. Haire, "Projective Techniques in Marketing Research," *Journal of Marketing,* **14:**649–
656, April 1950.

wants to know which specific values are being served or violated by the new product, so as to tell consumers that certain attributes will serve these values and thus help them to form appropriate choice criteria.

Third, if it is known which values are affected by the new behavior required for purchasing and consuming a new brand, decision makers can investigate these values to see whether they are subject to long-term trends. If they are, decision makers are in a better position to know whether the market for the product is likely to increase or decline over the next several years. As we saw in Chapter 5, the study of Nescafe made in 1948 suggests that the values which were violated by instant coffee in the late 1940s had changed by 1968, encouraging the development of a major market for instant coffee. This is an example of how syndicated value surveys (discussed at the end of Chapter 5) can probably indicate trends in values and thus guide decision makers.

Fourth, throughout this chapter it has been implicitly assuming that the product in question is a package good: a low-priced, frequently purchased item. Durables differ from such products in that they are more likely to involve EPS, as was emphasized in Chapter 5. This suggests that values are more likely to be important in EPS than in LPS. A review of the evidence indicates that internal variables, such as personality, do segment durable products better than nondurable products.[18] The greater involvement of the consumer where durables are concerned could be advanced to explain this. Greater involvement may cause greater efforts to relate purchase to values.

INFORMATION-PROCESSING CAPACITY

I believe that differences in the capacity to process information are a third type of individual difference which can help explain consumers' behavior. This seems to be true for at least four reasons.

First, information is of central importance, and its complexity of both content and form has been emphasized.

Second, we have seen some of the complications involved in processing information (especially in Chapter 6); for example, the abstractness of a message can distort inference.

Third, differences in information-processing ability have been shown by research. In one study, people were asked to paraphase compound names, such as "black bird house" that is, to provide a phrase that "meant about the same thing." Large differences were found among three groups: secretaries, undergraduate students, and graduate students.[19] The authors reported that "massive population differences in the ability to cope with paraphrastic relations were displayed."[20]

---

[18]Holbrook and Howard, op. cit.
[19]L. R. Gleitman and H. Gleitman, *Phrase and Paraphrase,* Norton, New York, 1970.
[20]P. 137.

Fourth, a number of standard psychological tests appear to show the willingness of people to subject themselves to cognitive strain and deal with it effectively. For example, the widely used Rotter scale,[21] which distinguishes between "externals" and "internals," is found to be a good predictor of information seeking.[22] Externals feel that they are controlled by their environment, whereas internals are inclined to think that they control themselves and are more inclined to seek information. I have in mind not the wide range of phenomena that are included under the rubric "cognitive style," but only those more limited aspects associated with information processing.

Not only does the capacity to deal with information distinguish individuals. Like concreteness-abstractness, it also appears to be related to personality characteristics, such as width of categories; leveling, assimilation, and contrast; cognitive simplicity; and open- and closed-mindedness, or dogmatism.[23] I believe that it may be a way to bring together in a systematic fashion the consumer's environment and values.[24]

Finally, it provides a way of empirically incorporating short-term memory (STM) into the system of consumer behavior indirectly, as an individual difference. As you will recall from earlier discussions, "cognitive strain" refers to the limited capacity of STM to handle information.

MARKET SPACE

Preceding chapters dealt mainly with the individual consumer; but in this chapter we have begun to discuss many consumers and how they differ. Also, the notion of several sellers has been introduced, along with the notion of a market. The case of many heterogeneous consumers and a few sellers with differentiated brands is brought to focus in the concept of market space. The analysis which follows is, of course, applicable only to RRB and LPS, where choice criteria exist.

In Chapter 3, the notion of a product space was developed: consumers are asked to rate a brand on choice criteria which constitute the dimensions of a product space. Now we can go one step further and ask consumers to rate their "ideal brand,"[25] making up a space which we can call a "consumer space." The location of this brand in space is called an "ideal point." When product space and consumer space are combined, so that competing brands and con-

---

[21]J. B. Rotter, "Generalized Expectancies for Internal versus External Control of Reinforcements," *Psychological Monographs*, **80**:1–28, 1960.

[22]G. Bridge, "The Utility of ECHO Surveys in Cross-Cultural Research on Values," Presented at the American Psychological Association, Washington, D.C., 1969, mimeographed, p. 14.

[23]R. Zajonc, "Cognitive Theories in Social Psychology," in G. Lindzey and E. Aronson (eds.), *The Handbook of Social Psychology*, 2d ed., Addison-Wesley, Reading, Mass., 1968, p. 335.

[24]L. E. Tyler, *The Psychology of Human Differences*, 3d ed., Appleton-Century-Croffs, New York, 1965, pp. 233–234.

[25]D. R. Lehmann, "Television Show Preference: Application of a Choice Model," *Journal of Marketing Research*, **8**:47–55, February 1971.

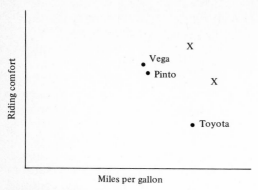

Figure 8-3   Market space.

sumers are located in the *same* space, we have a *market space*. (The more common term in the technical literature is "joint space"; but the term "market space" is used here in order to bring together economics, marketing, and psychology.) Market space is illustrated in Figure 8-3, which is simply an extension of the product space shown in Figure 3-9. In Figure 8-3, dots indicate positions of brands and crosses indicate positions of consumers in the space. The axes are, of course, choice criteria. The central principle of market space is that the closer a brand is to the consumer's ideal point, the more that brand is preferred. This is a powerful concept, as we will see.

Consumers could differ on where they locate an automobile, say, on a given criterion for a number of reasons. For instance, they may have been exposed to different environments, either by accident or because they searched differently. Also, some may be better able to process information than others and have consequently derived different brand concepts. And they may have paid attention to different pieces of information because their values differed. This last point touches upon an important issue which has so far been disregarded: different values would cause criteria to be weighted differently. (To simplify, this factor is neglected in Figure 3-9 and Figure 8-3.) Finally, we can presume that differences in the salience of choice criteria will often be important.

Some techniques have been developed to deal directly with locating consumers and brands in space. One is conjoint measurement, illustrated in Figure 8-4.[26] It incorporates the salience of choice criteria. Here, a spot remover for carpets and upholstery was assumed to be conceptualized by the consumer on five criteria. The number of possible units for each criterion was as follows: for package design, 3; for brand name, 3; for price, 3; for whether the Good Housekeeping seal is attached, 2; and for whether a money-back guarantee is offered, 2.[27]

[26]P. E. Green and V. R. Rao, "Conjoint Measurement for Quantifying Judgmental Data," *Journal of Marketing Research,* **8**:355–363, August 1971.

[27]P. E. Green and Y. Wind, "New Way to Measure Consumers' Judgments," *Harvard Business Review,* July–August, 1975, pp. 107–115.

Package designs

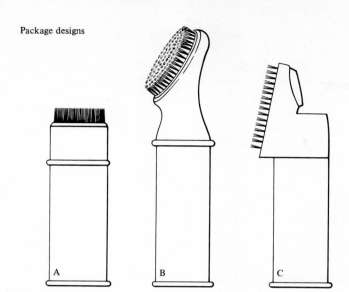

Orthogonal array

Package design	Brand name	Price	Good Housekeeping seal?	Money–back guarantee?	Respondent's evaluation (rank number)
1 A	K2R	$1.19	No	No	13
2 A	Glory	1.39	No	Yes	11
3 A	Bissell	1.59	Yes	No	17
4 B	K2R	1.39	Yes	Yes	2
5 B	Glory	1.59	No	No	14
6 B	Bissell	1.19	No	No	3
7 C	K2R	1.59	No	Yes	12
8 C	Glory	1.19	Yes	No	7
9 C	Bissell	1.39	No	No	9
10 A	K2R	1.59	Yes	No	18
11 A	Glory	1.19	No	Yes	8
12 A	Bissell	1.39	No	No	15
13 B	K2R	1.19	No	No	4
14 B	Glory	1.39	Yes	No	6
15 B	Bissell	1.59	No	Yes	5
16 C	K2R	1.39	No	No	10
17 C	Glory	1.59	No	No	16
18 C	Bissell	1.19	Yes	Yes	1*

*Highest ranked

Figure 8-4 Experimental design for evaluation of a carpet cleaner. *(P. E. Green and Y. Wind, "New Way to Measure Consumers' Judgments,"* Harvard Business Review, **53**:108, July–August 1975.)

Each consumer was asked to rank his or her evaluations of various combinations of these five characteristics. First, the ranking would presumably include the effect of the salience of each criterion; this is important theoretically. Second, to compare all possible combinations would indeed be difficult: $3 \times 3 \times 3 \times 2 \times 2 = 108$ brand concepts. But by means of a particular experiential design called an "orthogonal array" this number can be reduced to 18, as is seen in Figure 8-4; this is important methodologically. One consumer's ranking of the alternative brand concepts is shown in the column at the extreme right; notice that the highest-ranked concept was made up of package C, the brand name Bissel, a price of $1.19, the Good Housekeeping seal, and a money-back guarantee.

The ranked data (ordinal data) are converted by special computer programs to the equal-interval data necessary for locating a brand concept in space. From this ranking data it is also possible to derive the "utility" of each value on each criterion and thus to estimate consumers' preferences for concepts not included among the specific eighteen that the consumers were asked to rank. Deriving the utilities of untested concepts is, of course, a valuable result of the technique because some of the untested concepts may be preferred to those tested. (For the procedures, the reader is referred to the original source.)

As regards segmenting, if the consumers in the study had also been asked to rate the importance of their values, they could also be grouped by these ratings. The differences in values would presumably create differences in the salience of choice criteria. Each group would locate each brand concept in a different position in market space. This conclusion assumes, of course, that within each segment consumers are perfectly homogeneous with respect to their values. Typically, however, this is true only in a rough sense. A recent development has been to simplify the demands made on consumers by asking them to compare only two attributes at a time, instead of the five attributes shown in Figure 8-4.[28]

Utility derived by conjoint measurement does not distinguish between belief and salience. Thus the approach is plagued by the same problem that economists have confronted: the inability to separate, as they put it, the effects of changes in consumer technology (reflected in beliefs) from the effects of changes in preference (reflected in salience). Furthermore, no one has attempted to determine how closely the concept of utility derived in conjoint measurement conforms to that specified in economic theory as described by Lancaster.[29]

APPLICATION

Attempting to segment a market is a strategic decision because it has broad organizational implications and represents a long-term commitment. It is a *marketing* decision, however—not, typically, a matter of corporate strategy like

[28]R. M. Johnson, "Beyond Conjoint Measurement: A Method of Pair-wise Trade-off Analysis," *Proceedings of the Association of Consumer Research*, November 1975, Cincinnati, Ohio, pp. 353–358.

[29]K. Lancaster, "Theories of Consumer Choice from Economics: A Critical Survey," Project on Synthesis of Knowledge of Consumer Behavior, RANN Program, National Science Foundation, April 1975.

the decision to initiate an EPS product. (It can be a corporate decision, as was the case when Seven-Up was repositioned from a special drink to a general soft drink in 1968; but this is atypical.)

Differences among consumers are identified for a number of reasons, as was noted earlier in this chapter; but let us assume here that our purpose is to segment the market. In identifying market segments, one very important point is often neglected: the only differences that matter are those related to consumers' responses to marketing efforts. Differences that do not help us identify differences in response are irrelevant.

Segmentation always has one or both of two purposes: to increase marketing effeciency and to lessen competitive pressures. The first purpose exists because some segments are more responsive than others to marketing efforts—for example, to advertising. Therefore, a given advertising budget will yield a greater return in sales from some segments than from others. The second purpose exists when a company is better able than its competitors to serve a segment, such as by designing a product especially for that segment. In this situation a company can often make a higher profit because its competitors are not able to force it to reduce its price by cutting their own prices.

Because differences in responsiveness are crucial in segmentation, and because the purposes of segmentation are marketing efficiency and protection from competition, the concept of market space is particularly useful. It highlights these characteristics. If "sweetness" is one dimension (choice criterion) of the space, a consumer who values sweetness more than other consumers will be more responsive to information that a brand is sweet. An advertising budget devoted to telling consumers that it is sweet will yield a higher rate of return than a budget telling consumers that it is cheap, assuming that consumers do not place as high a value on cheapness as on sweetness. And if consumers locate themselves near a brand in a market space but at some distance from other brands, we can conclude that the company is protected from competitors because these consumers like the brand better than competitors' brands.

We are not yet able to apply the concept of market space perfectly. Nevertheless, the concept suggests a series of steps for application that can be useful in deciding what an appropriate marketing strategy should be.

Steps in Applying Market Space

Five steps are required to apply the concept of market space: (1) determining dimensions of the space—that is, the choice criteria that underlie it; (2) clustering consumers; (3) determining positions of brands in the space; (4) determining ideal points in the space; (5) developing prescriptive implications.[30]

Determining Dimensions   How are the dimensions of a market space determined? We have discussed product space and market space enough to know that space implies dimensions on which something is measured. All the research that

---

[30]Holbrook and Howard, op. cit.

has been done using the concept of product space has assumed that what is measured is positions on the consumer's evaluative or choice criteria. Thus it has implicitly assumed that the consumer has choice criteria already formed and so is either in LPS or in RRB. The research has usually also implied that it is possible to change a brand image either by changing the brand per se or by changing information about it; this really assumes LPS. In short, consumers must have previous knowledge of the brand. One check on whether the consumer knows the brand well enough for him or her to tell the researcher how well the brand is liked is whether there is a strong relation between the consumer's belief and the intention to buy.

How are these dimensions identified for a particular product class? At one extreme is the word-association technique for developing the meaning of a brand (Chapter 3). This is rough-and-ready but context-free. At the other extreme is the multidimensional scale, where the consumer is asked to rate pairs of brands: "Do you prefer A to B more than you do C to D?" All possible pairs are compared and by means of a computer program, the data can be converted to an interval metric scale and brands can be located in the derived space. Unfortunately, this method does not give us the name of a dimension; we must infer the choice criteria from other information. For example, if A and B are a long way apart in the space, and we know that they differ greatly in sugar content, we might infer that the dimension is sweetness. A third technique, more common in practice than either of the two just mentioned, is "focused group interviews." The respondents—homemakers, for example—are assembled in a group and asked to talk about a product class, the brands in it, how the brands are used, etc. A discussion leader tries to distill from the discussion what the criteria are. These distillations are then often subjected to factor analyses in order to group them into a few criteria.

Clustering Consumers   How do we cluster consumers in segments so that we can think of each cluster as a separate submarket? Lehmann suggests the use of various self-reported characteristics such as importance (salience) scores for the various choice criteria, ideal brand positions, and perceptions of real brand positions.[31] Ideal-point positions have the advantage of yielding homogeneous segments; but they yield segments which are not as useful as, for example, demographics.

Determing Positions of Brands   How do we place each brand in this space? We can assume that consumers are alike and use the mean position of consumers on each choice criterion. Or, if we already know how consumers are clustered, we need not assume that consumers are alike but can do a multidimensional scaling separately for each of the different segments.

Determining Ideal Points   If a sample is large—and it should be, to yield reliability—locating the ideal point of each respondent in space is not possible.

[31]Lehmann, op. cit.

Instead, respondents can be clustered by ideal points, and the mean for each cluster on each criterion can be used to develop the buyer space. Other methods have also been used.[32]

Developing Prescriptive Implications One of the most important decisions is the decision to reposition a brand. This is a particularly useful strategy when a product class is either approaching or in RRB. Not only is growth slowing down or stopping, but prices and profits are likely to be declining as a result of sharper competition. The concept of market space can show where a brand is now located and whether there is a position that represents a number of consumers but is devoid of brands. By either modifying a brand or telling customers about characteristics which it has but of which they are not aware, the brand may be moved to a more protected position and thus avoid some of the pressure on price.

If customers are not clustered but rather located at different positions in the space, the concept of market space can sharpen the identification of a market target. By repositioning a brand away from a major competitor and toward the ideal point of a major segment, a company can increase its share of the market.

It has been argued that the same kind of market-space analysis can be applied to data from product-concept tests, as in the use of conjoint scaling. In a concept test, consumers respond to a description, verbal or pictorial, of a proposed new product which has not yet appeared in the market.[33] The reliability of responses seems questionable in a single-response situation and where the brand itself is not available to build brand identification (the necessary foundation of a brand concept), as was discussed in Chapter 3.

Market Space and Planning

Once a strategic decision has been made, marketing efforts must be consistent with it. Even if there is to be no change in positioning, some shift in marketing effort may be suggested by the market space. In any event, detailed quantitative estimates of the elasticity of response to marketing effort are needed. Obtaining these estimates is dealt with in Part Two, Advanced Work.

Market Space and Information Structure

It was shown in Chapter 3 that a brand space specifies the content of the consumer's information structure and so tells us what information is needed if new consumers are to have an image of a brand in that brand space. Correspondingly, market-space analysis will tell us what information content is needed to move consumers to a particular position within that space. Also, with an understanding of information processing (Chapter 4), we can begin to make inferences about the best form for that information.

[32]Green and Wind, op. cit.; Johnson, op. cit.; L. A. Neidell, "The Use of Nonmetric Multidimensional Scaling in Marketing Analysis," *Journal of Marketing,* **33**:37–43, October 1969.
[33]Green and Wind, op. cit.

Market Space and EPS

Our discussion of market space has assumed either RRB or LPS. Do the principles also apply to the case of a radically new brand—that is, to EPS? There is apparently a product-class space where the consumer chooses among product classes. It would seem that this level of choice could be subjected to the same set of principles, but this is a task for the future.

CONCLUSIONS

At the outset of this chapter, several reasons were advanced for finding, and attempting to explain, individual differences in consumers' behavior. A body of theory has developed in the past decade that goes a substantial distance toward meeting the first reason: the need of practitioners for a theory. The other three reasons—segmentation, reduction of noise, and identification of a system—emphasize the need for explaining the differences found. When an explanation is given, we can know whether a difference has generality and, if so, under what conditions. In this way we can make greater progress in both research and practice.

For the sake of simplicity and coherence, the differences were summarized as springing from differences in environment, values, or information-processing capacity. All three constructs will require further development to be fully operational, especially the last. It was shown in Chapters 4 and 7, respectively, that individual differences provide a way of indirectly operationalizing short-term memory and arousal.

How individual differences affect the structure of consumer behavior given in Figure 7-2 was illustrated for values in Figure 8-1, where there is an arrow from "values" to "attitude." In line with the perceived-risk hypothesis (Chapter 7), it is postulated that differences in search arise from differences in the intensity of values and have an inverse relationship to confidence, but, in order to simplify, this relation is not shown in Figure 8-1. Other differences might have an impact elsewhere—as on brand identification, confidence, or intention, or even directly on purchase—depending on the causal mechanisms operating.

When this analysis is applied to another culture, such as a preindustrial or industrial country, Bridge's ECHO method can be used to identify the terminal and instrumental values.[34]

By extending the notion of semantic structure to include both identifying and evaluating features, an information-processing theory of personality was developed. According to this theory, personality can be viewed as a wheel that differs from person to person. For any one consumer, it is a wheel with uneven spokes, because each product may create a spoke of a different length.

Finally, the notion of market space was developed to focus individual differences on market segmentation. In discussing market space, conjoint measurement was suggested as a technique for measuring utility. This brings us

---

[34]Bridge, op. cit.

closer to the economist's way of conceptualizing consumers' behavior, but it has the disadvantage of not distinguishing between consumer technology and consumers' preferences, or—in marketing terms—between beliefs and the salience of choice criteria. Whether utility as used in conjoint measurement conforms to utility as specified in economic theory is an open question.

It is to be hoped that values can provide the necessary depth of understanding of the mechanisms operating in individual differences and that these values can be related to more operational variables, such as demographics, on which a great many data are available. (The U.S. Census provides a wealth of historical and current classificatory data.) In this way, we can have the best of both worlds: depth of understanding and practical application of that understanding.

QUESTIONS

1 Why is it useful to know about individual differences among consumers in studying consumers' behavior?
2 One reason often advanced for incorporating individual differences among consumers in an analysis of consumer behavior is to segment the market. What does this mean? Explain the benefits of market segmentation.
3 What is the relationship between the concept of a market space and market segmentation?
4 Explain how you could use the concept of market space.

SUGGESTIONS FOR FURTHER READING

Frank, R. E., W. F. Massy, and Y. Wind: *Market Segmentation*, Prentice-Hall, Inc., Englewood Cliffs, N. J., 1972.

Wells, W. D., and S. C. Cosmos: "Life Styles," in R. Ferber (ed.), *A Synthesis of Selected Aspects of Consumer Behavior*, U.S. Government Printing Office for National Science Foundation, Washington, D.C., in press.

Chapter 9

Social Structure

CONTENTS

Interpersonal Influence and the Stages of Decision

Elements of Social Structure
  Dyads
  Groups
    Group influences: Compliance, identification, internalization
    Example: A study in Cebu City
  Social Institutions
  Society as a Whole

Operation of Social Influence
  Social Influence in a Dyad: Salesperson and Buyer
  Social Influence in an Informal Group: The Family
  Social Influence in a Formal Group: The Organization
  Social Influence in an Industrial Society

Summary: Social Influence

Changing Values
  Measurement of Values
  Concepts

We must now drop the assumption made in Chapter 1 that social stimuli do not differ in kind from other stimuli in the buyer's environment. Social stimuli—other people—can be an especially important influence. "Interpersonal influence" is a term often used to describe these stimuli. Most interpersonal influence probably consists of spoken conversation, or "word of mouth" (WOM). Body language—kinesiology—has been receiving increased attention, but the analysis here will be confined to WOM.

It was noted in Chapter 7 that automobile buyers prefer information by WOM from noncommercial sources over all commercial sources. It was also noted that a number of studies provide evidence of the power of WOM.[1] This influence seems especially strong in the case of a radically new product—that is, when buyers are in EPS. Those who are involved in introducing a new product should ask themselves, "What is going on out there?" A company may have millions of dollars, and the reputations of its executives, at stake. If the program of a government agency fails, Congress will be asking questions and the agency's reputation will be tarnished. Thus decision makers need to understand the social process that is operating but hidden from view.

The influence of WOM is best described in terms of social structure. "Social structure" is defined as specific patterns of interaction among people; of course, we are concerned here only with people as consumers. Interaction is the pur-

---

[1]H. S. Jagpal, "The Formulation and Empirical Testing of a Dynamic Consumer Decision Process Model: A Simultaneous Equations Econometric Model," unpublished doctoral dissertation, Columbia University, 1974, pp. 3-44–3-50.

poseful, reciprocal influencing of two or more people by each other; it is generally carried out by means of symbols—language, for the most part—rather than physical contact. Interaction is often described quantitatively by a sociometric map, which shows who talks to whom and with what frequency. From such interaction consumers obtain much information and, as a result, new values. The acquisition of new values is especially important for our purposes. Much research has been done on the acceptance of new ideas, practices, and products; these investigations are called "diffusion studies" because they examine how ideas diffuse through a social structure.

In order to understand the role of social structure in consumers' behavior, and particularly in the process of changing values, it will be useful to consider interpersonal influence in the framework of the stages of decision; then to examine social structure more fully; then to discuss the process of changing values; and finally to consider diffusion studies as examples of how social structure operates over the product life cycle.

INTERPERSONAL INFLUENCE AND THE STAGES OF DECISION

To give ourselves a better background for thinking about the role of social structure in shaping consumers' behavior, let us review the information requirements of EPS, LPS, and RRB.

In RRB, the simplest case, information (such as price and availability) would seem to be so simple and clear that interpersonal influence would be no more effective than information from any other source. Trustworthiness and competence would not seem to be serious issues. Possibly, in the example of buying gasoline in Chapter 2, the decision about what price is "fair" might be affected by trustworthiness because it is an evaluative judgment, not a factual one. The consumer's confidence is higher, you will recall, when a distinctive difference exists, when the information has been consistent, and when there is consensus. In RRB, it seems that social influence would have some unique effect only as regards consensus.

In LPS, judgments about brand identification are agreed upon by different people and so are not much subject to interpersonal influence. Attitude, however, could be subject to interpersonal influence, especially when—as is often the case—the contribution of a product to choice criteria is unclear. Interpersonal choice criteria (discussed in Chapter 3) result from social influences. Confidence can be strongly influenced.

But it is in EPS that interpersonal influence can be strongest, even if we assume given values. What choice criteria should be used to judge a radically new brand? I suspect that social acceptability can be a strong force. In Chapter 5, for example, it was noted that some people believed buyers of instant coffee to be lazy, poor planners, spendthrifts, and poor homemakers. If we admit that it is possible for values to change, we must believe even more strongly in interpersonal influence.

ELEMENTS OF SOCIAL STRUCTURE

Chapter 5 discussed how consumers' information requirements change over the product life cycle (PLC) because the consumers are in different stages of decision. Communication to the consumer over the product life cycle occurs, of course, in a social structure. This structure shapes the process by which consumers move through the stages of decision over the cycle. We must therefore examine the nature of that structure, so that later we can turn to the diffusion studies to develop a more systematic account of the way consumers adapt to changes in the PLC and to other changes in their environment.

Social structure can be viewed at four different levels of abstraction: the dyad, the group, the social institution, and the society as a whole.

Dyads

The individual consumer as a socialized organism can, of course, carry out consuming activities alone. But when the individual interacts reciprocally with someone else in that process, a "dyad" is said to exist. Much of a consumer's information is obtained from simple dyadic relationships not connected to any more extensive social organization. For example, suppose that you are considering buying an automobile, and you recall seeing an acquaintence driving the make and model that interests you. You telephone this person for information. You have created a dyad.

Groups

Often, however, such interaction occurs in a situation where the dyad is part of a group. A "group" is defined as the coming together of people who are aware of each other and are ready to interact on the basis of distinctive, special expectations connected to the status they occupy within the group; "status" is simply a social position that sums up a bundle of expectations about a person. Groups permeate society. An important fact about them is that their members are likely to have common values, especially when they have come together to achieve a recognized, common goal.

An important implication of serving a common goal is conforming, to some extent, in behavior and values. Thus, consumers learn much about what brands are available, and what brands serve which choice criteria, and what choice criteria will serve which goals. But—more important—they learn what values and choice criteria to use if they want to remain members in good standing. The group, then, is a major source of change in values; of course, it can also prevent change in values.

Cohesion is a result of similarity of values. To emphasize the socially normative role of values, let us elaborate upon the definition of values that we have been using in previous chapters. Values (1) are widely held beliefs, (2) are thought to be desirable by members of the group, and (3) serve as general guides or premises for activities within the group.[2] To begin with, the members of a group tend to have *similar values;* thus they will apply roughly the same choice criteria. As a consequence, transmitting evaluations is greatly simplified: "This is good" means "This is high on choice criteria that are relevant for us." There is evidence that products diffuse faster among people who hold the same values. Furthermore, as people interact within a group, their values become still more similar, if only because group members talk more to each other than to outsiders, people with different values.

For our purposes, let us simplify and assume that a person is a member of one group only, and that this group is small. The group exists because it performs certain functions; for instance, a community group can do more to make the community a good place to live than all the members acting alone. To accomplish the functions, certain behaviors are more effective than others. Consequently, there is a tendency for the group to impose these behaviors on its members to ensure the survival of the group. As a result, especially as the group becomes larger, there is a tendency for its members to specialize their functions or roles. Economists call this "specialization of labor." Some members will work on beautifying the community, for instance, while others work to lower taxes. One specialized function is to provide information about new ideas to the group; the person who does this will probably be highly respected. Attached to each person's role are certain expectations about what the person will do. These expectations become premises—of others—about what he or she will and should do. Each person, then, has premises about others' behavior that partially shape his or her own behavior.

Group Influences: Compliance, Identification, Internalization   In a group, three types of social influences operate on a consumer's behavior.[3] First, the other members have the power to reward a consumer who conforms to their values and norms and punish one who violates them. This sort of influence is called "compliance" or "conformity." Norms are specific levels of values; we can think of norms as including the choice criteria for certain products. When consumers are confronted with a radically new brand, they will exhibit purchase behavior sanctioned by the group, even if such behavior is contrary to their personal values. For instance, if you are interested in a subcompact car but your group generally feels that subcompacts are for nonconformists, the effect will be to decrease your intention to buy.

A second type of influence can be seen, for example, in a work group. A buyer who likes and respects members of the work group and will strive to do those things—apply those choice criteria—that further his or her relationship with them. Such a buyer identifies with the group; and this kind of influence is

[2]F. Nicosia and R. Mayer, "The Sociology of Consumption: A Prospectus for Basic and Applied Research," Project on Synthesis of Knowledge of Consumer Behavior, RANN Program, National Science Foundation, April 1975, p. 8.

[3]J. A. Howard and J. N. Sheth, *The Theory of Consumer Behavior,* Wiley, New York, 1969, pp. 296–299.

called "identification." It leads to interpersonal choice criteria and to beliefs on those criteria; accordingly, in the consumer behavior model "attitude" is modified.

The third kind of influence occurs when, in normal day-to-day discussion, the buyer picks up value-free information from members of the group about which criteria will serve his or her values and which brand is good or poor on these and other criteria. The buyer internalizes such information; thus this type of influence is called "internalization." The individual's attitudes become similar to those of the group; moreover, as we noted in Chapter 3, this consensus increases confidence.

Example: A Study in Cebu City The relevance of group influences for consumers' behavior can be seen in a study of how social structure shapes the introduction of an innovation. People who are alike are likely to be attracted to each other, to interact, and to be members of the same group. This tendency is called the "principle of homophily."[4] If an innovation is to be generally accepted, it must gain access even to groups which typically discourage innovative behavior among their members. That is, a certain amount of heterophily—dyadic relationships between unlike people—is necessary for a innovation to gain entry into society. This is called the principle of the "strength in weak ties."

To test the principle of the strength in weak ties, a group of women ($N = 360$) were interviewed in Cebu City, Philippines, to determine how they had learned about various family-planning devices.[5] The women were from two kinds of communities—homogeneous lower-class communities and mixed (lower-class and lower-middle-class) communities. (In large cities in the Far East, different social classes often live together in the same neighborhood.) The study was confined to women who had had at least one pregnancy, had lived in Cebu City for at least five years, had resided at their present addresses for at least two years, were less than 46 years old, and resided with their spouses. Two measures of the effectiveness of communication were used: "heard of a method of family planning" and "learned how to use it." The two measures were not distinguished in the analysis, however. Mass communication had not been used and was not used during the study.

It was found that neighbors were the major source of information. A larger proportion of lower-class women learned of family planning methods from neighbors in the mixed neighborhoods than in the homogeneous lower-class neighborhoods or the predominantly middle-class neighborhoods. The researchers concluded that heterophilous communication—communication across social classes—facilitated learning about family-planning techniques for lower-class women. There was some question about the frequency of heterophilous communication, however: even in the mixed neighborhoods, lower-class women learned

[4]P. F. Lazarsfeld, W. H. Sewell, and H. L. Wilensky, *The Uses of Sociology,* Basic Books, New York, 1967, p. 816.
[5]W. T. Liu and R. W. Duff, "The Strength in Weak Ties," *Public Opinion Quarterly,* **36**:361–366, Fall 1972.

about the techniques more frequently from other lower-class women than from higher-class women. The frequency of heterophilous communication, then, is still less than that of homophilous communication. Nevertheless, although the heterophilous contacts were relatively infrequent, they were *strategic*.

In this study, the actual relationships were not traced out as is done in a sociogram; but we can speculate about the group influences. In some of the groups, values were probably favorable to adoption of a new product. In these, an innovation such as birth control would be accepted. In other groups, this was probably not so, and the innovation would be rejected. Another social unit—the social institution of religion—was also probably influential. We also know that if the receiving member of a dyad has a high status in the group, the adoption of an innovation will be facilitated. In the heterophilous dyad, what was the credibility of the sender of the message? Being of a higher class, she probably possessed higher credibility; this would enhance the impact of the message. Also, the higher-class women may have had more contact with doctors and would thus be rated high on competence. If mass media had been the source of information, the message probably would have been less credible. On the other hand, mass media could have reached a larger number of people; one task in desigining such messages for the mass media is to construct them in such a way that they will stimulate conversation similar to that in interaction.

Social Institutions

The third level of abstraction in the concept of social structure is the social institution. Social institutions are created when large numbers of people (groups) organize to serve goals that perpetuate society. They are composed of inter-related statuses instead of specific individuals. The members of a social institution typically share a geographic area and a common system of values. The major institutions of society are economic, political, family, and religious structures.

Society as a Whole

The fourth level of abstraction in examining social structure and its influence on consumers' behavior is society itself. When groups, including formal organizations, come together and form institutions serving to perpetuate social existence, a "society" is said to have developed. Within a society are subcultures, such as social classes. Social institutions make laws and change values as conditions confronting the society change.

OPERATION OF SOCIAL INFLUENCE

With this set of constructs and hypotheses, we are in a better position to discuss how social influence operates. Examples of how a dyad, an informal group, and a formal organization affect consumers' behavior will be given.

Social Influence in the Dyad: Salesperson and Buyer

In this section, in examining the dyadic relationship, we will assume that no other social influences operate on either party to the dyad.

A party to a dyad can act as a free agent, although part of a social group, probably only when the behavior involved is repetitive (RRB), so that the group has had the opportunity to work out rules. In this situation, a group can delegate a decision to a member as part of a dyad. There are many examples of this. Diplomacy is a dramatic example; two diplomats, representing two countries, have the task, as parties to a dyad, of reconciling differences between the countries. But each must work within well-defined limits set by his or her country.

An example which has been much studied is the salesperson-buyer dyad. This dyad was implied in Figure 7-1, where the automobile buyer evaluated different sources of information. There, "interaction" was a black box, telling us nothing about the process; here we will emphasize the process of interaction between salesperson and buyer.

Much of the research in this area has been done for a very important practical purpose: to select people for sales positions. Consequently, it focuses on the act of purchase. For our purposes, this is not so useful as research that focuses on the interaction process. I shall lean heavily here upon a splendid review of sales research by Capon, Holbrook, and Hulbert.[6]

One persistent debate in sales management is whether the soft sell or the hard sell is more effective. (In one study, it was found that the soft sell is more effective in changing preferences for owning various patterns of drinking glasses.) Another issue is whether a "canned" sales presentation or a "customer-specific" presentation is more effective. (In one study, a customer-specific message was found to be better for obtaining comprehension, but a canned presentation was more exciting and achieved greater intention to buy.) Another set of issues has involved the similarity of salesperson and buyer and the expertise of the salesperson. It was found in one study that both similarity and expertise had a positive effect upon sales of a tape-player cleaner, but the effect of expertise was stronger. When price was varied over four levels, high expertise was correlated with high sales at each of the four prices. It was also found that at lower prices expertise exhibited low negative price elasticity—that is, when price was lowered, sales tended to increase only slightly—whereas low expertise resulted in low positive price elasticity. This suggests there may have been a slight price-quality association.

Do the salesperson and the message interact? Do some salespersons do better than others with a particular message? They do in some cases. In selling magazines over the telephone, one salesperson did better with an interactive

---

[6]N. Capon, M. B. Holbrook, and J. M. Hulbert, "Selling Processes and Buyer Behavior: Theoretical Implications of Recent Research," Graduate School of Business, Columbia University, mimeographed, 1975.

approach, conversational give-and-take; another did better with a straightforward sales delivery; and a third did equally well with either. Thus, we find differences among salespersons regarding the kinds of message they are effective with.

Finally, it has been found that the salesperson, not the customer, may determine the extent of the search for and evaluation of alternatives, and thus can influence the customer's selection of particular attributes.

It should be noted that the client-salesperson dyad is probably not entirely representative of social influence generally, because the salesman is often rated low on credibility. But this is not always the case. Casual observation suggests that some salespersons are able to build a fine reputation with clients and consequently have high credibility. (Similarly, some diplomats are considered highly credible.)

It must also be pointed out that the discussion so far has assumed that a consumer is a member of a single group. It has assumed that this is his or her only reference group. This is a static view. But this assumption does not allow for the phenomenon of upward and downward social mobility. In a society where there is much social mobility, we should consider not only a consumer's present group but the group to which he or she aspires. For the upwardly mobile person, this second type of reference group may be more important in shaping behavior than the present group. Also, our discussion has not allowed for multiple reference groups. But in fact a consumer is often a member of more than one group, each exerting influence. Finally, we have not allowed for changes in values, which will be discussed under "Measurement of Values."

Social Influence in an Informal Group: The Family

In shaping consumers' behavior, one of the most significant social units is the family. For our purposes, the family is an informal small group; but it is sometimes treated in a more fundamental way as an institution.

The family is almost unique, it seems, in the lopsidedness of its structure of authority: society almost gives the parents carte blanche in regulating children's behavior. It is also a uniquely important unit for buying, because much purchasing is done for the home and because the wife does much of the purchasing of particular products for family members. In the following discussion, I make use of Davis' careful review of consumer behavior in the family.[7]

Let us examine how the husband-wife relationship in buying differs between durables and nondurables. In one study, the nondurables beer, liquor, and shaving cream were viewed as "masculine" products; the wife bought the brands which the husband requested. An important finding was the dependability of the information, as was shown by the high degree of agreement between husband and wife as to whose preferences were followed. Only 8 percent of the couples did not support each other's answer. It was consistently found in a number of

---

[7]H. L. Davis, "Decision Making within the Household," Project on Synthesis of Knowledge of Consumer Behavior, RANN Program, National Science Foundation, April 1975.

studies that although wives do most of the shopping for groceries, they do so with an awareness of products and brands their families like.

With durables, there was a tendency for the choice to be divided between husband and wife. In the purchase of housing, the husband's influence was greatest on decisions about the price range and whether to move; the wife was dominant in decisions about the number of bedrooms and similar features. In the purchase of automobiles, the husband was more dominant than for housing; but, as with housing, the stages of decision were divided between them.

In summary, there are great differences in the husband-wife buying relationship from product to product. This relationship also varies according to stage of decision; e.g., in one study 60 percent of the husbands were dominant as regards the brand of an automobile to be purchased, but only 25 percent were dominant regarding the color of an automobile to be purchased. There is also variation from family to family, of course.

When the process of decision making was examined, the husbands and wives were found to use different criteria. It has been said that "a man tolerates buying a house for the sake of a woman, while she tolerates the man for the sake of the home."[8] For example, in choosing housing even the criterion "convenience" was defined differently; women considered funtionality, but men considered closeness to work and suitability for relaxation.

The role of children is probably significant for some products. Teenagers, for example, were found to be particularly prominent in selecting new or different brands. The evidence here, however, is apparently much more sparse than the evidence regarding husbands and wives.

There is growing belief that the home is a poor environment for decision making. For one thing, family decisions usually occur late in the evening or early in the morning, when family members are tired or hurried. Also, some family decisions are taken mainly to perpetuate the group, and decisions may be delayed or avoided because of fear of conflict. This is true in many groups, but it may be especially true in the family unit. Finally, family decisions are not independent of each other, but rather are part of a continuous stream of activity; this complicates choice.

Different disciplines view the family unit quite differently; the view taken here is behavioral. Economists, however, have come to conceptualize the family as the consumer counterpart of the firm and to speak of "consumer technology," which is defined as the ratio of the quantity of a good to the quantity of its characteristics (see Chapter 1). But economists have difficulty separating changes in consumer technology from changes in consumers' preferences.[9] If we want to estimate the nonmarket components of national income, or what happens in the way of substitution with changing prices, the economists' view may well be the most useful. But if we are concerned with the process of change and

[8]Davis, op. cit., p. 34.

[9]M. Wilkinson, "Extension of Consumer Theory," Graduate School of Business, Columbia University, mimeographed, 1975, pp. 4–7.

thus with how families respond to information, the economists' view is not as appropriate. Perhaps the economic and behavioristic views should be combined. For example, substitution may occur quite slowly if prices of brands change sharply; but with better information, as from advertising, the consumer could be thrown into LPS and would respond much more rapidly.

Social Influence in a Formal Group: The Organization

Often, consumers—or buying units—are formal organizations, such as companies, churches, schools, government agencies, hospitals, and the like. A formal group is a more purposeful and cohesive group than is an informal group and has more thoroughly articulated goals.

For such formal organizations, the salesperson is often the dominant external influence. Internal social influence tends to be stronger in a formal organization than in a looser social structure like a neighborhood group, or even a voluntary community organization. For example, there is a well-defined status hierarchy, conformity is well enforced, compliance is common, specialization is prominent, dependable expectations are more essential, and there is less emphasis upon homogeneity of values. In a choice situation, this tighter structure can cause impersonal criteria—those attitudes toward product attributes which serve the organization's goals—and interpersonal criteria to dominate the buyer's personal criteria.

The role of impersonal choice criteria—or "professional goals," as they are often called—is illustrated in Figure 9-1, which shows an industrial buyer's decision process in RRB. The task was to buy fasteners for the company—fasteners being bolts, screws, rivets, etc.; anything that holds two things together. Notice that the criteria implicitly specified by the boxes (e.g., the relation between delivery date and lead time in box 2) are all rather clearly impersonal criteria. They are designed to serve the company's interests. It is difficult to imagine direct relations between these criteria and the buyer's motives. There is obviously an indirect relation, however; presumably, if the buyer serves these criteria well, he or she will be rewarded by the company. A complicating problem is that the company may have limited ability to properly evaluate the buyer's contribution.

Another difference often found between organizational buying and individual buying is that in organizational buying the object being bought is less separated in the buyer's mind from the seller as an organization. An individual buyer, for example, often may not even know what company produces a brand, although the brand name itself is quite important. This is much less true in organizational buying. The reason is partly that things like delivery time and services offered to buyers by the seller are important in organizational buying, whereas for many consumer products the brand is generally available in retail stores and service is irrelevant. Thus the organizational buyer's judgments of these qualities of the seller become essential parts of the concept of the product. This concept is more accurately described as a "product-supplier concept" than a "brand concept." The difference in the way a product is conceptualized makes

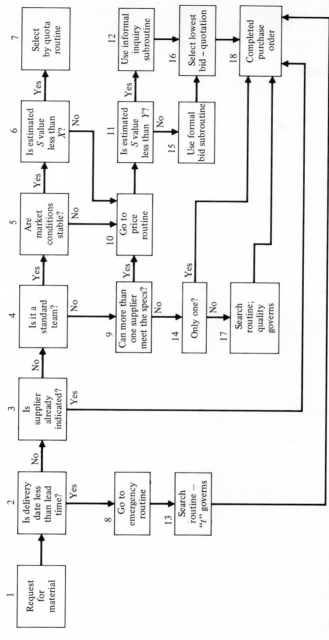

Figure 9-1 Industrial buying. (*J. A. Howard, Marketing Management, 3d ed., Irwin, Homewood, Ill., 1973, p. 67.*)

it necessary to redraw Figure 2-1 to incorporate impersonal criteria in the brand concept. Presumably, if we were to derive the meaning of a product supplier as the meaning of "asparagus" was derived in Chapter 3, the attributive words would include references to the qualities of the company as well as to those of the product.

When buying is repetitive (RRB), however, as it is in much organizational buying, the decision process appears to be much like that of individual buying. The process shown in Figure 9-1 is very similar to that shown in Figure 2-2. Figure 9-1 implies a definite order in which each decision rule is applied. It also indicates that the choice process is binary, not multivalued. Finally, in Figure 9-1, the process is factored into individual parts, as is indicated by the large number of boxes: that is, a large number of criteria are applied. The reason for this similarity is that when a product is bought repetitively (RRB), the buyer usually has complete control, but within limits defined by his or her superiors. When this responsibility was delegated to the buyer, certain criteria for choice were specified.

Sometimes the purchasing agent, or an assistant or assistants, is given responsibility for almost all buying in a company; sometimes the responsibility is dispersed among varying people. We will assume here, to simplify, that one person has this responsibility. What particular choice criteria are used by such a buyer?

To answer this question, let us examine the results of a study by Lehmann and O'Shaughnessy.[10] They asked purchasing agents to rate the seventeen attributes of product suppliers shown in Table 9-1 across four product types. O'Shaughnessy had concluded from his earlier research that there are roughly four different types of buying situations and that buyers tend to emphasize different criteria for each type.

The first type of buying situation occurs when the use of the product involves no problems of procedure or performance. This is RRB. The buyer would be expected to rate reliability of delivery and price as most important and would show a preference for current suppliers. As was predicted, reliability of delivery and price were rated first and second in this situation.

The second type of situation involves procedural problems. This is a kind of LPS buying. Here, employees must learn to use the product. As was expected in this case, the following three criteria were rated most important:

Technical service offered
Ease of operation or use
Training offered by supplier

Third, there are products involving problems of performance. This is another kind of LPS situation. Here, criteria which facilitate judgments about whether the supplier and its product can perform as indicated are rated high. The

[10]D. R. Lehmann and J. O'Shaughnessy, "Difference in Attribute Importance for Different Industrial Products," *Journal of Marketing,* **38**:36–42, April 1974.

Table 9-1   Seventeen Attributes Rated by Purchasing Agents

1 Overall reputation of the supplier
2 Financing terms
3 Supplier's flexibility in adjusting to your company's needs
4 Experience with the supplier in analogous situations
5 Technical service offered
6 Confidence in the salesman
7 Convenience of placing the order
8 Data on reliability of the product
9 Price
10 Technical specifications
11 Ease of operation or use
12 Preferences of principal user of the product
13 Training offered by the supplier
14 Training time required
15 Reliability of delivery date promised
16 Ease of maintenance
17 Sales service expected after date of purchase

Source: D. R. Lehmann and J. O'Shaughnessy, "Difference in Attribute Importance for Different Industrial Products," *Journal of Marketing,* **38:**36–42, April 1974.

following criteria were predicted to be most likely to function in this role, and in fact they were three of the four rated most highly:

> Technical service offered
> Flexibility of supplier
> Product reliability

The fourth, reliability of delivery, was more important than the other three, however.

Finally, there are products which involve political problems. These are products that are judged, regardless of application, on the basis of the interdepartmental conflict they encounter (such as conflict between marketing, production, and research and development). This is like an EPS situation in that conflict arises over what choice criteria will be used. The five most highly rated criteria for these products were:

> Price
> Reputation of supplier
> Data on product reliability
> Reliability of delivery
> Flexibility of supplier

These, too, appear to conform to the prediction.

In practice, the industrial buyer is not always as independent in decision making as I have implied. When a new product supplier comes along—especially if the product is radically new (EPS)—the buyer will usually be expected to consult with others in the company and get their agreement. Such joint decision making usually involves the production manager and engineering or research and development manager; and more and more frequently, the marketing manager is brought in. Thus joint decision making can be fraught with conflict.

The simplest problem arises when the parties have different beliefs about the contribution of the product supplier to given criteria; in this case, additional search will usually make agreement, and a decision, possible.

In other cases, however, there will be differences among the parties about the appropriate criteria. These differences arise largely because differences in the organizational reward structure have produced different motivations among the parties to the decision. The purchasing agent thinks in terms of economics or profit criteria. The production manager wants to avoid increasing costs of production. The engineer will be concerned with the quality of the product. The marketing manager will want criteria which have to do with effects on sales. If the criteria can be related to some common denominator, such as some more abstract measure of the company's welfare, persuasion will work to achieve agreement. If not, bargaining will take place. The production manager may remind the other three, for example, that the last time a buying issue was thrashed out among them, he was particularly generous.

Finally, the situation can become quite tense if each party is jockeying for power and trying to protect his or her position in the long run. In a company, a manager typically wants as much power as possible. Managers want to keep their options open—the greater the number of options, the less likelihood of being caught in a difficult position by some unexpected set of circumstances. For example, if the product manager can set criteria, then if for some reason the operation becomes less efficient, so that costs rise, the manager may be able to offset this inefficiency by demanding that a cheaper component be purchased. Thus, the norm has been changed. The same principle applies in each of the four areas of operations: purchasing, engineering, production, and marketing. In a situation like this, politicking will occur. Each party will try to invoke the support of higher management without seeming to do so. (In seeking help, one cannot be obvious, because this makes one vulnerable to the charge of incompetence.)

Social Influence in an Industrial Society

As was noted earlier, societies adjust values and make laws in response to changing conditions. In an industrial society some of these laws and values have the purpose of protecting consumers. In an advanced society, the flow of goods includes many new and unfamiliar products, and this makes new demands on consumers. For example, when technology creates such products as microwave ovens and pocket calculators, consuming becomes quite complicated.

In such a situation, traditional market regulation may no longer be appropriate. This issue is dealt with at length in Chapter 10.

SUMMARY: SOCIAL INFLUENCE

Social influences on the consumer in various settings—dyads, groups, social institutions, and society itself—have been examined. Some of the mechanisms by which this influence works have been delineated; many more have been implied. Three such mechanisms are compliance, identification, and internalization.

The role of common values within a group in shaping individual behavior has been emphasized. The most strategic influence of the group occurs, of course, by means of changes in values. Let us now examine the case of changing values, which has so far been avoided by assuming given values.

CHANGING VALUES

Sometimes a product is so radically new that consumers cannot adequately adapt to it merely by adopting new choice criteria; their instrumental values and even their terminal values may have to change. It has been mentioned several times that when instant coffee was introduced in the 1940s, a study by Haire showed that some people considered anyone who would buy such a product to be lazy, a poor planner, a spendthrift, and a poor homemaker. Apparently, some of the values underlying such a judgment had to change before the product could be widely accepted; this was suggested when Pechman and Webster repeated Haire's experiment in 1968. Although no direct evidence is available, I suspect that the change had to do with the instrumental value placed on convenience, perhaps traceable to a change in the terminal value of pleasure. One reason for the greater desire for convenience and the possibly greater emphasis on pleasure was probably the increase in the number of working wives. By 1959, 40 percent of all American wives were working outside the home.[11] The product life cycle for a successful product in EPS is probably a learning process taking place simultaneously within a more general change in values in the society.

In some cases, a government will make an effort to change values. This might happen with respect to nutrition, for example; thus the government might encourage consumers to place a higher value on nutrition than on taste in selecting and preparing foods. The worldwide food shortage makes it necessary to instill in consumers new values that stress certain nutritional aspects of food. People like meat because of its taste; but since 7 pounds of grain are required to produce 1 pound of beef, beef is much more expensive than cereal as a source of nutrition. In a sense, buying cheaper sources of protein would often imply changing choice criteria and thus a general change in values. The process of transmitting new values, however, is not well understood, despite the extensive research on diffusion of innovations. Until recently, not much of an effort had been made to fully conceptualize it, much less test the truth of any conceptualizations. In this regard, one of the most serious questions, as will be seen in Chapter 10, is: Who can best bring about changes in values? That is, who will educate—industry, government, schools, or families? A related question is: Who should bear the cost of this?

[11]H. P. Miller, *Rich Man, Poor Man,* Crowell, New York, 1964, p. 192.

Measurement of Values

A discussion of how to measure values will provide a better understanding of the process of changing values.

Measurement is not difficult if we accept Rokeach's list of values (see Chapter 5, page 93) as adequate for the population whose values we want to observe or change. We give the consumer a sheet of paper, with the eighteen terminal values listed alphabetically on the right-hand side and eighteen numbered boxes on the left-hand side, and eighteen gummed labels with one of the values printed on each. The consumer is asked to rank-order the values:

> Study the list carefully and pick out the one value which is the most important for you. Peel it off and paste it in box 1 on the left. Then pick out the value which is second most important to you. Peel it off and paste it in box 2. Then do the same for each of the remaining values. The value which is least important goes in box 18. Work slowly and think carefully. If you change your mind, feel free to change your answers. The labels peel off easily and can be moved from place to place. The end result should truly show how you really feel.[12]

The same procedure is applied to the instrumental values.

If the population consists of college students or others in a highly industrialized Western nation, Rokeach's list is probably appropriate. It is culture-bound, however, and limited to functionally literate people. Also, interpretation of the rankings requires extensive previous knowledge of the culture, and it produces only a weak, ordinal measurement.[13]

If the population is of a different culture, a method for measuring values described by Bridge will be more appropriate; this method applies to any culture and to illiterates. To obtain instrumental values, consumers are asked to respond to the following type of question:

> What is a good thing that a person like you could do?

To obtain terminal values, a question like this is asked:

> What is a good thing that could happen to a person like you?[14]

This second question elicits hopes and fears, which are manifestations of terminal values. Once answers have been obtained from a sample of the population, they are presented to another, small sample of the same culture, and the second group are asked to categorize the answers given by the first group. Once having

[12]M. Rokeach, *The Nature of Human Values,* Free Press, New York, 1973, p. 27. Subsequent references to Rokeach in this chapter are to this work.

[13]R. G. Bridge, "The Utility of ECHO Surveys in Cross-Cultural Research on Values," In S. Morris, *Assumptions and Problems in the Practical Application of Attitude and Value Research,* American Psychological Association, Washington, D.C., 1969.

[14]R. P. Barthol and R. G. Bridge, "The ECHO Multi-Response Method for Surveying Value and Influence Patterns in Groups," *Psychological Reports,* **22:**1345–1354, 1968.

categorized the answers, the second group are asked to put descriptive labels on each category. In the case of the "do" question, these labels are instrumental values; in the case of the "happen" question, they are terminal values. We might also want to ask for demographic data, for example, so as to identify groups with particular values for the purpose of segmentation (Chapter 8).

With a background on the measurement of values, one is in a position to determine whether values have been changed by using a before-and-after measure. Will knowing a consumer's values make it possible to predict a priori what choice criteria he or she will apply when exposed to a radically new brand? If so, it would immensely simplify the problem of bringing about change. To my knowledge, no systematic answer to this question has yet been attempted.

Concepts

The concepts needed to understand changes in values have already been presented, here and in earlier chapters; let us now review them and state them more systematically.

Self-concept, as described at length in Chapter 5, plays a role:

> The functions served by a person's values are to provide him with a comprehensive set of standards to guide actions, justifications, judgments, and comparisons of self and others and to serve needs for adjustment, ego defense and self-actualization. All these diverse functions converge into a single, overriding, master function, namely, to help maintain and enhance one's total conception of oneself.[15]

"Self-concept" as used here is very stable. Like any concept, it is made up of evaluational and referential elements, as is implied by the more general definition of "self-concept" that has been used throughout this book: the fullest description of himself (or herself) that a person is capable of making at any given time, including his feeling about what he considers himself to be.[16] Terminal values can be thought of as the evaluative dimensions of the self-concept, analogous to the brand concept. The referential dimensions of self-concept—the analogue of brand identification—are not well understood.[17] People do develop categories for identifying each other in social relations. The term "personality" is popularly used to mean the referential aspects of a person. Psychologists, who want to be more systematic in their referential descriptions, use "personality" to apply to a deeper level of analysis and describe this level by means of "personality traits." An enormous amount of research has been done in the past three decades on personality traits; but, unfortunately, the results have not been very consistent, with a few important exceptions (see Chapter 8).

---

[15]Rokeach, op. cit., p. 216.

[16]H. B. English and A. C. English, *Psychological and Psychoanalytic Terms,* McKay, New York, 1958, p. 456.

[17]R. B. Zajonc, "Cognitive Theories in Psychology," in E. Lindzey and E. Aronson (eds.), *Handbook of Social Psychology,* 2d ed., vol. 1, Addison-Wesley, Reading, Mass., 1968.

Creating Changes in Values

A basic premise of Rokeach's analysis is that self-concept is the element most stable and most difficult to change; attitude is the least stable and easiest to change; and values fall in between. The principle of change is that whenever a person finds either an attitude or a value incompatible with his or her self-concept, the contradiction will be removed by changing the attitude or the value to make it consistent with the self-concept. In other words, self-concept will at least be maintained, and if possible, strengthened.

The person will be led to remove the contradiction between attitude or value and self-concept as a result of experiencing of self-dissatisfaction. Dissatisfaction arises when a discrepancy is perceived between one's self-concept and one's performance on values or choice criteria. (Rokeach has not developed his work to the specific level of choice, and so he refers to attitudes instead of choice criteria.) This discrepancy leads to conflict. Although self-dissatisfaction motivates one to remove the contradiction, one must first identify the source; this is sometimes a difficult task. The perceived sources of self-dissatisfaction are perceived deficiencies, particularly in competence and morality:

> A person defines himself as incompetent in a given situation to the extent that he sees his performance to be deficient in skill, ability, intelligence, ability to appraise reality correctly, or in ability to play assigned roles in society successfully. A person defines himself as immoral to the extent that he sees himself as harming himself or others or as deficient in exercising impulse control over his thoughts or feelings.[18]

In discussing the elements of social structure, it was suggested that peers—group members—shape each other's choice criteria and values associated with product classes. An expert source, on the other hand, is believed to be more effective in strengthening the linkage—attitude—between already held cognitions and an object.[19] Thus, both peers and experts can be equally credible, but on different dimensions; they thus can have different effects. Peers are more important in changing values; experts are more important in creating beliefs.

This logic leads to a procedure for changing values. To change consumers' values, one should present them with the following, in the order shown: (1) Information about their values, their attitudes toward the product class, and the associated behavior. (2) Information about the analogous values and attitudes of people with whom the consumers could compare themselves and with whom they identify. (3) Information on the relationship between the analogous values and attitudes of others with whom they identify, and a brief interpretation of the data which draws attention to contradictions existing in the values of these other people. By implication, these contradictions may also exist within the consumers' own system of beliefs. This interpretation then can cause consumers to examine the relationship between their own self-concept, values, and choice

---

[18]Rokeach, op. cit., p. 228.
[19]E. E. Jones and H. B. Gerard, *Foundations of Social Psychology,* Wiley, New York, 1967, pp. 436–444.

criteria relevant to a brand. Thus they can become aware of discrepancies between self-concept and any or all of the three cognitions—values, choice criteria and beliefs. This will create self-dissatisfaction, and this in turn can motivate consumers to change the discordant values, choice criteria, or beliefs. It is crucial in this procedure that the consumers are in fact subject to the influence process of identification discussed earlier.

Using these principles, Rokeach was able to show change among students in terminal values, attitudes, and behavior for as long as fifteen months; these were defined as long-term changes. The values were equality (brotherhood, equal opportunity for all) and freedom (independence, free choice). The attitudes were toward equal opportunity for black people. Behavior measured was in terms of response to a solicitation to become a member of NAACP, register in ethnic-studies courses, and change to a major in social science or education. (Clearly, the ethical problems in the effort to change values are profound; but consideration of this issue is delayed until Chapter 10, where it can be discussed systematically.)

What does this tell us about buying behavior? One way to begin answering this question is to consider how human beings conceptualize an object. We return to the example of asparagus discussed in Chapter 3. Intuitively, one suspects that attitude toward the "equal rights of black people" is a name for a substantially more abstract concept—a concept higher in the structure—than "asparagus." Obviously, we would suppose that a person who thinks about blacks and their rights is more involved—has a more differentiated structure—than someone who thinks less about them (see Chapter 8). But let us assume away the problems posed by such individual differences.

We could conclude that it may be possible to bring about major innovations in behavior under certain circumstances by using the particular approach implied by the theory stated above. The necessary circumstances are, first, that some people in the peer group and preferably most of them already have the values that we wish our consumers to adopt; and, second, that we are able to convey this fact to our subjects with a high degree of credibility and understanding. These requirements suggest why it often takes so long for an innovation to diffuse through society. Moreover, these are only the basic forces that appear to operate; in order to simplify, secondary forces have been ignored. For example, a person with whom a consumer interacts can make a difference; expertise and trust were discussed earlier. These are details, however, that are best avoided in presenting the basic ideas.

The analysis does not tell us anything about the change from EPS to LPS. But this change, brought about simply by the reweighting of one or more choice criteria, is obviously important in practice. Attitude elements (beliefs), rather than a single-dimensional attitude, were used in Rokeach's study, and the values of the beliefs were only binary. This seriously limits the possibilities of analysis comparable to the two-level analysis of Chapter 5, and no attempt in this direction has been reported.

The study does lend support to the general principle of the means-end chain.

The chain is considered to be made up of links, some nearer to action and some farther from it; the farther from action, the more stable the link. Although Rokeach's analysis was applied to only one sample, it is nevertheless an important study. The behavior—such as changing a college major to social science or education—was similar to that occurring in a complex, real-world setting, as contrasted with the highly simplified laboratory settings often used for studying motivation: the "end" in the means-end chain.

Content of Future Values

The description of social structure has so far omitted one dynamic element: the general changes in values that pervade a society, particularly a postindustrial society. As was noted earlier, I believe that much EPS is successful because it takes place simultaneously with changes in values. Consequently, an important question is: What changes in values is our society in general likely to undergo?

An earlier generation of social philosophers assumed that the end of scarcity, as reflected in a high material standard of living, would bring a new set of values. It was thought that many of our social problems arose because of scarcity of resources, and that with improvements in the technology of production and the accumulation of capital this problem would be ameliorated and perhaps eliminated.

Today, it is no longer believed that such a solution is within our grasp. Any good has a cost; and if we think of scarcity in terms of cost, there is a whole new set of scarcities confronting us. By implication, these scarcities will influence our values. These new scarcities are:

Information—the centrality of information in postindustrial society creates new and different problems.

Coordination—the coordination of economic activity is shifted from the unseen hand of the market to the visible political arena.

Time—consumption itself requires time; and in a society of growing abundance, time is perhaps the scarcest commodity of all.[20]

The continuing existence of scarcities does not imply there will be no change in values; but it does suggest that changes in values will be less drastic than was thought.

Conclusion on Changes in Values

Sharply pointed research on changes in values and their relevance for the acceptance of new products is in its infancy. An attempt to use mass media to change health habits related to heart attacks is being made at Stanford University; the preliminary report is encouraging.[21] But an elaborate show on public television, "Feelin' Good," created to improve the health habits of Americans,

---

[20]D. Bell, *The Coming of Post-Industrial Society,* Basic Books, New York, 1973, pp. 466–475.
[21]*Advertising Age,* December 9, 1974, p. 36.

is generally agreed to have been poorly conceived, and thus provides no basis for conclusions about the potential of such efforts.[22]

DIFFUSION OF INNOVATIONS

Empirical research on marketing new products has been largely confined to particular brands. As a consequence, when the stage of the improved version of the product is reached (LPS), competition complicates the attempt to understand what is happening in the market. The concept of the product life cycle allows us to abstract from competitive relations, and it gives a highly useful view of the market over time.

Research on the diffusion of innovations has been centered on the innovation—EPS, or a new class concept—and has avoided the competitive complication of LPS. Unfortunately, the distinction between EPS and LPS has been accidental, not deliberate, in diffusion research, because such research grew largely out of rural sociology and geography. Clearly, in the diffusion of innovations we would expect special information requirements and also special variables for segmenting, as was discussed in Chapter 8.

The major development in studying how innovations diffuse through society was an analysis of how farmers in Iowa accepted an important innovation in food—hybrid seed corn—in 1943, as Rogers notes in describing the state of diffusion research.[23] Such research has become common as different types of innovations—such as family planning, health practices, and especially new technologies in developing countries—have been investigated; now some 1,800 research reports are available. By 1973, some 500 "knowledge-attitude-practice" (KAP) studies of family planning had been done in seventy-two countries.

The key ideas of diffusion research are: an *innovation,* defined as an idea, practice, or object as seen by an individual or some other relevant unit of adoption, which is *communicated* through certain *channels* over *time* among the members of a *social structure.*

Diffusion Analysis

The factor *time* in the concept of diffusion implies that not all people adopt a new idea simultaneously. The notion of the normal curve from learning theory is proposed as a description of the process, as is shown in Figure 9-2. In this illustration, we can see the proportion of people that adopted an innovation early and late according to their distance from the mean time of adoption (X). For example, 2.5 percent of the subjects adopted the innovation by the date represented by the mean minus 2 standard deviations. When the normal curve is stated cumulatively, the logistic curve shown in Figure 9-3 is obtained. This curve is obviously similar to some product life cycles.

[22]*New York Times,* January 13, 1975, p. 56.
[23]E. M. Rogers, "New Product Adoption and Diffusion," Project on Synthesis of Knowledge of Consumer Behavior, RANN Program, National Science Foundation, April 1975, pp. 3, 7.

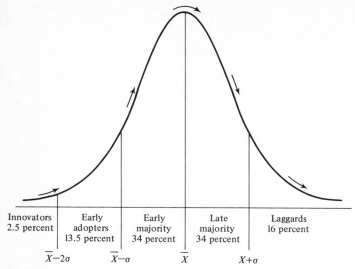

| Innovators 2.5 percent | Early adopters 13.5 percent | Early majority 34 percent | Late majority 34 percent | Laggards 16 percent |

$\overline{X}-2\sigma \qquad \overline{X}-\sigma \qquad \overline{X} \qquad X+\sigma$

Figure 9-2 Distribution of innovation acceptors. (*E. M. Rogers,* Diffusion of Innovations, *Free Press, New York, 1962, fig. 6-1, p. 162.*)

For more realism, one should allow for the time period involved, if necessary. In the study in Iowa, it was nine years. In the study of instant coffee discussed in Chapter 1, it was more than twenty years, but the curve was not adjusted for population growth; if it had been, it would have leveled off somewhat sooner.

Substantial research has been devoted to determining whether the normal curve really does describe the actual process in a wide number of products;[24] and in fact many cases were found to be approximated by this representation. One group of researchers concluded: "The logistic diffusion process is thus indicated by the data to be both robust and general."[25]

The descriptive stage of diffusion research resulted in many attempts to explain why a certain pattern existed, in the hope of speeding up the rate of acceptance. As is suggested by Chapter 8, the first approach might be to explain it in terms of differences among people, such as differences in personality. Second, we might explain it in terms of social environment, as is suggested by the earlier part of this chapter. Third, we could explain it in terms of people's limitations in the capacity to process information; this is suggested by the emphasis on communication in earlier chapters.

Individual Differences   Figure 9-2 shows that different people adopt an innovation at different times; that is, there are people, called "innovators," who

---

[24]E. M. Rogers, *Diffusion of Innovations,* Free Press, New York, 1962, chap. 6.
[25]R. L. Hamblin, R. B. Jacobsen, and J. L. L. Miller, *A Mathematical Theory of Social Change,* Wiley, New York, 1973, p. 4.

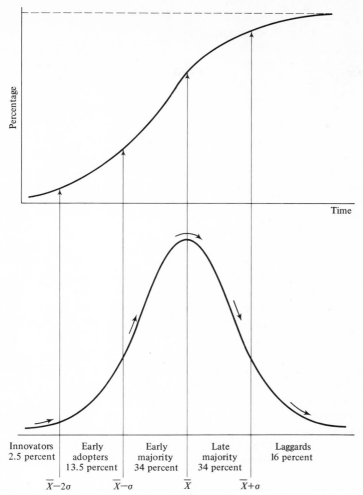

Figure 9-3 Cumulative distribution of adopters.

adopt it first. Supposedly, then, people move through the different stages at different speeds. From a review of 708 diffusion studies, it was concluded that adoption time, or adoption versus nonadoption, is related to education, income, and standard of living; knowledgeability, attitude toward change, and aspirations for upward mobility; cosmopoliteness (orientation outside one's social system); and exposure to mass media and to interpersonal communications.[26]

How well do these conclusions about individual differences accord with research in marketing? In general, the results of marketing research are much

[26]E. M. Rogers and J. D. Stanfield, "Adoption and Diffusion of New Products: Emerging Generalizations and Hypotheses," in F. M. Bass, C. W. King, and E. A. Pessemier, *Applications of the Sciences in Marketing Management,* Wiley, New York, 1968, pp. 227–250.

less clear-cut, especially as regards nondurables.[27] For durables there is somewhat closer conformity, possibly because durables are typically more involving and more likely to be "new" than nondurables. The greater likelihood of newness comes about because of technological change and infrequency of purchase. In this connection, it is possible that more of the marketing studies have concentrated on brands than on product classes; the brands could, then, be instances of LPS.

Social Structure Diffusion research has made some progress in dealing with social structure as an influence on the acceptance of innovations. The most encouraging approach has been "network analysis,"[28] in which sociometric data about communication flows and patterns are analyzed by the use of interpersonal relationships as the unit of observation. Briefly, specific message flows in a system are reconstructed with empirical data, and then the social structure is overlaid on this pattern of flows.

This approach allows us to understand how the social structure channels the process of diffusion. It also lets us analyze the data of a "who-to-whom" communication matrix; facilitates the identification of cliques within a total system; makes it possible to examine how such structural subgroupings affect the diffusion of an innovation; clarifies specialized communication roles, such as liaisons, bridges, and isolates; and allows communication analysis to be extended far beyond opinion leadership, which was its original focus. A "clique" is a subsystem whose elements interact with each other more frequently than with other members of the communication system. It is somewhat similar to what we have been calling a "group," except that a group is more loosely organized. A "liaison" is an individual who connects two or more cliques within a system without belonging to either. A "bridge" is an individual who is a member of a communication clique and has a link to another individual who is a member of a different communication clique. In the Cebu City study discussed earlier in the chapter, a member of the lower middle class who talked with a member of the lower class was either a liaison or bridge, depending on whether she was a member of the clique from which her information came. An "isolate" is, of course, an individual who has few communication contacts with the rest of the system.

These constructs underlie the development of various structural characteristics for subsystems or entire systems such as formal organizations and communities. The structural characteristics are "system connectedness," the degree to which the members of a system as a whole are linked with each other by communication flows; and "system openness," the degree to which a system exchanges information with its environment. One hypothesis is that the innovativeness of a system is positively related to its connectedness and openness.

---

[27]M. B. Holbrook and J. A. Howard, "Consumer Research on Frequently Purchased Nondurable Goods and Services: A Review," Project on Synthesis of Knowledge of Consumer Behavior, RANN Program, National Science Foundation, April 1975, pp. 73–77.

[28]C. Kadushin, "Introduction to the Sociological Study of Networks," Teachers College, Columbia University, mimeographed, October 1975.

Information Processing Although diffusion research has emphasized the influence of communication, this is largely a matter of information resulting from the social structure. The research has not attempted to develop an information-processing model by which an innovator receives information and forms certain cognitive structures which lead to behavior, adoption, or nonadoption. Moreover, in designing studies of the effects of communication, researches have not dealt specifically with the information-processing characteristics of potential innovators.

Evaluation of Diffusion Research

Rogers, who is one of the leaders in diffusion research, criticizes the field on three grounds; lack of process orientation, bias in favor of innovation, and psychological orientation.

As Rogers correctly points out, human communication implies a process.[29] Appropriate concepts and propositions in diffusion research have not been tested nearly as much as they should be.[30] Most of this book has been concerned with delineating these constructs and propositions, including information-processing characteristics, as the basis for studying this process in the individual. The diffusion studies can help us extend the constructs to social processes.

"Bias in favor of innovation" refers to the purpose of the studies. The purpose has been practical and immediate: to get people to accept an innovation, regardless of whether or not it is good for them. Not only have the innovators' interests been ignored, but this has also led to correlational studies and a tendency to ignore issues of causality. In this book, in order to analyze the individual, causality has been constantly emphasized; Part Two, Advanced Work, presents the methodology for discovering causation empirically. Marketing research for new products has suffered seriously from this bias for innovation; but this will be dealt with in Chapter 10 as part of the more general problem of the consumer's interest.

The psychological orientation is criticized because of its stress upon the individual instead of the group as the basic unit of analysis. The role of the group in shaping consumers' behavior is seen in the Cebu City study of "strength in weak ties." Some progress has been made toward understanding the role of groups, but not enough.

Conclusions on Diffusion

If the process approach to consumer behavior, with its emphasis on causality, is combined with the social-structure analysis of diffusion research, substantial progress in mapping relations seems to be possible. Social structure—interaction at any of the four levels—would operate on the model of consumer behavior by means of one or more of the three types of social influence: compliance, identification, and internalization. Compliance operates directly upon intention to

---

[29]Rogers, "New Product Adoption and Diffusion."
[30]G. Zaltman, "An Assessment of Diffusion Research in Marketing," in A. R. Andreasen and S. Sudman (eds.), *Public Policy and Marketing Thought*, American Marketing Associations, Chicago, Ill., 1976.

buy; identification affects interpersonal choice criteria; internalization operates like any normal information received from outside the social structure. Also, the individual differences which Rogers found that distinguish the early innovators from the late adopters can be introduced into the system of consumer behavior just as values were earlier, in Figure 8-1.

APPLICATION

Although social structure does have some influence in RRB, its effects are presumed to be small; to simplify, they will be ignored here. Social structure is considerably more influential in LPS than in RRB, and it is most influential in EPS; this discussion of application will therefore give most attention to EPS and as a result will be oriented toward top management and the long term.

Values and Higher Management

In the last decade, top management has become more and more concerned about the broader environment of the company and changes in people's values. This concern is relevant in setting corporate strategy, with its heavy emphasis on the probable future of its market. I. H. Wilson, of General Electric's Business Environmental Research operation, has said: "Identifying shifts in people's basic values is the single most important element in forecasting the environment in which organizations must operate in the future."[31] There are also new laws to be anticipated and dealt with, particularly regarding consumers. You will recall the quotation from Howard K. Smith, in Chapter 1, to the effect that the consumer will wield major power in the last third of the twentieth century.

To meet these needs, top management of a company often subscribes to commercial services which provide estimates of the current and future state of consumers' values. From this information, it tries to infer intuitively what changes in corporate strategy should be made. For example, one syndicated service establishes a trend and then proceeds to extrapolate from it. To simplify the analysis of data, respondents are put into the following five categories, the first three being "new values" and the last two, "old values":

The autonomous
New conformists
Forerunners
Traditionalists
Retreaters

By examining shifts in these categories over time, members of top management can presumably arrive at judgments about the direction of corporate strategy and the types of product development that should be undertaken; but the actual extent to which this sort of material is used is not known. A more explicit way to

---

[31]*Grey Matter,* **47**(1), 1976; Grey Advertising, New York.

relate data about values to consumer behavior has been suggested in Chapters 5, 6, and 8 to replace the current intuitive approach.

One of the major decisions a company will have to make is whether to attempt to change consumers' values. What we have seen of the influence of social structure suggests that such an attempt is fairly risky. Whether a company can accomplish it is doubtful. Although, as was noted earlier, salespersons in department stores can change the choice criteria emphasized by consumers, it is not certain that this involves changing even instrumental values. More likely, it was the choice criteria that changed. It must also be pointed out that changing values in a whole market would probably be far too expensive for any package goods. Finally, although expertise can be used to relate a brand and values—to build choice criteria—the low credibility that results from lack of trustworthiness suggests that a company probably would be unwise to attempt to change values. This is an open question, however.

Product Design

Planning a product for EPS requires long-term thinking. You will recall the example of instant coffee, which was introduced in the 1930s and exhibited absolute growth for more than twenty years. Production facilities for such a new product must also be planned over the long term.

Channel Design

A product in EPS requires careful attention to current and future marketing channels. For many companies, changing distribution channels is a slow, expensive process. If the company uses a wholesaler-retailer channel, for example, the acquisition of new channels means lengthy negotiating with many retail and wholesale units over a large area. Because a large investment and a long period of time are implied, long-term planning is essential.

As with establishing corporate strategy and product design, estimates of consumers' values several years hence are essential, even though these forecasts are subject to error.

Even if no change in channels is anticipated, a company will still want to know what the existing channels will be like ten and fifteen years in the future. Will in-home shopping (e.g., by telephone) be much more prevalent? If so, products which will be seen on a television screen must be designed differently from products which will be seen on a shelf in a store.

Design of Market Communication

By and large, market communication does not require the long-term planning that product design and channel design require. But major changes in communication technology are on the horizon; and some important changes, such as the increasing role of cable television and satellite television, are already under way.

Certain aspects of the social structure have an immediate relevance here. Most studies of the relationship of husband and wife as buyers were made by

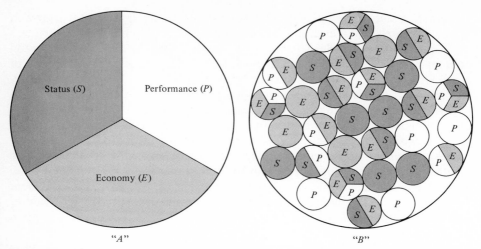

Figure 9-4 Hypothetical market segments for automobiles. (*H. L. Davis, "Decision Making within the Household," Project on Synthesis of Knowledge in Consumer Behavior, RANN Program, National Science Foundation, April 1975, unpublished.*)

companies in order to improve the targeting of marketing activities. The following points are particularly important:

1 Selecting the proper respondent in consumer research surveys.
2 Determining the content of advertising messages.
3 Selecting advertising media.
4 Guiding product designers to include features which appeal to those who are most influential in the purchase decision.
5 Assisting in the location of retail outlets.[32]

The significance of considering the family as the unit of purchasing can be illustrated with automobiles as in Figure 9-4. Status (*S*), economy (*E*), and performance (*P*) are the hypothetical choice criteria. In part *a* of Figure 9-4, we look at the market as individual behavior; there are three segments, each one preferring a particular characteristic. In part *b,* we look at the market as group behavior. For some percentage of households, the individual and group models of decision making are indistinguishable as far as goals are concerned; all three criteria are used. In the remaining households, however, members have differing goals; there can be disagreements between husband and wife about goals, and different decision strategies will be used. The effectiveness of advertising appeals, media, and even products is likely to differ among these different types of households.

CONCLUSIONS

Social structure consists of patterns of interaction. Social influence is transmitted mainly by word-of-mouth conversation. The hypothesis has been proposed that

[32]Davis, op. cit., p. 49.

it affects "information input" in the structure of consumer behavior shown in Figure 7-2. Consequently, it would be represented in the construct "information exposed." The usual content elements would be those affecting the brand concept. The source of the message is an important factor in word of mouth and would be treated as an element of the form of the message.

The nature of social structure is complex and not well understood,[33] but some encouraging progress has been made. A promising development seems to be the combination of systematic, causal process models developed for consumer behavior with the social-structure analysis of diffusion research supplemented by network analysis. This is even more promising if a further step is taken: adding the procedures for changing values.

Aside from its general influence on behavior and its implications for social policy, social structure has certain specific areas of application that are of immediate relevance in buying, such as the family and the formal organization (industrial buying).

Another area where the principles of social structure can be relevant is broad policy for society as a whole. For example, almost all countries experience inflation. Can social-structure analysis be used to develop social policies which will supplement fiscal and monetary policy in controlling inflation? Nicosia and Mayer raise this kind of question, in a more general way, for developing societies.[34] A particular kind of social policy that has become increasingly important in postindustrial society is the protection of consumers. For a number of reasons, protecting the consumer appears to have a higher priority in a postindustrial society characterized by private enterprise than in less developed societies. For a discussion of this, see Chapter 10.

QUESTIONS

1 List, describe, and explain the interaction of the elements of social structure.
2 What are the characteristics of values that cause them to be so central to the understanding of the influence of social structure upon consumers' behavior?
3 Describe the procedure for inducing changes in values.
4 Why has this chapter devoted so much attention to diffusion research when only a small proportion of this research deals with the marketing of new products?
5 What do we mean by "the strength in weak ties"? What is the significance of this notion?

SUGGESTIONS FOR FURTHER READING

D. B. Montgomery: "New Product Distribution: An Analysis of Supermarket Buyer Decisions," *Journal of Marketing Research,* **12**:255–264, August 1975.
T. S. Robertson: *Innovative Behavior and Communication,* Holt, Rinehart and Winston, New York, 1971.

[33]J. E. Stafford and A. B. Cocanougher, "Reference Group Theory," Project on Synthesis of Knowledge of Consumer Behavior, RANN Program, National Science Foundation, April 1975.
[34]Nicosia and Mayer, op. cit., pp. 3–4.

M. J. Ryan and E. H. Bonfield: "The Fishbein Extended Model and Consumer Behavior," *Journal of Consumer Research,* **21**:118–136, September 1975.

J. E. Stafford and A. B. Cocanougher: "Reference Group Theory," in R. Ferber (ed.), *A Synthesis of Selected Aspects of Consumer Behavior,* U.S. Government Printing Office for the National Science Foundation, in press.

Consumer Policy

CONTENTS

Up to this point we have assumed that our objective in learning about consumer behavior is to change buying—to make it different from what it would otherwise be. The question whether this objective is necessarily in the consumer's interest was not raised. Now, however, we must make the assumption that the consumer should not be manipulated. This view is sometimes called "macromarketing."

A number of institutions have evolved in our society to meet consumers' needs. One of these is the market. Jevons defined a market as "any body of persons who are in intimate business relations and carry an extensive transaction in any commodity."[1] But in most markets consumers are the weaker party because they are so numerous and lack access to information. Thus, there is concern for "protecting the consumer." Partly for this reason, other social institutions, such as those regulating markets, have evolved. Recommendations for change should be evaluated in the context of these existing institutions. Unfortunately, much of current research directed toward problems of consumers has been piecemeal. The purpose of this chapter is to review existing institutions and current policy, as a background for making recommendations for change. With a few explicit exceptions, we will deal here only with federal policy.

The statement by Howard K. Smith quoted in Chapter 1 deserves to be repeated here:

> The evolution of real power in this country in this century has a certain symmetry to it.
> The first third of the century we were ruled by our politicians chosen by Business. . . . In the second third, Business had to accept . . . Organized Labor as a counterforce in power. . . .
> In the final third, now, it seems clear that 200 millions in between, the broad public, [are] moving in. . . . [There is a need for] every President and Governor to have a consumer advocate on his staff.

[1]A. Gray, *The Development of Economic Doctrine,* Longmans Green, London, 1931, p. 341.

The implication of these remarks for us is that the design of consumer policy will be a continuing problem in the foreseeable future.

There has been much evidence of the consumer's coming to political power since truth-in-packaging in 1966, which was followed by truth-in-lending and a great variety of other regulatory innovations to protect the consumer: nutritional labeling, unit pricing, corrective advertising, comparative advertising, substantiation of advertising, etc. Nutritional labeling is a requirement by the Food and Drug Administration that the seller must tell the consumer the nutritional qualities of a product, in a certain standard format on the package. Unit pricing, a requirement in some states, requires the seller to specify the cost of a brand per unit weight or volume; this is intended to help the consumer make comparisons among brands. Substantiation of advertising is a requirement by the Federal Trade Commission that the seller must be able to support all advertising claims by objective data. Corrective advertising is another device to encourage truthful advertising; it requires the seller to say in future advertising that past advertising was untrue. Firestone Tire and Rubber Company, for example, was charged with failing to tell consumers that tires are not safe under all conditions. As a consequence, it has agreed to spend $750,000 to inform consumers that "no tires are safe under all conditions of use" and "proper tire safety depends upon the consumer taking specific steps."[2] Comparative advertising occurs when a seller's advertising compares the product explicitly with a competitor's product. Robert Pitofsky, Director, Bureau of Consumer Protection, Federal Trade Commission, has stated that comparative advertising, if it is truthful, not only is legal but is also in the consumer's interest.

All these devices were intended to better inform the consumer. But such new protective devices have been introduced hurriedly, and there has often been a tendency to ignore their cost. For example, a market research director for one of the large chemical companies told me that 80 percent of his budget is devoted to collecting information to show whether the company's advertisements are true. To say that cost is important is not to question the benefit of research; it is simply a matter of being rational. We must recognize that greater accuracy can be almost always obtained at greater cost, and try to determine the optimum balance.

The omission of cost is one of the largest problems in current "consumer policy." Such policy is built on a very special set of assumptions about how consumers respond to advertising and how consumers' behavior relates to competitive behavior and market structure. Unfortunately, these assumptions about consumer behavior have been implicit more often than they have been explicit; and this causes a variety of difficulties for both regulator and regulatee.

The Federal Trade Commission (FTC), as the chief source of federal consumer policy, seems to deal with most of the elements involved; consequently, the discussion here will be largely confined to the FTC. (However, the

[2]*Advertising Age,* February 23, 1976, p. 16.

FTC is not the sole source of federal consumer policy; the Attorney General's Office has much to do with antitrust, and the Food and Drug Administration deals with many issues of consumer protection.) Let us now examine FTC policy in order to gain perspective on the present and guidance for the future.

First, current policy will be briefly described; then it will be illustrated by a case of current interest involving breakfast cereal; then its evolution will be traced; finally, its consequences will be described.

BACKGROUND

Current Policy

Current policy is beginning to merge more traditional antitrust doctrine with consumer protection. Antitrust doctrine deals with the adequacy of consumers' *options;* consumer protection has to do with the adequacy of *information* available for choosing among those options. The three different views of the consumers' stages of decision—marketing, economics, and psychology—can be especially useful in considering this merger. Knowing the economists' viewpoint is essential here because, first, it provides a highly useful philosophic framework, and, second, lawyers working on regulations think like economists.

Until recently, antitrust activities and consumer protection have gone their separate ways. Increasingly, antitrust activities have had to do with prices and products; and antitrust doctrine has considered advertising as barring entry to markets, allowing higher prices, and encouraging trivial product competition. These are serious charges and should not be underestimated. Consumer protection has had to do with the informational role of advertising; specifically, doubts have been raised about whether advertising performs this role adequately.

The action taken by the FTC against the cereal industry, along with other cases and trade regulations, indicates the extent to which antitrust doctrine and consumer protection have now begun to merge. That the FTC's *intent* was to merge the two types of regulation in this instance is clearly suggested by the staff memorandum to the Commissioners which led to the citing of four cereal companies.[3] This memorandum goes to great lengths to show that the FTC—in contrast to its past history of taking action against predatory actions and other unlawful "conduct" by companies—is now paying attention to "product differentiation" as the source of industrial concentration "created and maintained by the advertising itself." The case of the cereal companies, as described in the complaint, will serve as an example of the principles of public policy and how they are administered; administration is sometimes just as important as principles.

Example: Cereal Companies The FTC has proposed that the cereal companies listed in Table 10-1 should be dissolved.[4] One of the charges given in support

[3]R. E. Wilson, "The FTC's Deconcentration Case against the Breakfast Cereal Industry: A New "Ballgame" in Antitrust?" *Antitrust Law and Economic Review,* 4:57–76, Summer 1971.
[4]Trade Regulation Reports, Commerce Clearing House, Inc. May 15, 1972, pp. 19898–19900.

Table 10-1   Cited Companies and Their Share of the Cereal Market

Company	Share as of 1970, percent
Kellogg	45
General Mills	21
General Foods	16
Quaker Oats	9
Total	91

of this action is that their advertising is excessive and untruthful. Ordinarily, dissolution is associated with conventional antitrust activities, and the charge of untruthfulness with consumer protection. The FTC holds in this case that excessive advertising is a barrier to entry into a market; the central role of excessive advertising has been further confirmed by the FTC staff economists since the case was initiated,[5] but there are differences of opinion within the FTC as to whether it has, in fact, acted as a barrier to entry. As far as the development of current policy is concerned, a more important charge is that advertising converts true product competition to trivial product competition, as is shown by the appearance of 120 new cereal products in the period from 1950 to 1970. There is also a question of how retail shelf space is allocated to the industry; but the nature of the arrangement, which is not well specified in the FTC complaint, is omitted from this exposition. Finally, the FTC complains that competitors have been bought up by the major companies over the thirty-year period—1940 to 1970—during which the industry's behavior was examined as the basis for the complaint. The FTC staff has proposed, specifically, that three new companies be made from Kellogg, that General Mills and General Foods each spin off one new company, and that Quaker Oats be left as is.[6]

Evolution of Policy

Understanding how current policy—a blend of antitrust measures and consumer protection—developed will help us estimate its consequences and predict its future direction. The current policy evolved when early, simplistic concepts of pure competition and monopoly were supplemented by a later, more realistic set of concepts called "market structure."

Pure Competition and Monopoly   Before 1930, the behavior of companies was considered mainly in terms of two concepts: pure competition and monopoly. "Pure competition" assumed that competitors were sufficiently numerous, and brands sufficiently alike, so that no one firm had control over the price of a

[5]*Advertising Age,* March 29, 1976, p. 3.
[6]*Advertising Age,* March 22, 1976, p. 1.

particular product class. "Monopoly" was the extreme opposite of pure competition; in a monopoly, one company sells an entire product class, so that it has control of price.

The task of serving the consumer was defined as maintaining competition. It was concluded that pure competition is good and monopoly is bad, and this bias has shaped consumer policy in the United States since the turn of the century. The implication for policy is that if an industry has departed from the model of pure competition and moved toward the model of monopoly, it should be forced to conform to the competitive model; dissolution is one way to achieve this end. When the degree of concentration in many industries is considered, however, the effort to achieve a purely competitive economy seems draconian. Even if such a goal is achievable, it might entail a degree of uncertainty among company decision makers that in itself would have highly undesirable results.[7]

There were at least two flaws in this early approach to providing consumers with adequate options. Lewis Engman, a former chairman of the FTC, phrased the first very well: "Because economic theory binds the means (structure of the market) and end (industrial performance) so tightly together into a causal relationship, we tend to measure only the causal factors, to focus on the means rather than the desired ends."[8] The significance of this simplification was that the goal became competition as such instead of the protection of the consumer. The second flaw was that additional theoretical market structures were needed to capture reality, since various states exist which fall between the two extremes of pure competition and monopoly.

Market-Structure Approach   These two flaws led to the development of the conventional market-structure approach, which, since 1950, has become the accepted doctrine of the FTC as well as the Attorney General's Office.

During the 1930s, Edward S. Mason and others added two key ideas to the established doctrine of regulation. First, they appropriated the notion of "monopolistic competition" from Chamberlin and Robinson and the notion of "oligopoly" from Cournot. On the basis of two dimensions—number of firms and degree of product differentiation among companies in an industry—five theoretical market structures were developed; these are shown in Table 10-2. These five structures were better able than the original two to encompass all possible competitive situations, particularly if some assumption was made about the buying side of the market (such as that competition existed among buyers).

Second, the notion of "workable competition" was introduced. This was perhaps most fully articulated by J. M. Clark:

> The main implication of a program of workable competition is to decide, on the basis of the specific information available for individual industries, what degree of competition is obtainable by methods of practical policy without substantial loss of techno-

---

[7]W. Fellner, *Competition among the Few,* Knopf, New York, 1949, pp. 288–291.

[8]Lewis Engman, before the Anti-Trust Section of the American Bar Association, Honolulu, August 14, 1974.

Table 10-2   Market Structures

	Many sellers	Few sellers	One seller
Undifferentiated product	Pure competition	Pure oligopoly	Monopoly
Differentiated product	Monopolistic competition	Differentiated oligopoly	Monopoly

Table 10-3   Analytic Framework of Modern Market-Structure Approach

Industry structure	Competitive behavior	Industry performance
Number of companies Degree of differentiation Barriers to entry	Dimensions of rivalry	Profit levels Progressiveness in cost reduction

logical efficiency at the time when the policy is adopted and does not presumably create a degree of uncertainty such as would offset the advantages.[9]

"Workable competition" provided an alternative to the older, more doctrinaire approach. It proposed that each industry be investigated, instead of maintaining that pure competition is necessarily good, that monopoly is necessarily bad, and that therefore the economy should be forced into the mold of pure competition.

The "market-structure economists"—or "industrial-organization economists," as they were often called—explicitly distinguished between structure of the market, competitive behavior, and market performance. Their basic assumption was that in a given industry structure led to certain competitive behavior, which in turn yielded a particular performance by that industry. Criteria were developed for applying each of these constructs to a particular industrial situation, as is illustrated in Table 10-3.

The structure was considerably elaborated by the inclusion of a number of other criteria, such as the nature of industry demand—expanding, stable, or contracting. This pragmatic view stimulated research projects which investigated a number of industries to test the validity of the market-structure concept. The structural view held substantial appeal for policy makers because it gave them a systematic rationale. It highlighted the possibility of taking action either (1) by changing the structure, and so changing behavior and improving performance, or (2) by acting directly upon behavior to improve performance.

Consequences of Policy

Let us examine the consequences of the policy for advertising (market information) that are implied by the case of the cereal companies. Traditionally, market information has not been considered in the market-structure approach. Since

[9]Fellner, op. cit., pp. 289–290.

1966, however, information has become the most important element of consumer protection. In this case, we see the first attempt to integrate the consumer's informational requirements into the modern market-structure view.

If the format of market structure is used, the analysis shown in Figure 10-1 seems implicit in the FTC's complaint. The logic is as follows. Concentrated structure is shown in the large market shares of the four companies, especially that of Kellogg. This concentration is a result of advertising, which acts as a barrier to entry—that is, prevents other companies from entering the market. This permits the existing companies to compete on dimensions other than price: advertising and change in the product. "Rivalry" on price is replaced by rivalry on less important dimensions, presumably supported by action in concert to avoid price competition in some unspecified way. Curiously, no explicit analysis is made as to why, in the presence of a furious pace of product innovation, no new firms and no private brands have penetrated the industry to any extent. Advertising is viewed as a particularly strong barrier to entry in this case, because it is untruthful, is directed to children (who are less discriminating than adults), and permits companies to compete on trivial instead of desirable changes in the product. The protection from competition afforded by this concentrated structure and by advertising as a barrier to entry in turn leads to excessive profits: a ten-year average of more than 20 percent after taxes on stockholders' equity. The FTC's proposed answer to this bad performance is to dissolve the companies.

An examination of this analysis raises the question whether the competitive behavioral theory implied under "competitive behavior" is truly descriptive of what goes on in the marketplace. For example, does heavy advertising necessarily lead to triviality in product development? Is this theory, which is largely implicit, a valid theory?

Furthermore, given our understanding of the consumer's capacity to acquire and process information, we may become skeptical about the nature of consumer theory implied in the analysis. Is advertising so powerful in shaping choice that it can block the market to competition and succeed in getting consumers to accept trivial new products?

If these two questions are answered negatively, will dissolution—change in structure—necessarily make a difference in behavior so as to achieve better performance for the consumer?

Summary: Current Policy

Historically, there have been two disparate elements in our national consumer policy: (1) Antitrust measures are intended to provide the consumers with adequate options in terms of price, quality, and number of products. (2) Consumer protection is intended to provide the consumer with adequate information for judging these options.

These two elements are now being merged, as is seen in the case of the cereal companies (Figure 10-1). Advertising is seen as a structural characteristic because it was viewed as a barrier to entry; informational criteria—truthfulness and the existence of children as an audience—are included as performance

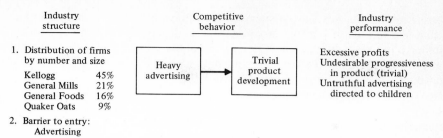

Figure 10-1   Market-structure analysis applied to cereals.

criteria. There seem to be two flaws in this case. First, companies do not necessarily compete only on trivial dimensions of a product as a result of advertising. Second, consumers are not so strongly tied to a company by advertising that it can be used as a barrier to entry, if we assume that parents buy with the welfare of their children in mind.

NEW DIRECTION OF POLICY

The two flaws in the underpinnings of current policy are an inadequate theory of competitive behavior and an inadequate theory of consumer behavior. I believe that they suggest directions for the development of new policy, similar to what occurred in an earlier period of our regulatory history. I suspect that in time these changes will in fact occur. The following sections indicate probable directions of change: first, in the theory of competitive behavior; and second, in the theory of consumer behavior.

Competitive Behavior: Supply

Schumpeter provides a model which appears to capture most of the essential ideas in the case of the cereal companies; thus it can represent much of heavy-advertising industry.[10] His basic idea is that innovation, especially product innovation, is a driving force in competition and also serves as the central element generating both the business cycle and economic development. Our interest here is only in its role in competition.

Product Innovation   When a company creates a "new commodity"—in our terms, a new product class—it must advertise heavily and engage actively in other promotions to get this radically new product accepted. As Schumpeter puts it: "The great majority of changes in commodities consumed have been forced by producers on consumers, who, more often than not, have resisted the change and have had to be educated up by elaborate psychotechnics of advertising."[11] An illustration of such innovation is instant coffee in 1949, when Mason Haire did his classic study indicating that some consumers felt that a homemaker who

[10]J. A. Schumpeter, *Business Cycles,* vol. 1, McGraw-Hill, New York, 1939.
[11]P. 87.

bought instant coffee was lazy, a spendthrift, a poor planner, and a bad wife—ideas that had to change before Nescafe could be accepted. Most new products are similarly initiated. Not all the 120 new products introduced into the cereal market between 1950 and 1970 by the four companies in Table 10-1 represented new product classes, but very probably some did.

Next, in order to compete effectively with the innovator, other companies each offer an improved product. As a result, innovations cluster in the industry, and consumers respond by changing their buying habits.

Thus, innovation and imitation of the innovator both impart a healthy dynamism to market behavior. The current market-structure view neglects this dynamism.

Product Life Cycle   By using the concept of the product life cycle we can elaborate Schumpeter's ideas. Let us use as an example the product life cycle for instant coffee shown in Figure 10-2.

The concept of the product life cycle (PLC) postulates four more or less distinct stages in the life of a product class: introduction, growth, maturity, and decline. The concept has often been criticized; but criticism falls on the fourth stage, and indeed the evidence suggests that the fourth stage is the least dependable, although a product often declines as in Figure 10-2.[12] The nature of the fourth stage is not crucial to the argument here and will not be discussed further. We could use the term "product growth curve"; but "product life cycle" has much greater currency, and a firm psychological and sociological foundation exists for it, as was seen in earlier chapters.

Schumpeter was probably not familiar with the PLC, but his ideas are consistent with it. His "new commodity" is the first brand in a new product class, as Nescafe was in the late 1930s. This is the introduction. Acceptance of this radically new product comes slowly, as the company learns to market it. Soon other companies begin to follow, each trying to introduce a superior product, not too different from the first but different enough. This is the period of growth. Finally, market saturation is achieved, and the stage of maturity is reached.

This model of competitive behavior is on the supply side of the market. We must now turn to the demand side of the market, where the second flaw in current market-structure theory appears. Unfortunately, Schumpeter dealt systematically only with supply.

Consumer Behavior: Demand

Economic Theory   The lack of a theory of consumer behavior in the current market-structure approach should not be surprising, because the market-structure approach evolved out of economics.

---

[12]M. B. Holbrook and J. A. Howard, "Consumer Research on Frequently Purchased Nondurable Goods and Services: A Review," Project on Synthesis of Knowledge of Consumer Behavior, RANN Program, National Science Foundation, April 1975, pp. 68–69.

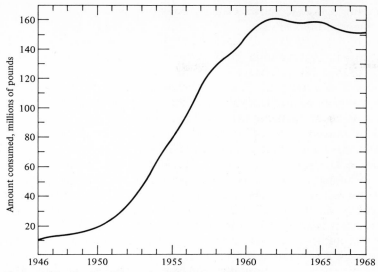

Figure 10-2 Product life cycle of instant coffee.

One of the leading economists of consumer demand, Kelvin Lancaster, has recently summarized the state of the field as follows:

> The economist's theory of consumer choice is built on the concept of the preferences of the individual and devotes great attention to the study of the presumed structure of these preferences. Are preferences innate? Are they entirely due to social conditioning? Can they be influenced by advertising or propaganda? Do individuals know their "real" preferences, or do they have to learn what they are from experience? How stable are these preferences? Do behavioral changes due to major environmental changes represent a shift in preferences or an adjustment within a grand pattern of preference? In spite of the crucial role of preference in economic theory, economists have no real answers to questions such as these, and generally speaking do not even ask them within the ordinary context of economic theory.[13]

Lancaster emphasizes that economists must understand how these preferences are formed in order to deal with many important problems. He also notes that the assumption of "separability"—the assumption that consumers can form a prod-uct-class concept—deserves much more attention than it has received.

In recent years, a few economists have attempted to develop a better understanding of the role of advertising in consumer behavior—for example, Comanor and Wilson, Grabowski, and Schmalensee.[14] Nelson has also made

[13]K. Lancaster, "Theories of Consumer Choice from Economics: A Critical Survey," Project on Synthesis of Knowledge of Consumer Behavior, RANN Program, National Science Foundation, April 1975, p. 50.

[14]S. F. Divita, *Advertising and the Public Interest,* American Marketing Association, Chicago, Ill., 1973.

progress.[15] Lancaster's review shows clearly, however, that there is no adequate economic theory in this area.

Marketing Theory   A substantial body of theory about consumer behavior has begun to emerge in marketing, as we have seen. A useful starting point is our familiar stages of decision: routinized response behavior (RRB), limited problem solving (LPS), and extensive problem solving (EPS).[16] As was noted repeatedly in earlier chapters, each of the stages of decision can be related to a stage of the product life cycle. Let us use this background on consumer behavior to fill in the demand side of the economic process represented in the product life cycle.

To facilitate the exposition, Figure 6-1 is repeated as Figure 10-3. When a new product representing a new product class like Nescafe in the late 1930s is introduced to the market, all consumers are obviously in EPS. They have seen nothing like the new product, and their information requirements are very heavy; the information content is specified at the lower left of Figure 10-3.

We know from diffusion studies (discussed in Chapter 9) that some consumers quickly accept a new product. Consequently, Figure 10-3 shows that in the early stages of the cycle most consumers will be in EPS; a few will be in LPS; and perhaps a very few will quickly become loyal to the first new brand and will thus be in RRB. This distribution is indicated at the lower left of the top half of Figure 10-3; it is the introduction stage of the cycle.

As more new brands appear—as happened with instant coffee in the 1950s—more and more of the consumers become familiar with some brand in the product class, and so fewer and fewer are in EPS. This is the growth stage. The distribution shown in the middle of the curve reflects this. Most consumers are in LPS, with some moving into RRB as they become loyal buyers. Information requirements are much less, as is shown; the content is specified in the lower middle of Figure 10-3.

Finally, there is the maturity stage, where almost all consumers are familiar with the class and most brands in it. As the distribution indicates, almost no consumers are in EPS; not many are in LPS; and most are in RRB. Information requirements are small, as is seen at the lower right of Figure 10-2, where the content is specified.

Having examined both sides of the product life cycle—supply and demand—separately, let us put them together. We now examine market behavior.

Market Behavior

At the bottom of Figure 10-3—EPS—we would expect Nestle to advertise heavily to meet the needs of the market. Consumers have much to learn about

[15]Phillip Nelson, "Information and Consumer Behavior," *Journal of Political Economy,* 78:311–329, 1970; "Advertising as Information," *Journal of Political Economy* 8:729–754, July–August 1974; "Consumer Information and Advertising," Economic Growth Institute, State University of New York, Binghamton, N.Y., January 1975.

[16]J. A. Howard and J. N. Sheth, *The Theory of Buyer Behavior,* Wiley, New York, 1969.

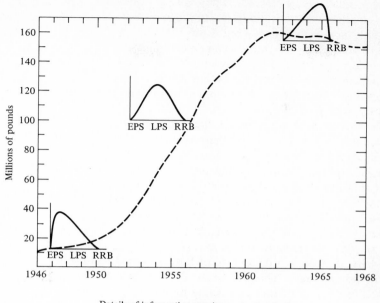

Details of information requirements at each stage

Product class choice

EPS

Terminal values	Choice criteria for product class	Salience of criteria	Beliefs about product class	Contribution
═══	═══	═══		
Attitude toward product class				

Brand choice

EPS

Instrumental values	Choice criteria for brand	Salience of criteria	Beliefs about brand	Contribution
═══				
Attitude toward brand				

LPS

Choice criteria for brand	Salience of choice criteria	Beliefs about brand	Contribution
═══	═══		
Attitude toward brand			

RRB

Choice criteria	
Brand concept	Nescafe
Impersonal criteria Availability Price	Yes No
Attitude toward brand	

Figure 10-3 Changing information requirements over the PLC.

this new product called Nescafe. They not only don't know how good it is; they don't even know what criteria to use to judge it. Not much empirical information is available about this stage; but Lutz offers some evidence that it is more difficult to change the weighting of a choice criterion than to change position on a choice criterion (attitude).[17] Many consumers will take some time to make up their minds to try a new product; in this instance, regular coffee has been doing a fairly good job for them, and they have many habits, including social relations, associated with it.

In the absence of mass media, the social structure must serve to diffuse a new product. As was seen in Chapter 9, heterophilous dyadic relations are essential to change and homophilous dyadic relations discourage it. Consequently, if communication is relegated to the social structure, diffusion will probably be slowed down substantially. As Schumpeter noted almost forty years ago, "psychotechnics of advertising" will be necessary to educate consumers.

Also, it will be necessary for the message to contain a great amount of redundancy because consumers lack the structure that would facilitate the receipt of meaning through attention and search (see Chapter 7).

Finally, if the new product is to be fully accepted, some change in values will probably be required. This evidently did occur with instant coffee, as was discussed in Chapter 9. But we assume that a company probably cannot change values by means of advertising, one reason being that its credibility is low. Thus, the need for a change in values will also act to retard diffusion.

As Schumpeter noted, other new brands will next begin to be introduced, and each new competitor will contribute to educating the market. Thus, the growth stage of Figure 10-3 develops. The appearance of still more new brands, with their own improvements—some of which may be trivial and fail—will stimulate the growth of the product. Consumers are now in LPS, and they respond more quickly. They have criteria by which to judge any new brand and therefore require less information: they can simply place a new brand on these well-established criteria.

Eventually, everyone will know about the new product: with Nescafe, this happened in the late 1950s, as Figure 10-3 indicates. Each consumer will have decided to use instant coffee, regular coffee, or neither. This is the maturity stage. Profits are still high, partly because of accounting arrangements. Earlier costs of development and introduction were written off against current operations; accountants believe that this is the correct procedure. As a consequence, however, current profits were then understated and are now being overstated. Although this procedure can mislead investigators for the Federal Trade Commission, it does not mislead potential introducers of new products, who decide that the future is not hopeful in the industry. This marks the end of the introduction of new products. Even improvements in products become minor; some would call them "trivial." As profits decline, companies that already have a product in

---

[17]R. J. Lutz, "Changing Brand Attitudes Through Modification of Cognitive Structure," *Journal of Consumer Research*, 1:49–59, March 1975.

the market will continue to advertise, but will probably reduce advertising, hoping to find a special segment which responds particularly well to their offering and which may be relatively inexpensive to reach if promotion and advertising media are judiciously chosen.

If profits seem to be excessive before this stage is reached, a part of the excess may be illusory and due to accounting procedures which fail to allocate costs in the appropriate time periods. Also, in the case of the cereal companies, if many of the 120 new products represented new product classes, we would expect an above-average rate of return in the industry as the product threw off rewards for successful innovation.

MARKET STRUCTURE VERSUS MODIFIED MARKET STRUCTURE

The picture of competitive behavior and consumer behavior that emerges as "market behavior" when more realistic models are introduced contrasts significantly with the picture implied in the case of the cereal companies, especially as regards advertising. Let us call this new picture "modified market structure." Using modified market structure, we can generalize from the case of the cereal companies to a wider range of situations.

Product Competition

Instead of lumping 120 new products together and labeling them "trivial product competition," as the FTC did, we should examine each one separately to determine which, if any, were the first products in a new product class (EPS) and which were imitative new products with improvements (LPS). If none of the new products was an EPS product, we would be seriously concerned. For those that were LPS products (a classification that could be verified by analysis of brand switching), we would carefully examine each brand as it appeared. The question would be: In what way is this an improvement over previous brands in the class? It is essential to bear in mind that in the stage of growth or product improvement (LPS), major changes in the product are not essential to benefit consumers; there need only be enough change to shift some consumers from one brand to another. These may make the market sufficiently dynamic. In the case of the cereal companies, this type of systematic analysis would probably reveal that some of the product changes were not as trivial as they appeared to be when all 120 products were lumped together.

We would also want to examine the advertising for each new brand to find out what attributes were considered relevant to consumers. We would expect different copy points for the EPS and the LPS products: in EPS, basic values would be stressed; in LPS, the stress would be on more immediate criteria.

Under current public policy, where product safety is concerned, competitive behavior is subject to direct regulation rather than the regulation represented by changing the structure. When consumers are not perfectly informed—which is particularly likely to be the case with infrequently purchased products such as durables—Gresham's law can operate: bad products can drive out good products. Recent changes in federal policy regarding product safety have had a profound impact upon some industries.

Advertising

It is useful to distinguish advertising as a barrier to entry from advertising as a source of information. The former aspect represents structure; the latter, competitive behavior with implications regarding performance.

Structure: Advertising as a Barrier to Entry For products in EPS, we would expect heavy advertising, although the same amount of advertising would be considered excessive for products in RRB. As was already indicated, consumers in EPS must both form new choice criteria and place the brand on these criteria. Thus substantially more information is required in EPS than in RRB. Furthermore, the social structure hinders rapid diffusion of a new product, especially where a change in values is involved. Finally, redundancy in advertising is essential because the buyer lacks a structure to guide attention and search.

Even in the stage of maturity we should not be surprised to find a considerable amount of advertising. Companies are searching for market segments that can protect them from sharp price competition in a dynamic market. Also, there will not necessarily be precise changes in the level of advertising over the product life cycle, because it may not be possible to know exactly where a product class is in the cycle. We cannot use a company's actual advertising as indicative of what would have been optimum; each company's knowledge of the effects of advertising is so limited that the "right amount" is unknown, although brand awareness is one measure of success.

Instead of viewing advertising as a barrier to entry, we might consider it *essential* to entry because without advertising the time required to introduce even a really superior product would probably be unprofitably long. If the introduction took extremely long, retailers would conclude that the product was a failure and remove it from their shelves.

This conclusion, however, is applicable only as regards the FTC's charge that advertising has the power to tie consumers to the seller. It is also possible that economies of scale exist in advertising; if so, these could be a barrier to entry. To correct a flaw in the original notion of market structure, the concept of "workable competition" was introduced. Under this concept, each industry would be investigated to determine what degree of competition might be possible without "substantial loss of technological efficiency." The idea is that in some industries the large firm has a cost advantage. Usually, such economy of scale is thought of only in terms of production; but economies of scale can apply just as well to the marketing side—particularly to advertising, where highly specialized skills are required. There is some evidence that economies of scale do exist in the use of media,[18] but economies of scale in marketing are not a well-explored area.

[18]M. E. Porter, "Interbrand Choice, Media Mix and Market Performance," *American Economic Review Supplement,* **66**:398–406, May 1976.

Performance: Informational Criteria Informational criteria should be added to the specifically consumer-oriented criteria introduced in the case of the cereal companies. In assessing the performance of an industry, these criteria supplement the traditional criteria: level of profits and progressiveness. With respect to the cereal companies, truthfulness and the use of children as a market segment were introduced as criteria. The term "vulnerable segments" would be more general than "children"; it could refer to any group whose capacity to handle information may be deficient—such as the very poor. Three additional informational criteria should, in principle, be added: relevance, clarity, and timeliness.[19] The qualification "in principle" is important; in our current state of knowledge of advertising, these criteria might be damaging if applied rigorously.

Truthfulness This criterion for evaluating information is not as simple as it might seem. Not only should information be objectively true, but the consumers should believe that it is true.

It is not easy to ensure objective truth, especially in EPS, where the consumer typically lacks a satisfactory frame of reference for dealing with information. A long exposition may be necessary; yet the consumer cannot handle information on a new subject rapidly: five to ten seconds are needed to store a piece of information in LTM. It is costly to substantiate advertising, but this seems to be a necessary policy: when consumers are not well informed, untruthful advertising can probably drive out truthful advertising. Some punishment for untruthful advertising also seems to be necessary; corrective advertising is one possible way of enforcing truthfulness.

Even if advertising is objectively true, it may still not be credible to consumers. Consumers may not trust advertising and rely more on word of mouth from friends (see Chapter 9). But distrust of advertising probably springs from experience with advertising in the past; to the extent that future advertisements are truthful, distrust may well disappear. Moreover, as regards word of mouth, there can always be doubt about the competence of the source.

LPS poses less serious problems, because the consumers have a frame of reference which gives them confidence in evaluating the truthfulness of information. Truthfulness is more obvious; accordingly, comparative advertising is probably helpful in LPS. The frequency of comparative advertising has increased, but companies and advertising agencies disagree on whether it is a desirable practice.

In RRB, truth is most obvious. A price, say, either is or is not 39¢. Here, untruthful but credible advertising can be especially damaging to the consumer. Repeat purchasing should act as a check, of course; but unfortunately many products—especially consumer durables—are purchased infrequently.

Finally, as far as truthfulness is concerned, it does not seem that the size of a company is relevant. Dissolution, then, would not be a remedy for untruthful advertising. Direct action on competitive behavior may be a solution—for example, the substantiation of advertising.

[19]J. A. Howard and J. Hulbert, *Advertising and the Public Interest,* Crain Communication, Inc., Chicago, Ill., 1973, chap. 8.

Vulnerable segments   Certain special segments of the population may be unable to process information critically. In the case of the cereal companies it is alleged that children are particularly misled by advertising. The poor are often said to be misled. Facts about the extent of these deficiencies in society are sparse; but to the extent to which they do exist, they should be given special consideration in evaluating the informational aspects of the marketing activity of each company which sells to them.

Relevance   Relevance has to do with the content of the message, in contrast to its form. If consumers are in EPS, does the message tell them by which criteria the product can be evaluated and which instrumental values these criteria serve? If so, does establishing this connection in a consumer's mind represent undue influence? This raises another question, a technical one: Can an advertiser have this much influence? It may be that consumers are perfectly willing to accept the advertiser's information as regards the positions of the brand on given criteria, but not to change their criteria. Some evidence, cited earlier, indicates that it is more difficult for advertising to change criteria than to change positions on criteria.

If the advertiser can change criteria, what can be said about the situation—common in EPS—where instrumental values themselves will have to be changed? Schumpeter said: "The great majority of changes in commodities consumed have been forced by producers on consumers who, more often than not, have resisted the change and have had to be educated up by elaborate psychotechnics of advertising."[20] It has already been noted that, in the case of instant coffee, Webster and Von Pechman's replication of Haire's study suggested that consumers' values had to change before instant coffee could be fully accepted.

Policy in this area is very unclear. In the past, the issues have not been articulated; but Chapter 5 enables us to do this now. We have assumed that companies cannot change consumers' values. The evidence is highly inadequate, however; and the attempt to change values is one of the most seriously criticized aspects of advertising.

In discussing the power of advertising for brands, McGuire notes that he is not concerned about advertising per se, but rather is worried about the *unintended* effects of mass media, including advertising. To illustrate, he considers the possible effect of television on violence, and from his review of the Surgeon General's study concludes: "My judgment is that the effect is statistically significant, and television contributes a small but unignorable portion of public mayhem."[21]

Another example of this problem can be found in nutritional advertising, although it does not seem to have been recognized as such. The staff of the

[20]Schumpeter, op. cit., p. 87.
[21]W. J. McGuire, "Psychological Factors Influencing Consumer Choice," Project on Synthesis of Knowledge of Consumer Behavior, RANN Program, National Science Foundation, April 1975, p. 26.

Federal Trade Commission recommended that when the food industry advertised the nutritional characteristics of its products, it should be required to give
the nutritional details now specified by the Food and Drug Administration for
labels falling under its jurisdiction.[22] One reason for this proposal was to force
the industry to educate consumers about nutrition. This would, in my opinion,
require a change in some of the instrumental values of a large proportion of
consumers. Thus, industry was being asked to do something for which it has
traditionally been seriously criticized. After more than a year of informal discussion and debate, there is now some tentative agreement on "a large-scale
industry-supported nutritional education effort utilizing the full resources of the
media."[23] In my judgment, individual companies probably cannot accomplish
this task, nor should they be permitted to try—this would entail undue use of
power by private parties. A group effort by the industry as a whole could be
justified, if representatives of the public were included in the design and administration of the program.

When we turn to LPS, the issues are clearer. The consumer needs information to form a brand concept: brand identification, attitude, and confidence. In
principle, the content of these has been specified; see especially Chapter 3.
Although application is not so easy, the guidelines are clear.

Relevant information in RRB, as we saw in Chapter 2, is probably easiest to
deal with. Informational requirements have to do with such matters as price and
availability; these are easy to identify and not particularly difficult to communicate. The structure of the relevant market is different here, however; local retail
markets are involved, and at this level information skills are often scarcer than at
the manufacturing level. Small independent retail stores, for example, may not
be able to afford expensive advertising talent.

Clarity Obviously, a message must be clear if the consumer is to grasp it
easily and quickly. Here we are concerned with the form of the message, not its
content; and not so much with physical form (although smudged print, for
example, could be a problem) as with more subtle elements of form. It was
repeatedly noted in earlier chapters that language, memory, and inference impose
special conditions on the form of a message, especially in EPS. For instance, a
"kernel sentence" communicates more quickly and easily than a complex,
negative, passive, or interrogative sentence. Also, short-term memory and long-
term memory require real time to operate; if the flow of information is speeded up,
the message will be less clear. As regards inference, perhaps the most important
consideration is the level of abstraction at which the message is written.

As far as clarity was concerned, the advertising of the cereal companies was
probably fairly good; copywriters seem to handle this intuitively in a sophisticated market. Nutritional advertising, however, is an example of a much more
complex situation, since it seems to involve changes in values. Bettman has

---

[22]Federal Trade Commission, *Food Advertising,* Washington, D.C., **39**(218), part II, November
11, 1974.

[23]*Advertising Age,* March 22, 1976, pp. 34, 36.

proposed that in addition to television advertisements, a format similar to the one presented for unit pricing in Chapter 4 (Table 4-1) might be used in retail stores—that is, at the point of purchase.[24] Television could be used to emphasize the benefits of nutrition and to direct consumers to the in-store displays of information which would show nutritional benefits across brands. This approach would substantially lighten the burden of processing information by making it possible for the consumer to bypass long-term memory, as we saw in Chapter 4. I suspect that a great variety of social institutions may have to be enlisted to accomplish the large task of nutritional education.

This brings up the matter of cost. There is a cost attached to providing information which is too often ignored but which should always be weighed against the benefit of the information in deciding what should be provided and who can best provide it. A cost-benefit analysis becomes especially difficult when it is found that only some consumers will benefit; in the case of unit pricing, for example, only one-third of the consumers benefited.[25] Of course, the direct benefit to those affected should be considered; and it should also be borne in mind that even a few may have a leverage effect on the market that helps to make it somewhat self-adjusting. By responding to the better-informed behavior of these few, sellers can benefit the market as a whole.

Timeliness Ideally, consumers are exposed to information only when they need it. Otherwise, the burden on their memory becomes increasingly heavy. (Probably the cereal industry would measure up relatively well on this criterion.) Also ideally, the information would appear at the point of purchase; but because the time spent by consumers in retail stores is valuable, advertising received on television at home is probably more convenient.

Applying informational criteria Information given to consumers is almost universally viewed as desirable in the abstract, but in practice it might be too much of a good thing. The burden of information processing which gives rise to cognitive strain has been emphasized repeatedly. Several experiments under the rubric of "information overload" have been done by Jacoby and others.[26] but firm conclusions about overload in a buying situation are not yet possible.

The benefits of information are also difficult to calculate, not only because these are different for different people, but also because the value of information is probably not well recognized by the recipient. Indeed, the consumer is often unconscious of using it. Even information of which one is conscious is typically a

[24]J. R. Bettman, "Issues in Designing Consumer Information Environments," *Journal of Consumer Research,* 2:169–177, December 1975.

[25]J. M. Carman, "A Summary of Empirical Research on Unit Pricing in Supermarkets," *Journal of Retailing,* 48:63–71, Winter 1972–1973.

[26]J. Jacoby, D. E. Speller, and C. A. Kohn, "Brand Choice Behavior as a Function of Information Overload: Replication and Extension." *Journal of Consumer Research,* 1:33–42, June 1974; J. E. Russo, "More Information Is Better: A Reevaluation of Jacoby, Speller and Kohn," Journal of Consumer Research, 1:68–72, December 1974; J. Jacoby, D. E. Speller, and C. A. K. Berning, "Constructive Criticism and Programmatic Research: Reply to Russo," *Journal of Consumer Research,* 2:154–156, September 1975.

discounted future benefit. For example, if you buy information you pay for it now but use it only in the future, when it is worth less.

CONCLUSIONS: MODIFIED MARKET STRUCTURE

The modified market structure not only provides an approach which includes structure, competitive behavior, and performance; it also implies a fundamental framework for rationally evaluating alternatives in consumer policy. This rational approach seems even more important when we consider the complicated institutional setting within which policy is formulated.

Often, large companies, organized in industrial trade associations, are advancing one view—a view that will best serve the stockholders' interests, of which they are the trustees. Consumer advocates, sometimes self-appointed but effective (such as Ralph Nader) but more often organized in local and national organizations, advance another view. Emotions run high, because beliefs about rightness and justice are involved. The consumerist advocates are usually less well organized than industry and have fewer resources, but they are attentively listened to by Congress and regulatory agencies. The rational framework of the modified market structure forces all participants to at least give lip service to a common goal: the efficient allocation of resources. If permitted to follow this goal, a regulatory agency can plan ahead and deal with those cases which will contribute most to an overall consumer policy that will best serve the consumers' interests. Without an overall goal, and in the face of strong pressures from industry and consumers' representatives, the regulatory agency must descend to the political level—winning cases only against conspicuous offenders and so gaining attention and justifying its budget. When this happens, the consumers' interests are served by accident, not by design; and in fact, the chances are slight that their interests will be served at all.

A goal also requires that proposals for providing adequate information to consumers will be evaluated not only in terms of their benefit to the consumers but also in terms of their cost. In addition to the cost-benefit principle, there is an "opportunity cost" principle, according to which a benefit should at least be greater than the most productive alternative use of the resources involved. Estimates of benefits to the consumer are badly needed because, as we have seen, economics does not provide the concepts for evaluating the effects of information. At the same time, the cost of providing information must be estimated. Approaching the issue in terms of "information overload," however, implies that information is cost-free: the only limit on providing information is that it must stop short of having a negative effect on the consumer. If the cost-benefit principle is used, one will always stop short of having no effect.

In summary, this chapter has merged economic and behavioral views. Economics provides an overall framework for thinking about problems of informing consumers in terms of costs and benefits. Behavioral science must show how much benefit will be obtained by the expenditure of how many resources. It must also specify the content and form dimensions of that information.

QUESTIONS

1 In terms of the consumer's interest, what is the goal of antitrust measures? What is the goal of consumer protection?
2 What were the inadequacies of the older market-structure view as regards antitrust doctrine?
3 What are the inadequacies of the current market-structure view for evaluating an industry's performance in terms of the consumer's interest?
4 Describe Schumpeter's theory of innovation.
5 Why should the marketing manager, the brand manager, or both be concerned with consumer policy and its rationale?

SUGGESTIONS FOR FURTHER READING

J. R. Bettman: "Issues in Designing Consumer Information Environments," *Journal of Consumer Research,* **21**:169–177, December 1975.
W. L. Wilkie: *Public Policy and Product Information: Summary Findings from Consumer Research* (NSF Report), U.S. Government Printing Office, Washington, D.C., 1975.

Conclusions to Part One

CONTENTS

The purpose of Part One has been to present a consistent point of view to facilitate application. At the end of each chapter, there has been a section on how the principles presented could be applied to real problems. These discussions were brief rather than exhaustive, because their purpose was simply to introduce problems, not to analyze them fully.

Principles are useful when applied only if the theory upon which they rest is a reasonable representation of how consumers behave. The theory and its application have been separated because in order to apply the theory, one must know it well. We must now consider whether the system described here captures relevant features of consumer behavior in most buying situations and yet is not so complex that it cannot be manipulated by the normal human mind.

TWO BENCHMARKS

For some readers, this chapter is the end of the book; for others, it is a way station. For both, it provides an opportunity to review our understanding of consumer behavior. But instead of merely reviewing the material covered so far, let us consider two external sources which will give us a more objective and broader view of where we are. First, we will compare the presentation of this book with the earlier works out of which it grew. Second, we will examine Wind's prediction about the future direction of research in this field. These two sources can be considered as benchmarks.

Blackwell's and Sheth's Reviews of Earlier Work

Each development in the field of consumer behavior—as in science generally— builds upon earlier work. This book can be compared with three earlier works out of which it developed: Howard, *Marketing Management* (first and second editions); Howard, *Marketing: Executive and Buyer Behavior;* and Howard and Sheth, *The Theory of Consumer Behavior.*[1] The comparison will give us a sense of where we now stand. Fortunately, there are two well-informed, objective reviews of this earlier work: one by Blackwell[2] and one by Sheth;[3] and, also fortunately, both use as a framework for analysis Zaltman, Pinson, and Angelmar's approach to evaluating theories, which gives the two evaluations a common focus.[4] Each criticism by Blackwell and Sheth will be examined in light of the structure proposed in this book; but it should be noted that the comments pertaining to modeling are dealt with more thoroughly in Chapter 15, after the discussion of modeling.

One of Blackwell's criticisms had to do with linguistic inexactness in the original theory: specifically, Blackwell found that the construct "perceptual bias" was not well defined. In reformulating the theory in terms of information processing centered in short-term memory, I found it was possible to eliminate

[1]J. A. Howard, *Marketing Management,* Irwin, Homewood, Ill., 1957, chap. 5; J. A. Howard, *Marketing Management,* 2d ed., Irwin, Homewood, Ill., 1963, chap. 3; J. A. Howard, *Marketing: Executive and Buyer Behavior,* Columbia University Press, New York, 1963; J. A. Howard and J. N. Sheth, *The Theory of Consumer Behavior,* Wiley, New York, 1969.

[2]R. D. Blackwell, " John Howard and Marketing Theory and Metatheory," in A. R. Andreasen and S. Sudman (eds.), *Public Policy and Marketing Thought,* American Marketing Association, Chicago, Ill., in press.

[3]J. N. Sheth, "Howard's Contribution to Marketing: Some Thoughts," in A. R. Andreasen and S. Sudman (eds.), *Public Policy and Marketing Thought,* American Marketing Association, Chicago, Ill., in press.

[4]G. Zaltman, C. R. A. Pinson, and R. Angelmar, *Metatheory and Consumer Research,* Holt, Rinehart and Winston, New York, 1973.

perceptual bias by elaborating upon the "coding" process that generates information inside a consumer's mind. Short-term memory—which largely replaces perceptual bias—can be indirectly operationalized, even in the field, by means of individual differences (as was seen in Chapter 8). Although Blackwell did not mention it, the failure to define "information" more carefully in the earlier work was also an instance of linguistic inexactness. The concept of "structure of information" has been developed here both to provide linguistic exactness and to measure information objectively.

Blackwell also noted that the distinction between "exogenous" and "endogenous" variables was not clear-cut. This lack of precision arose because the earlier work contained no theory of exogenous variables; the choice among exogenous variables was largely empirical. In this book, the stage has been set for the development of a theory of individual differences (in Chapter 8), but we are still some distance from a well-articulated rationale for individual differences.

Finally, Professor Blackwell questioned whether the earlier theory could be translated into workable relationships that would be testable and simple to apply. The problem of testability can be presented as follows: Is the theory well-enough *specified* to permit testing? One issue, for example, has to do with the concept of an "intervening variable." In the earlier work, an attempt was made to link, but distinguish between, the hypothetical construct and reality by inserting an intervening variable. Such a distinction was thought to be necessary because application encourages reification of the theory. In Chapter 3 of this book, an example of reification common throughout the literature in this field was noted: using "attribute" to mean the mental counterpart of a brand's attribute. The "intervening variable" is a sort of halfway point between a hypothetical construct and reality; it should not be confused with another use of the term, by which "intervening variable" refers to any variable linking two other variables. Since the field of consumer behavior has now matured substantially, the intervening variable is less necessary; and it has been omitted in this version of the theory. In general, then, this version is substantially better specified.

As regards simplicity of application, for most applications the theory does not need to be so complex as it is presented here. In fact, Figure 11-1, a stripped-down version of the theory, is adequate for verbal application and even for some quantitative application, such as monitoring a market. When it comes to diagnosing a problem as the basis for recommending action, however, you will find yourself utilizing additional elements of the theory, depending upon the situation. Typically, you will find yourself compromising between completeness and simplicity, and the exact point of compromise will depend upon such things as the time available, and the complexity and importance of the problem. But in any event, the total system defines the field, and you will often find that the unused elements provide implicit premises—premises which you are using in your analysis at the moment but of which you are not aware.

Sheth, whose critique is as thorough and objective as Blackwell's, raised another set of issues. One had to do with the narrow focus of the earlier work

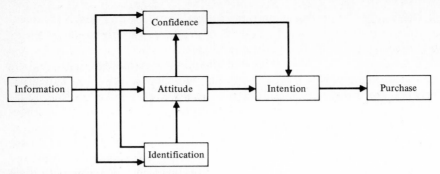

Figure 11-1   Reduced model of theory.

upon a "highly deliberative, cognitive and even rational decision-making process."[5] As you will recall from Chapter 7, this narrow focus was expanded in two ways: first, by the inclusion of motivational elements and the recognition that excessive motivation can distort information processing; second, by the inclusion of the case of insufficient motivation. But although these "irrational" processes are important in specific cases, I believe that they represent a small proportion of total buying.

A second criticism had to do with the failure to take up the joint decision making that characterizes much of family and organizational buying. That is dealt with in Chapter 9 of this book, but not as systematically as is necessary. Here, Davis's work on family decision making is quite helpful,[6] and there is also some current research on organizational buying. Sheth has proposed a structure for each of these two situations.[7]

A third criticism concerned another limitation on the earlier theory: it centered on the relation between attitude and behavior without incorporating situational variables and behavioral antecedents, which generate a need to choose. Both of these have now been given specific roles. Situational variables are captured in the environment as indicated in Chapter 8, and behavioral antecedents are incorporated by means of the definition of "need."

A fourth criticism was that static and dynamic constructs—specifically, learning and perceptual elements—were mixed together in the same system. Experience has suggested that at least one of the earlier perceptual variables (perceptual bias) is unnecessary, as was indicated above. The dynamic (motivational) element represented in perceptual mechanisms has been more systematically developed by means of the constructs of "arousal" and "values," which supplement "motives." This modification is most sharply seen in the discussion of attention and search (Chapter 7). Furthermore, learning itself has become

[5]Sheth, op. cit., p. 23.

[6]H. L. Davis, "Decision Making within the Household," Project on Synthesis of Knowledge of Consumer Behavior, RANN Program, National Science Foundation, April 1975.

[7]J. N. Sheth, "A Theory of Family Buying Decisions," in J. N. Sheth (ed.), *Models of Buyer Behavior,* Harper and Row, New York, 1974, pp. 17–33; "A Model of Industrial Buyer Behavior," *Journal of Marketing,* **37**:50–56, October 1973.

more motivational in this version. The effect of attitude upon intention to buy is a product of a belief and the salience of the choice criterion in which the consumer holds that belief; salience is a motivational element.

There was also the issue of the search process per se. In the present version, there is a more systematic development of attention processes and language, memory, and inference, which contributes indirectly to our understanding of search, particularly with respect to individual differences.

Sheth also pointed out that the earlier work said little about how a consumer codes (perceives) a message. The present version goes much further in explicating the coding process. The emphasis has been upon deeper information processing (Chapters 4 and 6) and attention and search (Chapter 7). Factors that create cognitive strain bear directly upon this issue. The way has now been cleared for more productive work on the coding process in both laboratory and field contexts. The concept of "structure of information," with its distinction between content and form dimensions, is an important step in providing a way to specify the message, which is essential to further development.

Finally, Sheth noted the managerial bias built into the early theory, which Rogers has called a "pro-innovation bias," as we saw in Chapter 9. The systematic introduction of economic concepts, particularly in Chapter 10, has done much to alleviate this bias, as have concept learning and the sociological concepts of Chapter 9.

Wind's Predictions about Future Research

Our second benchmark in discussing where we now are is Wind's judgments about the future directions of research. This is an essential complement to the reviews that have just been discussed, since Wind's commentary is more related to the field of consumer research as a whole.

Wind systematically reviewed (for a National Science Foundation symposium) fourteen issues having to do with the conceptual and methodological aspects of brand choice (purchase) as a criterion or dependent variable in consumer behavior. A judgment based upon such a review is particularly relevant here, because an emphasis upon purchase has been implicit throughout this book. Substantively, purchase is important to the manager. It is the consumer's act of purchasing that generates the essential revenue to which the manager is most sensitive. Methodologically, the act of purchasing is important because it serves to validate the role of earlier constructs in the system. Specifically, purchase is the final means of the means-end chain that has been a central theme in this book. The acid test of whether earlier constructs in the means-end chain actually exist is whether they can be shown to be related to the act of purchasing. Thus, the act of purchasing serves a central role in the development of the field.

Wind's conclusion was as follows:

> The large number of issues highlighted in this paper suggest that the most pressing need in the area of brand choice is a better conceptualization of the field. The availability of numerous stochastic brand choice models, literally thousands of

commercial brand choice studies, the richness of the *choice* literature in the behavioral science (especially psychology), the experience with consumer behavior models of brand choice such as the Howard and Sheth, and the availability of new measurement and analytical tools suggest that it is time for a major integrative effort of the work of the three groups of specialists—the behavioral scientists/consumer researchers, management scientists and the marketing researchers. Such integrative effort should be aimed at the development of operational (and to the extent possible) simple model(s) of brand choice which will solve the 14 sets of issues discussed in this paper and provide better understanding of the brand choice phenomenon (and the effect of various marketing stimuli on it) and high predictive efficacy."[8]

In terms of the goal enunciated by Wind, this book does offer a new conceptualization. The theory set forth in this book is designed to be operational, although it is incomplete as regards individual differences among consumers. To a considerable extent, its operationability will be documented in Part Two. With respect to simplicity, the system can be used in a quite parsimonious form (as in Figure 11-1), but additional elements can be included—especially if "predictive efficacy" is desired (this will be seen in later chapters). Finally, although the theory does not deal adequately with all fourteen issues raised by Wind (nor should it be expected to), it does make major contributions to a substantial number of them.

OTHER CONSIDERATIONS

In addition to the points raised by Blackwell, Sheth, and Wind, other developments have been incorporated into this version of the theory.

Stages of Decision

The systematic inclusion of information processing gives a much fuller understanding of the nature of buying behavior. This subfield is, of course, in its infancy; but it has permitted us to bring together the historically disparate fields of concept learning and attitude formation and change, and in this way the concept of structure of information—with its content and form elements—was formulated.

The three stages of decision have given a sharp focus to the analysis; but I suspect that they may have drawn our attention away from the continuity of learning. If we look at concept learning as a continuous process, the following is probably a reasonably accurate description, although not everyone will agree with it: When first confronted with a new product in a new product class, the consumer strives to infer a single most important choice criterion for evaluating the brand as indentification of the product class is developed. Other choice criteria are added, but at first their functioning tends to be heavily dependent upon the first. As more information is taken in, however, the criteria begin more

[8]Y. Wind, "Brand Choice," Project on Synthesis of Knowledge of Consumer Behavior, RANN Program, National Science Foundation, April 1975, p. 30.

and more to function independently of each other, particularly if instrumental values are constant so that weighting of choice criteria is stable. Once these choice criteria are well learned, there is a tendency to make them binary. Since binary choices are much easier to use, other criteria may well be added, making for a more elaborate decision, especially with complex products. However, the elements of the environment that are unstable—such as price (deals) in an oligopolistic market—may, because of their clarity and instability, remain multi-valued.

But although the concept of stages of decision may have hidden the continuity of concept learning, it has served the very important function of highlighting the lack of content of EPS in the previous work. The development of content for EPS has extended the theory to a much wider range of circumstances— situations that will become increasingly common in postindustrial society. There is also another benefit. The stages of decision enable us to describe the boundaries of the field. They encompass the highly unstructured situation of change in values as one extreme and repetitive behavior with homogeneous brands (classical demand theory) as the other.

Types of Problems

A book about application of theory should say something about *types* of problems to which the theory might be applied. At the outset, problems of consumer behavior were classified into three types: management, regulation, and buying. The managerial problems of the type encountered in private companies have been covered extensively although not in great depth. The "macromarketing" or "social" type of managerial problem has been given little attention, largely because to do so would seem repetitious: these two managerial problems are very similar, although they differ in detail. Regulatory problems were developed in Chapter 10. Problems of buying—how consumers should buy to serve their own interests—were given almost no attention. The importance of this area is not questioned, but my ability at the moment to say anything worthwhile about it can be questioned. Secondary schools are beginning to try to meet this need by offering courses in how to buy. The Educational Research Council of America, for example, in its Unified Science Program, is making available a consumer science program for grades nine through twelve. "Consumer science" is concerned with how to choose the best product and offers "guidelines for testing many common products."[9] The principles of information processing and concept learning emphasized throughout this book could be the foundation of such material.

Settings of Problems

The *setting* of a problem should also be relevant to any discussion about application. To indicate the possible range of problems, three settings were defined at the outset of this book: preindustrial, industrial, and postindustrial

---

[9]Educational Research Council of America, Rockefeller Building, Cleveland, Ohio.

societies. The less developed countries that are the preindustrial societies can, in a sense, be said to have no consumer problems other than supply. Most of the existing products have been bought for generations, and the culture contains a wealth of advice on buying them. However, we are beginning to see serious problems developing in such societies—for example, the decline in breast feeding of babies and consequent shift of consumption to prepared baby foods has been remarkable in the last twenty years.[10] In Chile, for example, in 1960, 95 percent of the mothers nursed their children. By 1969, this proportion had been reduced to less than 10 percent. This increases costs (because milk must be bought), infant malnutrition, and infant mortality. Advertising by manufacturers of baby food is thought by some to be a major cause of the decline in breast feeding, but dependable evidence is apparently lacking. In a setting like this, the need to understand the effects of various kinds and sources of information is obvious. In general, however, problems involving information are probably much less than in the other two settings.

The industrial societies are facing the problems that the United States has had in the past twenty years. Technological change is having an increasing impact on consumer products, and mass communication media are providing information. The problems used as illustrations in Chapter 10 characterize an industrial society with a private enterprise system. The task in such a society is to ensure freedom of choice for the consumer and freedom to innovate for the seller. If the economic framework, with its cost-benefit principle, is combined with the information processing of behavioral theory and with our concept of information structure, the probability would seem to be substantially greater that public policy will attain these two goals.

In postindustrial society, new technology promises to modify the nature and amount of information so that the *individual* consumer can take advantage of it in buying. With some assurance, we can assume that in the postindustrial setting all three types of problems—management, regulation, and consumption—will appear in new and often difficult forms.

SUMMARY

The commentary of Blackwell, Sheth, and Wind gives us a measure of the contribution of this book. It is summarized by a structure largely described in Figure 7-2 and supplemented in Chapters 8 and 9. That structure was mainly achieved by merging three points of view—marketing, psychology, and economics—and supplementing them with some sociological concepts.

We now have the exciting opportunity to apply this structure to some of our urgent private and social needs; the variety of possible applications is indicated by the differences among the three settings: preindustrial, industrial, and postindustrial societies.

Although the principles implied in the structure are general, each application

[10]A. Berg, *The Nutrition Factor,* Brookings Institution, Washington, D.C., 1973, chap. 7.

is specific and unique. Each application can be both interesting and useful for a wide range of people: product designers; brand managers; marketing managers; chief executive officers; managers of ballets, orchestras, and other fine arts groups; antitrust lawyers; copyright lawyers; consumer protection lawyers; commissioners and staff members of the Federal Trade Commission; judges; members of juries; members of Congress; teachers of how-to-buy courses; consumers; and others.

SUGGESTIONS FOR FURTHER READING

K. Lancaster: "Theories of Consumer Choice from Economics," in R. Ferber (ed.), *A Synthesis of Selected Aspects of Consumer Behavior,* U.S. Government Printing Office for the National Science Foundation, in press.

W. J. McGuire, "Psychological Factors Influencing Consumer Choice," in R. Ferber (ed.), *A Synthesis of Selected Aspects of Consumer Behavior,* U.S. Government Printing Office for the National Science Foundation, in press.

Part Two

Advanced Work: Modeling Consumer Behavior

Chapter 12

Modeling RRB: Stochastic and Deterministic Models

CONTENTS

Modeling consumer behavior has become a popular topic. To "model" a consumer is to describe his or her behavior in quantitative terms; here, we are concerned with modeling RRB, the behavior described by concept utilization.

In RRB, the buyer has already learned the concept of a brand, which implies a certain liking or preference for it, and only the conditions of purchase (such as price and availability) may be changed from time to time. You will recall from Figure 2-2 that if the conditions of purchase do not change—as may often be the case—the system is guided toward brand choice by the unchanging brand concept alone. Thus, under these circumstances, habit alone would explain behavior. A type of model that is consistent with this explanation is a particular kind of Markov model, and the Markov model is a type of stochastic model. Let us first discuss the general idea of a stochastic model; then illustrate the stochastic model hypothetically and practically; and then discuss deterministic models, which are an alternative to stochastic models.

STOCHASTIC PROCESSES

Techniques that will predict the behavior of buyers are useful to managers whether or not they offer much in the way of a supporting rationale or explanation. For example, consider a man who is introducing a new product this month. If he can predict with some accuracy how many people will be buying it a year hence, he can plan to meet that demand. As a result of this information, he can tell the production department how much to produce and the sales department how much to plan to sell. Because prediction is so helpful, several types of models have been developed in the past fifteen years whose main or sole purpose is prediction. They do not attempt to represent underlying processes—that is, they are not based on a theory—and so are less useful for diagnostic purposes than for prediction. They provide few hints for remedying unsatisfactory situations.

Stochastic processes represent one common type of predictive model. For a nontechnical discussion of these, see Montgomery and Ryans;[1] for a thorough discussion, see Massy, Montgomery, and Morrison.[2] A basic assumption of all stochastic models is that buyers behave in a stochastic manner: that is, their behavior can be described as a matter of chance. An example will clarify chance behavior and its significance for the manager.

The Markov Model

One type of stochastic model makes the assumption that the probability of the next purchase depends only on the last (most recent) purchase. For example, the consumer buys a product at time t, finds the price is low, and develops a more favorable impersonal attitude; thereafter, that purchase has no further effect.

[1]D. B. Montgomery and A. B. Ryans, "Stochastic Models of Consumer Choice Behavior," in S. Ward and T. S. Robertson (eds.), *Consumer Behavior: Theoretical Sources,* Prentice-Hall, Englewood Cliffs, N.J., 1973, pp. 521–576.

[2]W. F. Massy, D. B. Montgomery, and D. G. Morrison, *Stochastic Models of Buying Behavior,* M.I.T. Press, Cambridge, Mass., 1970.

This is called "first-order process," and models of this kind are named after the Russian mathematician Markov. Developing an arithmetic example of such a model will give us an intuitive idea of the nature of a stochastic model without involving us in mathematical complexities.

Since the stochastic model depends on chance, we must first to feed in some probabilities. Let us consider Spic & Span as an example. Several years ago, the management of the Spic & Span Division of Procter & Gamble Company wondered if Spic & Span, which had been advertised only for cleaning walls and woodwork, could find an expanded market as a floor cleaner. To get some measure of the market, the management decided to advertise it as a floor cleaner in two test markets, in Buffalo and Birmingham.

Suppose that, in order to estimate the future market, the two test markets were sampled after the advertising had run for one year, and that 100 homemakers who regularly cleaned their walls and woodwork were questioned. Each subject was asked what brand of cleaner he or she had bought most recently and what brand he or she had bought the time before that. If 50 of the subjects had bought Spic & Span before the last purchase and 50 had bought some other brand, we can construct the "brand-switching matrix" shown in Table 12-1. Of the 50 subjects who had bought Spic & Span the last time (t), 45 bought it again this time ($t + 1$), while 5 switched to some other brand. On the other hand, of the 50 who had bought some other brand last time (t), this time ($t + 1$) only 35 bought some other brand, while 15 switched to Spic & Span.

These data provide the basis for developing a first-order Markov model, which assumes that the consumer learns only from the first purchase. The relative frequencies in the brand-shifting matrix can be treated as probabilities; for example, $^{45}\!/_{50}$ = a probability of .9; $^{5}\!/_{50}$ = a probability of .1; $^{15}\!/_{50}$ = a probability of .3; and $^{35}\!/_{50}$ = a probability of .7. In standard terminology, these probabilities form a "transition matrix" or "matrix of transition probabilities" (Table 12-2) based on the brand-switching matrix (Table 12-1). For a consumer

Table 12-1 Brand-Switching Matrix

	S & S$_{t+1}$	Other$_{t+1}$	Total
S & S$_t$	45	5	50
Other$_t$	15	35	50

Table 12-2 Transition Matrix

Brand purchased at time t	Brand purchased at time $t + 1$		Total
	S & S	Other	
S & S	.9	1 − .9	1
Other	1 − .7	.7	1

Table 12-3   Changing Brand Shares with Constant Purchase Probabilities

Quarter	S & S	Other
1	50	50
2	$(50 \times .9) + (50 \times .3) = 45 + 15 = 60$	$(50 \times .1) + (50 \times .7) = 5 + 35 = 40$
3	$(60 \times .9) + (40 \times .3) = 54 + 12 = 66$	$(60 \times .1) + (40 \times .7) = 6 + 28 = 34$
4	$(66 \times .9) + (34 \times .3) = 59.5 + 10 = 69$	$(66 \times .1) + (34 \times .7) = 6.6 + 23.8 = 31$
5	$(69 \times .9) + (31 \times .3) = 62 + 9 = 71$	$(69 \times .1) + (31 \times .7) = 6.9 + 21.7 = 29$
6	$(71 \times .9) + (29 \times .3) = 63.9 + 8.7 = 73$	$(71 \times .1) + (29 \times .7) = 7.1 + 20.3 = 27$
7	$(73 \times .9) + (27 \times .3) = 65.7 + 8 = 74$	$(73 \times .1) + (27 \times .7) = 7.3 + 19 = 26$
8	$(74 \times .9) + (26 \times .3) = 66.6 + 8 = 75$	$(74 \times .1) + (26 \times .7) = 7.4 + 18 = 25$

who bought Spic & Span at t, there is .9 chance that Spic & Span will be bought at $t + 1$, and a .1 (1 − .9) chance that some other brand will be bought at $t + 1$. For a consumer who bought "Other" at time t, there is .3 (1 − .7) chance that Spic & Span will be bought at time $t + 1$ and .7 chance that "Other" will be bought. Thus, if we want to know what will happen to Spic & Span in the future, as Procter & Gamble did, we simply use the probabilities in the "S & S" column.

As was mentioned above, an important assumption of this model is that after the first effect of some event, such as buying a brand, nothing happens to change the consumer's behavior. Now, this assumption can be worded more precisely by saying that the probabilities in the transition matrix do not change. One other assumption is that all consumers are alike in their response patterns, but this is not so important an assumption, since in an RRB market buyers probably do tend to be much more alike than in LPS.[3]

It is now possible to sketch the future consumption pattern for Spic & Span; this is shown in the left-hand column of Table 12-3. There we see that in quarter 1, 50 people bought Spic & Span. In quarter 2, of the 50 who bought Spic & Span the last time, .9 (that is, 45) will buy it this time. Of the 50 who bought "Other" the last time, .3 (that is, 15) will buy Spic & Span this time. Thus, Spic & Span will obtain a total of 60 customers in quarter 2, or a market share of 60 percent. This process of applying the transition matrix from quarter to quarter is carried out until equilibrium or steady state is reached. Equilibrium occurs whenever an iteration does not change the total number of consumers buying Spic & Span; here, this happens in quarter 8. (To prove this to yourself, compute quarter 9 to see if it yields different results from quarter 8.) Steady state is attained when market share $t + 1$ is the same as it was in t. From this model, Procter & Gamble could conclude that in about two years it would have a 75 percent share of the market.

What can such a model contribute? In practice, of course, we would not expect Procter & Gamble's market share to come out exactly as predicted.

[3]D. G. Morrison, W. F. Massy, and F. N. Silverman, "The Effect of Non-Homogeneous Populations on Markov Steady State Probabilities," *Journal of the American Statistical Association*, **66**:268–274, June 1971.

Nevertheless, knowing the direction the market share will take and about how soon equilibrium will be reached can be highly useful. A benefit which may not be obvious is that the model provides a framework for organizing and interpreting a mass of data that would otherwise be very difficult to handle. For example, a sample of only 1,000 consumers purchasing coffee on the average of one purchase every two weeks will generate 26,000 purchases to be analyzed (1,000 $\times$ $^{52}\!/_2$). Using the brand-switching matrix for organizing data is no small benefit, since getting answers quickly is essential to managers.

The right-hand side of Table 12-3 results merely from applying the "Other" column of the transition matrix. It is, of course, a mirror image of the left-hand side and can be more easily computed by simply subtracting the figure in the left-hand column from 100. Normally, however, managers want to know what is happening to each of several other brands, so as to estimate competitive response. If it is known, for example, that one competitor has unfavorable costs, then it can be predicted that a decline in sales will affect that competitor's profits so adversely as to force a substantial price cut. Such considerations amount to supplementing the model with outside information. This type of analysis can be done very inexpensively, because the data are almost costless: they are purchase-panel data bought by many companies for another purpose—to monitor the market share of such products as foods and drugs.

As has been indicated, managers are implicitly assuming that the transition probabilities are constant. This can be a serious deficiency of the model, if, in fact, they are doing things to change the probabilities—altering advertising copy, for example, or raising or lowering price, or making brands more or less available in stores. Therefore, the prediction is really a conditional prediction, conditional upon no change in the probabilities. Changing elements can be incorporated, but one must be able to construct a pattern of the way in which they will change. Telser, Nakanishi, and Lilien, for example, have incorporated marketing variables directly into their stochastic models as exogenous variables to determine the effects of marketing variables.[4]

The Hendry Model[5]

So far, we have dealt only with the first-order Markov model. Another possibility is a zero-order model, which assumes that the consumer does not learn at all, even from the first event. In terms of the theory, this could be RRB in a constant environment. Even impersonal attributes are constant, so that the consumer is "fully learned." The Hendry model makes this assumption. It is probably the most widely used stochastic model. (For example, the director of stochastic modeling for one of the largest package goods companies reports that about 75 percent of the company's products are being analyzed by the Hendry model.)

---

[4]Montgomery and Ryans, op. cit.; G. L. Lilien, "A Modified Linear Learning Model of Buyer Behavior," *Management Science,* **20**:1027–1036, March 1974.

[5]M. U. Kalwani, and D. G. Morrison, "A Parsimonious Description of the Hendry System," *Management Science,* forthcoming.

Not only is it a zero-order model; it is heterogeneous and aggregate—that is, it does not assume that consumers are alike as regards the probability of response, and it analyzes aggregates of consumers rather than individual consumers.

In all stochastic analyses, the product class must be defined, because brand switching is meaningful only in terms of occurring within a given product class. This problem was ignored in the arithmetic example. The Hendry model can be said to be made up of two submodels, of which one defines the product class and the other deals with stochastic prediction. Let us first examine class identification.

Class Identification   What brands should be included in the brand-switching matrix, in terms of the manager's needs? The question here is: Who are my competitors? This is obviously a very important question; in fact, one of the most important criteria for a brand strategy is usually the relationship of the brand with competitors, as indicated by its market share. Consistent with RRB theory, the Hendry model assumes that consumers have in mind well-defined product classes and, specifically, that they do not substitute across classes, a point to be clarified below.

In each case, the product class is derived from actual behavior of consumers. The manager of brand A is first asked for a judgment about who are brand A's closest competitors. "Competitors" are defined as those brands that consumers view as most similar to A and, therefore, the brands they are more likely to switch to (away from A) and switch from (to A). The switching patterns among these brands are computed in a more elaborate version of Table 12-1 to determine how well the manager's judgment accords with the reality of the market. If there is not substantial switching among all the brands named by the manager, the manager is again consulted and asked to reconsider the judgment in light of the brand-switching evidence. This procedure is repeated until a satisfactory definition of the product class, in terms of the brands making it up, has been reached.

This "partitioning" of brands to correctly specify a product class—to estimate a semantic structure as described in Chapter 3—can be illustrated with a hypothetical example. In this example, the forms of the product can be thought of as constituting product classes, as was done with appliances in the example of two-level choice in Chapter 5. Also, choice among product classes can be considered first, as with EPS in Chapter 5, instead of choice within a product class (as in Chapters 2 and 3).

> For instance, in the margarine market, form of margarine (stick, cup, etc.) *might* represent the primary level of decision making. That is, a consumer decides first on the form of margarine she wishes to buy, and only then chooses a particular brand within that form. The structure of the market upon analysis may look [like Figure 12-1].
>
>   As shown in [Figure 12-1], in this form-primary margarine market, we assume there are two forms of margarine (cups and sticks) and three brand labels (1, 2 and 3).

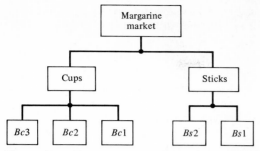

Figure 12-1 Form-primary market. (*M. U. Kalwani and D. G. Morrison, "A Parsimonious Description of the Hendry System," Graduate School of Business, Columbia University, Research Paper No. 82, March 1975, p. 16.*)

Brand labels 1 and 2 are sold in both forms, whereas Brand 3 margarine is sold only in cups.

. . . In the hypothetical illustration, above, each form of margarine would represent a separate partition with its own switching characteristics. The margarine market can, in such a case, be classified as form-primary. A consumer in such a form-primary market will have a very small preference for a brand which does not carry her margarine-form. That is, form of margarine would be the primary structural component because the consumer would first identify margarine as having a particular form.

The identification of the partitioning structure in a market has several practical implications. These implications can be best described by comparing the above structure with a brand-primary margarine market. Using the assumptions above, a brand-primary margarine market can be represented [as shown in Figure 12-2].

Firstly, in the form-primary market, the consumers exhibit lower brand-name loyalties than in the brand-primary market. Secondly, five separate brands are perceived by consumers in the form-primary margarine market. The firm manufacturing Brand 1 (say, Firm 1) has to promote its two forms of margarine separately. On the other hand, in the brand-primary case, Firm 1 could promote its two product types (Bc1 and Bs1) together. Finally, if Firm 3 wanted to introduce margarine in stick form in the brand-primary case, it would experience a certain amount of "cannibal-

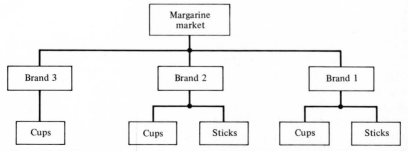

Figure 12-2 Brand-primary market. (*M. U. Kalwani and D. G. Morrison, "A Parsimonious Description of the Hendry System," Graduate School of Business, Columbia University, Research Paper No. 82, March 1975, p. 16B.*)

ism." On the other hand, in the form-primary case, if Firm 3 introduced margarine in stick form, it would end up getting a share in the 'sticks' partition which would be independent of its share in the 'cups' partition.[6]

So far, this discussion of the Hendry model fits smoothly into the framework of two-level choice given in Chapter 5—except, of course, that the mechanism must be approximately that of RRB. With this background on defining the product class, let us turn to the other submodel in the Hendry system: stochastic prediction.

Stochastic Prediction   The basic element of this submodel is the notion of a "purchase-probability distribution." This is a useful idea in thinking about consumers and an essential component of the Hendry model. In the literature it is referred to as a "preference distribution"; but this term is confusing because no independent measure is taken of the consumer's preference and correlated with the probability of purchase. A purchase-probability distribution is shown in Figure 12-3, where the vertical axis is percent of consumers and the horizontal axis is probability of purchase.

An important conclusion of the Hendry model is that the purchase-probability distribution will always have the shape of a "bathtub"—it is low in the middle and high on the sides. This means that for any brand, a large percent of consumers will have a very low probability of buying it, some consumers will have a level of probability varying between the two extremes of high and low, and a large percent will have a high probability of buying it. This polarization for and against a brand has not been explained but has been accepted. Later, we will discuss why it may be true under some conditions but not others, and thus when the model is and is not a valid description of consumer behavior.

The assumption that most buyers become polarized as regards a brand— have either a low probability or a high probability of purchase—is viewed as affecting the degree of leverage available for changing consumers' behavior by means of marketing. The more that consumers are polarized for each brand, to the exclusion of other brands in the market, the harder it is to change their behavior and thereby change market shares.[7]

To repeat: the Hendry model results in a bathtub shape for the distribution of purchase probabilities, and then makes predictions from this distribution about actual results in a market. The important point is that these predictions, although not necessarily incorrect, follow mathematically from a basic assumption instead of being based on empirical facts. The bathtub shape has intuitive appeal because we know there are many people who never buy a brand and many who buy only one brand. And in fact this phenomenon has been tested empirically, not only with regard to package goods but also for television viewing and magazine

[6]Ibid.

[7]H. E. Kropp, "Determining How Much to Spend for Advertising—Without Experimental Testing," presented at Association of National Advertisers Advertising Research Workshop, New York, February 28, 1974.

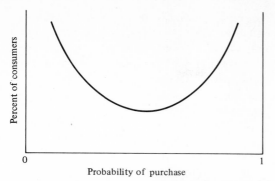

Figure 12-3 Bathtub-shaped purchase-probability distribution for brand *A*.

readership.[8] Morrison has proposed three procedures for testing the assumption of a zero-order process, which underlies a number of stochastic models, including the Hendry model.[9]

The reliability of the partitioning of a given market is tested by repeating the analysis used in developing the first acceptable partition, as was discussed earlier. However, this is a test of reliability, not a test of the validity of the construct. The Hendry model is only one way of partitioning a market; and there is no single "best way" to partition across all consumers and all products. Hence, it is recommended that a manager try more than one way and compare the resulting structures. If two or more techniques yield similar results, the manager can be more confident that the true structure has been identified.

Conclusions on Stochastic Models

We have seen how two types of stochastic models can be useful. A first-order model (Markov model) assumes that one event causes change and proceeds to generate equilibrium. A zero-order model (Hendry model) assumes that past choices do not affect future choices: in psychological terms, that consumers do not learn. As you will recall from Chapter 2, this assumption does describe RRB behavior in a stable environment. Another type of stochastic model, often discussed (although not discussed here), is the negative binominal developed by Ehrenberg.[10]

More complex models have been developed. These can provide some predictions and offer some insights into the structure of buying behavior.[11] For example, three kinds of stochastic models were applied to Crest toothpaste when a supporting statement by the American Dental Association was used in the advertising. The "probability-diffusion" model, which assumes that all effects are due to factors in the environment (such as advertising), found that the

[8]D. J. Sabavala, and D. G. Morrison, "Television Show Loyalty: A Beta Binomial Model Using Recall Data," *Journal of Advertising Research,* forthcoming.

[9]Massy, Montgomery, and Morrison, op. cit., chap. 3.

[10]A. S. C. Ehrenberg, "The Pattern of Consumer Purchases," *Applied Statistics,* **8**:26–46, March 1959.

[11]Montgomery and Ryans, op. cit., pp. 572–574.

endorsement had a much greater effect on the ability of Crest to *hold* customers than on its ability to attract new customers. The "linear-learning" model, which assumes that all past purchases are the causal mechanism, found that purchase did have a positive effect on future purchase. But the "dual-effects" model, which incorporates both environmental effects (such as advertising) and purchase feedbacks, found a *negative* purchase feedback, which is to say that past purchase negatively affects future purchases. From the results of these three models, the conclusion was drawn that the advertising was strong enough to overcome the negative effect of trying the brand, which in this case may have been due to a taste disadvantage. How to choose among the three models is a difficult problem, however. It is almost impossible to discriminate statistically among competing models.[12]

Aside from these exceptions, however, none of the stochastic models explains behavior in terms that are useful to the manager—that is, none relates purchase to some condition internal or external to the consumer. Managers need diagnostic help. They want to know not only what will happen if nothing changes, but what will happen if, for instance, advertising is changed in some way. For this, a theory is needed. This is where marketing expertise lies, and where managers need some evaluation of their creative efforts to guide them in future decisions.

As we saw with both the Markov model and the Hendry model, a stochastic model can be useful in structuring a situation so as to see a problem clearly. It can also show the *direction* of change, even though a specific prediction may be incorrect.

For a number of reasons, these strictly "chance" models approximate the reality of RRB. First, a bathtub-shaped probability distribution may often be found, especially if the product class is not particularly involving, so that preferences are not strong—since low motivation discourages sharp discrimination among brands. With frequently purchased products, habit is encouraged. Second, differences between brands have probably become minimal as the brands have matured, because technology is stable and competitors have copied each other's technology. It is generally agreed that the Hendry model fits best where brands are most alike. Third, a few companies, through internal growth and acquisition, may come to dominate an industry, so that they each have good distribution (availability). Since simple price competition can be dangerous in a market verging on pure oligopoly, it will probably not be used unless some major development occurs which allows cost reduction. Coupons and other promotional techniques which are hidden price cuts may be used because the consumer responds more slowly to them than to a simple price change. Limited advertising can be used to call the consumers' attention to a brand, and attention to the brand is about all that matters in the choice here. It is easy to overspend on advertising

[12]D. G. Morrison, "The Uses and Limitations of Brand-Switching Models," in H. L. Davis and A. Silk (eds.), *Symposium on Behavioral Science and Management Science in Marketing,* Ronald Press, New York, 1976.

in this situation, because there is nothing much to tell consumers that they want to know, other than that the product is available (although sheer familiarity can to some extent create liking, as we saw in Chapter 3). Under these circumstances, then, a "bathtub" may not be an inaccurate representation. To simplify an uncertain decision—one where all alternatives are satisfactory—a consumer is likely to be loyal to one brand and ignore other brands.

One user of the Hendry model states: "We know how to determine advertising expenditure levels for businesses without experimentation. We know how because we have in Hendry a good theory—and because we have a conviction in the theory, we use it in planning and evaluating business operations."[13] Kalwani and Morrison's article on the Hendry model, however, closes with a pertinent comment: "We believe the Hendry (and other similar) approaches are nothing more than parsimonious *descriptions*; albeit very useful and insightful descriptions. Other argue strongly that these approaches constitute a *theory* of switching behavior."[14] Kalwani and Morrison's own view seems to be correct. What is lacking is a description—a theory—of why a particular pattern of behavior occurs at any time. A theory about habitual behavior may be implicit in stochastic models, but it is not specific enough to be useful. Deterministic models can provide a fuller explanation of buying behavior.

DETERMINISTIC MODELS OF RRB

Deterministic models for RRB are an alternative to stochastic models. A deterministic model relates some specific internal or external condition or conditions to the consumer's purchasing behavior in exact, nonprobabilistic terms. There are two general types of deterministic models: estimation and structural.

Estimation Models

Estimation models are not concerned with causal relations per se. For example, we can estimate the relation between a consumer's exposure to advertising and his or her behavior by means of regression analysis; the relation will tell us nothing about the causal process, however. In fact, there is evidence to suggest that in LPS advertising does not cause purchase directly (as we will see in Chapter 13). An analogous process is expected in RRB with respect to conditions of purchase. The consumer is not an automaton: there is a thinking process that intervenes between exposure to advertising and the act of purchase. The value of estimation models is a matter of how efficient and accurate they are, not whether they can explain a process.

Structural Models

Structural models do attempt to represent actual causal processes—for example, what takes place between exposure to advertising and purchase. For fitting a

---

[13]Kropp, op. cit., p. 13.
[14]Kalwani and Morrison, op. cit.

structural model to data in order to test the model, we must have a theory of the process, and the goal is to define a set of equations derived from the theory. Defining a causal structure requires specifying the network of causal paths that exist between variables and identifying the parameters of causation so that we know how much one variable affects another.

Example: Decision-Net Models   One kind of structural model is the decision-net model with which we are already familiar. Figure 2-2, for example, represented a consumer buying gasoline; this type of idiosyncratic (descriptive of a single buyer), sequential, satisficing process model has been extensively used. Most such models have not been developed beyond flowcharts,[15] but Russ has fitted a variety of models to this kind of data and has concluded that a satisficing, lexicographic, semiorder model fits best. [16] A "lexicographic" model assumes that the criteria can be ordered in terms of their importance. Alternatives are first compared on the most important criterion. If brand A is considered better than B on this criterion, A is preferred over B, irrespective of how B is rated on the other criteria. If A and B are viewed as equal on the most important attribute, they are then compared on the next most important attribute, and so on. In a lexicographic "semiorder" model, the brands are compared on the second most important criterion not only where the values for the two brands are the same on the first criterion, but in all cases where the difference on the first criterion is not significant or not noticeable. In a "satisficing" lexicographic, semiorder model, all alternatives not meeting minimally acceptable levels for each criterion are eliminated before the lexicographic semiorder tests are applied.

Decision-net modeling is highly useful in understanding the decision-making process; but it has been little used by managers, who must deal with large numbers of customers, because idiosyncratic processes are time-consuming to map and too complex to model easily.

Theory of Consumer Behavior   As you will recall from Chapter 2 (Figure 2-1), RRB postulates causal relations in buying a brand. This is shown in Figure 12-4. To capture these causal relations in a model, a number of equations are needed.

First, information, or facts, that the consumer is exposed to (F) affects impersonal attitudes toward price (Pri) and availability (Av) of the brand. Thus:

$$Pri = f(F) \tag{1}$$
$$Av = f(F) \tag{2}$$

[15]J. A. Howard and W. M. Morgenroth, "Information Processing Model of Executive Decision," *Management Science,* **14**:416–428, March 1968.

[16]J. R. Bettman, "Decision Net Models of Buyer Information Processing and Choice," in G. D. Hughes and M. L. Ray (eds.), *Buyer/Consumer Information Processing,* University of North Carolina Press, Chapel Hill, N.C., p. 62.

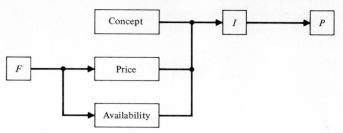

Figure 12-4   Model of RRB.

The brand concept contains a "liking" or attitude element. We will use personal attitude (*A*) to represent this. Intention to buy (*I*), then, is caused by personal attitude and the two impersonal attitudes:

$$I = f(A, \; Pri, \; Av) \tag{3}$$

Finally, purchase (*P*) is caused by intention to buy (*I*):

$$P = f(I) \tag{4}$$

Equations (1) to (4) make up the causal system, although the exogenous variables needed to identify the system have been omitted in order to simplify. The next step, applying the model and showing concretely how it is superior to stochastic models in designing marketing programs, requires substantial background; this will be provided in Chapter 13.

COMPARISON OF RRB AND LPS

Before we go on to modeling LPS (Chapters 13 and 14), our understanding of both RRB and LPS may be increased by examining briefly an insightful study which compares the two.

Using conditions that describe LPS instead of RRB, Beckwith generated a number of hypothetical probability distributions. None of them conformed to the bathtub shape.[17] Going further, he used data from an experiment by McConnell[18] in which sixty students at Stanford University who drank beer were offered regularly, twenty-four different times, one of three "brands" of beer. Actually, all the beer was the same; the brand name was hidden from the students, and the bottles were labeled "M," "L," or "P." A probability distribution was computed for the last twelve trials, and it did resemble a

[17]N. E. Beckwith, "Stochastic Implications of Brand Choice: Models on the Distribution of Brand Purchase Probabilities," Graduate School of Business, Columbia University, mimeographed, 1975.

[18]P. Charlton and A. S. L. Ehrenberg, "McConnell's Experimental Brand Choice Data," *Journal of Marketing Research,* **10**:302–307, August 1973.

bathtub. However, the distribution computed for the first twelve trials definitely did not conform to the bathtub shape. Rather, it resembled the hypothetical shapes that Beckwith had generated assuming LPS.

These results are consistent with the idea that models of brand preference based on information, like the multiple-attribute model, should explain consumers' initial choices while they are learning about a brand. After the initial learning, consumers' choices may be better described by probabilistic models which recognize each individual's routinized selection among a subset of brands.

CONCLUSIONS

For some products, and for consumers in late stages of learning, some kinds of stochastic models can be useful in predicting purchasing behavior from past experience. Bass has made a strong case for recognizing the stochastic element in consumers' behavior, but his evidence is from products that fall under RRB.[19] Products and models should be carefully selected and matched so that particular models are applied only where the conditions are appropriate. The stochastic models do not work well, for example—their predictions are less accurate— where there are differences between brands; but this is precisely the situation that is most important for a manager: a brand that is viewed as favorably different by buyers offers the greatest marketing opportunity. The limitations of these models would also seem to be substantial as regards the introduction of new products, although they have been used to forecast expected volume for new convenience products (Massy's STEAM model, for example).[20]

There is some indication that stochastic models can be used to evaluate a given marketing effort—as when three models were applied to Crest toothpaste. But for guidance in designing a marketing mix, a more fundamental level of understanding is desirable. Also, there is an urgent need to satisfy the requirements of public policy concerning the informing of consumers (see Chapter 10). Finally, consumers need to learn to buy more effectively. To meet these needs, structural models are essential.

SUGGESTIONS FOR FURTHER READING

F. M. Bass: "Analytical Approaches in the Study of Consumer Purchase Behavior and Brand Choice," in R. Ferber (ed.), *A Synthesis of Selected Aspects of Consumer Behavior*, U.S. Government Printing Office for National Science Foundation, in press.

The Hendry Corporation: *Speaking of Hendry*, 1976. A compilation of speeches describing the Hendry Marketing Support System.

[19]F. M. Bass, "The Theory of Stochastic Preference and Brand Switching," *Journal of Marketing Research*, **11**:1–20, February 1974.

[20]W. F. Massy, "Forecasting the Demand for New Convenience Products," *Journal of Marketing Research*, **6**:405–413, November 1969.

Modeling LPS: Linear, Recursive, Homogeneous Models

CONTENTS

Complex Causal Modeling of LPS
Steps in Modeling
Specification of the model
Operationalization of the specified model
Collection of data
Analysis of data
Conversion of the model to estimating form
Description and interpretation of results
Limitations—Alleged and Real
Implications

Market Simulation
Specification
Estimation of Parameters
Stability of Relationships
Simulation Model
Stability of the System

Conclusions

Suggestions for Further Reading

Modeling LPS yields a greater payoff than modeling RRB, because in LPS there are more points of leverage for changing behavior; particularly, the brand concept itself can be changed in LPS. In Chapter 12, two ways of modeling RRB were discussed: stochastic and deterministic. For modeling LPS, a deterministic approach is required, although stochastic elements can be included. Causation can be determined by experimenting, by using cross-lagged correlation over time,[1] or by applying a theory that is assumed to be true and estimating its relations for the data. It is this last course that we will follow here.

The general approach set forth here was referred to in 1966 by William J. McGuire, a psychologist at Yale University, as "more-than-faint rumblings of approaching breakthrough." He described it as dealing with the problem of measurement in natural settings instead of in the laboratory—"the detection of the crucial factor among too many unknowns and uncontrollable variables." The major problem in nonexperimental research, he said, is "teasing out causal direction among covariants, none of which we can manipulate."[2] In economics this is called "econometrics"; in sociology, it is called "path analysis." Econometrics and path analysis, although not identical, are very similar.[3] We will take an econometric approach; for a path-analysis approach to the same system, using the same data, see Klahr.[4]

COMPLEX CAUSAL MODELING OF LPS

The discussion of RRB models in Chapter 12 all but ignored several steps that are in fact necessary for modeling any stage of purchasing behavior. These are: specifying the model, operationalizing the specified model, collecting the data, analyzing the data, converting the model to an estimating form, describing the results, and interpreting the results. Chapter 12 was concerned with only two steps: analysis of the data and interpreting the results. The other steps, though not as exciting, are nonetheless essential, and the kind of modeling that will be discussed here quickly shows up weaknesses that can occur in carrying out the other steps.

The theory described in Figure 13-1 will here be applied to a brand of instant breakfast food, Post Instant Breakfast (PIB).[5] Carnation Instant Breakfast (CIB) had been in the market for about two years when two new brands—PIB, by General Foods Corporation, and Foremost Instant Breakfast (FIB), by Foremost Dairies—were introduced into a test market in Portland, Oregon, in the summer

---

[1]D. R. Lehmann, T. V. O'Brien, J. U. Farley, and J. A. Howard, "Some Empirical Contributions to Buyer Behavior Theory," *Journal of Consumer Research,* 1:43–55, December 1974.

[2]W. J. McGuire, "Theory-Oriented Research in Natural Settings: The Best of Both Worlds for Social Psychology," in M. Sherif and C. W. Sherif (eds.), *Interdisciplinary Relationships in the Social Sciences,* Aldine, Chicago, Ill., 1966, pp. 37 and 38.

[3]H. M. Blalock (ed.), *Causal Models in the Social Sciences,* Aldine Atherton, New York, 1971, p. 74.

[4]M. W. Klahr, A Comparison of Two Buyer Behavior Models, unpublished doctoral dissertation, Columbia University, 1974.

[5]M. Laroche and J. A. Howard, "Non-Linear Relations in a Complex Model of Buyer Behavior," Graduate School of Business, Columbia University, mimeographed, 1975.

of 1966. About 1,100 homemakers were interviewed at four different times (waves). The facts here were collected on the third wave (approximately July 15)—with the exception of purchase, which was for the succeeding period, July 15 to October 1.

The model given here will have the following characteristics:

Linearity: Its relations will be straight-line.
Recursiveness: It contains no feedbacks.
Homogeneity: It assumes that all buyers are alike except for their current information.

Steps in Modeling

Specification of the Model   The first step in applying a theory is to specify it—to describe it—as precisely as possible. The concept of a flowchart, used in earlier chapters to describe the system (Figures 2-1, 3-4 and 4-3) contributes substantially to the precise description needed for modeling. In Figure 13-1, the boxes represent the constructs, and the arrows indicate the paths of causation among the boxes. The arrows show that change in one construct will cause change in a subsequent construct or constructs. The $A \rightarrow C$ relation has been omitted, because at the time of the study (1973) no explanation for it was available. Satisfaction has also been omitted, because as a feedback it will be dealt with in Chapter 14. The direct relation from memory (F) to intention (I) was included because in 1973 it was believed to be appropriate.

For simplicity, the names of constructs have been replaced with symbols:

Permanent memory	F
Brand identification	B
Attitude	A
Confidence	C
Intention	I
Purchase	P

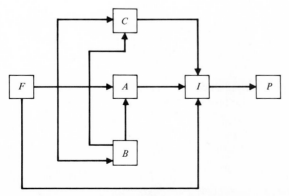

Figure 13-1   LPS model specified for instant breakfast food.

Operationalization of the Specified Model   Once the model is fully specified, the next question is: How do we ask questions of the consumer to elicit numbers for each of the boxes? Here, we are concerned with designing a questionnaire for collecting data from which the numbers to be inserted in the equations can be derived.

For memory (F), we are concerned with the effects of information, including advertising. The questions were (slightly paraphrased): "In how many media have you seen any PIB advertised during the past two weeks?"; "Have you talked with anyone about PIB?"; "Have you received a sample of PIB?" The answers were converted to an index number.

For brand identification (B), the questions were: "Do you think Instant Breakfast comes as a powder? In a box? In many flavors? As a drink? Packaged in individual portions?" Correct items were summed.

For attitude (A), the question was: "Will you indicate on the scale how much you like PIB? The scale is 1 to 7 with 'like' at one end and 'dislike' at the other."

Confidence (C) involved a scale of 1 to 5; the question was: "Rate on the scale your confidence in judging the quality of PIB."

For intention (I), the question was: "Indicate on the scale how likely you are to buy PIB in the next month." The respondent was presented with a five-point scale which read: "definitely will," "probably will," "not sure," "probably will not," and "definitely will not."

Finally, for purchase (P), the question was: "How many times have you bought PIB in the past month?"

Collection of Data   The questions noted above were put together to constitute a questionnaire. A questionnaire can be administered by personal interview, mail, or telephone. Each method has its advantages and disadvantages. Mail, for example, is cheap, but the nonresponse rate can be very high. Telephoning is more expensive, and limits each interview to perhaps fifteen minutes, but the nonresponse rate is low. The personal interview is very expensive, but it usually has a still lower nonresponse rate and provides a very comprehensive coverage of the subject matter. In this case, interviews were conducted by telephone.

Once the questionnaire has been made up and the method of interviewing has been decided on, there is still the matter of the sample. The two most important questions are: How big should the sample be? How much attention will be paid to its representativeness? The sample in this case was originally 1,100; but it was reduced to about 550 to include only subjects who had answered each of three waves of interviews after the introduction. To ensure representativeness, the names were drawn at random from telephone directories in the Portland, Oregon, area. Only homemakers were included.

For a full description of data collection, see Day.[6]

---

[6]G. S. Day, "A Description and Evaluation of the Design of the Buyer Behavior Research Project," in J. U. Farley, J. A. Howard, and L. W. Ring (eds.), *Consumer Behavior: Theory and Application,* Allyn and Bacon, Boston, 1974, pp. 33–43.

Analysis of Data   To guide the analysis, the model in Figure 13-1 is recast into the following set of symbolic equations (these are implied by the specification):

$$B = f(F) \tag{1}$$
$$A = f(F,B) \tag{2}$$
$$C = f(F,B) \tag{3}$$
$$I = f(F,A,C) \tag{4}$$
$$P = f(I) \tag{5}$$

The letter f stands for "function of." For example, in equation (1), brand identification (B) is caused by—is a function of—information (F). In each equation, the variable at the left is called the "dependent" (caused) variable, and the variable or variables at the right are called "independent" (causal) variables.

Conversion of the Model to Estimating Form   To fit the model to the data, we must convert the symbolic equations into a form for which we can get the numbers—in technical language, a form for which we can estimate the relations. Thus:

$$B = a_1 + b_1F \tag{1}$$
$$A = a_2 + b_2F + b_3B \tag{2}$$
$$C = a_3 + b_4F + b_5B \tag{3}$$
$$I = a_4 + b_6F + b_7A + b_8C \tag{4}$$
$$P = a_5 + b_9I \tag{5}$$

In these equations, the a's are constants and the b's are coefficients. Our task is to obtain estimates of each a and b. If we can do this, we can, for example, assert from equation (1) that if F increases by x percent, B will increase by y percent. A number of conditions have to be met,[7] but, for our purposes, let us simplify by assuming that they are met. (These issues are dealt with in econometrics and need not detain us here.)

The system must also be properly identified. This has to do with the requirement that in a system of simultaneous equations the necessary condition is that the number of exogenous and lagged endogenous variables excluded must

---

[7]The following assumptions give the method quantitative validity:

(1) Change in one variable in this system always occurs as a linear function of change in other variables and, in this case, change in one dependent variable occurs as a linear function of one or more independent variables.

(2) The system is recursive; it contains no reciprocal causation or feedback loops. That is, if x causes y, y cannot affect x, either directly or through a chain of other variables.

(3) The causal laws governing the system—the theory—are established sufficiently to specify the causal priorities among variables in a way that is undebatable.

(4) The disturbances of dependent variables are uncorrelated with each other or with the inputs; thus, it is necessary that *all* system inputs be explicitly entered into analyses.

(5) The usual methodological assumptions of multivariate regression analyses are met: sample units are independent, measurements are at least interval, homoscedacity is required, multicollinearity not a problem (there is sufficient independent variation).

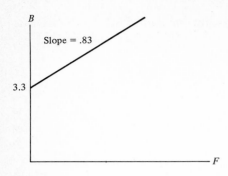

Figure 13-2 Relationship between information and brand identification.

equal or exceed the number of endogenous variables included minus 1. In the form applied here, the system is identified, but this is a technical issue that is better dealt with elsewhere.[8]

This set of equations can be solved simultaneously. However, it so happens that (with assumption 4 in footnote 7) we can proceed by solving each equation at a time. Estimating the a's and b's then becomes a simple problem of computing five regression analyses, one for each equation. Equation (1) can be estimated as follows:

$$B = 3.3 + .83F$$

and shown in graphic form (Figure 13-2). The regression coefficient is 0.83, and the constant is 3.3. This tells us that if we increase F by 10 percent, other things being equal, B will increase by 8.3 percent—almost as much. We can make this statement because, and only because, we accept the model as theoretically correct and quantitatively valid. As was noted above, this is ensured if the assumptions are true; the theory is the foundation of the quantitative tools.

In a similar fashion, each of the other equations was solved to obtain a and b. This completed the analysis of the data.

Description and Interpretation of Results   *Description.* The results of the analysis are summarized in Table 13-1. For any of the equations, -1 indicates that the variable in that column is the dependent variable and all the other variables in the same row are the independent variables.

For a clearer picture of the results, see Figure 13-3, where the coefficient for each independent variable is shown on the arrow from that variable to the one it influences. This allows us to compare the strengths of the various causal paths through the system if the coefficients are standardized as in path analysis.

Interpretation. Figure 13-3 shows that information has a strong effect on brand identification and a substantial effect on confidence and attitude: 0.83, 0.25, and 0.33, respectively. Specifically, we can say that if information was increased by 10 percent on this scale, brand identification would increase by 8.3

---

[8]L. J. Parsons and R. L. Schultz, *Marketing Models and Econometric Research,* North Holland, New York, 1976, pp. 58–65; C. F. Christ, *Econometric Models and Methods,* Wiley, New York, 1966, especially chap. 8.

Table 13-1   Coefficients of the Instant Breakfast Model

Equation	F	B	A	C	I	P	Constant	R_2
1	.83	−1					3.3	0.10
2	.33	.12	−1				3.2	0.13
3	.25	−.05		−1			3.0	0.10
4	−.21		.22	.31	−1		0.8	0.25
5					.10	−1	− .15	0.04

Note: Some segmenting variables were included to properly identify the equations, but to simplify they are omitted here. Their coefficients, though usually significant, were small.

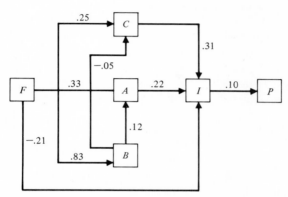

Figure 13-3 LPS model with coefficients.

percent. Corresponding statements can be made about all the other relationships.

A comparison of coefficients for brand identification, confidence, and attitude suggests that the message was designed to affect brand identification rather than confidence and attitude. On the other hand, it could be that none of the sources of information contained evaluative information; this would account for the low coefficient of $F \rightarrow A$. The negative relation between information and intention is surprising; nevertheless, it is consistent with other analyses using the same specification. It probably captures effects otherwise omitted from the system. The negative effect of B on C is unusual, but the coefficient is small. A and C have similar effects on I. Finally, intention has a definite positive effect on purchase, but it is small.

Limitations—Alleged and Real

Like any method, complex causal modeling is subject to limitations—some only alleged, others real.

A criticism sometimes heard is simply that one cannot model consumer behavior. The comment appears to be made in two quite different senses. First, it can be a moral imperative: one ought not try, because human behavior is sacrosanct. In answer to this, we can say that public and private policies are being made; and unless consumers' behavior is better understood, these policies, though designed to help consumers, may actually injure them. The second sense in which this criticism is made is that, because consumer behavior is too complex to understand, any attempt to model it is doomed to failure. But there has been remarkable progress in the past decade toward understanding the consumer which controverts this belief.

What actually limits modeling depends on how the system is being used. Empirical research is done on consumer behavior for two major reasons: to test theory and to use it. If, for example, one's purpose is to test the theory that has been laid out in Chapters 1 through 8, then the assumption of linearity is a limitation. The relations previously discussed imply not only linearity, but also that there are no interactions among the independent variables. As was suggested theoretically in earlier chapters and will be seen in Chapter 14, neither of these implications is strictly true, but linearity immensely simplifies the analyses and provides a highly useful first approximation for the scientist. McGuire, however, has commented, "The model is so robust that one can use the freedom in setting the parameters so as to be able to account for just about any outcome without disproving the model. . . ."[9] This issue will be dealt with in Chapter 14. For application—for using the theory—linearity is not so serious a limitation, because it is more economic and presents a more easily understood description of the consumer. There are times, however, as we will see in Chapter 14, where a linear model can be misleading in practice.

Two standard questions have to do with validity and reliability. Does the mathematical model really capture the empirical counterpart of the theoretical structure? If repeated measurements are taken, will essentially the same results occur?[10] Let us deal first with the question of validity.

We assume that the questions do elicit from the consumer the content specified by the appropriate construct in the theory. This is a matter of judgment. Except for the information variable, I suspect that the variables are good representations of the constructs. (Information is, in my judgment, open to question.) In other applications of the theory, which incorporate more of the total system, the operational definitions are more questionable than the central constructs used in the simplified version of complex causal modeling discussed here.

As regards validity, it has been said that this way of analyzing the data, which involves analyzing the system as a whole, is not useful for understanding how the consumer processes information.[11] This criticism must be taken seriously. The answer lies, in part, in the definition of information processing. If it is defined at the traditional attitudinal level, the system is adequate to deal with information processing. But if it is defined at a more physiological level, as in Chapters 4 and 6, the criticism is more valid. And in fact a physiological approach is essential; it articulates the opportunities and limitations for acting upon consumers' behavior more fully than the traditional cognitive approach.

[9]W. J. McGuire, personal communication, February 14, 1975.

[10]J. A. Howard, "Introduction: Noisy Data—A Common Problem in Social Research," in J. U. Farley and J. A. Howard (eds.), *Control of "Error" in Market Research Data,* Lexington Books, Lexington, Mass., 1975, pp. 1–9.

[11]F. A. Russ, "On Econometric Analysis of Consumer Information Processing: A Discussion of the Dominguez Paper," in G. D. Hughes and M. L. Ray (eds.), *Buyer/Consumer Information Processing,* University of North Carolina Press, Chapel Hill, N.C., 1974, pp. 51–58.

Chapter 14 shows, however, how econometric modeling can help here. Also, the major alternative to complex causal modeling is realistic experimentation in the field, which entails the problem of obtaining enough control to make results statistically significant. Chapter 14 presents substantial evidence that the nonlinearities, interactions, and feedbacks postulated here must, if known, be built into experimental design in order to obtain the necessary controls. Without these controls, experiments are likely to yield contradictory results. McGuire has emphasized that conditions require us to examine the entire process of communication and influence.[12] The comprehensive model, combined with econometric techniques or the similar techniques of path analysis from sociology, provides a way of doing this and of determining the factors that must be controlled for in field or laboratory experimentation.

It might seem that we are confronted with a dilemma: it is necessary to incorporate many variables, but if we do, we are unable to handle all of them. In the early chapters of this book, we can see a way out of this dilemma. From our understanding of the theory and of each element of information processing—language, memory, and inference—we can make predictions about the effects of messages with different content, form, media, and timing. These predictions can be tested in a simplified model. At the same time, we retain the capacity to determine interactions and feedbacks, as will be shown in Chapter 14, which discusses nonlinear, nonrecursive, heterogeneous versions of the model.

We now turn to the question of reliability: How dependable are these relations? First, all the relations are statistically significant at the level of .05 or better; and most of them are significant at the level of .01. Second, an important consideration is the values of R^2. These show the proportion of variance explained by the independent variables in the equation; when subtracted from 1.0, they provide the amount of unexplained variance, or the coefficient of nondetermination. In equation (1) in Table 13-1, $R^2 = 0.10$. Thus, 90 percent of the variance is unexplained. Equations (2) and (3) perform similarly. Equation (4) does well. In equation (5), however, R^2 has a low value, 0.04. In summary, the relations are real, but other factors are operating in addition to the variables included in Figure 13-1.

Some of the factors omitted from Figure 13-1 could, if included, account for some of the unexplained variance. First, there is price. From other analyses of the same data, it is clear that price matters substantially to the consumer. Second, availability of the brand in grocery stores was omitted, but we know that it mattered here because two competing brands appeared at the same time in the test market. (General Foods was able to obtain distribution in only 60 percent of the stores, and consumers were often confronted with "not available.") Third, it was assumed that all consumers were alike except with respect to the information to which they were exposed. But this is not so; in Chapter 14, for example, we will see that size of family makes a big difference in response. Fourth, a recursive model was assumed; that is, it was assumed that all relations work

[12]W. J. McGuire, "Psychological Factors Influencing Consumer Choice," Project on Synthesis of Knowledge of Consumer Behavior, RANN Program, National Science Foundation, April 1975.

forward throughout the system, with none working backward upon earlier variables (no feedbacks). But in Chapter 14 we will see that feedbacks do matter in some cases. Fifth, it was assumed that people think in terms of equal intervals. When they are asked to rate a brand on a scale, for instance, we assume that a distance of x at one position on the scale represents the same psychological distance as the same distance at another position. Without this assumption, we could not use the powerful statistical technique of multiple regression in analyzing the data. But are the scales really equal-interval, as assumed? This is not known. However, "Cliff has demonstrated that these quantifiers (slightly, quite, extremely) do provide approximately equal intervals when combined with a large variety of evaluative adjectives."[13]

The issues that have been discussed so far have to do largely with basic research. When we turn to application, an important question for managers is whether these relations are really *response functions*. That is, will a change in a prior variable necessarily cause a change in its successor? The data in Table 13-1 are given for a single point in time, so that the analysis is across consumers; this is called "cross-section" analysis. According to the theory, however, a single buyer will behave in the specified way *over time*. Thus we are assuming that different buyers in our sample are simply at different stages of the decision process. Does this assumption affect whether or not our relations are response functions?

Consider the following case. Advertising will usually increase awareness of a brand by most people in the market, although those who, for instance, find the product class not to their liking are less likely to become aware of it (as was seen in Chapter 6). Of the people who are aware of the brand, some simply do not like it. In Figure 13-4, people who like the brand are represented by o's and people who do not by x's. This is the problem of individual differences in buyers (see above and Chapter 8); more specifically, it is a result of the feedback from attitude to attention (discussed theoretically in Chapter 7 and quantitatively in Chapter 14). For practitioners this difference is typically not very relevant, because for a market as a whole the relation will be as indicated by the slope of the regression line, although it does understate advertising effects. The main consequence is that the value of R^2 for the equation will be lower. But repeated applications with consistent results give us confidence that a relation does represent a response function.[14] Also, the examples of further specifications omitted here but given in Chapter 14 are especially significant in increasing R^2. Finally, the coefficients of nondetermination $(1 - R^2)$, which are, in general, quite high, are much less important to the manager. First, R^2 measures the ability to predict an *individual* consumer's behavior; but in fact, managers are not interested in the behavior of any particular consumer; their problem is to predict the average (mean) behavior for a market or a particular segment, and this can be predicted

[13]C. E. Osgood, "Psycholinguistics," in S. Koch (ed.), *Psychology: Study of a Science,* McGraw-Hill, New York, 1963, p. 271.
[14]J. U. Farley, J. A. Howard, and D. R. Lehmann, "A 'Working' System Model of Car Buyer Behavior," *Management Science,* forthcoming.

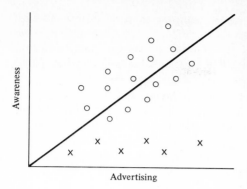

Figure 13-4 Individual differences in potential for awareness.

with far greater accuracy than individual behavior. Second, the values of R^2 have been substantially higher in some other studies, as will be seen in Chapter 14.

Implications

In order to understand more realistically what this system can do for the manager, let us examine information input (F). The operational definition used here was the sum of the number of media seen (WOM and television) multiplied by the number of times each was seen plus whether a coupon was received (1, yes; or 0, no). If we want to know what aspect of our message had an effect, in order to design better messages in the future, we will use our concept of structure of information to analyze the advertising. Various contents and forms of our advertising will be specified, and their impacts will be shown by the model.

This discussion has focused on only a single brand. Managers, however, also want to know the same thing about their competitors—that is, what their advertising is accomplishing. Now, in questioning a sample of consumers one does collect the same data on at least some of the competing brands; this is done to prevent the biased answers that will be given if respondents recognize that the questioner is interested in a particular brand. Thus, the data on important competitors are already in hand, and at no extra cost. All the various brand models can be put together into a single system.

Finally, the emphasis so far has been upon the use of the principles of consumer behavior for explanatory purposes, to support diagnoses. Obviously, however, managers also need predictions. They want to know what the market will buy during some period, given their own marketing activities. In Chapter 12, we saw how a stochastic model can be used predictively. The predictive use of the structural model will be shown in the discussion of simulation.

MARKET SIMULATION

The proceding discussion gives rise to additional questions. For example, we may ask about the generality of the modeling procedures: Is the theory valid only in the American culture? As regards this, the procedure has been applied to a new soap in Argentina[15] and to male contraceptives in rural Kenya,[16] with similar success. Other questions are these: Is the theory applicable to expensive consumer durables, such as automobiles, in contrast to nondurables like instant breakfast food, shampoo, and soap? Are the relationships stable and dependable, or are they unstable (and so useless for prediction)? Can the theory be used as a simulation in a computerized marketing information system to answer questions about what will happen if certain activities are undertaken? (For example, "If we increase advertising 10 percent, what will happen to sales?") These last three questions will be answered in the affirmative in this section.

In 1970, a new subcompact car was introduced; a panel of consumers was interviewed at five different times over an eighteen-month period.[17] The discussion which follows is based on this study.

On the basis of a substantial amount of complex causal modeling (some of which was shown earlier in this chapter), a "working model" was formulated with the following characteristics in mind:

1 The working model should involve constructs which are important to the marketing decisions to be made over the tracking period (here, the period of introduction) and which also can be measured with an acceptable degree of validity and reliability.

2 The model should be developed in such a way that systems parameters can be estimated.

3 The model should have a parametric structure at least qualitatively and preferably quantitatively comparable over time, over brands, and over any subsamples which might form natural subgroupings of the data base.

4 The model should, when combined with actual parameter estimates, behave "reasonably"—i.e., it should not blow up under boundary values of input variables and it should yield reasonable predictions under less extreme conditions.[18]

Specification

The model was specified somewhat differently from Figure 3-4. As can be seen in Figure 13-5, the arrow from "information" to "attitude" was accidentally omitted in the original study. "Attitude to confidence" was not included and "information to intention" was included because the rationale for this system was not as fully developed as those in previous chapters. "Purchase" was omitted during the earlier period because advertising was introduced before the automobile was available (that is, purchase was not possible). The reduction in the size of the model was deliberate. For practical purposes, it nevertheless captures much of

[15]J. U. Farley, J. A. Howard, and D. R. Lehmann, "Evaluating Test Market Results: Buyer Behavior Analysis in Argentina," *Journal of Business Administration,* **5:**69–88, Spring 1974.

[16]T. R. L. Black and J. U. Farley, "An Awareness-Knowledge-Trial System Model of a Subsidized Contraceptive Test Market in Kenya," *Journal of Advertising Research,* forthcoming.

[17]Farley, Howard, and Lehmann, *Management Science.*

[18]Ibid.

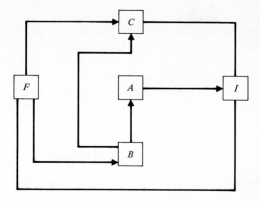

Figure 13-5 Specified model of sub-compact.

the essential elements of the much more complex system, such as Figure 7-2. Segmenting variables were included, but we will ignore them here and treat the model as homogeneous. (Heterogeneity will be dealt with in Chapter 14.)

Estimation of Parameters

When the set of four equations implied by the model specified in Figure 13-5 are fitted to the data, the following results are obtained:

$$B = .886 + .084F \tag{1}$$
$$A = 3.356 + 1.412B \tag{2}$$
$$C = 4.351 + .251F + .252B \tag{3}$$
$$I = .300 + .099A + .016C + .044F \tag{4}$$

As an aid in interpreting the results, the coefficients are shown on the diagram of the model in Figure 13-6. As with the model for instant breakfast food, increasing the causal or independent variable by one scale point increases the caused or dependent variable by the amount of the coefficient shown in Figure 13-6.

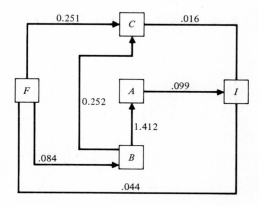

Figure 13-6 Graphic view of subcompact model.

Stability of Relationships

To evaluate the meaningfulness of the relations in the system, the statistical significance of the coefficients and the amount of variance explained were used, as in the study of instant breakfast food. Another indication of whether or not the relationships mean anything is their stability or instability. In this study there was a good opportunity to evaluate the stability of relationships by checking them over time (five waves); over brands (seven brands); over the two methods of ordinary-least-squares (OLS) regression versus two-stage least squares (TSLS), which takes account of simultaneous causality among endogenous variables; and over people (the sample at the beginning was 1,700 consumers).

   1   In terms of signs, there was little variation of relationships over time and brands, especially those involving endogenous variables.
   2   The relationships did vary across people (exogenous); but this we would expect because of individual differences (Chapter 8).
   3   There was some variation over method, with ordinary-least-squares regressions (OLS) giving better results than two-stage least squares (TSLS).

Simulation Model

From this model for a subcompact automobile, a predictive simulation model can be devised. It is of the type required in a computerized information system to provide a manager with answers to "what if?" questions, such as "If we increase advertising by 100 percent, what will happen to sales?"

   Let us assume that in this case the managers do want to know the consequence of increasing advertising; and that they know that increasing advertising by \$1 million will increase the consumer's recall of having received information about the automobile by 5 points on a 16-point scale.

   The following results would be obtained by multiplying through the coefficients in Figure 13-6:

$$B \text{ increases by } (.084 \times 5) = 0.42 \tag{1}$$
$$C \text{ increases by } (.252 \times .42) + (.251 \times 5) = 1.36 \tag{2}$$
$$A \text{ increases by } (1.412 \times .42) = 0.59 \tag{3}$$
$$I \text{ increases by } (.099 \times .59) + (.016 \times 1.36) + (.044 \times 5) = .30 \tag{4}$$

Increasing advertising by 5 points increases B by 0.42 because the coefficient relating F to B is .084. C increases by the direct effect of the increase in F (.251 $\times$ 5) plus the indirect effect of the increased value of B (.252 $\times$ .42). In this manner we can work our way through the complete analysis step by step.

   From this analysis, we obtain a summary response function for the system as a whole, in which the regression coefficient is divided by 5 to reduce the change to a per unit change:

$$I = 0.30 + \frac{0.30F}{5} = 0.30 + 0.06F \tag{5}$$

The constant is that for I as originally derived. The coefficient for F is the one derived by multiplying the coefficients as above and giving the answer to equation (4). This simple equation—equation (5)—summarizes the results of the four-equation system and can be used to answer the question, "What happens if advertising is increased so as to increase F by 2 points?" The answer is:

$$I = 0.30 + 0.06F$$
$$= 0.30 + 0.06(2)$$
$$= 0.42$$

Thus, if F is increased by 2 memory units, intention to buy (I) will increase by 0.42 intention units.

If this change in advertising were actually implemented, consumers would not be expected to change instantaneously from the existing equilibrium; they would require some time to reach a new equilibrium, just as was true with the arithmetic example of the stochastic model in Chapter 12. The model given here has no feedbacks; but according to the theory postulated in Chapter 3, the consumer learns from the experience of buying and consuming the brand. Specifically, there are arrows from "purchase" to "satisfaction" and from "satisfaction" to "attitude" and "confidence." If satisfaction were included here to convert the recursive model to a nonrecursive model, a still longer time would be required to reach equilibrium. The direct effect of advertising on attitude, confidence, and intention as shown here would, with the inclusion of satisfaction, have a further effect on attitude and confidence. When these indirect effects of satisfaction were worked out, we could speak of a long-term equilibrium. (Modeling feedbacks will be discussed in Chapter 14.)

A simulation is sometimes said to have four uses.[19] First, it contributes to understanding; for example, in Figure 13-6 the paths of effect can be traced. Second, it aids in the development of alternative plans and can open up creative opportunities by allowing us to go beyond generally accepted premises; this can be called a "diagnostic" role. Third, it can be used to evaluate the merits of alternative actions—that is, to answer "what if?" questions. This is its predictive role. Fourth, it can be used for verification and control; for example, it can be used to set norms so that managers will be alerted to violations. In this role, it would warn managers that the nature of the market has changed.

Stability of the System

Another test of a system is whether or not it will blow up if extreme values are fed into it. This is a particularly important question to ask about a linear system beyond their natural bounds, because the endogenous variables might, by implication, increase beyond their natural bounds for some conditions that might arise. There are no changes in the slopes of the relations to prevent it.

The possibility that the system discussed here will blow up can easily be checked by choosing the most extreme values of the independent variables in each equation to predict values for the dependent variables. None of the constructs blows up badly; only attitude fractionally exceeds its minimum base. Thus, even the linear approximation has reasonable system properties.[20]

CONCLUSIONS

It is clearly possible to quantitatively model the system of buyer behavior begun in Chapter 12 (RRB) and carried forward here (LPS).

Also, the model of LPS can be of a much reduced size, which immensely simplifies understanding and applying it. Figure 13-1 requires five equations; but in the study of the subcompact we have dealt with as few as four equations.

Modeling can give us both understanding, which aids diagnosis, and prediction, which can guide immediate action. Diagnosis stimulates creative strategies and plans. Prediction answers "what if?" questions.

An alternative to the kind of modeling that we have been discussing is the "decision calculus" approach.[21] It "is not unreasonable, however, to expect that these two streams of market modeling philosophy may converge more closely in future applications as the decision calculus approach becomes more data-oriented and buyer behavior models become more functionally explicit."[22]

Finally, we could view the homogenous, linear, recursive model as the end result of several processes delineated at the outset of the chapter. It does yield useful results. Alternatively, we can view it as the beginning point for further specification to capture more of the complications of reality. Sometimes relations are nonlinear instead of linear; some variables that are assumed to be independent of each other, in fact, do interact; substantial interpersonal differences can exist among consumers; and consumers do exhibit feedbacks. These further complications are dealt with in Chapter 14.

SUGGESTIONS FOR FURTHER READING

J. U. Farley, J. A. Howard, and D. R. Lehmann: "A 'Working' System Model of Car Buyer Behavior," *Management Science,* forthcoming.

L. J. Parsons and R. L. Schultz: *Marketing Models and Econometric Research,* North Holland, New York, 1976.

[20]Farley, Howard, and Lehmann, *Management Science.*

[21]J. D. C. Little, "Models and Managers: The Concept of Decision Calculus," *Management Science,* **16**:466–485, April 1970.

[22]Farley, Howard, and Lehmann, *Management Science.*

Modeling LPS: Heterogeneous, Nonlinear, Nonrecursive Models

CONTENTS

A linear, recursive, heterogeneous model is the simplest of the structural models. A number of instances, however, raise doubts about whether this model adequately captures reality. First, in Chapter 8 we discussed the need for segmenting variables. Since consumers may respond differently from each other, how do these fit into a quantified system? In a technical sense, this is the most essential modification to make because exogenous variables are essential for identifying the system. Second, feedback loops do, in fact, occur in a number of places in the theory, making it a nonrecursive system (as was noted in Chapters 3, 4, and 7). Third, there is the question whether the relations are always linear. According to the theory, some are not. Nonlinear relations allow us to deal with the related question of interdependence among the independent variables in a multiple relation. The theory postulated in Chapter 3, for example, holds that attitude and confidence are interdependent in causing intention.

HETEROGENEOUS MODELING OF LPS

The models discussed in Chapter 13 were all heterogeneous; but to simplify, they were discussed as though they were homogeneous. Now, we will deal with some of the complexities of individual differences among consumers (discussed in Chapter 8). For practical purposes, the most important aspect of individual differences is the possibility of segmenting a market. In addition, however, they are a means of reducing noise and providing variables to identify the system for the purpose of structural modeling.

A specific and extensive example of individual differences will illustrate some of the complexities.

Example: Data, Operationalization, Specification, Analysis

The same raw data are used here as in the study of instant breakfast food in Chapter 13. The sample consisted of 1,100 homemakers in a test market in Portland, Oregon, in 1966. At this time, Post Instant Breakfast (a new brand) was being introduced after Carnation Instant Breakfast (an established brand) had been on the market for about two years. The variables were operationalized as described in the appendix to this chapter.

The model specified by Jagpal[1] is shown in Table 14-1, where the eight constituent equations are displayed as columns 2 through 9. In column 2, for example, the dependent variable is recall of media and the independent variables are attitude, age, and lagged satisfaction (line 28). A nonrecursive version is used because it allows a comparison between the model with individual-difference (exogenous) variables and the model without them; such a comparison shows the contribution that individual-difference variables make to the system. Also, the same model can then be used to deal explicitly with nonrecursive systems (this is discussed in the next section).

[1]H. S. Jagpal, "The Formulation and Empirical Testing of a Dynamic Consumer Decision Process Model: A Simultaneous Equations Econometric Model," unpublished doctoral dissertation, Columbia University, 1974.

For analysis of the data, ordinary-least-squares (OLS) regression was used. Two-stage least squares (TSLS) was also tried, but OLS consistently gives better results.[2]

The results of the analysis are shown in Table 14-1. The first number in each cell is the regression coefficient; the number immediately below in parentheses is the t-test value for that regression coefficient. Following are the one-tailed t-test significance limits for interpreting these coefficients:

1.29 indicates a significance level of 10 percent
1.64 indicates a significance level of 5 percent
2.33 indicates a significance level of 1 percent
3.09 indicates a significance level of 0.1 percent

Beginning at line 11 in Table 14-1 are the socioeconomic and personality variables; these continue to line 25. Thus fifteen such variables are entered into various equations (as you can see by looking across lines 11 to 25), specifying a total of twenty-three relations. The logic of this particular specification is based on a variety of sources.[3] No attempt will be made to describe them here; but, as was seen in Chapter 8, the theory for specifying individual differences has been weak.

According to Table 14-1, ten of the fifteen socioeconomic and personality variables are statistically significant at the 10 percent confidence level ($t > 1.29$) or better somewhere in the system. If the regression coefficients had been standardized, we could go a step further and compare the relative strengths of these variables; but it has not been usual in econometrics to standardize regression coefficients, as it has in path analysis.

The major practical interest of individual differences is for segmenting purposes. A variable to be used for segmenting must, of course, be some characteristic by which consumers can be identified in the market; it must also be powerful enough to justify making a market effort in terms of it. Unless individual differences can be identified in such a way that the marketing program can be tailored to them, they are not useful. For example, how does one reach people who are high on opinion leadership with a particular message? Self-selection is a possibility—as was implied in Chapter 7 when feedbacks to attention were discussed—but self-selection is probably an inefficient way to reach people. A direct approach would be more desirable.

Another purpose of individual-difference variables is to increase R^2 so as to improve prediction. What can such variables do to reduce noise? That is, how much do they increase our ability to predict and our confidence that we have incorporated into the system most if not all of the major forces bearing on the consumer's choice? To answer this question, we apply the same type of analysis to a system with such variables (Table 14-1) and a system without them (Table 14-2, which is homogeneous, with the minor exception of income in row 14).

[2]J. U. Farley, J. A. Howard, and D. R. Lehmann, "A 'Working' System Model of Car Buyer Behavior," *Management Science,* forthcoming.
[3]Jagpal, op. cit., chap. 4.

Table 14-1 Ordinary-Least-Squares Estimates of Structural Parameters in a Linear, Nonrecursive, Heterogeneous Model of Consumer Behavior for an Established Brand

(1) Variables	(2) Media recall	(3) Word of mouth	(4) Brand identification	(5) Attitude	(6) Intention	(7) Confidence	(8) Purchase	(9) Satisfaction
Endogenous								
1 (Media) recall	—	0.007 (0.85)	−0.220 (−12.72)	0.064 (1.81)	−0.285 (−14.99)	0.089 (4.41)	—	—
2 Word of mouth	—	—	0.310 (3.27)	0.361 (2.17)	—	0.241 (2.53)	—	—
3 Brand comprehension	—	—	—	0.067 (0.84)	—	0.111 (2.36)	—	—
4 Attitude	0.115 (2.02)	0.020 (1.90)	—	—	0.161 (5.11)	—	0.170 (4.99)	—
5 Intention	—	—	—	—	—	—	—	—
6 Confidence	—	—	—	—	0.229 (4.22)	—	—	0.421 (8.11)
7 Purchase	—	—	—	—	—	—	—	—
8 Satisfaction	—	—	—	—	0.30 (7.67)	—	0.30 (8.39)	—
Marketing								
9 Price	—	—	0.441 (3.81)	—	0.037 (0.26)	—	—	—
10 Sample	—	—	—	—	—	—	—	—
Exogenous								
11 Age	−0.095 (−16.80)	—	0.028 (9.66)	−0.015 (−2.71)	—	—	—	—
12 Education	—	—	0.009 (5.42)	—	—	—	—	—
13 Household size	—	—	—	—	—	—	1.540 (1.32)	—
14 Income	—	—	—	−0.087 (−2.45)	—	—	−0.056 (−2.60)	—
15 Nutrition-consciousness	—	—	—	0.094 (1.19)	—	—	—	—

	(1)	(2)	(3)	(4)	(5)	(6)	(7)	(8)
16 Generalized self-confidence	—	−0.005 (−0.63)	—	—	—	0.067 (3.10)	—	—
17 Gregariousness	—	0.001 (2.23)	—	—	—	—	—	—
18 Innovativeness	—	—	—	0.049 (1.41)	—	0.015 (0.74)	—	—
19 Opinion leadership	—	0.129 (3.05)	—	—	—	—	—	—
20 Product importance	—	0.028 (1.98)	—	—	—	0.055 (1.66)	—	—
21 Deal-proneness	—	−0.006 (−1.16)	—	—	—	—	0.004 (0.31)	—
22 Price-consciousness	—	—	—	—	—	—	−0.041 (−2.55)	—
23 Store loyalty	—	—	—	—	—	—	0.370 (1.87)	—
24 Household skills	—	—	—	0.017 (0.42)	—	—	—	—
25 Food-innovativeness	—	−0.006 (−0.14)	—	—	—	—	—	—
Lagged endogenous								
26 Confidence	—	0.027 (1.55)	—	—	—	—	—	—
27 Purchase	—	—	0.252 (4.65)	—	—	—	—	—
28 Satisfaction	0.198 (2.51)	0.021 (1.38)	−0.003 (−0.11)	0.741 (15.54)	0.025 (0.59)	0.362 (13.00)	—	—
29 **Constant**	4.151 (12.09)	−0.215 (−2.52)	2.983 (21.06)	3.052 (7.80)	1.175 (7.21)	1.520 (5.85)	−0.072 (−0.67)	1.661 (23.79)
30 R^2	0.382	0.094	0.636	0.391	0.468	0.383	0.215	0.099

Note: Figures in parentheses denote *t*-values.
Source: H. S. Jagpal, "The Formulation and Empirical Testing of a Dynamic Decision Process Model: A Simultaneous Equations Econometric Model," unpublished doctoral dissertation, Columbia University, 1974, pp. 5-9 and 5-10.

Table 14-2 Ordinary-Least-Squares Estimates of Structural Parameters in a Linear, Nonrecursive, Homogeneous Model of Consumer Behavior (Including Only Marketing-Controlled Variables) for an Established Brand

(1) Variables	(2) Media recall	(3) Word of mouth	(4) Brand identification	(5) Attitude	(6) Intention	(7) Confidence	(8) Purchase	(9) Satisfaction
Endogenous								
1 (Media) recall	—	-0.017 (-2.84)	-0.357 (-22.72)	0.102 (3.08)	-0.285 (-14.99)	0.110 (5.82)	—	—
2 Word of mouth	—	—	0.465 (4.36)	0.365 (2.20)	—	0.269 (2.82)	—	—
3 Brand comprehension	—	—	—	0.026 (0.42)	—	0.050 (1.41)	—	—
4 Attitude	0.251 (3.66)	0.019 (1.85)	—	—	0.161 (5.11)	—	0.253 (8.68)	—
5 Intention	—	—	—	—	—	—	—	—
6 Confidence	—	—	—	—	-0.229 (4.22)	—	—	—
7 Purchase	—	—	—	—	—	—	—	0.421 (8.11)
8 Satisfaction	—	—	—	—	—	—	—	—
Marketing								
9 Price	—	—	—	—	0.300 (7.67)	—	—	—
10 Sample	—	—	0.473 (4.11)	—	0.037 (0.26)	—	—	—
Exogenous								
11 Age	—	—	—	—	—	—	—	—
12 Education	—	—	—	—	—	—	—	—
13 Household size	—	—	—	—	—	—	—	—
14 Income	—	—	—	—	—	—	-0.059 (-2.73)	—
15 Nutrition-consciousness	—	—	—	—	—	—	—	—

276

	1	2	3	4	5	6	7	8
16 Generalized self-confidence	—	—	—	—	—	—	—	—
17 Gregariousness	—	—	—	—	—	—	—	—
18 Innovativeness	—	—	—	—	—	—	—	—
19 Opinion leadership	—	—	—	—	—	—	—	—
20 Product importance	—	—	—	—	—	—	—	—
21 Deal-proneness	—	—	—	—	—	—	—	—
22 Price-consciousness	—	—	—	—	—	—	—	—
23 Store loyalty	—	—	—	—	—	—	—	—
24 Household skills	—	—	—	—	—	—	—	—
25 Food-innovativeness	—	—	—	—	—	—	—	—
Lagged endogenous								
26 Confidence	—	0.033 (1.88)	—	—	—	—	—	—
27 Purchase	—	—	0.262 (4.26)	—	—	—	—	—
28 Satisfaction	0.312 (3.27)	0.016 (1.06)	−0.023 (−0.73)	0.765 (16.17)	0.025 (0.55)	0.386 (14.23)	—	—
29 **Constant**	0.255 (0.83)	0.013 (0.23)	4.551 (54.35)	2.977 (9.56)	1.18 (7.21)	2.119 (11.86)	−0.131 (−1.35)	1.661 (23.79)
30 R^2	0.090	0.042	0.556	0.375	0.468	0.371	0.112	0.099

Note: Figures in parentheses denote t-values.

Source: H. S. Jagpal, "The Formulation and Empirical Testing of a Dynamic Decision Process Model: A Simultaneous Equations Econometric Model," unpublished doctoral dissertation, Columbia University, 1974, pp. 5-53, 5-54.

Table 14-3 Comparison of R_2 to Show Effects of Individual Differences

	(2) Media recall	(3) Word of mouth	(4) Brand identification	(5) Attitude	(7) Confidence	(8) Purchase
Table 14.1	0.38	0.09	0.64	0.39	0.38	0.22
Table 14.2	0.09	0.04	0.56	0.38	0.37	0.11

Compare line 30 of Table 14-1 with line 30 of Table 14-2, omitting intention (column 6) and satisfaction (column 9) because they contain no exogeneous (segmenting) variables. You will find that in all six equations, the value of R^2 is improved by the inclusion of these segmenting variables. The question now is, By how much? This comparison is shown in Table 14-3, where the columns are numbered in the same way as those of Tables 14-1 and 14-2. Columns 2, 3, and 8 were substantially improved and column 4 was somewhat improved; but for attitude and confidence (colums 5 and 7), the improvement was not significant. The results in column 3 are at least partially explained by the mere inclusion of additional variables. What is surprising is that R^2 for media recall more than quadrupled in Table 14-1 (column 2, line 30). Age (line 11) was the only segmenting variable assigned to media recall; here, the negative relationship in Table 14-1 is fairly strong and its significance is very high. One might infer that older people did not bother to pay attention to the brand, because they did not like it, as would be indicated by the negative effect on attitude (column 5, line 11). The coefficient between brand identification and age (column 4, line 11) is highly significant. Perhaps older people quickly learned about the brand and decided they didn't like it.

To simplify, the effects of segmentation variables on the new brand are not shown; but the results are quite similar to those shown here for the established brand.

Summary: Heterogeneity

It is especially important to make use of individual-difference variables, because, as Wilkie and Pessemier have pointed out,[4] without them there is some question about the validity of the cross-sectional analysis that is heavily relied on in this chapter and in Chapter 13. Also, they can be used for segmenting, to make marketing efforts more efficient; but, in practice, we also need to know whether their relations are nonlinear, so as to maximize the individual functions. (For simple ways of checking for nonlinearity, see Lehmann.[5]) Use of these variables can also improve prediction. Finally, there is a technical, econometric issue: identifying the system. Of these reasons for using individual differences, the two

[4]W. L. Wilkie and E. A. Pessemier, "Issues in Marketing's Use of Multi-Attribute Attitude Models," *Journal of Marketing Research*, **10:**428–441, November 1973.

[5]D. R. Lehmann, "Some Alternatives to Linear Factor Analysis for Variable Grouping Applied to Buyer Behavior Variables," *Journal of Marketing Research*, **11:**206–213, May 1974.

most important for our purposes are segmenting a market and reducing noise so that prediction can be improved. As regards prediction, however, we must bear in mind that (as was mentioned in Chapter 13) practitioners are interested not in predicting an individual's behavior but in predicting the behavior of groups—the mean of a segment, for example.

One caveat is necessary. Segmenting variables do not capture all individual differences within a linear model. They capture differences only in levels of variables, not in the slope. If nonlinear relations are used, segmenting variables can capture differences in the shapes of the functions as well and thus yield different response functions. Segmentation is useful only if there are differences in response functions among the segments.

NONRECURSIVE MODELING OF LPS

The theory described in Chapters 3, 5, and 7 postulates two kinds of feedbacks: one from the satisfaction of buying and consuming a brand to attitude and confidence; the other from various endogenous variables to the attention and search process. Not all such feedbacks are captured in the system specified here, but enough are to illustrate how they can be modeled.

Specification of Feedback Elements

Specification of the incomplete, nonrecursive model for an established brand is shown in Table 14-1, which also contains the results of analyzing the data; the same data and analysis will be used in this section. To clarify an otherwise complex discussion, however, it is helpful to show the feedback elements from Table 14-1 separately; this is done in Figure 14-1.

The dashed lines in Figure 14-1 show the feedbacks from satisfaction specified in the model. The dashed-and-dotted lines show the only feedbacks specified to the attention and search process: namely, from "attitude" to "media recall" and to "word of mouth" and from "confidence" to "word of mouth."

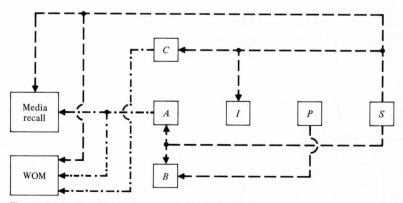

Figure 14-1   Feedback elements in nonrecursive model.

Results

Figure 7-3 showed a feedback from "attitude" to "attention." This is also seen when "media recall"—column 2 in Table 14-1—is examined and attitude is related to media recall with a regression coefficient of 0.115, which is significant. The measurements of attitude and media recall were taken at the same time and so imply a simultaneous feedback. Confidence was also specified to feed back to WOM, but with a lag. Specifically, confidence was measured eleven weeks before WOM.[6] In Table 14-1, confidence (line 26) is shown as having a small but significant positive lagged effect. A negative effect was postulated; but this assumes that the purpose of WOM is to get information, and the operationalization of WOM does not distinguish between getting and giving information, as can be seen in the appendix to this chapter. (See Lampert for a detailed analysis.[7])

Satisfaction, according to the theory, feeds back to attitude and confidence (see Chapter 3). Here, it is specified to feed back, after a lag, in all the equations except purchase (and, of course, satisfaction). As with confidence, the lag was eleven weeks. As can be seen in Table 14-1 (line 28), its effect on media recall (indicated by the size and significance of the regression coefficient) is substantial. Except for media recall, however, the theory holds: the feedback to attitude (column 5, line 28) is highly significant, and the feedback to confidence (column 7, line 28) is almost as significant. The theory does not postulate feedbacks to identification and intention, or a feedback from purchase to brand identification. Only the latter (column 4) is significant.

Nonrecursiveness can also be evaluated in terms of its effect on prediction, as indicated by R^2. When a recursive model is compared with the nonrecursive model, in Table 14-4, the nonrecursive model shows some improvement in the predictive power of the brand identification equation. The effect is much greater for the attitude and confidence equations, as is to be expected because of the large regression coefficients. The remaining three equations are largely unchanged.

A question that can be raised is whether the feedback effects of satisfaction are different at different stages of learning. To answer this, the results for each of the two methods with the new brand (Post Instant Breakfast) are compared in Table 14-5. The pattern of effects is the same as in Table 14-4, but the magnitude of differences between recursive and nonrecursive methods is substantially less for the new brand. The effects on the established brand could be so much stronger because the disequilibrium—a state of disturbance from the normal position—of the established brand is much less and thus more quickly restored.

---

[6]G. S. Day, "A Description and Evaluation of the Design of the Buyer Behavior Research Project," in J. U. Farley, J. A. Howard, and L. W. Ring (eds.), *Consumer Behavior: Theory and Application,* Allyn and Bacon, Boston, 1974, p. 36.

[7]S. I. Lampert, "Word of Mouth Activity During the Introduction of a New Food Product," in J. U. Farley, J. A. Howard, and L. W. Ring (eds.), *Consumer Behavior: Theory and Application,* Allyn and Bacon, Boston, 1974, pp. 67–88.

Table 14-4   Values of R^2 for Established Brand

	B	A	C	I	P	S
Recursive system	0.62	0.14	0.21	0.47	0.21	0.10
Nonrecursive system	0.64	0.39	0.38	0.47	0.22	0.10

Table 14-5   Values of R^2 for New Brand

	B	A	C	I	P	S
Recursive system	0.65	0.22	0.31	0.32	0.37	0.10
Nonrecursive system	0.66	0.25	0.34	0.33	0.37	0.10

In more psychological terms, the consumer has much more structure (to provide feedback) for the established brand than for the new brand.

Summary: Nonrecursive Models

Consistent with the theory, a nonrecursive model of satisfaction shows strong improvement over a recursive model; but this improvement is greater for a stable brand than for a new brand.

Nonrecursive modeling is somewhat more complicated than recursive modeling. As we have seen, interpretation is somewhat more difficult. Also, the length of time required for the process to take place raises important questions as regards nonrecursive models. We should know the length of the lag and collect data in terms of it. Specifically, the time elapsed between collections of data should equal either (1) the time required for the change or (2) some multiple of that time; otherwise, the data do not conform to the theory. Here, eleven weeks elapsed between collections of data. The results seem to justify the additional effort.

Unfortunately, the data did not permit testing of the other feedbacks to attention and search processes. These should be investigated because they should be much better understood. The theory suggests, for example, that communicating to a consumer in LPS is much easier than communicating to a consumer in EPS because the feedbacks are much more operative in LPS.

NONLINEAR MODELING OF LPS

We have been assuming so far in this chapter, as in Chapter 13, that the relations are linear. This assumption greatly simplifies the task of modeling, but it probably misses some of reality. To determine how much of reality it does miss, let us examine an instance of nonlinear modeling.

In Chapter 3, it was asserted that information has a nonlinear effect: that is, consumers take in more information until they have learned about a brand and thereafter take in less. Also, in Chapter 7 a nonlinear relation was postulated between purchase and satisfaction because of the consumer's level of aspiration.

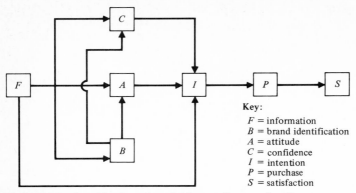

Key:
F = information
B = brand identification
A = attitude
C = confidence
I = intention
P = purchase
S = satisfaction

Figure 14-2 Specification of model for nonlinear estimation.

When a nonlinear relation exists, the effect of a change in the independent variable is greater at one level of the independent variable than at another level. When linear relations are used, it is implicitly assumed that among the endogenous variables one independent variable does not interact with other independent variables in the same equation. With nonlinear relations we can determine to what extent independent variables do interact with each other, but this can also be done with a statistical technique called the ANOVA model without computing nonlinear relations. An illustration will clarify this problem of interaction. According to the theory in Chapter 3, a buyer's attitude and confidence both cause intention to buy. If attitude and confidence exerted independent effects on intention, being highly confident would not cause attitude to be any more or less effective. But, as was discussed in Chapter 3, attitude and confidence do interact; there is an arrow from "attitude" to "confidence" in Figure 3-4, which implies that they operate jointly to cause intention.

For the nonlinear analysis presented here, the data from the study of instant breakfast food discussed in Chapter 13 are again used. Laroche carried out two analyses together, in order to show the advantage of estimating nonlinear relations.[8] The specification in Figure 14-2 is identical to that of Figure 13-1; but at a more detailed level of specification the shapes of the functions may be nonlinear, as will be seen later.

Relations

The relations used in Chapter 13 are listed below, with the addition of feedback from satisfaction:

$$B = f(F) \tag{1}$$
$$A = f(F,B) \tag{2}$$
$$C = f(F,B) \tag{3}$$

[8]M. Laroche, "A New Approach to Non-Linear Consumer Behavior and Market Segmentation by the Use of Orthogonal Polynomials," unpublished doctoral dissertation, Columbia University, 1974.

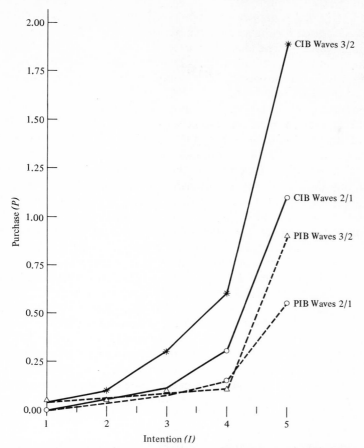

Figure 14-3 Conditional means in the relationship between purchase and intention. *(M. Laroche and J. A. Howard, "Nonlinear Relations in a Complex Model of Buyer Behavior," Graduate School of Business, Columbia University, mimeographed, 1975.)*

$$I = f(F,A,C) \tag{4}$$
$$P = f(I) \tag{5}$$
$$S = f(P) \tag{6}$$

F is an exogenous variable; but to simplify, exogenous variables included to identify the system are omitted here. (For a complete list of the variables used in the study, see Laroche and Howard.[9])

Procedure for Fitting Nonlinear Relations

The form of each function was obtained in two steps. First, conditional means were obtained for each relation. This is illustrated in Figure 14-3, where "CIB

[9]M. Laroche and J. A. Howard, "Non-Linear Relations in a Complex Model of Buyer Behavior," Graduate School of Business, Columbia University, mimeographed, 1975.

waves 3/2,'' for example, refers to data on intention collected on July 15 (wave 2) and data on purchase collected for the subsequent period, beginning July 15 and ending in early October (wave 3). The analysis is over two waves of interviewing and over two brands: Carnation and Post. Except for the intention-purchase equation, only waves 1 and 2 are involved in the comparison. The "conditional mean" is the mean of the values of the dependent variable (purchase) for each value of the independent variable (intention). In the intention-purchase equation, $P = f(I)$, there is the one independent variable, intention. In the attitude, confidence, and intention equations, however, there are two or more independent variables; when this analysis is done for one of them, the other independent variables in the equation are held constant. As is shown in Figure 14-3, this first step provides insight into the shape of the relationship. The relation is obviously upwardly convex.

Second, the four curves of Figure 14-3 must be reconciled into one functional form. The form selected to represent the intention-purchase relation from Figure 14-3 was:

$$\text{Log } (P + 0.05) = \exp I + \text{constant}$$

Results

Graphing the results makes them easier to understand and reveals the nature of both the nonlinearities and the interactions.

For example, let us consider Figure 14-4, which repeats a relation postulated in Chapter 3 and shown there as Figure 3-6. In Chapter 3 it was said that in order for attitude to form, brand identification must form first. Briefly, information is a necessary but not sufficient condition for concept attainment; brand identification must also be present $[A = f(F,B)]$. First, as can be seen in Figure 14-4, where $B = 5$, the relation is strongly nonlinear. A nonlinear model for such a relation, instead of a linear model, could substantially improve the fit of the model to the data. Second, brand identification has an independent, positive effect upon attitude, as is shown by the differing intercepts with different values of brand identification. Third, brand identification and information have a joint effect upon attitude. When brand identification is low ($B = 0$), additional information has no effect on attitude; but as B becomes larger, information has a greater effect. At $B = 5$, information has a very strong effect, especially at lower levels of information.

The point made in Chapter 13, that it is essential to study the system as a whole to determine factors that must be controlled when a single relation is studied, now becomes clearer. For instance, imagine an experiment on the information-attitude relation. If most of the sample happened to have a brand identification of 0 to 1, you would come to quite different conclusions about the effect of information than if most of the sample had a brand identification of 5. More important, from a theoretical point of view, the relation is consistent with the hypothesis that brand identification is a necessary condition to the formation of attitude. In examining Figure 14-5, you should ask the three questions im-

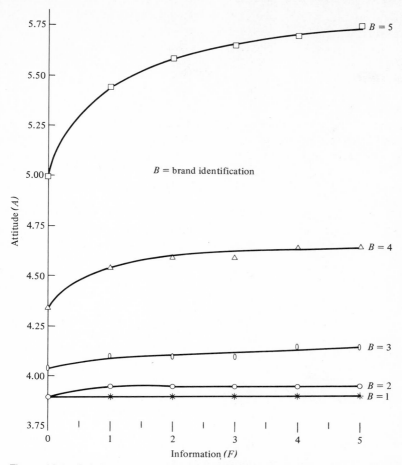

Figure 14-4 Relationship between information and attitude with information interacting with brand identification. *(Laroche and Howard, 1975.)*

plied above: Is the relation nonlinear? Does the second independent variable have an effect upon the dependent variable? Do the independent variables have a joint effect upon the dependent variable?

Not all the relations we are concerned with are interdependent, however. In Figure 14-5 there are strong nonlinearities in the relation between brand identification and attitude but almost no interaction. Here we see how useful nonlinear analysis can be. Suppose that a manager increases advertising, so that brand identification increases to a level of 2. Attitude does not increase; the manager may therefore assume that the advertising was wasted. But as Figure 14-5 shows, this need not be true. There is a level of brand identification, about 2, that must be attained before brand identification affects attitude. Any increase beyond this would have a strong effect on attitude. This example is especially important because attitude is used as a common measure of the effect of advertising.

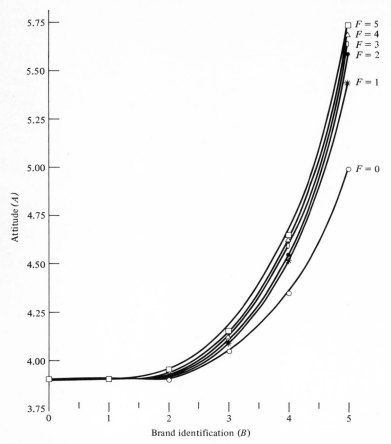

Figure 14-5 Relationship between brand identification and attitude with brand identification interacting with information. *((Laroche and Howard, 1975.)*

Figure 14-6 shows the relation between intention and purchase; this was hinted at in Figure 14-3, where the procedure for deriving nonlinear relations was illustrated. This relationship is surprisingly nonlinear, and it too illustrates the usefulness of nonlinear analysis for the manager. A manager could erroneously conclude that an increase in intention had no effect on purchase and, accordingly, stop spending money to increase intention. A manager who was further out on the curve might conclude that a small increase had an enormous effect on intention and thus exaggerate the overall power of advertising.

The purchase-satisfaction relation shown in Figure 14-7 (page 288) is quite nonlinear. Early purchases have a strong effect; later purchases, a weaker effect. This could be interpreted as a result of levels of aspiration (discussed in Chapter 7): with additional experience the consumer's level of aspiration rises, so that a brand becomes less satisfying with additional purchases.

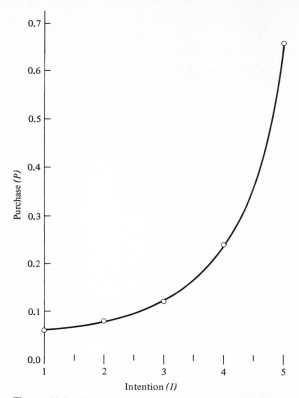

Figure 14-6   Relationship between purchase and intention. *(Laroche and Howard, 1975.)*

Summary: Nonlinear Models

Only a few of the relations in the model have been examined. (To investigate the others, see Laroche and Howard.[10]) Enough were shown, however, to illustrate how nonlinear relations can be derived and how fruitful they can be.

We begin to see, for example, why it is so difficult to interpret facts in a market without a theory. To illustrate, let us return to an example discussed in connection with Figure 14-6. Because of the shape of the intention-purchase relation, a manager could increase advertising and have a substantial effect on buyers' intentions with no effect on purchase. The conclusion that advertising was having no effect would be erroneous; in other words, it may be erroneous to use only sales as a measure of the effectiveness of advertising.

As regards basic research, we see how important the complete nonlinear analysis can be in showing what variables should be controlled for in an experiment on a single relation. Also, we have seen more evidence that it is necessary to specify a model fully in order to test its truth. The use of flowcharts contrib-

[10]Ibid.

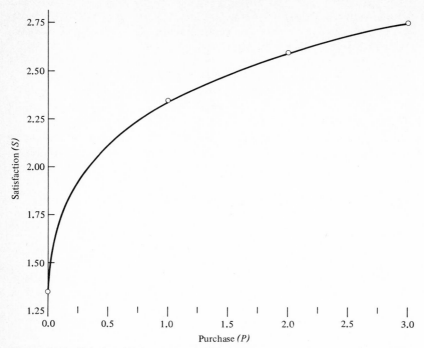

Figure 14-7   Relationship between satisfaction and purchase. *(Laroche and Howard, 1975.)*

utes greatly to the precise description needed for modeling, but it still leaves questions about the shapes of the relations.

Finally, a nonlinear model does complicate analysis and interpretation; but fortunately, only a few of the relations appear to be strongly nonlinear.

CONCLUSIONS

This chapter is relevant for both practice and basic research.

As regards practice, the flexibility of the system is conspicuous. A very simple system can be used, as in Chapter 13, to facilitate introducing a system into practice (as for monitoring a test market). But we are now in a better position to appraise the limitations of such a system and determine the cost we are paying for simplicity. From our fuller knowledge of the total system we are better able to interpret results. If, for example, purchase does not increase with increased attitude, we will suspect a nonlinear relation and ask where we are on the curve.

If additional information is needed for diagnosis, as it usually is, a more complex system can be developed. The key point is that now we are in a much better position to know how to complicate the system in order to gain certain advantages while avoiding the cost of unnecessary complexity. For example, feedbacks from satisfaction are very important, but only to attitude and confidence.

In Chapter 13, the question of whether the functions in the system really are response functions was raised. This, of course, entails the question of whether the relations are causal: Will an increase in an independent variable necessarily raise the value of the dependent variable? That question can now be answered in the affirmative. There are times, as we saw, when the dependent variable does not respond, but this is because of the state of some other part of the system. Increasing information, for example, is not likely to increase attitude unless brand identification is greater than zero, as was seen in Figure 14-4.

In practice, prediction is important. Unless a relationship can be depended upon, it is not very useful. We want our system to capture as much as possible of the forces playing on the consumer. This is where R^2 becomes relevant; Table 14-6 compares values of R^2 from studies across three models and two brands.

If the improvements in R^2 that occur with nonlinear relations were added to the values of R^2 for the linear, nonrecursive, heterogeneous model in the four equations that are greatly improved, we can expect that this would result in still better values of R^2 for the established brand. This assumes that the other equations are linear and would not profit from nonlinear fitting.

Some problems of estimating and testing complex structured models have been omitted here; these have to do with the conditions listed in Chapter 13, none of which is insurmountable. (Complications posed by multicollinearity, for example, are a common problem.) Also, nothing has been said about using a variety of multivariate statistical techniques in developing operational definitions; but this is especially important in conducting diagnoses—that is, determining why we find what we do in a particular situation and what action we should suggest. This can be considered part of the general problem of noise reduction.[11]

As regards basic research, we can now be more sympathetic to McGuire's plea that we look at the total process from availability of information to action.[12] Even if we study only a single relation in the laboratory, we can improve the chances of success because we know better what to control for.

Structural modeling sharply highlights the intimate, powerful, mutually reinforcing relationship between theory and measurement. In the interaction between the two, we can see in Chapters 13 and 14 substantial support for the theory, although this was not their main objective. The need for further development is obvious, and one can think of numerous suggestions in this regard. For example, certain nonlinear and nonrecursive features should be combined into a single model, and better individual-difference variables should be combined with both.

We are now ready to go on to the next stage of development—to go beyond estimating relations to testing hypotheses about the specific shapes of the relations.

[11]J. U. Farley and J. A. Howard (eds.), *Control of "Error" in Market Research Data*, Lexington Books, Lexington, Mass., 1975.

[12]W. J. McGuire, "Psychological Factors Influencing Consumer Choice," Project on Synthesis of Knowledge of Consumer Behavior, RANN Program, National Science Foundation, April 1975.

Table 14-6 Comparison of R_2 Obtained in Three Multiple-Equation Process Models of Consumer Behavior Using the Same Data

Endogenous variables	Established brand			New Brand	
	Linear, recursive, heterogeneous*	Nonlinear, recursive, heterogeneous‡	Linear, nonrecursive, heterogeneous¶	Nonlinear, recursive, heterogeneous‡	Linear, nonrecursive, heterogeneous¶
Media recall	0.06	—	0.38	—	0.48
Word of mouth	0.07	—	0.09	—	0.28
Brand comprehension	0.10	0.32	0.64	0.12	0.66
Attitude	0.14	0.18	0.39	0.14	0.25
Confidence	0.02	0.30	0.38	0.11	0.34
Intention	0.42	0.45	0.47	0.28	0.33
Purchase	0.15	0.13	0.22	0.11	0.37
Satisfaction	0.25	0.06	0.10	0.05	0.10

*J. U. Farley and L. W. Ring, "An Empirical Test of the Howard-Sheth Model of Buyer Behavior," *Journal of Marketing Research*, **7**:427–438, November 1970

‡M. Laroche and J. A. Howard, "Non-Linear Relations in a Complex Model of Buyer Behavior," Graduate School of Business, Columbia University, mimeographed, 1975.

¶H. S. Jagpal, "The Formulation and Empirical Testing of a Dynamic Consumer Decision Process Model: A Simultaneous Equations Econometric Model," unpublished doctoral dissertation, Columbia University, 1974.

APPENDIX: Definitions of System Variables and Their Empirical Measurement

EXOGENOUS VARIABLES

Socioeconomic, Demographic, and Nonpersonality Factors

"Age of homemaker": in years

"Education of homemaker": in years

"Household size": number of members.

"Sample receipt":
>Have you ever received a free sample or coupon in the mail? (Yes or No)

"Total income of the household":
>(1)   under $2,500
>(2) $2,500–$3,999
>(3) $4,000–$5,999
>(4) $6,000–$7,999
>(5) $8,000–$9,999
>(6) $10,000 and over

"Price": Average price paid per unit
>(NOTE: A unit is defined as a standard size for each brand to allow for unequal sizes of packages.)

Personality Variables

"Nutrition-consciousness": defined as the sum of the following—
>I never give a thought to proper foods. (Yes or No)
>I plan my meals so that my family gets proper nutrition. (Yes or No)
>I often go out of my way to buy nutritious food. (Yes or No)

"Generalized self-confidence":
>Do you like to have the help of others in deciding what to do?
>Do you often hesitate to speak up or express yourself in a group?
>Do you see yourself as a person who introduces new things to your friends?

"Gregariousness": sum of the following—
>Not counting members of your immediate family, about how many people do you talk to during an average week?
>How many times in the past seven days have you had visitors at your home or had an informal get-together there?
>How many times in the past seven days were you invited out for an evening with some friends or to have a dinner at their house?

"Innovativeness": sum of answers to the following—
>How likely are you to try a car that can be steered by an electric eye?
>An effective pill for the prevention of colds and minor respiratory ailments?
>Visual telephones (so that you can see the person to whom you are talking)?
>(Scale of 4, "very likely," to 1, "unlikely")

Personality Variables (Continued)

"Food-innovativeness": sum of the following—
> When I am in a grocery store, I am likely to reach out and pick up new foods. (Yes or No)
>
> I am the kind of woman who, just for the fun of it, will try almost any new food once. (Yes or No)
>
> I will try almost any new food once. (Yes or No)

"Opinion leadership":
> Do you like to be leader of the group you are in? (Yes or No)

"Product importance":
> How interested are you in brand differences for milk additives?
> (5, "very interested," to 1, "not at all interested")

"Deal-proneness": Total units purchased on deals in a given period.

"Price-consciousness": sum of the following—
> I check the prices of food items I buy all of the time ( ), most of the time ( ), sometimes ( ), never ( ).
>
> The difference in price between the various brands of packaged food interests me a great deal ( ), quite a lot ( ), only a little ( ), not at all ( ).
>
> I go to stores where I don't usually shop in order to take advantage of food sales every chance I get ( ), almost every chance ( ), seldom ( ), never ( ).

"Store loyalty": Number of stores where respondent shops
> (NOTE: This is an inverse relation.)

"Household skills": sum of the following—
> How good are you at cooking?
> How good are you at other tasks of homemaking?
> (Scale of 1 to 6)

ENDOGENOUS VARIABLES

"Media recall": defined as the sum of the following—
> Have you seen the brand advertised in newspapers or magazines? (Yes or No)
>
> Have you heard the brand advertised on radio? (Yes or No)
>
> Have you heard the brand advertised in other sources? (Yes or No)
>
> Number of times the respondent remembers seeing the brand advertised on television.

"Word of mouth": defined as the sum of the following—
> Have you discussed the brand with your husband? (Yes or No)
>
> Have you discussed the brand with your children? (Yes or No)
>
> Have you discussed the brand with a friend or friends? (Yes or No)

"Brand comprehension": defined as summated index based on correct responses to the following questions—
> In your opinion, is the "instant breakfast" product we have talked about a food which:
> > (a) Is frozen, powdered, or natural?
> > (b) Comes in a can, bottle, or box?

ENDOGENOUS VARIABLES (Continued)

(c) Comes in many flavors or one flavor?

(d) Is drunk or eaten with a spoon?

(e) Is packaged in individual portions or in bulk?

(NOTE: Brand comprehension is approximated by product comprehension owing to unavailability of data.)

"Attitude":

How do you rate the brand overall?

(7, "like it very much," to 1, "do not like it very much")

"Intention to buy":

How likely are you to buy the brand in the next month?

(5, "definitely will," to 1, "definintely will not")

"Confidence":

How confident are you in your ability to judge the brand?

(5, "extremely confident," to 1, "not confident at all")

"Purchase": defined as the number of units of the brand bought in a given period.

(NOTE: A standard unit is defined to allow for unequal package sizes.)

"Satisfaction":

How satisfied are you with the brand?

(4, "extremely satisfied," to 1, "not satisfied")

SUGGESTIONS FOR FURTHER READING

J. U. Farley and J. A. Howard (eds.): *Control of "Error" in Market Research Data,* Lexington Books, Lexington, Mass., 1975.

J. Jacoby, G. J. Szybillo, and C. K. Berning: "Collection of Data on Consumer Behavior: Use of Time," in R. Ferber (ed.), *A Synthesis of Selected Aspects of Consumer Behavior,* U.S. Government Printing Office for the National Science Foundation, Washington, D.C., in press.

Modeling EPS; Conclusions

CONTENTS

Modeling EPS

Structural Modeling: Evaluation

Other Developments

Implications of Merging Three Points of View

Philosophical Implications of Consumer Behavior

Suggestions for Further Reading

In this chapter, modeling EPS will be discussed briefly; progress in modeling the theory will be evaluated; three other developments will be examined; the merging of three points of view will be summarized; and, finally, some philosophical implications will be noted.

MODELING EPS

Modeling extensive problem solving is in its infancy. For a restricted case—constant consumer values—some progress is indicated by the example of two-level choice for consumer durables in Chapter 4.[1] Bhandari's work on family planning in India is also helpful.[2] But for the more complex case—changing values—there is little besides Rokeach's work,[3] which unfortunately is not cast in a systematic framework of choice.

One of the difficulties in modeling EPS is the tendency of values to group. Religious values are an example; in Chapter 8, real differences in values among people of three religious faiths were noted. This produces a high degree of collinearity and makes it necessary, when dealing with values associated with a given choice criterion, to separate the relevant value very carefully from the irrelevant but collinear values.

Another problem is to determine when a particular model of a particular stage is appropriate in a given market. This problem is complicated by the fact that, often, not all consumers are at the same stage at the same time in a given market; that is, consumers are heterogeneous in this respect. And, of course, learning is not discontinuous, as our three stages imply; rather, it is a fairly continuous process. Beckwith has suggested how one can distinguish between LPS and RRB, as we saw in Chapter 12. An analogous distinction needs to be developed for LPS and EPS. Some limited research suggests that consumers' confidence in judging a brand might be used for a given product class. The mean level of confidence, however, seems to vary substantially across product classes. Our earlier discussions of the three types of societies suggests that EPS would be more common in a postindustrial society, LPS in an industrial society, and RRB in a preindustrial society; but this cannot be taken as an ironclad rule.

The attempt to model EPS reemphasizes the point, made in Chapter 11, that EPS completes the boundaries of consumer behavior. Routine, impulsive, highly structured behavior has long been accepted as one extreme; but otherwise there have been no boundaries to limit this subject. The other extreme, we can now say, exists where values are changing and behavior is highly unstructured. Such a boundary can be useful for research on the system and communication about it. For example, if economists had not set a boundary of "given preferences" but rather had become involved with defining "change in preferences," they might not have developed the splendid modeling techniques that they have.

STRUCTURAL MODELING: EVALUATION

Having examined structural modeling in Chapters 12, 13, and 14, let us return to the commentary of Blackwell, Sheth, and Wind on the testing of theory. As in Chapter 11, we will use Blackwell's and Sheth's views as a benchmark. The

[1] A. S. Boote, "An Exploratory Investigation of the Role of Needs and Personal Values in the Theory of Buyer Behavior," unpublished doctoral dissertation, Columbia University, 1975.

[2] L. Bhandari, "Communications for Social Marketing: A Methodology for Developing Communication Appeals for Family Planning Programs," unpublished doctoral dissertation, Columbia University, 1976.

[3] M. Rokeach, *The Nature of Human Values,* Free Press, New York, 1973.

reader must bear in mind, however, that Blackwell and Sheth were commenting on earlier work and did not have access to three relevant studies.[4]

Blackwell stated: "[Howard] has offered researchers no equations to explain the main effects or interactions of the input, output, or intervening variables."[5] Chapters 13 and 14 meet this criticism.

Blackwell also raised a question by noting that "applying the model empirically or physically to the consumer behavior process is difficult because the parts of the model that are observable are the input and outcome variables and even some of these are not directly observable."[6] The elimination of the intervening variable between the hypothetical construct and reality (described in Chapter 11) does much to minimize this problem. It is true that some of the variables are still unobservable; but as long as there is a rationale for their existence and we can infer them consistently, there is no difficulty.

Another criticism was that "from the outset, serious problems have confronted researchers who have attempted to mathematize and empirically test the Howard-Sheth model."[7] After reviewing the two earliest studies[8] and others' comments on them, Blackwell concluded: "From this stream of research, comments and replies, considerable doubt emerges about the potential of testing the model as a whole."[9] Chapters 13 and 14 and the studies upon which they are based do much to answer this criticism. Although the system, as revised, has not been tested in its entirety, major portions of it have been tested, particularly some of its nonlinear and nonrecursive elements. This suggests that the system as a whole can be tested. But it has become clear that for most applied work, the entire system is not only unnecessary but much too burdensome.

Sheth stated: "A related problem to operationalization of the theory constructs is the need for a priori homogeneous segments of consumers to avoid the problems of statistical artifacts due to aggregation."[10] It was seen in Chapter 14 that individual differences do matter, and Chapter 8 does lay a foundation for developing a priori notions about them. More theoretical development and more

---

[4]J. U. Farley, J. A. Howard, and D. R. Lehmann, "A 'Working' System Model of Car Buyer Behavior," *Management Science,* forthcoming; H. S. Jagpal, "The Formulation and Empirical Testing of a Dynamic Consumer Decision Process Model: A Simultaneous Equations Econometric Model," unpublished doctoral dissertation, Columbia University, 1974; M. Laroche, "A New Approach to Non-Linear Consumer Behavior and Market Segmentation by the Use of Orthogonal Polynomials," unpublished doctoral dissertation, Columbia University, 1974.

[5]R. D. Blackwell, "John Howard and Marketing Theory and Metatheory," in H. R. Andreasen and S. Sudman (eds.), *Public Policy and Marketing,* American Marketing Association, Chicago, Ill., 1976.

[6]Blackwell, op. cit., p. 37.

[7]P. 39.

[8]J. U. Farley and L. W. Ring, "An Empirical Test of the Howard-Sheth Model of Buyer Behavior," *Journal of Marketing Research,* 7:427–438, November 1970; D. R. Lehmann, J. U. Farley, and J. A. Howard, "Testing of Buyer Behavior Models," *Association for Consumer Research Proceedings,* 1971, pp. 232–242.

[9]Blackwell, op. cit., p. 40.

[10]J. N. Sheth, "Howard's Contribution to Marketing: Some Thoughts," in A. R. Andreasen and S. Sudman (eds.), *Public Policy and Marketing Thought,* American Marketing Association, Chicago, Ill., 1976, p. 25.

empirical research will be required to deal with the problem adequately, however.

It is now possible to say more about Wind's commentary, cited in Chapter 11. The integration suggested by Wind now appears to be more feasible and to have greater potential than it did before the modeling of RRB and LPS was examined. The operationality of at least major parts of the system has been established, as was seen in Chapter 14. Stochastic models can have an important role, as was indicated in Chapter 12. The structure of consumer behavior, as shown in Figure 7-2 and modeled in Chapters 13 and 14, can be seen as analogous to the management scientists' "decision calculus."[11] Although these two approaches represent different philosophies of market modeling, they may come closer together as the decision calculus-approach becomes more data-oriented and the consumer behavior model becomes still more functionally explicit (as it might, for example, when hypotheses about the parameters are tested).

OTHER DEVELOPMENTS

Three additional points can be raised in connection with the discussion of modeling.

First, we have dealt only with estimating the parameters of the system. Should we not, however, also consider testing hypotheses about the parameters of those relations? Testing hypotheses is an important further step; it will provide estimates of the ranges of those parameters.

Second, a central tenet of this book—represented in the stages of the decision process—is that the consumer changes over time. This idea pervades much of the literature on consumer behavior, but it is considered a difficult problem to deal with. Rogers' summary of research on innnovation, for example, emphasizes this (see Chapter 9); and Jagpal's nonrecursive model[12] is the beginning of an effective effort to deal with time in a field context (see Chapter 13). The time-oriented stochastic models, which have been applied independently of theoretical developments, have now been brought within our framework (as seen in Chapter 2). Earlier consumer research dealt with similar problems, but not within a systematic, theoretical framework; for example, see Palda's work with a distributed-lag model.[13] Obviously, to incorporate time adequately, more attention must be given to specifying the length of lags and to collecting data in terms of those specified lags; nevertheless, a beginning has been made.

Third, it is probably true, as Slovic and Lichtenstein have pointed out,[14] that

[11]J. D. C. Little, "Models and Managers: The Concept of a Decision Calculus," *Management Science,* **16**:B-466–B-485, April 1970.

[12]Jagpal, op. cit.

[13]K. S. Palda, *The Measurement of Cumulative Advertising Effects,* Prentice-Hall, Englewood Cliffs, N.J., 1964.

[14]P. Slovic and S. Lichtenstein, "Comparison of Bayesian and Regression Approaches to the Study of Information Processing in Judgment," *Organizational Behavior and Human Performance,* **6**:649–744, 1971.

correlation research, which incorporates much of current attitude research, may be yielding better predictions than explanations. They urge that future research examine concept formation and information processing in more detail. Consistent with this prescription, a central theme of this book has been to bring together two traditional approaches to information processing: attitude formation (so well articulated by McGuire,[15]) and concept learning (exemplified by the research of Bruner, Goodnow and Austin), which introduces the notion of cognitive strain[16] and by Simon's work on memory, as discussed in Chapter 4). A natural extension of this kind of work is cognitive strategies, which here have been more implicit than explicit. For an application to consumer behavior, see Peter Wright.[17] Such developments represent a search for conceptually unifying and simplifying principles; they are in line with Suppes' view, which, although propounded in 1966, can still serve as a goal for most behavioral scientists, including consumer researchers:

> Many scientists working on these problems [perception and concept formation] feel we are getting very close to hitting on the one or two fundamental ideas needed to move rapidly ahead. If so, the theory of information processing and concept formation might even given quantum mechanics and molecular biology a run for their money for the title of most important scientific development of the twentieth century.[18]

Suppes had the insight to envision the power of concept learning, and especially its less developed form—concept formation, which has been conceptualized here as EPS. We have seen how concept learning links the two levels of information processing. The resulting whole becomes far more explanatory than the sum of the parts. Let us examine why the resulting structure should be so powerful, so that we can understand what it may portend.

"Identification," as used here (the phenomenon studied in traditional research on concept attainment), is only a part of cognitive structure. Another part is, of course, "liking" for a concept, which brings to bear the structure of attitude and the process of attitude formation represented in value-expectancy models. Implied in "attitude" is the process of motivation, which is largely provided by the research on values. As Feather has noted, "There is no reason why values should not be treated as basic personality characteristics similar and perhaps identical to motives, and integrated into expectancy value models in the

[15]W. J. McGuire, "The Guiding Theories Behind Attitude Research" in C. W. King and D. J. Tigert (eds.), *Attitude Research Reaches New Heights,* American Marketing Association, New York, 1971, pp. 26–48.

[16]J. S. Bruner, J. J. Goodnow, and G. A. Austin, *A Study of Thinking,* Wiley, New York, 1956.

[17]Peter Wright, "Consumer Choice Strategies: Simplifying versus Optimizing," *Journal of Marketing Research,* **12**:60–67, February 1975.

[18]P. Suppes, "Information Processing and Choice Behavior," Technical Report No. 91, Institute for Mathematical Studies in the Social Sciences, Stanford University, January 31, 1966, pp. 26–27.

same way that motives have been included in the past. . . .[19] Since Feather's work had not yet appeared while this book was being written, I was unable to take advantage of it; but his formulation and mine are almost identical.

Concept attainment links two approaches—attitude formation and concept learning—each of which deals with a different aspect of a brand concept. In addition, research on concept attainment presents a way of dealing precisely with information processing, as we saw in the example of the standard concept-attainment experiment in Chapter 3. Connecting traditional research on attitudes to the specification of information is especially important because the resulting theory can guide future research on the effects of messages. We now know very little about specific effects of messages, although the general effect of information on behavior has become increasingly apparent.

If the specification of information is to function effectively in guiding research on the effects of messages, it must be linked more closely to deeper information processing (discussed in Chapters 4 and 6). Here, the concept of structure of information, with its content and form dimensions, is a beginning; but the full explication of this concept, which will help specify this linkage, is yet to come. Elements of the concept, of course, will be language, memory and inference. Linguistics specifies the surface structure excellently, as we saw in Chapter 4, but it fails to link surface structure with deep structure (it comes near to doing this but is incomplete). In fact, memory and inference are deep structure. A structure begins to appear when a model of memory with an explanation of retrieval links memory and inference processes, as in Chapter 4.

Motivation appears to play a strong role in information processing. We have seen this in attention and search, in Chapter 7, but the specific role of motivation in linguistic processing, memory, and inference is also still to be developed. For laboratory research in this area, arousal provides a good starting place.

Finally, the substantive elements that we have been discussing will help us meet the challenge implicit in Suppes' comment; but the methodology of complex causal modeling discussed in Chapters 12, 13, and 14 is equally important. The method provides a means for the researcher to move easily and productively between the control of the laboratory and the realism of field research. It is important to bear in mind that laboratory researchers are likely to be productive only insofar as they have a well-developed structure to guide them. Field research can be exceedingly useful in identifying those elements that must be specified for effective control in a laboratory experiment. It is true that in the current state of knowledge we have no direct way of empirically specifying motivational capacity (arousal) and information-processing capacity (short-term memory) in a field study; but, as was indicated in Chapter 8, they can be dealt with indirectly as individual differences. As was noted in Chapter 4, there is evidence of "massive" interpersonal differences in information-processing capacity.

[19]N. T. Feather, *Values in Education and Society,* Free Press, New York, 1975, p. 300.

In summary, a strong foundation is being formed on which researchers in consumer behavior can build to meet Suppes' implicit but exciting challenge.

IMPLICATIONS OF MERGING THREE POINTS OF VIEW

In Chapter 1, a goal was set: to merge the marketing, psychological, and economic points of view. Since 1969, "marketing" has become "macro-marketing" and thus far more inclusive, although it is still confined to the relation between the provider and the user of a service or product.[20] Consistent with this broader interpretation, "marketing" has been used here to describe not only activities of private companies but, more generally, an orientation to action combined with a simplistic view of the "consumer." The intention has been to merge the orientation toward action and the simplistic view of consumer behavior with two disciplines—economics and psychology—so as to elaborate the simplistic view into a structure that is easily applied. In this process, not only was a structure formulated but substantial cross-fertilization among the three areas was observed. At least six important implications can be noted.

First, for the manager of a public or private organization, concept learning provides a set of powerful ideas linking many psychological processes to the action orientation, as we have seen. Thus the simplistic ideas of marketing are given an intellectual foundation which gives the manager a good basis for adapting to the market. This has been a successful integration. It is not complete (as the state of EPS shows), but it represents very real progress. It is useful here and now, for both planning action and modeling, and it can also guide the development of market or operating research techniques to deal with EPS situations. (Current techniques have been developed with only RRB and LPS in mind.)

Second, modeling of concept learning in a field context also has something to offer the psychologist. An orientation toward action is implied in the research, and action requires a complex theory. True, a simpler theory is adequate for monitoring (as was discussed in Chapter 13); but diagnostic inferences are often made from the data collected in the process of monitoring the market. Diagnosis does require a complex theory. Psychologists usually do not think in terms of an explicit complex theory, but their ideas would be more quickly accepted by nonpsychologists if they did. Furthermore, McGuire strongly argued that for social psychologists theory-oriented research in a naturalistic setting is the best of both worlds—the laboratory and the real world—for testing their hypotheses derived from theory. One of the reasons why he was optimistic about such ventures is that he saw the potential of the types of structural modeling described in Chapters 13 and 14. The sociologist's path analysis has similar implications for the psychologist; but path analysis has been directed more to building theory than to testing it. The psychologist is less comfortable with this path-analytic

---

[20]P. Kotler and S. J. Levy, "Broadening the Concept of Marketing," *Journal of Marketing,* **33**:10–15, January 1969.

philosophy of building theory than with testing theory. Thus, the structure and its modeling have a double implication for the psychologist: hypotheses can be tested in a real-world context if the psychologist will think in terms of an explicit complex theory.

Third, economics has contributed its normative orientation, which is highly useful in making a framework for public policy (see Chapter 10) and in providing some essential ingredients (such as the concept of market structure and Schumpeter's theory of innovation). Also, economics has much to say about organizing markets in preindustrial societies to improve the welfare of consumers (as with food), although it does not deal well with vertical market structures.[21] Furthermore, economics has provided a powerful methodology for structural modeling. But some relevant areas of economics have been omitted. For example, the concept of price elasticity was not introduced in Chapter 2; and the general notion of elasticity, which is more widely applicable, has also been omitted. Another omission has to do with a more contemporary development—substitute and complementary relations among product classes. Chapter 5 dealt only with substitute relations where choice of one product class is competitive with choice of another. It is true that this relation represents an important area, "interindustry competition." But complementary relations—as with gasoline and automobiles— can exist and may be important. Since the mid-1950s, economists have forged a powerful set of tools, called "functional structure and duality," for estimating these types of relations. Nevertheless, by assuming that preferences are *latent* and that *process* does not matter in consumers' choices, economists have defined their science so as to exclude most of what this book is about. By making the first assumption, they have assigned to someone else the task of explaining changes in preferences. Lancaster, who has developed the major set of ideas that come close to the problem of consumer behavior, has stated: "Economists cannot escape the criticism, however, that they know remarkably little about something on which their whole theory of individual behavior is founded." And, more specifically: "As the [economic] theory expands to cover larger situations, such as lifetime choice, and more resources come to be devoted to empirical estimates based upon past behavior, questions of the formation and stability of preferences become much more important."[22] This need to deal with changing tastes is seen, for example, in Crockett's review of choice between spending and saving, and in Huang's review of purchase of durables.[23] By making the second assumption—that *process* is unimportant and can be ignored—economists have greatly limited their ability to explain how consumers choose when confronted

[21]H. H. Baligh and L. E. Richartz, *Vertical Market Structures,* Allyn and Bacon, Boston, 1967.

[22]K. Lancaster, "Theories of Consumer Choice from Economics: A Critical Survey," Project on Synthesis of Knowledge of Consumer Behavior, RANN Program, National Science Foundation, April 1975, pp. 50–51.

[23]J. Crockett, "The Choice between Spending and Saving," Project on Synthesis of Knowledge of Consumer Behavior, RANN Program, National Science Foundation, April 1975, p. 43; D. Huang, "Consumer Purchase of Durables," Project on Synthesis of Knowledge, RANN Program, National Science Foundation, April 1975, p. 51.

with a new product in an existing product class. Also, in the new economic theory of the household, which treats the household as a production function, it is necessary, under certain conditions, to separate the effects of consumer technology from consumer tastes,[24] and thus the book provides a theoretical basis and an operational means for doing so. For this reason, the structure proposed here has something to offer economists, who must inevitably deal with changes in preference. A related question of interest to economists (as we saw in Chapter 5) is: Why are intentions to act a substantially better predictor of behavior at the brand level of choice than at the product-class level of choice?

Fourth, economics has contributed to psychology by providing the technology for modeling and also by emphasizing the role of the environment as a determinant of behavior.

Fifth, the contribution of psychology to economics is an understanding of the processes of change in preferences and tastes.

Sixth, marketing contributes to economics because the concept of the product life cycle provides a way of thinking about long-run changes in the market. Specifically, the concept is badly needed in dealing with antitrust problems and issues of consumer protection, as was indicated in Chapter 10. It can perhaps be as powerful here as Raymond Vernon has found it to be in developing international trade theory.[25] The product life cycle was used there with the traditional economic theory of demand. If the structure of Figure 7-2 had been used also, the analysis of international trade could probably have been substantially more revealing.

PHILOSOPHICAL IMPLICATIONS OF CONSUMER BEHAVIOR

At a time when philosophical issues are being reexamined by society, it may not be inappropriate to discuss the philosophical relevance of even buying behavior.

In evaluating Levi-Strauss's work, Bell pointed out, "For the past hundred years a single powerful concept has infused almost every doctrine in the social sciences. This is the idea that under the rational surface appearance of the world is an underlying structure of irrationality."[26] The major sources of this view are Marx, Freud, Pareto, and Weber. I have, on the contrary, implicitly postulated that, as buyers, people are—at least in their intentions—rational; and I have presented some empirical evidence for this view. For example, feedbacks from satisfaction to attitude are seen in Chapter 13 to have a powerful effect on shifting beliefs; this is consistent with the idea of rationality. Even more significantly, consumers' choices appear to be consistent with their beliefs, choice criteria, and values—and it is in such terms that we define rational behavior in the first place.

[24]R. A. Pollak and M. L. Wachter, "The Relevance of the Household Production Function and Its Implications for the Allocation of Time," *Journal of Political Economy,* **83**:255–277, April 1975.
    [25]R. Vernon, "International Investment and International Trade in the Product Cycle," *Quarterly Journal of Economics,* **53**:191–207, May 1966; *Manager in the International Economy,* 2d ed., Prentice-Hall, Englewood Cliffs, N.J., 1972.
    [26]D. Bell, Review of *Structural Anthropology,* vol. 2, by Claude Lévi-Strauss, *New York Times Book Review,* March 14, 1976, pp. 23–24.

Bell's interpretation of Levi-Strauss's implicit view is that being human is also being moral. I do not know that human beings as consumers are moral; but I do implicitly postulate that they are by accepting Rokeach's modified consistency theory of motivation. Human beings are motivated by conflicts in cognitions, but only in their personal cognitions—cognitions about their competence and *morality*. The extremely high ranking placed upon the instrumental (or more behaviorally oriented) value of being honest—irrespective of age, income, sex, education, or race—suggests that people must be moral. Being forgiving or helpful, although it has a somewhat lower priority than being honest—never falls below the mean of all instrumental values.[27] What this means for consumer behavior is interesting to consider. It is contrary to what psychologists have taught; as D. T. Campbell has asserted, "Psychology and psychiatry . . . not only describe man as selfishly motivated, but implicitly or explicitly teach that he ought to be so."[28] It is also clearly at variance with the economists' view that human beings are always selfishly motivated. That economists might be holding an incorrect view was recently suggested by a distinguished economist who shows the similarity of the sociobiologists' concept of group rationality to the economists' concept of individual rationality in that both can lead to altrustic rather than selfish behavior.[29] Perhaps a market need not be the cold and cruel mechanism that we have often thought it to be. Beyond consumer behavior, of course, the implications may be immense.

SUGGESTIONS FOR FURTHER READING

A. C. Kerckhoff: "Marriage and Family Formation and Dissolution," in R. Ferber (ed.), *A Synthesis of Selected Aspects of Consumer Behavior,* U.S. Government Printing Office for the National Science Foundation, Washington, D.C., in press.

A. Levine: "Educational and Occupational Choices," in R. Ferber (ed.), *A Synthesis of Selected Aspects of Consumer Behavior,* U.S. Government Printing Office for the National Science Foundation, Washington, D.C., in press.

[27]Rokeach, op. cit, chap. 3.

[28]Donald T. Campbell, presidential address before the American Psychological Association: "On the Conflicts between Biological and Social Evolution and between Psychology and Moral Tradition," *American Psychologist,* **30**:1104, December 1975.

[29]G. S. Becker, "Altruism, Egoism, and Genetic Fitness: Economics and Sociobiology," *Journal of Economic Literature,* **14**:817–826, September 1976.

Glossary
of System Constructs

Ambiguity of information   The lack of clarity with which the content and form dimensions of environmental events are communicated.

Arousal   The consumer's readiness to respond, which is a manifestation of his or her internal state of tension.

Aspiration level   The consumer's standard of adequacy in judging expected satisfaction from an attribute of the brand when the brand is consumed.

Attention   The active selection of, and emphasis on, a particular component of a complex experience, and the narrowing of the range of objects to which the consumer is responding.

Attitude   A cognitive state of the consumer that on a number of dimensions reflects the extent to which the buyer expects the brand to yield satisfaction if purchased. The term can apply to either a brand or a product class.

Belief   Cognitive state of the consumer, which reflects his or her evaluation of a brand in terms of a particular choice criterion that is personal, impersonal, or interpersonal. It can apply to either a brand or a product class.

Brand concept   The subjective meaning of a brand that arises, not from sensory data about the brand per se, but from applying the processes of abstraction and generalization to the sensory data in such a way that the sensory data are linked by words stored in memory. Brand concept consists of three elements: identification, attitude, and confidence.

Choice criterion   A cognitive state of the buyer, which reflects an attribute of the brand that is salient in the buyer's evaluation because it relates to motives relevant for this product class in the sense that brands in the product class have the potential for satisfying those motives. It can be personal, impersonal, or interpersonal. It can apply to either a brand or a product class.

Confidence   The degree of certainty that a consumer subjectively experiences with respect to satisfaction expected if a brand is purchased.

Evoked set   The subset of brands that a consumer considers buying out of the set of brands that he or she is aware of in a given product class.

Identification   A cognitive state of the consumer that reflects the extent to which he or she has sufficient knowledge to exhibit well-defined criteria for recognizing, not evaluating, a particular brand.

Information available   Some physical event in the consumer's environment to which the sense organs may be exposed, and definitely will be exposed if the consumer searches for information about the brand. It has both content and form characteristics; "content" has to do with the meaning of the brand or product class, and "form" has to do with the manner in which the meaning is conveyed.

Information exposed   External events with which the consumer's sense organs have come into contact. Descriptively, they are typically symbols that represent the brand; they may be linguistic (spoken word), orthographic (printed word), or pictorial (picture or cartoon). They may also be the physical brand itself. Analytically, they have content and form characteristics; "content" refers to the elements that convey the nature of the concept, and "form" refers to the manner in which the concept is conveyed.

Intention   A cognitive state that reflects the consumer's plan to buy some specified number of units of a particular product or brand in some specified time period.

Long-term memory   Storage of events which is more or less permanent. An event that is recalled from long-term memory has been absent from consciousness and belongs to the psychological past. Recall from long-term memory requires effort. Long-term memory is full of gaps and distortions.

Motive   A fundamental and relatively permanent disposition of the buyer to act, which is manifested through arousal and gives weighting to the subjective attractiveness of specific outcomes. It may be genetic or learned.

Overt search   Movement of the consumer's body, including the head, to bring the sense organs into contact with some aspect of the environment.

Product class concept   The subjective meaning of a class of similar brands which arises, not from the sensory data per se, but from applying the processes of abstraction and generalization to the sensory data in such a way that the sensory data are linked by words stored in memory.

Purchase   The point at which the consumer has paid for a product or has made a financial commitment to buy some specified amount during some specified period.

Satisfaction   The consumer's mental state of being adequately or inadequately rewarded for the sacrifice he or she has undergone in buying a product.

Short-term memory   A working memory which is a channel transmitting information from sensory memory to long-term memory, monitoring the transmission by internal control processes. It is a faithful record of events just perceived.

Value   An enduring belief that a specific mode of conduct or state of existence is personally and socially preferable to the opposite mode of conduct or state; a type of learned motive.

Bibliography

Advertising Age, December 9, 1974, p. 36; March 10, 1975, p. 51; February 23, 1976, p. 16; March 22, 1976, p. 1; March 22, 1976, pp. 34–36; March 29, 1976, p. 3.

Baligh, H. H., and L. E. Richartz: *Vertical Market Structures,* Allyn and Bacon, Boston, 1967.

Banks, S., and E. W. Hart: "Factors Influencing Consumer Choice: Promotional Methods," in R. Ferber (ed.), *A Synthesis of Selected Aspects of Consumer Behavior,* U.S. Government Printing Office for National Science Foundation, Washington, D.C., in press.

Barker, R. G., and A. W. Wicker: "Commentaries on Belk, Situational Variables," *Journal of Consumer Research,* **2**:165–168, December 1975.

Barthol, R. P., and R. G. Bridge: "The ECHO Multi-Response Method for Surveying Value and Influence Patterns in Groups," *Psychological Reports,* **22**:1345–1354, 1968.

Bass, F. M: "Analytical Approaches in the Study of Consumer Purchase Behavior and Brand Choice," in R. Ferber (ed.), *A Synthesis of Selected Aspects of Consumer Behavior,* U.S. Government Printing Office for National Science Foundation, in press.

———: "The Theory of Stochastic Preference and Brand Switching," *Journal of Marketing Research,* **11**:1–20, February 1974.

Bauer, R. A.: "Consumer Behavior as Risk Taking," in D. F. Cox (ed.), *Risk Taking and Information Handling in Consumer Behavior,* Graduate School of Business Administration, Harvard University, 1967.

Becker, G. S., "Altruism, Egoism, and Genetic Fitness: Economics and Sociobiology," *Journal of Economic Literature,* **14**:817–826, September 1976.

Beckwith, N. E.: "Stochastic Implications of Brand Choice: Models on the Distribution of Brand Purchase Probabilities," Graduate School of Business, Columbia University, mimeographed, 1975.

——, and D. R. Lehmann: "The Importance of Halo Effects in Multi-Attribute Attitude Models," *Journal of Marketing Research,* **12**:265–275, August 1975.

Bell, D.: *The Coming of Post-Industrial Society,* Basic Books, New York, 1973.

——: Review of *Structural Anthropology, II,* by Claude Lévi-Strauss, *New York Times Book Review,* March 24, 1976, pp. 23–24.

Belk, R. W.: "Situational Variables and Consumer Behavior," *Journal of Consumer Research,* **2**:157–164, December 1975.

Bennett, P. D., and R. M. Mandell: "Pre-Purchase Information Seeking Behavior of New Car Purchasers—The Learning Hypothesis," *Journal of Marketing Research,* **6**:430–433, November 1969.

Berg, A.: *The Nutrition Factor,* Brookings Institution, Washington, D.C., 1973, chap. 7.

Berlyne, D. E.: "Curiosity and Exploration," *Science,* **153**(3731):25–33, July 1, 1966.

——: "Motivational Problems Raised by Exploratory and Epistemic Behavior," in S. Koch (ed.), *Psychology: The Study of a Science,* vol. 5, McGraw-Hill, New York, 1963.

Bettman, J. R: "Decision Net Models of Buyer Information Processing and Choice," in G. D. Hughes and M. L. Ray (eds.), *Buyer/Consumer Information Processing,* University of North Carolina Press, Chapel Hill, N.C., 1974.

——: "Issues in Designing Consumer Information Environments," *Journal of Consumer Research,* **2**:169–177, December 1975.

Bhandari, L.: "Communications for Social Marketing: A Methodology for Developing Communication Appeals for Family Planning Programs," unpublished doctoral dissertation, Columbia University, 1976.

Birch, D., J. W. Atkinson, and K. Bongort: "Cognitive Control of Action," in B. Weiner (ed.), *Cognitive Views of Human Motivation,* Academic Press, New York, 1974.

Birdwell, A. E.: "Automobiles and Self-Imagery: Reply," *Journal of Business,* **41**:486–487, October 1968.

Black, T. R. L., and J. U. Farley: "An Awareness-Knowledge-Trial System Model of a Subsidized Contraceptive Test Market in Kenya," *Journal of Advertising Research,* forthcoming.

Blackwell, R. D.: "John Howard and Marketing Theory and Metatheory," in H. R. Andreasen and S. Sudman (eds.), *Public Policy and Marketing Thought,* American Marketing Association, Chicago, Ill., 1976, pp. 27–42.

Blalock, H. M. (ed.): *Causal Models in the Social Sciences,* Aldine-Atherton, New York, 1971.

Boote, A. S.: "An Exploratory Investigation of the Role of Needs and Personal Values in the Theory of Buyer Behavior," unpublished doctoral dissertation, Columbia University, 1975.

Bourne, L. E., and R. L. Dominowski: "Thinking," *Annual Review of Psychology,* **23**:110–126, 1972.

Brehm, J. W., and A. R. Cohen: *Explorations in Cognitive Dissonance,* Wiley, New York, 1962.

Bridge, G.: "The Utility of ECHO Surveys in Cross-Cultural Research on Values," presented at the American Psychological Association, Washington, D.C., 1969, mimeographed.

Brown, Roger: *Social Psychology,* Free Press, New York, 1965.

Bruner, J. S., J. J. Goodnow, and G. A. Austin: *A Study of Thinking,* Wiley, New York, 1956.

Buell, V. P.: *Changing Practices in Advertising Decision-Making and Control,* Association of National Advertisers, New York, 1973.

Buzzell, R. D.: "Competitive Behavior and Product Life Cycles," in J. S. Wright and J. L. Goldstucker (eds.), *Proceedings of American Marketing Association,* Chicago, Ill., 1966.

Campbell, D. T.: "On the Conflicts between Biological and Social Evolution and between Psychology and Moral Tradition," *American Psychologist,* **30**:1103–1126, December 1975.

Capon, N., M. B. Holbrook, and J. M. Hulbert: "Selling Processes and Buyer Behavior: Theoretical Implications of Recent Research," Graduate School of Business, Columbia University, mimeographed, 1975.

Carman, F. M.: "A Summary of Empirical Research on Unit Pricing in Supermarkets," *Journal of Retailing,* **48**:63–71, Winter 1972–1973.

Carroll, J. B.: "Words, Meanings and Concepts," in J. A. Emig, J. T. Fleming, and H. M. Popp (eds.), *Language and Learning,* Harcourt, Brace & World, New York, 1966.

Charlton, P., and A. S. C. Ehrenberg: "McConnell's Experimental Brand Choice Data," *Journal of Marketing Research,* **10**:302–307, August 1973.

Chomsky, N.: *Aspects of the Theory of Syntax,* M.I.T. Press, Cambridge, Mass., 1965.

——: *Syntactic Structures,* Mouton Press, The Hague, Netherlands, 1957.

Christ, C. F.: *Econometric Models and Methods,* Wiley, New York, 1966.

Claycamp, H. J.: "Dynamic Effect of Short Duration Price Differentials on Retail Gasoline Sales," *Journal of Marketing Research,* **3**:175–178, May 1966.

Cliff, N.: "Adverbs as Multipliers," *Psychological Review,* **66**:27–44, 1959.

Cofer, C. N., and M. H. Appley: *Motivation,* Wiley, New York, 1964.

Coleman, J., E. Katz, and H. Menzel: "Social Processes in Physicians' Adoption of a New Drug," *Journal of Chronic Diseases,* **9**:1–19, January, 1959.

Cox, D. F.: "The Measurement of Information Value: A Study in Consumer Decision-Making," in W. S. Decker (ed.), *Emerging Concepts in Marketing,* Proceedings of the Winter Conference of the American Marketing Association, 1962, pp. 413–421.

Cox, Keith: "The Effect of Shelf Space upon Sales of Branded Products," *Journal of Marketing Research,* **7**:55–58, February 1970.

Cox, W. E., Jr.,: "Product Life Cycles as Marketing Models," *Journal of Business,* **40**: 375–384, October 1967.

Crockett, J.: "The Choice between Spending and Saving," Project on Synthesis of Knowledge of Consumer Behavior, RANN Program, National Science Foundation, April 1975.

Davis, H. L.: "Decision Making within the Household," Project on Synthesis of Knowledge of Consumer Behavior, RANN Program, National Science Foundation, April 1975.

Day, G. S.: "A Description and Evaluation of the Design of the Buyer Behavior Research Project," in J. U. Farley, J. A. Howard, and L. W. Ring (eds.), *Consumer Behavior: Theory and Application,* Allyn and Bacon, Boston, 1974.

————: *Buyer Attitudes and Brand Choice Behavior,* Free Press, New York, 1970.

Deese, James: *Psycholinguistics,* Allyn and Bacon, Boston, 1970.

————: *The Structure of Associations in Language and Thought,* Johns Hopkins Press, Baltimore, Md., 1965.

Divita, S. F.: *Advertising and the Public Interest,* Chicago, Ill., American Marketing Association, 1973.

Dolich, I. J.: "Congruence Relationships between Self-Images and Product Brands," *Journal of Marketing Research,* **6**:80–84, February 1969.

Doob, A. N., J. M. Carlsmith, J. C. Freedman, T. K. Landauer, and S. Toin, Jr.: "Effect of Initial Selling Price on Subsequent Sales," *Journal of Personality and Social Psychology,* **9**:3–8, 1969.

Ehrenberg, A. S. C.: "The Pattern of Consumer Purchases," *Applied Statistics,* **8**:26–46, March 1959.

English, H. B., and A. C. English: *Psychological and Psychoanalytic Terms,* McKay, New York, 1958.

Engman, Lewis: Before the Anti-Trust Section of the American Bar Association, Honolulu, August 14, 1974.

ERC Reports, **12**(2), December 1974, Educational Research Council of America, Rockefeller Building, Cleveland, Ohio.

Farley, J. U., and J. A. Howard (eds.): *Control of "Error" in Market Research Data,* Lexington Books, Lexington, Mass, 1975.

————, and D. R. Lehmann: "A 'Working' System Model of Car Buyer Behavior," *Management Science,* forthcoming.

————: "Evaluating Test Market Results: Buyer Behavior Analysis in Argentina," *Journal of Business Administration,* **5**:69–88, Spring 1974.

Farley, J. U., and L. W. Ring: "An Empirical Test of the Howard-Sheth Model of Buyer Behavior," *Journal of Marketing Research,* **7**:427–438, November 1970.

Feather, N. T.: *Values in Education and Society,* Free Press, New York, 1975.

Federal Trade Commission, *Food Advertising,* vol. 39, no. 18, part II, Washington, D.C., 1974.

Fellner, W.: *Competition among the Few,* Knopf, New York, 1949.

Ferguson, James L.: in *Advertising Age,* December 22, 1975, p. 29.

Fillenbaum, S. F., and A. Rapoport: *Structures in the Subjective Lexicon,* Academic Press, New York, 1971.

Frank, R. E., and W. F. Massy: "Shelf Position and Space Effects on Sales," *Journal of Marketing Research,* **7**:59–66, February 1970.

Gardner, D. M.: "The Role of Price in Consumer Choice," Project on Synthesis of Knowledge of Consumer Behavior, RANN Program, National Science Foundation, April 1975.

————: "The Role of Price in Consumer Choice," in R. Ferber (ed.), *A Synthesis of Selected Aspects of Consumer Behavior,* U.S. Government Printing Office for the National Science Foundation, Washington, D.C., in press.

Gleitman, L. R., and H. Gleitman: *Phrase and Paraphrase,* Norton, New York, 1970.

Goldman, Arieh: "Do Lower-Income Consumers Have a More Restricted Shopping Scope?" *Journal of Marketing,* **40**:46–54, 1976.

Granbois, Donald: "Consumer Shopping Behavior and Preferences," Project on Synthesis of Knowledge of Consumer Behavior, RANN Program, National Science Foundation, April 1975.

————: "Consumer Shopping Behavior and Preferences," in R. Ferber (ed.), *A Synthesis of Selected Aspects of Consumer Behavior,* U.S. Government Printing Office for the National Science Foundation, in press.

Gray, A.: *The Development of Economic Doctrine,* Longmans Green, London, 1931.

Green, P. E., and V. R. Rao: "Conjoint Measurement for Quantifying Judgmental Data," *Journal of Marketing Research,* **8**:355–363, August 1971.

Green, P. E., and Y. Wind: "New Way to Measure Consumers' Judgments," *Harvard Business Review,* **53**:107–115, July–August 1975.

————, and A. K. Jain: "Analyzing Free-Response Data in Marketing Research," *Journal of Marketing Research,* **10**:45–52, February 1973.

Greene, J.: *Psycholinguistics,* Penguin Books, Baltimore, Md., 1972.

Greenwald, A. G.: "Cognitive Learning, Cognitive Response to Persuasion and Attitude Change," in A. G. Greenwald, T. C. Brock, and T. M. Ostrom (eds.), *Psychological Foundations of Attitudes,* Academic Press, New York, 1968.

Grey Matter, **47**(1):9, Grey Advertising, New York, 1976.

Grubb, E. L., and H. L. Grathwohl: "Consumer Self-Concept, Symbolism and Market Behavior: A Theoretical Approach," *Journal of Marketing,* **31**:22–27, October 1967.

Guilford, J. P.: *The Nature of Human Intelligence,* McGraw-Hill, New York, 1967.

Haire, M.: "Projective Techniques in Marketing Research," *Journal of Marketing,* **14**:649–656, April 1950.

Hamblin, R. L., R. B. Jacobsen, and J. L. L. Miller: *A Mathematical Theory of Social Change,* Wiley, New York, 1973.

Hansen, F.: "Psychological Theories of Consumer Choice," Project on Synthesis of Knowledge of Consumer Behavior, RANN Program, National Science Foundation, April 1975.

Haskins, J. B.: "Predicting Interest in Messages," *Journal of Advertising Research,* **15**:31–35, October 1975.

Hebb, D. O.: "Concerning Imagery," *Psychological Review,* **75**:466–477, 1968.

————: Personal communication, April 25, 1975.

Holbrook, M. B., and J. A. Howard: "Consumer Research on Frequently Purchased Nondurables and Services: A Review," Project on Synthesis of Knowledge of Consumer Behavior, RANN Program, National Science Foundation, April 1975.

Houthakker, H. S.: "The Present State of Consumption Theory," *Econometrica,* **29**:704–740, 1961.

Howard, J. A.: "Introduction: Noisy Data—A Common Problem in Social Research," in J. U. Farley and J. A. Howard (eds.), *Control of "Error" in Market Research Data,* Lexington Books, Lexington, Mass., 1975.

————: *Marketing: Executive and Buyer Behavior,* Columbia University Press, New York, 1963.

————: *Marketing Management,* Irwin, Homewood, Ill., 1957.

————: *Marketing Management,* 2d ed., Irwin, Homewood, Ill., 1963.

————, and J. Hulbert: *Advertising and the Public Interest,* Crain Communications, Chicago, Ill., 1973.

Howard, J. A., and W. M. Morgenroth: "Information Processing Model of Executive Decision," *Management Science,* **14**:416–428, March 1968.

Howard, J. A., and J. N. Sheth: *The Theory of Consumer Behavior,* Wiley, New York, 1969.

Huang, D.: "Consumer Purchase of Durables," Project on Synthesis of Knowledge of Consumer Behavior, RANN Program, National Science Foundation, April 1975.

Irwin, F. W., and W. A. S. Smith: "Further Tests of Theories of Decision in an 'Expanded Judgment' Situation," *Journal of Experimental Psychology,* **52**:345–348, 1956.

————, and J. F. Mayfield: "Tests of Two Theories of Decision in an 'Expanded Judgment' Situation," *Journal of Experimental Psychology,* **51**:263–268, 1956.

Jacoby, J., D. E. Speller, and C. A. K. Berning: "Constructive Criticism and Programmatic Research: Reply to Russo," *Journal of Consumer Research,* **2**:154–156, 1975.

Jacoby, J., D. E. Speller, and C. A. Kohn: "Brand Choice Behavior as a Function of Information Overload: Replication and Extension," *Journal of Consumer Research,* **1**:32–42, June 1974.

Jacoby, J., G. J. Szybillo, and C. K. Berning: "Collection of Data on Consumer Behavior: Use of Time," in R. Ferber (ed.), *A Synthesis of Selected Aspects of Consumer Behavior,* U.S. Government Printing Office for the National Science Foundation, Washington, D.C., in press.

Jagpal, H. S.: "The Formulation and Empirical Testing of a Dynamic Consumer Decision Process Model: A Simultaneous Equations Econometric Model," unpublished doctoral dissertation, Columbia University, 1974.

Jarvis, L. P., and J. B. Wilcox: "Evoked Set Size—Some Theoretical Foundations and Empirical Evidence," mimeographed, 1974.

Johnson, R. M.: "Beyond Conjoint Measurement: A Method of Pair-Wise Trade-Off Analysis," *Proceedings of Association for Consumer Research,* Cincinnati, November 1975, pp. 353–358.

Jones, E. E., and H. B. Gerard: *Foundations of Social Psychology,* Wiley, New York, 1967.

Kadushin, C.: "Introduction to the Sociological Study of Networks," Teachers College, Columbia University, mimeographed, October 1975.

Kahneman, D.: *Attention and Effort,* Prentice-Hall, Englewood Cliffs, N.J., 1973.

Kalwani, M. E., and D. G. Morrison: "A Parsimonious Description of the Hendry System," *Management Science,* forthcoming.

Kerckhoff, A. C.: "Marriage and Family Formation and Dissolution," in R. Ferber (ed.), *A Synthesis of Selected Aspects of Consumer Behavior,* U.S. Government Printing Office for the National Science Foundation, Washington, D.C., in press.

Klahr, M. W.: "A Comparison of Two Buyer Behavior Models," unpublished doctoral dissertation, Columbia University, 1974.

Kotler, P., and S. J. Levy: "Broadening the Concept of Marketing," *Journal of Marketing,* **33**:10–15, January 1969.

Kropp, H. E.: "Determining How Much to Spend for Advertising—without Experimental Testing," presented at Association of National Advertisers Advertising Research Workshop, New York, February 28, 1974.

Krugman, H. E.: "The Impact of Television Advertising: Learning without Involvement," *Public Opinion Quarterly,* **29**:349–356, Fall 1965.

Lampert, S. I.: "Word of Mouth Activity During the Introduction of a New Food Product," unpublished doctoral dissertation, Columbia University, 1969.

————: "Word of Mouth Activity during the Introduction of a New Food Product," in J. U. Farley, J. A. Howard, and L. W. Ring (eds.), *Consumer Behavior: Theory and Application,* Allyn & Bacon, Boston, 1974.

Lancaster, K.: *Consumer Demand: A New Approach,* Columbia University Press, New York, 1971.

————: "Theories of Consumer Choice from Economics," in R. Ferber (ed.), *A Synthesis of Selected Aspects of Consumer Behavior,* U.S. Government Printing Office for the National Science Foundation, in press.

————: "Theories of Consumer Choice from Economics: A Critical Survey," Project on Synthesis of Knowledge of Consumer Behavior, RANN Program, National Science Foundation, April 1975.

Lanzetta, J. T.: "Uncertainty as a Motivating Variable," Conference on Experimental Social Psychology, Vienna, Austria, mimeographed, 1967.

Laroche, M.: "A New Approach to Non-Linear Consumer Behavior and Market Segmentation by the Use of Orthogonal Polynomials," unpublished doctoral dissertation, Columbia University, 1974.

————, and J. A. Howard: "Non-Linear Relations in a Complex Model of Buyer Behavior," Graduate School of Business, Columbia University, mimeographed, 1975.

Lazarsfeld, P. F., W. H. Sewell, and H. L. Wilensky: *The Uses of Sociology,* Basic Books, New York, 1967.

Le Grand, B., and J. G. Udell: "Consumer Behavior in the Market Place," *Journal of Retailing,* **40**:35, Fall 1964.

Lehmann, D. R.: "Some Alternatives to Linear Factor Analysis for Variable Grouping Applied to Buyer Behavior Variables," *Journal of Marketing Research,* **11**:206–213, May 1974.

————: "Television Show Preference: Application of a Choice Model," *Journal of Marketing Research,* **8**:47–55, February 1971.

————, J. U. Farley, and J. A. Howard: "Testing of Buyer Behavior Models," *Association for Consumer Research Proceedings,* 1971, pp. 232–242.

Lehmann, D. R., T. V. O'Brien, J. U. Farley, and J. A. Howard: "Some Empirical Contributions to Buyer Behavior Theory," *Journal of Consumer Research,* **1**:43–55, December 1974.

Lehmann, D. R., and J. O'Shaughnessy: "Difference in Attribute Importance for Different Industrial Products," *Journal of Marketing,* **38**:36–42, April 1974.

Levine, A.: "Educational and Occupational Choices," in R. Ferber (ed.), *A Synthesis of Selected Aspects of Consumer Behavior,* U.S. Government Printing Office for the National Science Foundation, Washington, D.C., in press.

Lilien, G. L.: "A Modified Linear Learning Model of Buyer Behavior," *Management Science,* **20**:1027–1036, March 1974.

Little, D. C.: "Models and Managers: The Concept of a Decision Calculus," *Management Science,* **16**:B-466–B-485, April 1970.

Liu, W. T., and R. W. Duff: "The Strength in Weak Ties," *Public Opinion Quarterly,* **36**:361–366, Fall 1972.

Lutz, R. J.: "Changing Brand Attitudes Through Modification of Cognitive Structure," *Journal of Consumer Research,* **1**:49–59, March 1975.

Lynn, R.: *Attention, Arousal and the Orientation Reaction,* Pergamon Press, New York, 1966.

Massy, W. F.: "Forecasting the Demand for New Convenience Products," *Journal of Marketing Research,* **6**:405–413, November 1969.

————, D. B. Montgomery, and D. G. Morrison: *Stochastic Models of Buying Behavior,* M.I.T. Press, Cambridge, Mass., 1970.

May, F. E.: "Buying Behavior: Some Research Findings," *Journal of Business,* **38**:379–395, 1965.

McClelland, D. C.: *The Achieving Society,* Van Nostrand, Princeton, N.J., 1961.

McGuire, W. J.: "The Guiding Theories behind Attitude Research," in C. W. King and D. J. Tigert (eds.), *Attitude Research Reaches New Heights,* American Marketing Association, New York, 1971.

———: Personal communication to J. A. Howard, February 14, 1975.

———: "Psychological Factors Influencing Consumer Choice," Project on Synthesis of Knowledge of Consumer Behavior, RANN Program, National Science Foundation, April 1975.

———: "Psychological Factors Influencing Consumer Choice," in R. Ferber (ed.), *A Synthesis of Selected Aspects of Consumer Behavior,* U.S. Government Printing Office for the National Science Foundation, in press.

———: "Theory-Oriented Research in Natural Settings: The Best of Both Worlds for Social Psychology," in M. Sherif and C. W. Sherif (eds.), *Interdisciplinary Relationships in the Social Sciences,* Aldine, Chicago, Ill., 1966.

McNeil, J.: "Federal Programs to Measure Consumer Purchase Expectations, 1946–1973: A Post-Mortem," *Journal of Consumer Research,* **1**:1–15, December 1974.

Meyer, D. E., and R. W. Schvaneveldt: "Meaning, Memory Structure and Mental Processes," *Science,* **192**:27–33, 1976.

Miller, H. P.: *Rich Man, Poor Man,* Thomas Y. Crowell, New York, 1964.

Miller, G. A., and D. McNeill: "Psycholinguistics," in G. Lindzey and E. Aronson (eds.), *The Handbook of Social Psychology,* vol. 3, Addison-Wesley, Reading, Mass., 1969.

Modigliani, F., and K. J. Cohen: *The Role of Anticipations and Plans in Economic Behavior and their Use in Economic Analysis and Forecasting,* University of Illinois Bulletin 58, January 1961.

Montgomery, D. B., and A. B. Ryans: "Stochastic Models of Consumer Choice Behavior," in S. Ward and T. S. Robertson (eds.), *Consumer Behavior: Theoretical Sources,* Prentice-Hall, Englewood Cliffs, N.J., 1973.

Morrison, D. G.: "The Uses and Limitations of Brand-Switching Models," in H. L. Davis and A. Silk (eds.), *Symposium on Behavioral Science and Management Science in Marketing,* Ronald Press, New York, 1976.

———, W. F. Massy, and F. N. Silverman: "The Effect of Non-Homogeneous Populations on Markov Steady State Probabilities," *Journal of the American Statistical Association,* **66**:268–274, June 1971.

Myers, J. H., and J. Gutman: "Life Style: The Essence of Social Class," in W. D. Wells (ed.), *Life Style and Psychographics,* American Marketing Association, Chicago, Ill., 1974.

Neidell, L. A.: "The Use of Nonmetric Multidimensional Scaling in Marketing Analysis," *Journal of Marketing,* **33**:37–43, October 1969.

Nelson, P.: "Advertising as Information," *Journal of Political Economy,* **81**:729–754, July–August 1974.

———: "Consumer Information and Advertising," Economic Growth Institute, State University of New York, Binghamton, N.Y., January 1975.

———: "Information and Consumer Behavior," *Journal of Political Economy,* **78**:311–329, 1970.

Newell, A., and H. A. Simon: *Human Problem Solving,* Prentice-Hall, Englewood Cliffs, N.J., 1972.

New York Times, January 13, 1975, p. 56.

Nicosia, F., and R. Mayer: "The Sociology of Consumption: A Prospectus for Basic and Applied Research," Project on Synthesis of Knowledge of Consumer Behavior, RANN Program, National Science Foundation, April 1975.

Norman, D. E., *Memory and Attention,* Wiley, New York, 1969.

Osgood, C. E.: "Psycholinguistics," in S. Koch (ed.), *Psychology: A Study of a Science,* vol. 6, McGraw-Hill, New York, 1963.

Palda, K. S.: *The Measurement of Cumulative Advertising Effects,* Prentice-Hall, Englewood Cliffs, N.J., 1964.

Parsons, L. J.: "The Product Life Cycle and Time-Varying Elasticities," *Journal of Marketing Research,* **12**:476–480, November 1975.

———, and R. L. Schultz: *Marketing Models and Econometric Research,* North Holland, N.Y., 1976.

Peterson, D. R.: "Scope and Generality of Verbally Defined Personality Factors," *Psychological Review,* **72**:48–49, 1965.

Pollak, R. A. and M. L. Wachter: "The Relevance of the Household Production Function and Its Implications for the Allocation of Time," *Journal of Political Economy,* **83**:255–277, April 1975.

Porter, M. E.: "Interbrand Choice, Media Mix and Market Performance," *American Economic Review Supplement,* **66**:398–406, May 1976.

Ray, M. L., and W. L. Wilkie: "Fear: The Potential of an Appeal Neglected by Marketing," *Journal of Marketing,* **34**:54–62, January 1970.

Rhine, R. J.: "A Concept-Formation Approach to Attitude Acquisition," *Psychological Review,* **65**:362–370, 1958.

Rich, S. U.: "Shopping Behavior of Department Store Customers," Division of Research, Graduate School of Business, Harvard University, 1963.

Rogers, E. M.: *Diffusion of Innovations,* Free Press, New York, 1962.

———: "New Product Adoption and Diffusion," Project on Synthesis of Knowledge of Consumer Behavior, RANN Program, National Science Foundation, April 1975.

———, and J. D. Stanfield, "Adoption and Diffusion of New Products: Emerging Generalizations and Hypotheses," in F. M. Bass, C. W. King, and E. A. Pessemier, (eds.), *Applications of the Sciences in Marketing Management,* Wiley, New York, 1968.

Rokeach, M.: *The Nature of Human Values,* Free Press, New York, 1973.

Rosenberg, M. J.: "Cognitive Structure and Attitudinal Effect," *Journal of Abnormal and Social Psychology,* **53**:367–372, 1956.

Ross, I.: "Self-Concept and Brand Preference," *Journal of Business,* **44**:38–50, 1971.

Rotter, J. B.: "Generalized Expectancies for Internal versus External Control of Reinforcements," *Psychological Monographs,* **80**:1–28, 1960.

Russ, F. A.: "On Econometric Analysis of Consumer Information Processing: A Discussion of the Dominguez Paper," in G. D. Hughes and M. L. Ray (eds.), *Buyer/Consumer Information Processing,* University of North Carolina Press, Chapel Hill, N.C., 1974.

Russo, J. E.: "More Information Is Better: A Reevaluation of Jacoby, Speller and Kohn," *Journal of Consumer Research,* **1**:68–72, December 1974.

———, G. Krieser, and S. Miyashita: "An Effective Display of Unit Price Information," *Journal of Marketing,* **39**:11–19, April 1975.

Sabavola, D. J., and D. G. Morrison: "Television Show Loyalty: A Beta Binomial Model Using Recall Data," *Journal of Advertising Research,* forthcoming.

Schultz, R. L.: "The Use of Simulation for Decision Making," *Behavioral Science,* **19**:344–348, September 1974.

Schumpeter, J. A.: *Business Cycles,* McGraw-Hill, New York, 1939.

Sethna, B. N.: "A Control System Approach to Consumer Behavior," unpublished doctoral dissertation, Columbia University, 1976.

Sherif, C. W.: "Social Categorization as a Function of Latitude of Acceptance and Series Range," *Journal of Abnormal and Social Psychology,* **67**:148–156, 1963.

Sherif, M., and C. W. Sherif, *Social Psychology,* Harper and Row, New York, 1969.

Sheth, J. N.: "A Model of Industrial Buyer Behavior," *Journal of Marketing,* **37**:50–56, October 1973.

———: "A Theory of Family Buying Decisions," in J. N. Sheth (ed.), *Models of Buyer Behavior,* Harper and Row, New York, 1974.

———: "Howard's Contribution to Marketing: Some Thoughts," in A. R. Andreasen and S. Sudman (eds.), *Public Policy and Marketing Thought,* American Marketing Association, Chicago, Ill., 1976, pp. 17–26.

Simon, H. A.: "How Big is a Chunk?" *Science,* **183**:482–484, 1974.

———: "Motivational and Emotional Controls of Cognition," *Psychological Review,* **74**:29–39, 1967.

———: *The Sciences of the Artificial,* M.I.T. Press, Cambridge, Mass., 1969.

Slovic, P., and S. Lichtenstein: "Comparison of Bayesian and Regression Approaches to the Study of Information Processing in Judgment," *Organizational Behavior and Human Performance,* **6**:649–744, 1971.

Smith, H. K.: "Consumer's Third of a Century," *Christian Science Monitor,* June 12, 1975, p. 17.

Stafford, J. E., and A. B. Cocanougher: "Reference Group Theory," Project on Synthesis of Knowledge of Consumer Behavior, RANN Program, National Science Foundation, April 1975.

———: "Reference Group Theory," in R. Ferber (ed.), *A Synthesis of Selected Aspects of Consumer Behavior,* U.S. Government Printing Office for the National Science Foundation, in press.

Steffire, Volney: "Market Structure Studies: New Products for Old Markets and New Markets (Foreign) for Old Products," in F. M. Bass, C. W. King, and E. A. Pessemier (eds.), *Applications of the Sciences in Marketing Management,* Wiley, New York, 1968.

Sternthal, B., and C. S. Craig: "Fear Appeals: Revisited and Revised," *Journal of Consumer Research,* **1**:22–34, December 1974.

Stokes, R. C.: "Unit Pricing, Differential Brand Density and Consumer Deception," Consumer Research Institute, Washington, D.C., June 1973.

Suppes, P.: "Information Processing and Choice Behavior," Institute for Mathematical Studies in the Social Sciences, Technical Report No. 91, Stanford University, January 31, 1966.

Tate, R. S.: "The Supermarket Battle for Store Loyalty," *Journal of Marketing,* **25**:8–13, October 1961.

Thompson, Bryan: "An Analysis of Supermarket Shopping Habits in Worcester, Massachusetts," *Journal of Retailing,* **43**:18, Fall 1967.

Trade Regulation Reports, Commerce Clearing House, Inc., May 15, 1972, pp. 19898–19900.

Tyler, L. E.: *The Psychology of Human Differences,* 3d ed., Appleton-Century-Crofts, New York, 1965.

Van de Geer, J. P., and J. F. W. Jaspars: "Cognitive Functions," *Annual Review of Psychology,* **17**:149–150, 1966.

Vernon, R.: "International Investment and International Trade in the Product Cycle," *Quarterly Journal of Economics,* **53**:191–207, May 1966.

———: *Manager in the International Economy,* 2d ed., Prentice-Hall, Englewood Cliffs, N.J., 1972.

Vitz, P. C., and D. Johnston: "Masculinity of Smokers and the Masculinity of Cigarette Images," *Journal of Applied Psychology,* **49**:155–159, 1965.

Washington Post, June 18, 1975, p. A-2.

Wason, P. C., and P. N. Johnson-Laird: *Psychology of Reasoning,* Harvard University Press, Cambridge, Mass., 1972.

Webster, F. E., Jr., and F. von Pechman: "A Replication of the 'Shopping List' Study," *Journal of Marketing,* **34**:61–77, April 1970.

Wells, W. D.: "Psychographics: A Critical Review," *Journal of Marketing Research,* **12**:196–213, May 1975.

———: "Life Style and Psychographics: Definitions, Uses and Problems," in W. D. Wells (ed.), *Life Style and Psychographics,* American Marketing Association, Chicago, Ill., 1974.

———, and S. C. Cosmos: "Life Styles" in R. Ferber (ed.), *A Synthesis of Selected Aspects of Consumer Behavior,* U.S. Government Printing Office for National Science Foundation, Washington, D.C., in press.

Wickelgren, W. A.: *How to Solve Problems: Elements of a Theory of Problems and Problem Solving,* W. H. Freeman, San Francisco, Calif., 1974.

Wilkie, W. L.: *Public Policy and Product Information: Summary Findings from Consumer Research* (NSF Report), U.S. Government Printing Office, Washington, D.C., 1975.

———, and E. A. Pessemier: "Issues in Marketing's Use of Multi-Attribute Attitude Models," *Journal of Marketing Research,* **10**:428–441, November 1973.

Wilkinson, M.: "Extension of Consumer Theory," Graduate School of Business, Columbia University, mimeographed, 1975.

Wilson, R. E.: "The FTC's Deconcentration Case against the Breakfast-Cereal Industry: A New Ballgame," in *Antitrust Law and Economic Review,* **4**:57–76, Summer 1971.

Wind, Y.: "Brand Choice," Project on Synthesis of Knowledge of Consumer Behavior, RANN Program, National Science Foundation, April 1975.

Wright, Peter: "Consumer Choice Strategies: Simplifying versus Optimizing," *Journal of Marketing Research,* **12**:60–67, February 1975.

Zajonc, R. B.: "Cognitive Theories in Social Psychology," in G. Lindzey and E. Aronson (eds.), 2d ed., vol. 1, *Handbook of Social Psychology,* Addison-Wesley, Reading, Mass., 1968.

———, and D. W. Rajecki: "Exposure and Affect: A Field Experiment," *Psychonomic Science,* **17**:216–217, 1969.

Zaltman, G.: "An Assessment of Diffusion Research in Marketing," in A. R. Andreasen and S. Sudman (eds.), *Public Policy and Marketing Thought,* American Marketing Association, Chicago, Ill., 1976.

———, C. R. A. Pinson, and R. Angelmar: *Metatheory and Consumer Research,* Holt, Rinehart and Winston, New York, 1973.

Name Index

Lanzetta, J., 140
Laroche, M., 256, 282, 283, 287, 296
Lazarsfeld, P. F., 181
Le Grand, B., 135
Lehmann, D. R., 80, 167, 172, 188, 256, 264, 266,
    270, 273, 278, 296
Levine, A., 303
Levy, S. J., 300
Lichtenstein, S., 80, 163, 297
Lilien, G. L., 245
Little, J. D. C., 270, 297
Liu, W. T., 181
Lutz, R. J., 124, 220
Lynn, R., 142

McClelland, D. C., 94
McGuire, W. J., 40, 41, 102, 224, 237, 256, 262,
    263, 289, 298
McNeil, J., 107
McNeill, D., 74
Mandell, R. M., 141
Massy, W. F., 175, 242, 244, 249, 254
May, F. E., 36, 37
Mayer, R., 180, 205
Mayfield, J. F., 56
Menzel, H., 141
Meyer, D. E., 77
Michigan, University of, 55
Miller, G. A., 74
Miller, H. P., 191
Miller, J. L. L., 198
Miyashita, S. M., 81
Modigliani, F., 107
Montgomery, D. B., 205, 242, 245, 249
Morgenroth, W. M., 252
Morrison, D. G., 242, 244, 245, 248–251
Myers, J. H., 161

NAACP, 195
Neidell, L. A., 173
Nelson, Phillip, 150, 217–218
Newell, A., 71
Nicosia, F., 180, 205
Norman, D. A., 75, 128

O'Brien, T. V., 256
Osgood, C. E., 10, 52, 264
O'Shaughnessy, J., 188

Palda, K. S., 297
Parsons, L. J., 125, 260, 270
People's Republic of China, 156
Pessemier, E. A., 63, 278
Peterson, D. R., 160

Philippines, 181
Pinson, C. R. A., 230
Pitofsky, Robert, 209
Pollak, R. A., 302
Posner, M. I., 128
Procter & Gamble Company, 243

Rajecki, D. W., 54
Rao, V. R., 168
Rapoport, A., 46
Ray, M. L., 137
Rhine, R. J., 48
Rich, S. U., 135
Richartz, L. E., 301
Ring, L. W., 296
Robertson, T. S., 205
Robinson, Joan, 212
Rogers, E. M., 197, 198, 201
Rokeach, M., 92, 97, 109, 139, 160, 161,
    192–194, 295, 303
Rosenberg, M. J., 92
Ross, I., 90
Rotter, J. B., 167
Russ, F. A., 262
Russo, J. E., 81, 226
Ryan, M. J., 206
Ryans, A. B., 63, 242, 245, 249

Sabavala, D. J., 249
Schmalensee, Richard, 217
Schultz, R. L., 260, 269, 270
Schumpeter, J. A., 215, 224
Schvaneveldt, R. W., 77
Sethna, B. N., 141
Sewell, W. H., 181
Sherif, C. W., 35, 60, 95
Sherif, M., 95
Sheth, J. N., 3, 46, 180, 218, 230, 232, 296
Silverman, F. N., 244
Simon, H. A., 65, 71, 75, 96, 131, 145, 156
Slovic, P., 80, 163, 297
Smith, H. K., 2
Smith, W. A. S., 56
Speller, D. E., 226
Stafford, J. E., 205, 206
Stefflre, V., 89
Sternthal, B., 18, 137
Stokes, R. C., 65
Suppes, P., 298
Szybillo, G. J., 293

Tate, R. S., 36
Thompson, B., 135
Tom, S., Jr., 61
Tyler, L. E., 167

Subject Index